American Medical Association
Physicians dedicated to the health of America

W9-BRO-768

Mastering

the Reimbursement Process

Third Edition

L. Lamar Blount, CPA, FHFMA
President
Healthcare Management Advisors, Inc

Joanne M. Waters, CHFP
Senior Vice President
Healthcare Management Advisors, Inc

CONTRIBUTORS
Robert S. Gold, MD
Vice President, Clinical Consulting Services
Healthcare Management Advisors, Inc

Bruce A. Gramlich, RN, BSN, MA, CPHQ, CPUR
Senior Consultant
Healthcare Management Advisors, Inc

Sherry Huffman, CPC
Consultant
Healthcare Management Advisors, Inc

James S. Kennedy, MD
Physician Consultant
Healthcare Management Advisors, Inc

Mastering the Reimbursement Process, Third Edition

©2001 by the American Medical Association
All rights reserved
Printed in the United States of America

Internet address: www.ama-assn.org

This book is for informational purposes only. It is not intended to constitute legal or financial advice. If legal, financial, or other professional advice is required, the services of a competent professional should be sought.

No part of this publication may be reproduced, stored in a retrieval system, or transmitted, in any form or by any means electronic, mechanical, photocopying, recording, or otherwise, without the prior written permission of the publisher.

Additional copies of this book may be ordered by calling 800-621-8335. Secure on-line orders can be taken at www.ama-assn.org/catalog. Mention product number OP08000.

All Physicians' Current Procedural Terminology® (CPT®) five-digit numeric codes, descriptions, numeric modifiers, instructions, guidelines, and other materials are copyrighted 2001 by the American Medical Association.

Healthcare Management Advisors, Inc (HMA) provides education and technical support in the areas of clinical data quality, practice improvement, and regulatory compliance for physicians, hospitals, and other health care providers. HMA can be reached at 770 751-1199 or www.hma.com.

ISBN 1-57947-142-0
BP48:168A-00:2/01

Contents

2 Types of Insurance and Third-Party Payers

3 Electronic Claims Processing 79

4 The Coding Systems 97

5 Insurance Processing—Managing Insurance and Patient Accounts

After Submission of Claims 221

7 Insurance Accounts Receivable Management 229

8 Requests for Review and Appeals 239

About the Authors

L. Lamar Blount, CPA, FHFMA, President—During his 26 years serving the health care industry, Lamar has provided and directed consulting services for more than 300 clients in 30 states. He is the president and founder of Healthcare Management Advisors (HMA), a consulting firm providing extensive clinical data, compliance, and financial expertise to providers nationwide. He directs HMA's 40-plus-person practice, which provides services in compliance programs, diagnosis related group and Current Procedural Terminology® data quality improvement, medical record and utilization reviews, and litigation support. He has served multifacility groups, as well as individual urban medical centers, rural hospitals, nursing homes, home health agencies, and physicians.

His experience includes directing the litigation support for the defense of physician groups, hospitals, and individual physicians, including criminal and civil Medicare fraud cases.

Prior to founding HMA in 1990, Lamar directed the health care consulting practice for the tenth largest Atlanta CPA firm, which he cofounded in 1981. From 1983 to 1990, he was also president of Hosplan Micro Systems, which developed and distributed decision support software to more than 600 hospitals. Previously he was with a Big-Five CPA firm from 1974 to 1981, where he supervised substantially all of their Georgia health care audits and reimbursement consulting engagements, and he assisted their national office in the development of health care training programs.

Lamar is a past president of the Georgia Rural Health Association, is a Fellow and Certified Healthcare Financial Professional in the Healthcare Financial Management Association, and has been an advisor to the Council on Finance of the Georgia Hospital Association. He is also a member of the Health Care Compliance Association, American Institute of CPAs, the Georgia Society of CPAs, the Association of Certified Fraud Examiners, and the American Health Lawyers Association. Lamar is a certified public accountant and holds a BBA from Georgia Southern University.

In addition to writing articles for various national publications, Lamar has been the publisher of HMA's biweekly *Strategy Advisor* newsletter and the HMA.com and eMD solutions.net/md/ Web sites. He has served on the editorial advisory boards for the nationally recognized *Report on Medicare Compliance*, *Briefings on Coding Compliance*, *Medical Records Briefing*, *Physician's Payment Update*, and *Medical Office Manager*. Lamar is also a frequent speaker on compliance issues and health care financial and reimbursement topics.

Joanne M. Waters, CHFP, Senior Vice President—Joanne is the chief operating officer for HMA and is involved in client development and project management. In this strategic role, she uses her 17 years of experience in health care, including patient financial services, diverse financial management of integrated delivery systems, medical facilities and multiphysician practice management, external and internal financial reporting, capital and operational budgeting, third-party reimbursement, managed care, and general accounting.

Before joining HMA, Joanne was director of patient financial services at Southwest Hospital and Medical Center in Atlanta. Additionally, she worked for more than 10 years in the Finance Division of South Fulton Medical Center, where she had responsibilities in both the Accounting and Patient Financial Services Departments. Previously, she was an office manager for a specialty surgeon's practice in Tampa, Florida, and was with the University of South Florida College of Medicine.

Joanne is an active member of the Healthcare Financial Management Association and the Health Care Compliance Association. She previously served as co-chairperson of the Managed Care Education Committee for the Georgia Chapter of Healthcare Financial Management Association and is currently serving as chairperson of the Georgia HFMA Chapter Web Committee. She graduated from Georgia State University with a BBA in accounting. Joanne is a certified health care financial professional with a specialty area in patient financial services and has completed the managed care certificate program conducted by the Georgia Healthcare Financial Management Association and Mercer University.

Joanne has written articles for the Healthcare Financial Management Association on compliance issues in patient financial management, and she coauthored the previous edition of this book.

CONTRIBUTORS

Robert S. Gold, MD, Vice President of Clinical Consulting Services—
Dr Gold provided overall editorial reviews and contributed to multiple sections. He has more than 30 years of experience as a physician, medical director, and

consultant. At HMA, he directs the professional staff of MD, RN, RHIA, CPC, CCS, and MT credentialed consultants in projects including clinical data quality improvement programs, coding audits, coder and case manager training, physician liaison training, and litigation support. His clients have included multihospital systems, teaching hospitals, integrated delivery systems, and physician practice groups. Dr Gold has extensive experience in clinical documentation and resource utilization, quality reviews, coding and documentation audits, compliance assessments and risk support.

Dr Gold has been involved in medical staff education and physician behavior modification for improved clinical documentation and resource utilization. He also has provided quality reviews, coding and documentation audits, compliance assessments, and risk and training in clinical aspects to health information management personnel. Previously, as a general surgeon and Captain in the US Navy, Dr Gold aided in the development of quality efforts in its federally monitored healthcare delivery system as department head, chief of clinical services and chairman of many quality, risk and utilization committees.

Dr Gold graduated from Hahnemann Medical College and Hospital in Philadelphia and trained in General Surgery in the Navy and under the tutelage of such mentors as C. Everett Koop, MD, and Brook Roberts, MD.

Dr Gold has developed several innovative analytical tools and methods of demonstrating the accuracy and risk factors associated with DRG coding as well as quality measures to modify these risk factors. In addition to developing numerous educational programs for HMA's consultants and others, Dr Gold has authored articles for *Report on Medicare Compliance* and HMA's *Strategy Advisor* newsletter. Dr Gold is also a frequent speaker on clinical data quality, coding, and compliance issues.

Bruce A. Gramlich, RN, BSN, MA, CPHQ, CPUR, Senior Consultant—
Bruce has more than fifteen years of health care experience in case management/utilization review and coding. He provides training in the proper physician documentation requirements for coding, billing and regulatory compliance.

Prior to joining HMA, Bruce was a project leader with the Georgia Medical Care Foundation. He has provided physician education on Evaluation and Management coding and billing guidelines.

Bruce is a member of the Case Management Society of America, Case Management Society of Georgia and a member of the National Association for Healthcare Quality. Bruce is a Certified Professional in Healthcare Quality

(CPHQ) and a Certified Professional in Utilization Review (CPUR). He is also a Diplomat of the American Board of Risk Management (DABRM).

Bruce received a Bachelor of Science in Nursing degree from the University of Texas at El Paso and received an MA in Health Services Management from Webster University.

Sherry Huffman, CPC, Consultant—Sherry provides CPT coding and consulting services for HMA. She has more than 10 years of coding, auditing, and billing experience. Recent engagements include litigation support projects involving review of clinical documentation and appropriateness of CPT coding. Previously, Sherry served as the compliance specialist for a group of 45 family physicians as well as providing claims auditing services for 125 affiliates. In addition Sherry has developed and taught classes on ICD-9-CM and CPT coding.

Sherry is a Certified Professional Coder and attended West Virginia University. Sherry also holds a certificate in paralegal studies. Sherry is a member of the American Academy of Professional Coders. She has also served as a coding panel member for Independent Practices Physician groups.

James S. Kennedy, MD, Physician Consultant—Dr Kennedy contributed to Chapters 2, 4, and 5. He is a physician consultant for HMA and has more than 17 years of health care experience, both as a practicing physician and as a consultant. Dr Kennedy's consulting services include hospital and medical practice assessment, clinical practice review, and clinical productivity management.

Dr Kennedy has served as an internist and secretary-treasurer of MedCore Medical Group in Franklin, Tennessee, where he facilitated the expansion of Vanderbilt University Medical Center's clinical outreach program. Dr Kennedy served as the medical examiner of Williamson County, Tennessee, and contributed to Tennessee's current medical examiner handbook.

Dr Kennedy is board certified in internal medicine and serves as clinical assistant professor of medicine at Vanderbilt University. He is an active member of the American Medical Association, the American College of Physicians, and the American College of Physicians Executives. Dr Kennedy graduated from the University of Tennessee, Knoxville, and received his MD degree from the University of Tennessee, Memphis.

Introduction

This third edition of *Mastering the Reimbursement Process* includes many new and updated pages, reflecting the fact that the US health care system continues to become more complex and demanding. Despite the Health Insurance Portability and Accountability Act (HIPAA) "Administrative Simplification" provisions passed by Congress in 1996, dealing with reimbursement issues has continued to become more and more complicated for physicians and their staff members.

Healthcare Management Advisors' (HMA's) staff of physicians, billing specialists, coding professionals, attorneys, and financial consultants have endeavored to make the complex reimbursement process more understandable. Considering the seeming absence of logic in many government health care regulations and the regulators' tendency to continuously revise and modify the rules, this task was substantial.

The Office of Inspector General (OIG) itself admits that the complexity of Medicare's rules results in some billing errors. The OIG's most recent report on Medicare fee-for-service error rates found that over $13.5 billion (or about 8%) was improperly paid in 1999. Physician services accounted for the third largest category (after Home Health and Durable Medical Equipment) with the most common errors being related to the adequacy of documentation and appropriate coding of services.

Many people now investigate physicians and other providers who have questionable billings. Just within Medicare alone, more than 1,000 private whistleblower cases have been filed against physicians and other health care providers since 1996, and Medicare Contractor Fraud Control Units have referred more than 1,600 civil and criminal cases in the past 2 years alone. In addition, every state Medicaid agency and most insurance companies also have their own fraud control units, all staffed with investigators, analysts, and attorneys seeking to find improper claims.

Because of the increasing allegations of improper claims, it is only prudent that physicians and practice managers learn as much as possible about the reimbursement process. Failure to understand specific billing requirements could become "reckless disregard," exposing physicians to federal False Claim Act charges.

Additionally, by better understanding the reimbursement process, physicians and practice managers should be able to obtain the full reimbursement to which they are legitimately entitled for their services.

This third edition contains significant new material about Medicare program changes in Chapter 2, patient confidentiality in Chapter 4, sample position descriptions in Chapter 5, and tips on appeals in Chapter 7. In addition, three entirely new chapters have been added. Chapter 3—Electronic Data Interchange—provides comprehensive information on electronic claims submissions. Chapter 8—Compliance Programs and the OIG—explains the "Goldilocks Quality of Care Standard," outlines the steps to implementing a compliance program, includes a simplified internal control checklist, and identifies specific OIG targets. Finally, Chapter 9—Privacy, Confidentiality, and HIPAA—explains the background of HIPAA, potential conflicts with other laws mandating disclosure, the five newest principles of privacy legislation and physician practice requirements.

The third edition also contains four appendices. This material will help readers familiarize themselves with the unique terminology of health care reimbursement as well help them access many other resources.

- The Glossary of Terms (Appendix A) has been greatly expanded and updated to include definitions for more than 180 of the latest terms used in physician reimbursement and practice management.

- Internet Resources (Appendix B) provides web sites that are particularly helpful for physicians, coders, billers, and practice managers, including compliance resources, government agencies, professional associations, state medical boards, coding resources, and more. Because the Internet changes so rapidly, this appendix will be maintained at www.hma.com/md/www and www.eMDsolutions.net.

- OIG's Physician Compliance Program (Appendix C) is the full text of these final guidelines. Although compliance programs are not statutorily required, prudent practice managers and physicians must seriously consider the substantial risk of not having one.

- Medicare Carriers (Appendix D) includes a state-by-state listing of Medicare carriers, as well as their toll-free and local telephone numbers.

In addition to contributions from each of the listed authors and contributors for this edition, a special thanks goes to Gail Luxenberg, Elise Schumacher, Anne Serrano, Rosalyn Carlton, and Ronnie Summers at the AMA for their guidance and support. We also thank the administrative support staff at HMA for their countless hours of data entry, printing, and proofreading.

1 Understanding Insurance Basics

Objectives

After completing this chapter, you should be able to:

- Explain the difference between group plans and individual insurance plans.
- Understand the methods of reimbursement.
- Understand the Resource Based Relative Value Scale (RBRVS) fee schedule.
- Explain the difference between contracted rates and capitated rates.
- Understand the processing of claims.
- Understand what each modifier means and which modifier can be used for different specialties.

Introduction

Health insurance has traditionally been made available to help offset the expenses of the treatment of illness or injury. At its most basic, an "indemnity" health insurance plan pays for hospital stays and services provided by physicians and other health care providers. The purchaser of the health insurance (often the patient's employer) pays the insurance company a fixed amount, referred to as the premium, every month. In return for premiums paid, the health insurance company or carrier promises, following the terms set out in the insurance policy, to pay for the medical services provided to those covered under the insurance policy, often called "beneficiaries."

With the meteoric expansion of managed care, traditional indemnity health insurance is no longer the norm for most beneficiaries. However, the basic concept of health insurance has not changed, ie, a premium is paid by a beneficiary or another (such as an employer) on behalf of a beneficiary in return for which the insurance company agrees to pay for defined medical services provided to the beneficiary. Managed care organizations and plans now offer different types of health plans that vary in coverage and level of patient financial responsibility or shared payments such as copayments and deductibles.

According to the US Census Bureau, 83.7% of Americans had some type of health insurance in calendar year 1998, the last year for which data were reported. Payments from government and private insurance accounted for 70% of physicians' bills and more than 90% of all hospital bills. Table 1.1 illustrates the payer-mix sources from 1998.

Table 1.1   **Sources of Provider Payments**

Type of Health Insurance	Percentage of U.S. Population with Coverage
Private insurance plan	70.2
Medicare	13.2
Medicaid	10.3
Military health care	3.2
No insurance coverage	16.3

Source: US Census Bureau, 1998.
Note: Because some have insurance from both private and government sources, these figures exceed 100%.

It is important to note that the percentages in the table are constantly changing. Both private and public insurance programs are redesigning their products and offering more options for health care delivery. For example, both Medicare and many state Medicaid programs, with varying degrees of success, have designed and implemented managed care options to replace the traditional fee-for-service programs. Further, new types of programs, such as provider-sponsored organizations (PSOs), are themselves becoming insurance plans. Therefore, in the future, the traditional separations between insurance plans and providers will continue to merge.

Types of Health Insurance Plans

Insurance plans come in many forms. Certain plans, such as point-of-service (POS) plans, may be considered to be subclassifications of other types of insurance, modified to meet the needs of the marketplace. The changes and permutations will continue. Health insurance can be purchased in two ways: (1) by individuals, for themselves and their families, or (2) by a group that then offers the insurance to its members.

Both individuals and groups can purchase different types of insurance that can be broadly grouped into indemnity insurance and managed care. Within managed care, in particular, there are a number of differences between the types of plans. Below are definitions and discussions of the most prevalent type of managed care plans, ie, health maintenance organizations (HMOs), preferred-provider organizations (PPOs), and POS.

Ways to Purchase Health Insurance

Individual Insurance

Individual insurance is purchased by individuals on their own behalf. Generally, they are also entitled to ensure their primary family members under this coverage. Individual insurance plans are often more expensive than policies purchased through a group because of the concept of risk sharing: when an individual purchases insurance, the risk is not spread among many people and, thus, each individual assumes the full risk of his or her health status without benefit of pooling of individuals or a large group, which can spread the risk over many people.

Group Insurance

Group insurance is purchased through a group, which can be an employer, a trade association, or a professional association. The insurance is purchased by the group itself and is then offered to members of that group. Group insurance, like individual policies, generally also permits coverage of primary family members. Group policies are generally less expensive than individual coverage because the risk of adverse claims is spread across a larger number of people than with an individual policy.

Types of Insurance

Notwithstanding the method by which the insurance is purchased, there are alternative types of insurance available. Broadly distinguished between indemnity and managed care, they can be briefly defined as follows:

Indemnity Insurance

This insurance is also known as fee-for-service (FFS). Under traditional indemnity insurance there are no restrictions on beneficiaries as to the physician, hospital, or other health care provider they may use. Preapproval of medical visits is not required. After receiving medical care, the beneficiary submits a bill to the indemnity insurance carrier, which then pays the charges. Each year, the beneficiary must meet his or her deductible, which is the amount the beneficiary must pay out of pocket before the insurance company begins paying for medical services. After the deductible is met, the indemnity insurance carrier will pay the entire cost of medical services except for the following points: (1) There is generally a copayment or coinsurance for each service. For example, an 80-20 coverage would require the beneficiary to pay 20% of each dollar of medical care provided; the insurance carrier usually pays on usual, customary, and reasonable (UCR), as described in the section below titled "Methods of Insurance Reimbursement." (2) The beneficiary is responsible for, in addition to the copayment, any difference between UCR and the amount billed by the physician or other health care provider. (3) There are limitations on the type of care covered; for example, until recently, chiropractic care was often excluded from coverage. (4) There may not be coverage for preventive care such as well-baby checkups and mammograms. (5) There may be other restrictions in the insurance coverage.

Managed Care Organizations (MCOs)

MCOs enter into contracts with physicians, hospitals, and other health care providers. In each contract, the physician or other health care provider agrees to provide defined medical services to beneficiary members who have purchased insurance from the MCO. The physicians and providers agree to give a discount off their normal charges in exchange for being included by the MCO on their list of approved providers. MCOs tend to be less costly to the beneficiaries in exchange for certain limitations of beneficiary access to the physicians, providers, or services. Types of MCOs include the following.

Health Maintenance Organizations   HMOs are the most restrictive health plans but are also generally the least costly for the beneficiary. In HMOs, a beneficiary pays a premium for health care; services available to beneficiaries may be quite broad and may include benefits such as preventive care and prescriptions; and the beneficiary is restricted as to which physician he or she may see for care. Most HMOs have a "gatekeeper" concept that requires the beneficiary to initially visit a primary care physician for all care. Only if that gatekeeper-physician refers the beneficiary to another physician or prescribes other medical services will the HMO be responsible to pay for such services.

Staff-model HMOs restrict the beneficiary to HMO-employed physicians who are located in medical offices or clinics owned and managed by the HMO. HMOs based on independent practice associations (IPAs) or other networks will permit a beneficiary to use physicians in private practice, not employed by the HMO but under contract with the HMO. These private physicians will also see patients from other MCOs and indemnity plans and also self-pay patients. For each patient, the type of coverage purchased, eg, HMO, indemnity, PPO, will determine the type and perhaps amount of bill the physician will submit. While some insurance carriers require that its own forms be used for submission of claims, many now accept the standard HCFA 1500 form.

Out-of-pocket costs to the beneficiary for health care services are usually minimal, typically $5 to $10 per doctor visit, and may also have a prescription benefit that limits the out-of-pocket costs for approved drugs. If a beneficiary goes to a physician without the approval of the gatekeeper-physician or if the beneficiary visits a physician who is not under contract with the HMO, then the beneficiary will be responsible for all costs for that care.

Preferred Provider Organizations   As in an HMO, physicians and other health care providers enter into contracts with managed care plans to provide health care services to the beneficiaries of the PPO. However, unlike the HMO, PPOs are generally more flexible and give more options to the beneficiary. For this flexibility and options the beneficiary pays a higher premium than for an HMO. Under a PPO, the physician and other providers agree to a reduction in their normal fees and charges in exchange for being listed in the materials published by the PPO as a provider who has a contract with that PPO, which may be referred to as an "in-network" physician. PPOs do not use gatekeeper-physicians, allowing the beneficiary to determine from whom to seek services as long as the physician and other providers are in-network. PPOs generally require a yearly deductible and copayments or coinsurance for each visit. However, if the beneficiary visits a physician or provider who is not in the PPO network, the beneficiary will be responsible for all costs associated with that physician's services and charges.

Point of Service   The newest of the managed care plans discussed in this chapter, the POS has been called a "leaky HMO" or "gatekeeper PPO." Beneficiaries, if they receive medical care from in-network physicians, will receive benefits similar to those of an HMO, ie, if they first go to the gatekeeper-physician, do not self-refer to other specialists, and only seek that care that has been approved by the gatekeeper-physician, then all care is covered under the terms of the POS agreement between the beneficiaries and POS. However, if a beneficiary sees a physician who is not in-network, then, unlike a PPO or HMO, the POS plan will still pay the physician or other provider, but at a rate usually significantly less than that for care provided by physicians within the POS network. The difference between the POS plan payment and billed charges is the responsibility of the beneficiary. Unique to POS plans, beneficiaries may decide each time they seek care whether they will stay within the POS network, for maximum benefits, or go outside the POS network for greater options but reduced benefits.

As health insurance plans mature, the distinction between and among the various plans is becoming less distinct and the "labels" that describe a plan may not accurately reflect the plan and its coverage.

Methods of Insurance Reimbursement

Payments to physicians and other providers differ depending on whether the patient has insurance and, if so, the type and extent of coverage. Most commonly, the provider bills a standard fee to the patient and/or files a claim to the patient's insurance carrier. With the advent of managed care, payments may be determined by a contracted discount rate, a fee schedule, a case rate, or a capitated rate. For example, Medicare payments are determined on the basis of a national fee schedule. Each of these payment methods is discussed below. The traditional indemnity health plan is based on predefined payment allowances that may vary by provider specialty and/or geographic location. Data may be generated from within the plan's own records or obtained from outside.

Fee Schedules

The Usual, Customary, and Reasonable (UCR) Method

Historically, commercial and Blue Shield plans have based provider payments on the lowest of the following:

- The provider's most frequent charge for the service (usual).
- The average charge by providers in the area (customary).
- The actual charge appearing on the claim for the service (reasonable).

This method of determining payment is called the usual, customary, and reasonable method, or UCR. Each component amount is calculated on the basis of previous charges submitted to the insurer. For individual providers, a profile of all charges submitted is maintained, and the most frequent charge is identified to determine the usual charge. All charges of providers within a specified area are collated and averaged to determine a customary charge. To arrive at a payment amount for a claim, the carrier then compares the physician's most frequent charge (the usual), the average charge of all providers in the area (the customary), and the actual charge submitted on the claim (which, if submitted by a provider, must be reasonable to that provider). Whichever amount is the lowest is used as the basis for payment (the allowable charge).

For example, a physician usually charges $100 for a procedure and the average charge of providers in the geographic area is $105. The physician submits a charge of $120 on a particular claim. For that claim, payment will be based on $100, which is the lowest of the usual ($100), customary ($105), and actual ($120) charges.

Relative Value Payment Schedules Method

Another method used by insurance plans to develop payment schedules for provider services involves the use of "relative value scales." The Medicare Resource Based Relative Value Scale (RBRVS) is the best-known relative value scale. Other relative value scales include St Anthony's Relative Value for Physicians (RVP) (formerly known as McGraw-Hill's Relative Value for Physicians) and the Florida Medical Association's Florida Relative Value Scale.

Relative value scales assign a relative weight to individual services according to the basis for the scale. Some relative value scales are based on the cost of resources used and on the physician's effort and intensity. Some are based on a combination of both, as in the case of Medicare's RBRVS. Services that are more difficult, time consuming, or resource intensive to perform typically have higher relative values than other services. Payments are determined by multiplying a code's relative value by a constant dollar amount called the conversion factor or multiplier. For example, if a procedure has a relative value of 10 and the conversion factor is $20, the fee for the service would be $200 (10 x $20). Third-party payers using relative value systems often also apply additional methods, such as UCR, to determine payment limits.

Conceptually, the St Anthony RVP and the Medicare RBRVS are similar, but they differ in their design. Following is a discussion of each of these relative value scales.

Medicare's RBRVS Payment Schedule   On January 1, 1992, Medicare began implementation of a national provider payment schedule using the RBRVS. The RBRVS was developed for the Health Care Financing Administration (HCFA) under contract by researchers at Harvard University and continues to be refined. Under RBRVS, a procedure's relative value unit total is the sum of three elements: the provider's work (time and intensity) (RVUWK), the practice expense related to performing the service (RVUPE), and malpractice costs associated with the service (RVUMP).

To account for economic variation across different areas of the country, the Medicare RBRVS applies a geographic component called the geographic practice cost index (GPCI). GPCIs were developed for each of the 210 Medicare payment localities. These localities were established in the early 1960s and are based on historical circumstances. HCFA plans to review the current payment localities for further refinements.

Medicare conversion factors (CFs) used to calculate annual payment amounts are determined annually by HCFA in cooperation with Congress. Previous values are shown in Table 1.2.

Table 1.2   **Medicare Conversion Factors, 1996–2000**

Conversion Factors	1996	1997	1998	1999	2000
Primary care	$35.42	$35.77	$36.69	$34.73	$36.61
Surgical	$40.80	$40.96	$36.69	$34.73	$36.61
Nonsurgical	$34.63	$33.85	$36.69	$34.73	$36.61

The Medicare RBRVS payment schedule formula elements—the conversion factors, relative value units, and geographic adjustment factors—are continually reviewed for refinements. For example, Congress and the Physician Payment Review Commission (PPRC) make recommendations for the annual update of conversion factors, while the AMA/Specialty Society RVS Update Committee (RUC) and HCFA suggest refinements in service RVUs. The RVU updates are published in an issue of the *Federal Register* in late October or early November and go into effect the following January 1. Local Medicare carriers annually publish this calculated fee schedule and distribute it with their Medicare participation agreements.

The St Anthony Relative Value for Physicians (RVP) (Formerly the McGraw-Hill RVP).   In many respects, the RVP is simpler than the RBRVS. It has no geographic adjustment factors or individual RVU components to calculate. The relative value given by RVP is the number used to decide both fees and conversion factors. A drawback of the RVP is that, for each major category of procedures, a separate conversion factor needs to be developed. For example, the CF developed for surgical procedures (CPT codes 10000 through 69999) cannot be used with the pathology codes (80000 through 89999).

The fee amount for the RVP is calculated by means of the same basic principles as those used in the RBRVS, with the exception of the location and component characteristics. For example, procedure code 99204 has an RVU of 20. If we were to take the fee for this procedure, accepted at $80, and divide it by the RVU (20), we can calculate the CF, $4 in this case. Then, to establish the fee for other procedures in this category (those from 90000 to 99999), you simply multiply the procedure-specific RVU by the CF of $4.

Use of Relative Value by Other Payers

Relative value scales are important not only for programs like Medicare, but also to manage reimbursements from Medicaid, Blue Cross Blue Shield, and other commercial payers. Recent studies have shown that a significant number of insurers are currently using or are considering implementing a payment system similar to RBRVS.

In 1998, the American Medical Association (AMA) conducted a national survey of 222 public and private payers to assess the use of RBRVS by non-Medicare payers. The following results were reported in the AMA's publication *Medicare RBRVS: The Physicians' Guide:*

- The survey showed that 63% of respondents use the RBRVS in at least one product line. This compares with a 32% adoption rate from the 1993 Deloitte and Touche survey and a 28% adoption rate from a Physician Payment Review Commission (PPRC) study for its 1995 Annual Report to Congress.

- Of the 63% currently using the RBRVS, 89% have adopted and fully implemented it and 11% are undergoing implementation, meaning that phase-in or full use will begin within a year. In addition, 12% of those familiar with the RBRVS are considering their potential use of it. This indicates that 75% of respondents who are familiar with the RBRVS are either using it or actively considering its use. Only 10% of those familiar with the RBRVS have considered it but decided not to adopt, and 15% have not considered it at all. This can be compared to the 1993 Deloitte and Touche survey, which found that 72% of their respondents were using the RBRVS or actively considering its use, 32% had implemented it, and 40% were considering its use.

- Fee-for-service is the single most prominent use of the RBRVS. However, managed care is an area that has adopted the payment system to a significant degree. In fact, RBRVS is currently being used more commonly with HMOs, PPOs, POS, and managed fee for service.

- An area of concern with non-Medicare use of the RBRVS is the conversion factor and associated payment policies. The fear is that the RBRVS will be used solely to contain costs. This could have negative consequences for patient access.

- The adoption rate varies among four types of payers: Blue Cross Blue Shield (BCBS), Medicaid, workers' compensation, and other non-Medicare. A significant number, 87%, of BCBS plans in the survey use the RBRVS, while 55% of Medicaid and 44% of other non-Medicare plans use the RBRVS.

- A large percentage of BCBS plans use the RBRVS for fee-for-service medicine and managed care services. In fact, the largest single use of the RBRVS was for HMOs (61%), followed by PPO plans (52%), POS plans (41%), and traditional fee-for-service plans (41%).

- The greatest use of the RBRVS was for HMOs at 84%, followed by PPOs at 65% and then POS at 47%.

- Medicaid programs used the RBRVS mainly, 96%, for fee-for-service. They did not use the RBRVS at all for PPOs or POS and used it only minimally for HMOs (13%).

- Other payers' conversion factors, which are used to define physician payment, often differ significantly from Medicare's conversion factor.

This survey indicates a continuing trend toward increased non-Medicare use of the RBRVS. This recent survey by the AMA shows that all non-Medicare users of the RBRVS had a high adoption rate of Medicare payment policies, indicating a high probability for incorporating new policies. It also showed the users' willingness to adapt the RBRVS to their own needs. These results confirm the need to maintain the RBRVS as an accurate, comprehensive standard, uniformly containing all medical services nationwide.

Contracted Rates With Managed Care Organizations

A major tool in managed care is negotiations with physicians and other providers for reduced fees in exchange for the promise of patient volume. A physician may agree to provide services at a discount of his or her normal fee with the understanding that the MCO will refer patients to the provider or provide the provider with a pool of existing patients. The physician or practice may also accept a capitated rate and elect to take financial risk to improve patient volume or practice profitability.

Capitated Rates

A common payment arrangement between physicians and MCOs is a capitation plan. Capitated health plans contract with select physicians, usually primary health care providers who are charged with managing the health care delivery of their members. Under capitation, the physician provides the full range of contracted services to covered patients for a fixed amount on a periodic basis. For instance, the physician will be paid an amount per member per month (PMPM). As an example, if an MCO has 300 patients who selected Dr Smith as their primary provider, and the plan agreed to pay Dr Smith $12 per patient per month, Dr Smith would be paid $3600 each month regardless of the number of patients seen or treatments provided. While guaranteed a fixed amount each month, Dr Smith assumes the risk that the cost of providing care to these patients may exceed the payment amount, for which Dr Smith will not receive additional reimbursement. The physician's only additional charge may be a predetermined copayment and/or deductible coinsurance payment.

The positive aspects of a capitation arrangement are a guaranteed fixed payment, no bad debt, and an assured cash flow; however, the provider can lose money if its services are utilized heavily. To succeed under capitation, the physician must fully understand the contract before it is signed. Capitation agreements range from risk for services performed only in the physician's office to assumption of risk for all health care services provided to the patient.

The MCO will set the capitation rate after detailed evaluation of the number and type of services likely to be provided to patients covered by the plan. The physician must know in detail his or her costs for services, provided by CPT code, to ensure that the capitation amount is adequate. If the physician is at risk for out-of-office services, he or she may also be required to negotiate with a hospital or specialist for a rate for the services that may be needed by a patient. Since capitation contracts are variable, the services of an experienced health care attorney and practice manager will be significant in the success of the physician's negotiation.

Physicians must manage their costs through controlled service utilization, emphasis on preventive health care service, and the use of cost-effective tests, supplies, and allied health personnel such as nurse practitioners (NPs) and physician assistants (PAs). Primary care providers are encouraged to avoid the overutilization of ancillaries, eg, radiology and laboratory or high-cost procedures that have limited positive clinical outcomes. Outside costs are managed by prudent selection of consultants, facilities, and clinical services.

Accounting controls are vital. For example, if an at-risk test or procedure is ordered for which the physician will be financially responsible for payment in the next accounting period, it must be recorded as an "incurred but not reported" (IBNR) item; otherwise the accounting at the end of the period may show a false profit. Costs for compliance with utilization review and quality assurance must be taken into account; close monitoring of these reports is vital.

The two most important questions are "How much do I get?" and "What services am I required by the contract to provide to the patient?"

How Claims Are Processed by Insurance Carriers

Provider insurance claims are sent in two ways—paper claims that are mailed or faxed to the plan and electronic claims stored on computer media (disks, tapes, or CD-ROMs) transmitted via modem.

Paper Claims

Claim Preparation   The paper claim is the traditional method for physicians and other health care providers to submit their charges to insurance companies. The Universal Claim Form (HCFA-1500) is the most common form used, though individual companies may have their own forms. A sample of the HCFA-1500 form is shown in Exhibit 1.1. Relatively few health plans still accept a physician's charge ticket (often termed a superbill or encounter form) as a billing record for services provided to a patient. All claim forms must provide the information essential to process the claim, such as the name of the payer, patient, provider, place of service, date of service, description of the service provided, ie, diagnostic codes and procedure codes, and the charges.

A sample encounter form is shown in Exhibit 1.2. Each practice must create its own encounter form listing information and codes relevant to its needs. A trained consultant familiar with coding issues and payer requirements along with a printer who is familiar with the purpose and needs of the physician will facilitate the effective design of an encounter form. All encounter forms must include, at a minimum, the information requested on the HCFA-1500. Since coding requirements change at least annually, periodic updating of all encounter forms is mandatory. A poorly designed encounter form can adversely affect the physician's third-party payments.

Medicare will accept paper claims only on the HCFA-1500 form and will not accept encounter forms or charge tickets. HCFA discourages the use of paper claims, strongly preferring electronic claims. As a disincentive to the use of paper claims, Medicare and some other payers may process paper claims less quickly than electronic claims. Since virtually all third-party payers accept the HCFA-1500 form, thorough knowledge of this form is necessary for proper billing operations. To review how to complete a HCFA-1500 form, see Chapter 5.

Paper Claim Processing   Processing a paper claim involves the following fundamental steps:

1. Paper claims are received through the mail and microfilmed or microfiched by the payer. Any attachments accompanying claims are separated for microfilming. Since the payer may receive and film thousands of claims each day, they may be unable to match attachments to their associated claims if the following information is not provided on the attachments:

   Physician name

   Physician identification number

   Patient name

   Patient policy number

   Date of service

   Failure to include the above information on attachments may result in claim delays, requests for additional information from the payer, or claim denials.

Exhibit 1.1   Sample HCFA-1500 Form

APPROVED OMB-0938-0008

PLEASE
DO NOT
STAPLE
IN THIS
AREA

CARRIER

◻◻ PICA

HEALTH INSURANCE CLAIM FORM

PICA ◻◻

1. MEDICARE   MEDICAID   CHAMPUS   CHAMPVA   GROUP   FECA   OTHER

◻ (Medicare #)   ◻ (Medicaid #)   ◻ (Sponsor's SSN)   ◻ (VA File #)   ◻ HEALTH PLAN (SSN or ID)   ◻ BLK LUNG (SSN)   ◻ (ID)

1a. INSURED'S I.D. NUMBER   (FOR PROGRAM IN ITEM 1)

2. PATIENT'S NAME (Last Name, First Name, Middle Initial)

3. PATIENT'S BIRTH DATE
MM   DD   YY   SEX
M ◻   F ◻

4. INSURED'S NAME (Last Name, First Name, Middle Initial)

5. PATIENT'S ADDRESS (No., Street)

6. PATIENT RELATIONSHIP TO INSURED
Self ◻   Spouse ◻   Child ◻   Other ◻

7. INSURED'S ADDRESS (No., Street)

CITY   STATE

8. PATIENT STATUS
Single ◻   Married ◻   Other ◻

CITY   STATE

ZIP CODE   TELEPHONE (Include Area Code)
(   )

Employed ◻   Full-Time Student ◻   Part-Time Student ◻

ZIP CODE   TELEPHONE (INCLUDE AREA CODE)
(   )

9. OTHER INSURED'S NAME (Last Name, First Name, Middle Initial)

10. IS PATIENT'S CONDITION RELATED TO:

11. INSURED'S POLICY GROUP OR FECA NUMBER

a. OTHER INSURED'S POLICY OR GROUP NUMBER

a. EMPLOYMENT? (CURRENT OR PREVIOUS)
◻ YES   ◻ NO

a. INSURED'S DATE OF BIRTH
MM   DD   YY   SEX
M ◻   F ◻

b. OTHER INSURED'S DATE OF BIRTH
MM   DD   YY   SEX
M ◻   F ◻

b. AUTO ACCIDENT?   PLACE (State)
◻ YES   ◻ NO

b. EMPLOYER'S NAME OR SCHOOL NAME

c. EMPLOYER'S NAME OR SCHOOL NAME

c. OTHER ACCIDENT?
◻ YES   ◻ NO

c. INSURANCE PLAN NAME OR PROGRAM NAME

d. INSURANCE PLAN NAME OR PROGRAM NAME

10d. RESERVED FOR LOCAL USE

d. IS THERE ANOTHER HEALTH BENEFIT PLAN?
◻ YES   ◻ NO   *If yes*, return to and complete item 9 a-d.

READ BACK OF FORM BEFORE COMPLETING & SIGNING THIS FORM.
12. PATIENT'S OR AUTHORIZED PERSON'S SIGNATURE I authorize the release of any medical or other information necessary to process this claim. I also request payment of government benefits either to myself or to the party who accepts assignment below.

SIGNED _____   DATE _____

13. INSURED'S OR AUTHORIZED PERSON'S SIGNATURE I authorize payment of medical benefits to the undersigned physician or supplier for services described below.

SIGNED _____

PATIENT AND INSURED INFORMATION

14. DATE OF CURRENT: ILLNESS (First symptom) OR
MM   DD   YY   INJURY (Accident) OR
                      PREGNANCY(LMP)

15. IF PATIENT HAS HAD SAME OR SIMILAR ILLNESS.
GIVE FIRST DATE   MM   DD   YY

16. DATES PATIENT UNABLE TO WORK IN CURRENT OCCUPATION
MM   DD   YY   MM   DD   YY
FROM   TO

17. NAME OF REFERRING PHYSICIAN OR OTHER SOURCE

17a. I.D. NUMBER OF REFERRING PHYSICIAN

18. HOSPITALIZATION DATES RELATED TO CURRENT SERVICES
MM   DD   YY   MM   DD   YY
FROM   TO

19. RESERVED FOR LOCAL USE

20. OUTSIDE LAB? $ CHARGES
◻ YES   ◻ NO

21. DIAGNOSIS OR NATURE OF ILLNESS OR INJURY. (RELATE ITEMS 1,2,3 OR 4 TO ITEM 24E BY LINE)

1. ⌞___ . __   3. ⌞___ . __

2. ⌞___ . __   4. ⌞___ . __

22. MEDICAID RESUBMISSION
CODE   ORIGINAL REF. NO.

23. PRIOR AUTHORIZATION NUMBER

24.	A DATE(S) OF SERVICE						B Place of Service	C Type of Service	D PROCEDURES, SERVICES, OR SUPPLIES (Explain Unusual Circumstances) CPT/HCPCS MODIFIER	E DIAGNOSIS CODE	F $ CHARGES	G DAYS OR UNITS	H EPSDT Family Plan	I EMG	J COB	K RESERVED FOR LOCAL USE
	From MM	DD	YY	To MM	DD	YY										
1																
2																
3																
4																
5																
6																

25. FEDERAL TAX I.D. NUMBER   SSN ◻ EIN ◻

26. PATIENT'S ACCOUNT NO.

27. ACCEPT ASSIGNMENT? (For govt. claims, see back)
◻ YES   ◻ NO

28. TOTAL CHARGE
$

29. AMOUNT PAID
$

30. BALANCE DUE
$

31. SIGNATURE OF PHYSICIAN OR SUPPLIER INCLUDING DEGREES OR CREDENTIALS
(I certify that the statements on the reverse apply to this bill and are made a part thereof.)

SIGNED _____   DATE _____

32. NAME AND ADDRESS OF FACILITY WHERE SERVICES WERE RENDERED (If other than home or office)

33. PHYSICIAN'S, SUPPLIER'S BILLING NAME, ADDRESS, ZIP CODE & PHONE #

PIN#   GRP#

PHYSICIAN OR SUPPLIER INFORMATION

(APPROVED BY AMA COUNCIL ON MEDICAL SERVICE 8/88)   ***PLEASE PRINT OR TYPE***

FORM HCFA-1500 (12-90), FORM RRB-1500,
FORM OWCP-1500

Exhibit 1.2   Sample Encounter Form (Superbill)

Jane Doe, M.D.
Internal Medicine
300 Practitioner Road
Smallville, State 99999

Telephone: (555) 555-1212

DATE:

LAST NAME	FIRST	ACCOUNT#	DOB	☐ Male ☐ Female
INSURANCE		PLAN#	SUBSCRIBER#	GROUP#

OFFICE CARE

√	DESCRIPTION	CPT-MOD		
	NEW PATIENT			
	Focused	99201		
	Expanded	99202		
	Detailed	99203		
	Comprehensive-Mod.	99204		
	Comprehensive-High	99205		
	ESTABLISHED PATIENT			
	Minimal	99211		
	Focused	99212		
	Expanded	99213		
	Detailed	99214		
	Comprehensive-Mod.	99215		
	Comprehensive-High	99216		
	CONSULTATION OFFICE			
	Focused	99241		
	Expanded	99242		
	Detailed	99243		
	Comprehensive-Mod.	99254		
	Comprehensive-High	99265		
	Dr.			
	Post-op Exam	99024		
	EVALUATION/MANAGEMENT			
	Brief - 30 minutes	99361		
	Intermediate - 60	99362		
	Telephone-Brief	99371		
	Telephone-Intermed.	99372		
	Telephone-Complex	99373		

PROCEDURES

√	DESCRIPTION	CPT-MOD		
	Treadmill	93015		
	24 Hour Holter	93224		
	Recording only	93225		
	Interp. & Report	93227		
	EKG and interp.	93000		
	EKG (Medicare)	93005		
	Sigmoidoscopy	45300		
	Sigmoidoscopy (flex)	45330		
	Sigmoid (flex) w/bx	45331		

DIAGNOSIS

052.9	Chickenpox, NOS	266.2	B12 deficiency w/o anemia	309.9	Adjustment reaction, unspecified
111.9	Dermatomycosis, unspecified	276.5	Dehydration	305.00	Alcohol abuse, unspecified
009.1	Gastroenteritis, infectious	250.91	Diabetes mellitus, I, compl	303.90	Alcoholism, unspecified
007.1	Giardiasis	250.01	Diabetes mellitus, I, uncompl	331.0	Alzheimers
098.0	Gonorrhea, acute, lower GU	250.90	Diabetes mellitus, II, compl	307.1	Anorexia nervosa
054.9	Herpes simplex, any site	250.00	Diabetes mellitus, II, uncompl	300.00	Anxiety state, unspecified
053.9	Herpes zoster, NOS	250.13	Diabetic ketoacidosis	314.01	Attention deficit, w/ hyperactivity
042	HIV Disease	271.9	Glucose intolerance		
V08	HIV positive, asymp	240.9	Goiter, unspecified	314.00	Attention deficit, w/o
136.9	Infectious/parasitic dis unspec	274.9	Gout, unspecified		hyperactivity
487.1	Influenza w/ upper resp sx	275.42	Hypercalcemia	307.51	Bulimia
007.9	Intestinal protozoa, NOS	276.7	Hyperkalemia	312.90	Conduct disorder, unspecified
088.81	Lyme disease	276.0	Hypernatremia	311	Depressive disorder, NOS
055.9	Measles, NOS	252.0	Hyperparathyroidism	305.90	Drug abuse, unspecified

DIAGNOSIS		☐ Cash
RETURN APPT	REFERRING MD	SIGNATURE
		☐ Check ☐ Credit

Source: HMA

Do not write comments on the HCFA 1500 form in red ink, as it generally will not show up when claim is microfilmed.

2. After the claim has been microfilmed, it will be sent to the claims processing department. Some payers may first have the claim screened. Screeners review basic claims data to verify:

   - that the patient or provider is eligible.

   - that the policy is in effect.

   - that services provided are covered by the patient's contract.

   - that required preoperative clearances were obtained.

   - any other information determined pertinent by the payer.

   Increasingly, computers handle the screening functions at the time the claim is entered. Some payers use optical scanners to process HCFA-1500 forms. The scanners digitize the data on the claim form into their claims processing system for adjudication.

3. Claims processors enter the information on the claim into the payer's computer system. Because of the vast number of claims the payer must process each day, the claim may spend only 2 or 3 minutes with the processor. If the information the physician has provided is incomplete or illegible, the claim may be delayed, suspended for manual review, or denied. Paper claims have a significantly higher data error entry rate than electronic claims.

   If there are unusual facts surrounding the claim, it is important to include any supporting documentation at the time the claim is submitted. A processor may then send the claim to his or her supervisor, who will make a payment decision or forward the claim to the payer's medical review staff. Because claims processors and their immediate supervisors may have limited training in medical terminology, they may not fully understand operative reports and other supporting documentation. The physician may then be required to submit additional documentation to explain or justify the services, including a brief cover letter describing what was done, why it was done, and the unusual facts that affected the physician's services.

Common Problems of "Clean" Paper Claim Processing   Many claim delays and denials result from improper, incomplete, or inaccurate information on claims. These are sometimes called "dirty claims." The following types of problems are often the cause of dirty claims:

1. Illegible handwriting

2. Lack of provider name, identification, or signature

3. Lack of patient name or policy number. Note that the name of the patient submitted for Medicare must be identical to the name on the Medicare card, including middle initials.

4. Out-of-date patient information

5. Outdated codes (CPT, HCPCS, and ICD-9-CM)

6. Improper place-of-service code

7. Lack of name or identification of any referring provider name or identification

8. Illogical relationships between patient diagnoses and services provided

9. Service that does not match Medicare utilization screening criteria

10. Lack of necessary provider identification numbers (PINs or UPINs)

Many practice management computer systems and electronic claims submission programs facilitate cleaner submission of claims by requiring that basic claim information be included. A basic physician office policy should require that all claims submitted have complete, correct, and current information.

Processing of Electronic Claims

An alternative to paper claims is electronic claims submitted to the payer either directly by the physician or through a claims clearinghouse. The electronic process requires a computer, modem, and special software. Many firms offer simple terminals or data entry devices specifically for the purpose of submitting claims. Most provider practice management computer systems have capabilities for electronic claims submission. Computer vendors, BCBS, Medicare, and other organizations can provide information about setting up an electronic claims submission (ECS) system. ECS has several advantages over paper claims.

On average, ECS claims are paid more quickly than paper claims. Medicare, for example, is mandated to pay ECS claims within 14 days, while the paper claim threshold is 27 days. ECS claims are less likely to be rejected by payers. Most ECS software contains claim-editing features that detect and report incomplete claims, invalid codes, and other problems that will cause the claim to be rejected. These are basic edits that flag or reject claims such as a prostatectomy in a female or a Pap smear in a male. This edit feature forces the practice to file cleaner claims.

Most practices have found that ECS is about one-third less expensive than processing paper claims. Third-party payers also realize cost savings through the receipt of electronic claims. Payment posting and reconciliation of claims is far superior with the use of ECS. ECS allows a tape-to-tape rollover, eg, Medicare to Medicaid, that cannot be accomplished with paper claims. In summary, electronic claims are easier to submit and are more likely to be paid.

However, it should be noted that ECS has some shortcomings. Claims that require documentation must still be filed by the paper claim method. As ECS systems begin to accommodate the electronic transmission of reports, radiographs, and related information, however, claims may be generated in the future from an electronic medical record, which will enhance proper documentation. Also, start-up costs for ECS may be significant.

When ECS is evaluated, several methods of submitting claims electronically may be considered:

- Use software that allows the submission of claims directly to major third-party payers, such as Medicare and BCBS.

- Use software to submit claims electronically to a clearinghouse that in turn routes the claims electronically to various third-party payers.

- Send paper claims to a service bureau that enters the claims in their computer and submits them electronically on behalf of the physician.

- Use a combination of all three.

Because not all third-party payers accept electronic claims, even the most automated practices, clearinghouses, and service bureaus must still produce and mail a large number of paper claims. In most systems, a paper claim may be produced from the electronically stored data.

2 Types of Insurance and Third-Party Payers

Objectives

After completing this chapter, you should be able to understand:

- Commercial carriers' nondisclosed payment allowances.

- What distinguishes Blue Cross and Blue Shield plans from other commercial insurance carriers.

- The services covered under Medicare Parts A and B and how to file claims with Medicare.

- How Medicare + Choice provides managed care in the Medicare program.

- The Medicaid program including eligibility and scope of services.

- The basics of the CHAMPVA and CHAMPUS (TRICARE) programs.

- Alternate health plans including health maintenance organizations (HMOs) and preferred provider organizations (PPOs).

- What workers' compensation insurance covers

Introduction

In the United States, there are more than 3000 organizations that may be classified as third-party payers, each offering a variety of health-care benefit packages. They range from small corporate self-funded plans to Medicare. This chapter describes the different types of third-party payers, both public and private.

Commercial Carriers

Background Information

Commercial carriers are private, for-profit organizations that sell health insurance policies to groups (usually employers) and/or individuals. In return for premiums paid by employers or employees, they determine a defined set of health benefits, which may vary on a company-by-company or individual-by-individual basis. Major insurance companies such as Aetna, Cigna, Prudential, and Travelers are examples of commercial carriers.

Commercial insurance companies operate in the private sector and offer a number of different health insurance benefits plans to serve the needs of employers, business, and government. Generally, physicians do not have special contract agreements with commercial carriers, so the patient bears the ultimate responsibility for the bill and the filing of the claim. Some providers may want to file for the patient to ensure a clean, timely claim. Most providers do not require payment from the patient beyond the deductible and coinsurance if the patient is insured. Therefore, the risk of an "aged claim" falls on the provider.

The term *commercial insurance* has historically been used to refer to traditional indemnity health plans that reimburse fee-for-service, generally based on an 80/20 split, with the insurance covering 80% of the allowable charge and the patient being responsible for the remaining 20% coinsurance. Most commercial insurance plans have predefined patient deductibles and coinsurance provisions. The physician's office staff is responsible for contacting the plan to determine the patient's deductible and coinsurance status before rendering services. However, the copayment amount is often listed on the patient's insurance card.

Commercial Insurance "Nondisclosed" Payment Allowance

The traditional indemnity plan is based on predefined payment allowances that may vary by physician specialty and/or geographic location. Results of a recent survey show that 80% of indemnity insurers rely on at least one outside source of information, such as the Health Insurance Association of America or the St Anthony Relative Value for Physicians, to establish or evaluate their physician payment allowances.

Most commercial health plans do not release a fee schedule to physicians as the Medicare, Medicaid, and workers' compensation programs do, so physicians do not usually know what they will be paid before billing the claim. Physicians should pay close attention to commercial payment explanation of benefit (EOB) reports to see how close payments are to charges. This comparison will be helpful for future charge adjustments.

It is important that billing for any service be the same for all carriers. Medicare does not allow different billing for their services from those of commercial payers. The allowed payments may differ, but the amount billed may not. Also remember that all services rendered by physicians may not be covered by all insurance plans. Coverage for health services is defined in the patient's health insurance policy, which is based on a contract between the insurance company and the patient or employer. Therefore, each insurance company health plan offers different levels of medical and financial coverage.

Coordination of Benefits

The majority of commercial insurance health plans have coordination of benefits (COB) clauses that help to define primary and secondary payer status for a pending claim. Many plans also utilize the "gender rule" or the "birthday rule" to assign primary responsibility. Under the gender rule, the male of the household is first in line. Under the birthday rule, the plan of the spouse whose birthday falls earlier in the year is primary to the plan of the spouse whose birthday falls later in the year, referring to the month and day. If both spouses have the same birthday, then the plan that has covered one of them the longest is primary.

Relationship to Other Health Insurance Programs

- **Medicare.** Commercial insurance is almost always primary to any public program, including Medicare. Therefore, beneficiaries aged 65 years or older who are covered by an employer health plan should use the commercial payer as the primary insurer.

- **Medicaid.** If a person is eligible for Medicaid as well as commercial insurance benefits, commercial insurance is always primary.

- **CHAMPUS.** When a beneficiary is covered under another medical insurance plan, the Civilian Health and Medical Program of the Uniformed Services (CHAMPUS) is always secondary, except for Medicaid, the Indian Health Service, or any plan that is specifically designated as a CHAMPUS supplement.

- **Workers' Compensation.** Expenses for medical care related to job-connected illness or injury are paid by the workers' compensation program. Only when benefits are exhausted under the workers' compensation program does commercial insurance assume responsibility for the balance.

- **Private Automobile Insurance.** Any amounts paid by commercial insurance resulting from an automobile accident when the claims are also payable under a policy of automobile insurance may be subject to recovery under the Federal Claims Collections Act.

Claim Submission

It is the responsibility of physicians to accurately report the level or type of service they provide to patients according to CPT coding guidelines and reimbursement rules of the payer. Through accurate coding, the health plan's claim adjudication division will attempt to process the physician's claim and the physician will receive appropriate reimbursement.

Most commercial insurance companies are required to accept the HCFA-1500 for claims processing. Most commercial insurance companies have claim deadlines or a set time limit for which the claim is "processable." The period usually starts on the date of the physician service and may continue for 3 months, 6 months, or a year, depending on their policy. It is recommended that claims for patients with commercial insurance be filed within 4 to 6 days after the date of service. A claim filed on time but not settled expediently because of administrative delays should still be paid, even if the processing time extends beyond the filing date. Proof of filing may be necessary, as well as evidence that the claim continues to be actively pursued. Failure to meet this objective may indicate serious billing problems.

Blue Cross and Blue Shield Plans

Blue Cross and Blue Shield plans are a federation of individual, generally non-profit community corporations that contract with physicians, hospitals, and various other health entities to provide services to their insured companies and individuals. Blue Cross and Blue Shield refers to the persons they insure as subscribers, not policyholders, and they are issued a certificate, not a policy. The certificate defines the health-care benefits and obligations of the medical plan. The word *plan* refers to each separately incorporated, locally administered corporation authorized to use the Blue Cross and Blue Shield name and symbol.

Currently, there are 47 Blue Cross and Blue Shield Member Plans in the United States, Puerto Rico, and the District of Columbia.

Blue Cross primarily covers hospital services, outpatient care, some institutional services, and home care. By contrast, Blue Shield typically covers physician services and, in some cases, dental, outpatient, and vision care.

Collectively, Blue Cross and Blue Shield Member Plans provide health care coverage for more than 75 million, or one in four people in the 50 states, the District of Columbia, and Puerto Rico. This enrollment represents 27% of the total US population. In the United States, more than 80% of hospitals and nearly 90% of physicians contract directly with Blue Cross and Blue Shield Member Plans. Collectively, Blue Cross and Blue Shield Member Plans make up the nation's largest provider of managed care services. More than 52 million people—roughly one in six Americans—are enrolled in a Blue Cross and Blue

Shield managed care plan. Blue Cross is also the nation's largest processor of Medicare Part A (89%) and Part B (59%) claims.

The Blue Cross and Blue Shield Association of America coordinates activities of Blue Cross and Blue Shield plans nationally. Blue Cross and Blue Shield plans are organized locally, and, in some states, both Blue Cross and Blue Shield share offices. In other states, they are entirely separate organizations. The national organization coordinates services and benefits among different Blue Cross and Blue Shield plans for those with offices in multiple states as well as providing other related services.

Blue Cross and Blue Shield plans differ from commercial carrier plans in that they can operate as nonprofit corporations and write contracts directly with providers. If nonprofit, the Blue Cross and Blue Shield plan must obtain approval from its state insurance department before raising rates or changing coverage. Most Blue Cross and Blue Shield plans offer health maintenance organizations (HMOs), preferred provider organizations (PPOs), and point-of-service (POS) plans, which cover 29.8, 15.7, and 7.2 million Americans, respectively, in addition to group and individual fee-for-service (FFS) plans.

Physician reimbursement under Blue Shield plans has historically been based on the usual, customary, and reasonable (UCR) payment method. Under UCR, the allowable charge is the lower of the physician's charge for a service or the physician's UCR amount, or the "average" charge for the service by other physicians in the community who provide the same services. More plans are using the Resource Based Relative Value Scale (RBRVS) to define payment schedules, while other plans use a fixed rate per patient, called capitation. Blue Shield plans, like other commercial insurance plans, will continue to shift their reimbursement methods away from UCR to RBRVS and capitated methods.

Types of Accounts

The majority of Blue Cross and Blue Shield business can be classified into the following types of accounts:

1. Local or regular business

2. Federal Employee Program (FEP)

The following sections describe each type of account and provide procedures for filing claims.

Local or Regular Business Accounts   Local accounts are those in which plan members are located within the geographic territory of the plan. Blue Cross and Blue Shield issues identification cards locally, and all identification contract numbers will be preceded by the local plan's three-letter prefix.

When a patient presents a local or regular business ID card, transmit the following information from the card to the claim form.

1. Subscriber's name

2. Subscriber's contract number, alpha prefix, and other suffixes

3. Subscriber's group number

4. Blue Cross and Blue Shield plan code

This is just one example of information provided on the back of a Blue Cross card. Be sure to review the back of each card. Instructions may differ among the various Blue Cross groups. Exhibit 2.1 shows a copy of a sample Blue Cross and Blue Shield ID card.

Exhibit 2.1   Sample Blue Cross and Blue Shield ID Card

✚ 🛡 BlueCross BlueShield of Kansas City

Precertification required for inpatient hospitalization.
Call 1-800-992-5498.

Identification No.

Group No.   BC Plan   BS Plan

Coverages   See reverse side.

Service Phone Numbers
(314) 395-3674
1-800-892-6048

Providers: Payment of benefits will be based on the patient's eligibility at the time services are received.

Mail claims to:
Blue Cross and Blue Shield of Kansas City
P.O. Box 419169
Kansas City, MO 64141-6169

® Registered Marks Blue Cross and Blue Shield Association

Federal Employee Program (FEP)   The Blue Cross and Blue Shield Association, on behalf of all Blue Cross and Blue Shield plans, contracts with the US Office of Personnel Management (OPM) to provide government-wide service benefit plan coverage to 3.5 million federal employees, dependents, and retirees through the FEP. Forty-six percent of these individuals are members of the FEP. Each year the benefits and premiums are renegotiated with OPM. Benefits and rates for Blue Cross and Blue Shield employees are the same nationwide.

The FEP identification card is a nationally recognized card with the words "Government-Wide Service Benefit Plan" across the top. The card aids in admissions to hospitals without having to check with the patient's employer or make other financial arrangements. All claims are processed through the local plan's office. There is a toll-free customer service number that all customers may use for the claims filing procedures, requests for additional claim forms for patients, and benefits information. A sample of the FEP ID card is shown in Exhibit 2.2.

Exhibit 2.2   **Sample Federal Employee Program ID Card**

BlueCross
BlueShield

Government-Wide Service Benefit Plan

R99999999

FEP102   10/01/9x

TO THE HOSPITAL OR DOCTOR
Please notify your local Blue Cross or Blue Shield Plan on its regular claim form when services are provided.
TO THE FEDERAL EMPLOYEE OR ANNUITANT
1. The Government-Wide Service Benefit Plan Brochure (BRI 41-25) provides information regarding benefits of the Program and how they may be obtained.
2. Whenever you inquire about your coverage, please contact the Blue Cross or Blue Shield office serving the area where you live or work, or Blue Cross and Blue Shield Federal Employee Program,. 550 12th Street, S.W., Washington, D.C. 20024. Always give your identification number and the enrollment code which appear on the face of this card.
3. Coverage normally ceases for children who marry or attain the age of 22 years. To continue protection, they should apply promptly to their local Blue Cross and Blue Shield Plan for a conversion contract.

	ENROLLMENT CODES	
	HIGH OPTION	LOW OPTION
SELF ONLY	101	104
FAMILY	102	105

Employees may select from various options. The following list of coverage classification codes is used to identify the type of benefit option:

101	Self Only/High Option
102	Self and Family/High Option
104	Self Only/Standard Option
105	Self and Family/Standard Option

All FEP ID cards for federal employees are issued by the FEP Operations Center in Washington, DC. Employees can get replacement cards by writing to:

Blue Cross and Blue Shield Federal Employee Program
550 12th St SW
Washington, DC 20065
Attention: FEP Source Records Department.

Traditional Insurance Option

The traditional insurance option generally provides the same scope of benefits available to enrollees through their previous Blue Cross and Blue Shield coverage. However, full benefits for inpatient hospital services will be provided only after predetermination approval.

Members covered under the PPO option use the local plan's PPO network, while HMO members may have different plans depending on where they live. Mental health and substance abuse coverage information, if provided, is stated at the bottom of the enrollee's identification card.

Medicare

Background Information

Medicare is the federal government's health insurance program created by Title XVIII of the Social Security Amendment of 1965, titled "Health Insurance for the Aged and Disabled." The Medicare program is divided into two parts: Part A and Part B.

When Medicare began on July 1, 1966, there were 19.1 million persons enrolled in the program. By the end of 1975, there were about 24 million enrollees; in 1985, almost 30 million enrollees; and in 2000 there are 40 million enrollees in Part B of the Medicare program.

To be enrolled in the Medicare program, persons must be 65 or older, retired on Social Security benefits, the spouse of a person paying into the Social Security system, or those having received Social Security disability benefits for a 2-year period. Special eligibility provides coverage those diagnosed with end-stage renal disease (ESRD), the medical expenses of kidney donors to persons with ESRD, the spouses and dependent children of workers who paid into Social Security, and retired federal employees of the Civil Service Retirement System (CSRS) and their spouses. Everyone eligible for Social Security benefits is automatically enrolled in Part A, which covers institutional care, although Part B coverage must be elected and paid for with additional premiums. Beneficiaries are responsible for a deductible, copayments, and monthly premiums for Part B.

Part A

The Part A portion of Medicare, also called Hospital Insurance (HI) for the Aged and Disabled, covers institutional providers for inpatient, hospice, and home health services.

Individuals who did not pay Medicare taxes while working and those individuals having less than 30 quarters of coverage must pay a premium to obtain Part A benefits.

A deductible is required for each episode of illness and is currently $776. In addition, if a participant is hospitalized for more than 60 days, a coinsurance applies as well. The daily coinsurance is $194 for the 61st through 90th days and $388 for the 91st through 150th days.

For those individuals not eligible for Social Security, voluntary enrollment in Part A is available. However, applicants must be at least 65 years old and a US resident, ie, either a citizen or an alien lawfully admitted for permanent residence for not less than 5 years immediately prior to the application. Also, the individual must enroll in Part B.

Part B

The Part B portion, also called Supplementary Medical Insurance (SMI) Benefits for the Aged and Disabled, provides benefits for noninstitutional health care providers, most notably physician services. Table 2.1 defines and summarizes Part B service coverage and payment provisions.

Table 2.1   **Medicare Part B: Covered Services for 2000**

Services	Benefit	Medicare Pays	Patient Pays
Medical Services Physicians' services, except for intern and resident medical and surgical services and supplies incident to physician services, therapy, diagnostic tests, durable medical equipment, and other services	Unlimited if medically necessary	80% of approved amount (after $100 deductible); 50% of approved charges for most outpatient mental health services	$100 deductible, plus 20% of approved amount and limited charges above approved amount for "nonparticipating" providers
Clinical Laboratory Services Blood tests, urinalysis, and more	Unlimited if medically necessary	Generally 100% of approved amount according to a fee schedule	Nothing for services
Home Health Care Part-time or intermittent skilled care, home health aide services, durable medical equipment and supplies, and other services	Unlimited as long as Medicare conditions are met	100% of approved amount based on diagnosis; 80% of approved amount for durable medical equipment	Nothing for services; 20% of approved amount for durable medical equipment and osteoporosis devices
Outpatient Hospital Treatment Services for the diagnosis or treatment of illness or injury	Unlimited if medically necessary	Medicare payment to hospital based on ambulatory payment classifications	20% of approved amount (after $100 deductible)
Blood	Unlimited if medically necessary	80% of approved amount (after $100 deductible and starting with 4th pint); unless replaced satisfied under Part A	First 3 pints plus 20% of approved amount for additional pints (after $100 deductible)
Pneumococcal and Influenza Vaccines		100% of approved amount	Nothing for service
Screening Mammography Pap and Pelvic Exam		100% of approved amount	No deductible but 20% coinsurance applies

Medicare Part B premiums are usually deducted from the enrollee's monthly Social Security check. Enrollees who do not receive Social Security benefits can pay monthly premiums in order to receive Part B Medicare. Currently, the monthly premium is $45.50 and the annual deductible is $100.

Part B participants must also pay 20% coinsurance.

Table 2.2 contains examples of items not covered by Medicare.

Table 2.2	**Examples of Items Not Covered Under Medicare Part B**
	• Interns and residents providing services that are part of their teaching program
	• Services or items that are not medically necessary
	• Routine checkups, custodial care, and cosmetic surgery
	• Administrative services (not patient care) such as hospital committee work
	• Phone calls between physicians and beneficiaries, except in some cases for patient consultations in rural areas with a shortage of health care professionals
	• Patient visits solely for obtaining or renewing a prescription, without an examination of the patient
	• Services to hospice patients by physicians employed by the hospice (this is Part A service)
	• Preventive immunizations for smallpox, polio, diphtheria, etc, except for injuries or direct exposure, unless provided in a federally qualified community health center. Also, pneumococcal pneumonia, hepatitis B, and influenza virus vaccines are covered services
	• Self-administerable drugs or biologicals, unless administered to a patient in an emergency situation, and except for immunosuppressive drugs for transplant patients for 44 months, erythropoietin for dialysis patients, and certain other specific drugs
	• Eye exams, glasses, and contact lens
	• Hearing exams, hearing aids
	• Routine foot care, with a few specific exceptions
	• Dental services, unless hospitalization is required

Table 2.3 describes the condition for which Medicare covers the most common preventive services.

Who Is a Physician?

Medicare defines "physicians" to include these professionals:

- Doctors of medicine
- Psychiatrists
- Doctors of osteopathy
- Dentists

Table 2.3 **Medicare Covered Preventive Services**

Medicare generally does not cover preventive services, but here are the major exceptions for tests and a physician's interpretation of the results:

- *Screening Mammography.* Women aged 35 to 39 are covered for one screening, women 40 and older are covered for one screening per year. Part B deductible is waived and payment is $67.81.

- *Pap Smears, Pelvic and Breast Exams.* These tests are covered at 3-year intervals, with annual exams covered for women at high risk of cervical or vaginal cancer or who are of childbearing age with an abnormality detected during the past 3 years.

- *Colorectal Screening Test.* Anal fecal occult blood tests for those aged 50 and older, flexible sigmoidoscopy every 4 years for those aged 50 and older, colonoscopy every 2 years for high-risk individuals, screening barium enemas every 4 years for those 50 and older not at high risk and every 2 years for high-risk patients.

- *Bone Marrow Measurement.* These tests are covered for certain at-risk patients after a need for the test has been determined. Tests may be performed biannually or more often in certain cases.

- *Prostate Cancer Screening.* Anal digital rectal exams and prostate-specific antigen blood tests are covered for men over 50.

- *Diabetes Self-management.* Education and training are covered if certified under a physician's comprehensive plan of care. Blood glucose monitors and testing strips are covered as durable medical equipment.

- Optometrists
- Chiropractors

Medicare coverage is available only for those physicians licensed by the state in which they practice and only for services authorized by the state licensing agency and covered by Medicare. Physicians performing services in hospitals operated by the federal government within the scope of their federal employment are also covered even if not licensed by the state.

Intern and resident services that are part of an approved teaching program are covered under Part A, although the teaching physicians may bill under Part B for direct patient care provided certain documentation is maintained.

Medicare is administered by the Health Care Financing Administration (HCFA), a federal agency in the Department of Health and Human Services (DHHS). Large regional insurance companies, such as Blue Cross and Blue Shield plans, that have been awarded Medicare contracts conduct the actual day-to-day operations of Medicare Part B on a local basis. These companies are called Medicare carriers (see Appendix for a list of all carriers). Most of a physician's contact with Medicare will be through the local carrier's provider representative. All physicians and health care providers are required by law to bill Medicare for services rendered by completing the HCFA-1500 claim form at no charge to the patient.

Medicare Part B reimburses physician services according to the allowances defined in the Medicare Fee Schedule (MFS), which is based on the Resource Based Relative Value Scale (RBRVS). Under RBRVS, physician payment allowances for the same service may vary from one locality to another because of the localities' geographic practice cost index (GPCI); however, all physicians in the same locality, regardless of their specialty, receive the same payment for the same service. Payment variations for a Medicare service within a region depend on (1) whether or not the physician participates with Medicare, (2) the facility where the service is performed, and (3) whether or not the claim is assigned.

Medicare Physicians' Fee Schedule

Physicians are paid by Medicare on a national fee schedule, which applies to all "physician" services (see definition of physicians earlier in this chapter) and some services by other health care professionals, such as:

- Supplies and other service furnished incident to a physician's professional service provided they are integral in the patient's diagnosis or treatment

- Outpatient physical, occupational, and speech therapy

- Diagnostic x-rays and other diagnostic tests other than clinical lab, which has its own fee schedule

- Radioactive therapies, including materials and technicians

The Medicare Part B carrier generally pays 80% of the lower of the fee schedule amounts or the actual physician's charge, with 20% of the "allowed" amount being due from the patient. The fee schedule amounts are determined by multiplying the relative value by the geographic adjustment factor and the conversion factors.

The relative value is set by HCFA and is a relative ranking of the resources required for that procedure compared to all other procedures.

The relative value reflects:

- The value of the physician's professional time

- The physician's practice expense

- A factor for malpractice insurance costs

The geographic adjustment factor is a relative ranking of labor cost in each area (metropolitan statistical area, rural, etc) compared to all other areas.

The conversion factor is a dollar amount annually set by HCFA; the conversion factor for 2000 is set at $36.6137.

All participating physicians, regardless of specialization, in a given area are paid the same amount for the same service. Nonparticipating physicians are paid 5% less than participating physicians.

Adjustments to the Medicare Fee Schedule

In addition to the 5% discount for nonparticipating physicians, these other adjustments apply:

- *Anesthesiologists.* Medical direction is paid for at 50% when a single procedure is involved.

- *Assistants-at-Surgery.* Payment under Part B is prohibited for physician assistants-at-surgery in hospitals with approved teaching programs. Otherwise, the lower of 16% of the fee schedule or the actual charge is paid for these physician services, provided the services are required because of exceptional medical circumstances, complex medical procedures are performed requiring more than one physician, and certain other conditions are met.

- *Physician Assistants.* These professionals are paid 80% of the lesser of 85% of the Medicare fee schedule or the actual charges. If performing as an assistant-at-surgery, the payment is the lesser of the actual charge or 85% of the amount payable if the service was provided by a physician serving in the same role.

- *Nurse Practitioners and Clinical Nurse Specialists.* These professionals are paid at 80% of the lesser of the actual charge or 85% of the fee schedule.

- *Clinical Psychologists.* These professionals are paid at 100% of the fee schedule.

Understanding Medicare Participation

Each year, HCFA invites every physician to "participate" or discontinue "participation" by December 31. Medicare participation means that the physician agrees to accept assignment for all Medicare claims and to accept Medicare's allowable charge as payment in full for his or her services. Physicians who elect not to participate (referred to as "nonpar" physicians) can still see Medicare patients and accept assignment on a claim-by-claim basis.

The number of physicians electing to participate in Medicare has steadily increased during the past 10 years. Agreeing to participate means:

1. The physician agrees to accept assignment for all Medicare services provided. Assignment means the physician requests direct payment from Medicare and Medicare pays 80% of the fee schedule to the physician.

2. The physician agrees to accept Medicare's payment and the patient's deductible and coinsurance as payment in full for the services, regardless of the charge he or she makes.

3. The physician agrees not to bill the patient for services determined by Medicare to be noncovered services or certain elective procedures. However, the physician may bill the patient for other noncovered services provided notice of noncoverage was provided and the patient's signature obtained before services were rendered.

Electing not to participate with Medicare means the physician has the choice, on a claim-by-claim basis, to accept assignment.

Payments to nonparticipating (nonpar) physicians on assigned claims are 5% less than payments to participating physicians. For example, if the fee schedule amount for participating physicians is $100, the amount paid to a nonparticipating physician's assigned claim will be $95.

For unassigned claims, the physician must adhere to *limiting charge* limitations, also referred to as balance billing limits, determined by Medicare. The limiting charge is 115% of Medicare's allowable charge for participating physicians. Violation of the charge limitations is considered a violation of Medicare regulations, and overcharges must be refunded to the patients within 30 days. Physicians can obtain the limiting charge amounts from their local Medicare carriers.

Advantages and Disadvantages of Participation

1. Effective September 1, 1990, *regardless of the assignment status* of a claim or the participation status of a physician, *all physicians must submit bills to Medicare* on behalf of their patients. What used to be an advantage for nonparticipating physicians has equalized, resulting in the same time and costs to all practices.

2. On assigned claims, reimbursement is sent directly to the practice. This guarantees at least partial payment and can simplify bookkeeping procedures for the staff. Additionally, the remittance advice received with the check provides important feedback to the practice in terms of accuracy of coding, coverage information, and regulatory information, which is vital to improving reimbursements. This important information is lost when the nonparticipating practice does not accept assignment on the claim.

On unassigned claims, however, because payment can be collected "at time of service," the staff does not have to perform the extra record-keeping step of updating the financial record when the payment is received. The record can be marked paid at that time and put away, thus saving time, increasing efficiency, and possibly avoiding mistakes.

Although the nonparticipating physician who does not accept assignment on a claim can collect the fee at the time of service, many do not. What this means for the practice is that the Medicare payment sent to the patient may be spent on something other than the physician's fee. Because collection is only as effective as the staff has time to make it, this could become a burdensome and costly process. At least for assigned claims, the only amount to be collected is the coinsurance and deductible amounts. The practice is assured it will receive at least part of the reimbursement.

3. Collection from the patient poses less of a problem for the participating physician and those who accept assignment. In many circumstances, collection from the patient is avoided as many Medicare enrollees carry supplemental insurance, which pays for some or all deductible and coinsurance balances. Most carriers have an arrangement whereby they will send the necessary information to the appropriate supplemental insurer, thus eliminating this process for the office staff or the patient. (This advantage is usually only available to participating physicians.) Even though the practice must collect from two sources, it does usually collect the total approved fee.

   For a nonparticipating physician who does not accept assignment, the total limited fee can be collected at the time of service—which means no waiting, speedy cash flow, and no cost of collection. But again, if the fee is not collected from the patient at the time of service, the practice runs the risk of collecting substantially less money or no money at all from the patient and must cover the cost and time of collection efforts. Also, subsequent medical necessity denials cause the practice to have to refund to the patient any amounts previously collected.

4. Nonparticipating physicians have additional requirements that participating physicians do not, such as the completion of the elective surgery advance notice.

5. Carriers maintain and distribute a listing of all participating physicians, groups, and clinics. This annual listing, called the Medicare Participation Directory or MEDPARD, contains the name, address, and phone number of all physicians, groups, and clinics who have elected participation for a calendar year. The vast distribution of MEDPARD could help increase the participating physician's patient base.

6. When referring a Medicare patient to a nonparticipating physician for outpatient care, hospitals are required to also provide, where practical, the name of a participating physician qualified to perform the same services.

7. Medicare includes, on all explanation of Medicare benefits statements for unassigned claims, a statement reminding the patient about the participation program. Some carriers point out the amount of money the patient could have saved with a participating provider.

8. While this consideration may not be paramount to all practices, it is important to think about how physicians' participation status affects physicians' Medicare patients. Many Medicare beneficiaries do not understand the participation program or assignment agreement, and an explanation does not always help them understand it better. Participation removes a burden from these patients, possibly helping them focus on getting well rather than worrying about how to pay for it.

Medicare Outpatient Deductibles and Copayment

The 2000 Medicare Part B outpatient deductible is $100 per year, and the beneficiary coinsurance responsibility is 20% of the MFS payment allowance. However, the payment rules vary according to physician participation status and whether the claim was taken under assignment.

If a participating physician charges $100 for a service and the participating allowance is $60, Medicare will reimburse directly to the physician 80% of $60, or $48. The patient is responsible for 20% of $60, or $12, and the remaining $40 in excess of the allowance will be written off as a Medicare participation contractual allowance.

Under the same scenario, except for a nonparticipating physician not accepting assignment, the MFS has a nonparticipating limiting charge allowance that is calculated at 115% of the participating allowance. This limiting charge value represents the charge amount the nonparticipating physician cannot exceed when billing Medicare beneficiaries without facing possible Medicare fines and penalties.

The limiting charge for the service with the $60 participating allowance is equal to (115% × $60) or $69. Thus, the nonparticipating physician's charge cannot exceed $69. When billed to Medicare at $69, Medicare pays 95% of the 80 percent or $52.44. The beneficiary is responsible for 20% of the allowance or $13.80, plus the nonparticipating physician can collect the balance of the $69 charge ($69 minus [$52.44 + $13.80], or $2.76) from the patient.

Coordination of Benefits—Medicare as Secondary Payer

Basically, the Medicare secondary payer (MSP) program's function is to coordinate the coverage of health benefits between the Medicare program and other health insurers, with particular emphasis on employer group health plans.

Services payable under workers' compensation plans or the Federal Black Lung Program, or authorized by the Veterans Affairs, have always been excluded from primary payment under Medicare but may coordinate secondary payer benefits.

There are four types of insurance coverage circumstances that make Medicare benefits (payments) secondary to other forms of insurance. They include coverage by:

1. Employer group health plans (EGHP) insurance for working aged beneficiaries over 65 or the spouse of an employed individual of any age, and the beneficiary is covered under an EGHP.

2. Liability or "no-fault" insurance for automobile, homeowners, or property claims that provides personal injury or medical expense coverage.

3. Disability insurance for beneficiaries under age 65 and disabled, who are covered by a large group health plan (LGHP).

4. Work-related illness/injury insurance such as workers' compensation, Black Lung, or the Veterans Affairs.

The reporting of Medicare as secondary payer has been mandated by HCFA; therefore, physicians must take an active role in the identification of MSP claims before billing Medicare as primary. This can be accomplished by having the patient fill out the MSP questionnaire that asks a series of questions about the four categories of "other" insurers. Exhibit 2.3 is a sample MSP admission questionnaire.

Since both the MSP questionnaire and billing procedures for each of the four circumstances have been published in most of the Medicare carrier newsletters, reviewing the physicians' carrier newsletters may be beneficial. Practices that fail to follow MSP requirements will experience Medicare denials, accumulated accounts receivable, irritated beneficiaries, and less than optimal reimbursement.

If physicians determine the beneficiary has EGHP insurance that makes Medicare the secondary payer, physicians must bill the private insurance first for all the services and supplies provided during the patient encounter. Because Medicare is not the patient's primary insurer, physicians are not obligated to bill the physicians' "Medicare rates" or limiting charges, nor are physicians obligated

Exhibit 2.3   Sample MSP Admission Questionnaire

MEDICARE SECONDARY PAYER QUESTIONNAIRE

Part I

1. Is the patient receiving Black Lung (BL) benefits? _____ yes _____ no
BL IS PRIMARY ONLY FOR CLAIMS RELATED TO BL.

2. Has the Department of Veteran Affairs (DVA) authorized and agreed to pay for care at this facility?____yes (DVA IS PRIMARY FOR THESE SERVICES) _____ no.

3. Was the illness/injury due to a work-related accident/condition? _____ yes _____ no
If YES, record date of Injury/Illness. WC IS PRIMARY PAYER ONLY FOR CLAIMS RELATED TO WORK RELATED INJURIES OR ILLNESSES. **GO TO PART III** If NO, **GO TO PART II.**

Part II

1. Was illness/injury due to a non-work related accident? ___ yes ___ no If NO, **GO TO PART III.**

2. What type of accident caused the illness/injury?___automobile___non-automobile
NO FAULT INSURER IS PRIMARY PAYER FOR THOSE CLAIMS RELATED TO THE ACCIDENT. GO TO PART III.

3. Was another party responsible for this accident? _____ yes _____ no
LIABILITY INSURER IS PRIMARY ONLY FOR THOSE CLAIMS RELATED TO THE ACCIDENT. GO TO PART III

Part III

1. Is the beneficiary entitled to Medicare based on:
___Age. **Go to Part IV** ___Disability. **Go to Part V** ___ESRD. **Go to Part VI**

Part IV – Working Aged

1. Does the patient have current employment status? _____ yes _____ no

2. Does the patient's spouse have current employment status? _____ yes _____ no
IF PATIENT ANSWERED NO TO BOTH NUMBERS 1 & 2, MEDICARE IS PRIMARY UNLESS THE PATIENT ANSWERED YES TO QUESTIONS IN PART I OR II. DO NOT PROCEED ANY FURTHER.

3. Does the patient have Group Health Plan (GHP) coverage based on his/her own or a spouse's current employment status?
___yes ___no If NO, STOP. MEDICARE IS PRIMARY PAYER UNLESS THE PATIENT ANSWERED YES TO QUESTIONS IN PART I OR II.

4. Does the employer that sponsors the patient's GHP employ 20 or more employees?___ yes ____ no
If YES, GROUP HEALTH PLAN IS PRIMARY
If NO, STOP. MEDICARE IS PRIMARY UNLESS THE PATIENT ANSWERED YES TO QUESTIONS IN PART I OR II.

Part V – Disability

1. Does the patient have current employment status? ____ yes _____ no If No, record date of retirement.

2. Does a family member of the patient have current employment status? __ yes __ no If No, record date of retirement. IF THE PATIENT ANSWERED NO TO BOTH NUMBERS 1 & 2, MEDICARE IS PRIMARY UNLESS THE PATIENT ANSWERED YES TO QUESTIONS IN PART I OR II. DO NOT PROCEED ANY FURTHER.

3. Does the patient have GHP coverage based on his/her or family's employment status? ___ yes ___ no
If NO, STOP. MEDICARE IS PRIMARY UNLESS THE PATIENT ANSWERED YES TO QUESTIONS IN PART I OR II.

4. Does the employer that sponsors the patient's GHP employ 100 or more employees?___ yes _____ no
If YES, GROUP HEALTH PLAN IS PRIMARY.
If No, STOP. MEDICARE IS PRIMARY UNLESS THE PATIENT ANSWERED YES TO QUESTIONS IN PART I OR II.

Part VI – ESRD

1. Does the patient have group health plan coverage? _____ yes _____ no
If No, STOP. MEDICARE IS PRIMARY.

2. Is the patient within the 30-month coordination period?__ yes ___ no STOP. MEDICARE IS PRIMARY.

3. Is the patient entitled to Medicare on the basis of either ESRD and age or ESRD and disability? ___yes ___no. STOP. GHP IS PRIMARY DURING THE 30-MONTH COORDINATION PERIOD.

4. Was the patient's initial entitlement of Medicare (including simultaneous entitlement) based on ESRD?
___yes STOP GHP CONTINUES TO PAY PRIMARY DURING THE 30-MONTHS.
___no. INITIAL ENTITLEMENT IS BASED ON AGE OR DISABILITY.

5. Does the working aged or MSP disability provision apply (i.e. Is the GHP primary based on the age or disability entitlement)?___yes STOP. GHP CONTINUES TO PAY PRIMARY DURING 30-MONTH COORDINATION PERIOD. ___no MEDICARE CONTINUES TO PAY PRIMARY.

IT IS IMPORTANT TO REMEMBER TO ACQUIRE DATES AND INFORMATION RELATING TO EMPLOYMENT AND BENEFITS COVERAGE. THIS INFORMATION WOULD INCLUDE RETIREMENT, ACCIDENT, AND START DATES FOR BENEFITS AS WELL AS NAME AND ADDRESS OF INSURANCE CARRIERS AND EMPLOYERS, POLICY OR IDENTIFICATION NUMBERS, GROUP IDENTIFICATION NUMBERS, NAME OF POLICY HOLDER, RELATIONSHIP TO PATIENT, AND CLAIM NUMBERS.

Copyrighted 1998 by HMA.

to abide by Medicare service and supply coverage limits, unless so defined by the primary insurer. Physicians should bill the physicians' standard or private insurance charges.

Practices unfamiliar with the MSP program assume that if the primary insurance payments exceed the Medicare allowable(s) for services rendered, the billing and collection process has been completed. This assumption not only prevents Medicare from tracking beneficiary coordination of benefits, deductible, and coinsurance liabilities, but also reduces legitimate payment optimization efforts.

The amount of the Medicare secondary payment (per service) is based on several factors. Medicare will pay the lowest of the following values:

1. The billed charge minus the primary insurer's payment

2. The amount Medicare would have paid as primary (ie, 80% of the MFS allowable amount)

3. The higher of (*a*) the fee schedule amount or (*b*) the other insurer's approved charge minus the amount the other insurer actually paid

What Can the Patient Be Charged?

If the claim is assigned, the beneficiary's obligation remains 20% as a coinsurance plus any unmet deductible. The physician can charge the patient only if the primary insurer's payment is less than the patient's Medicare coinsurance and deductible.

The patient's coinsurance (20% × $125) of $25 cannot be collected from the patient, as the primary payment ($120) satisfies this obligation. If the primary payment does not satisfy the beneficiary's obligation (ie, the primary payment was only $20), the physician can bill up to the deductible and coinsurance due, or $5.

Expenses that meet the beneficiary's Part B $100 deductible are credited to the deductible even if the primary insurer paid the entire bill and there is no Medicare benefit payable. The Part B deductible is credited on the basis of Medicare allowable charges, rather than the amount paid by the primary insurer.

A sample of the Medicare beneficiary health insurance ID card is shown in Exhibit 2.4.

The Medicare ID card has four key areas to understand and utilize for efficient claim submission:

1. Beneficiary name

2. Medicare beneficiary health insurance claim number (HICN). This is the beneficiary's unique identification number. It closely matches his or her

Exhibit 2.4   **Medicare Beneficiary Health Insurance ID Card**

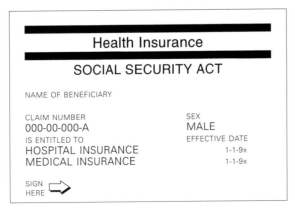

nine-digit Social Security number, plus a one- or two-digit alphanumeric modifier (discussed later)

3. Entitlement. This defines what the beneficiary is entitled to. "Hospital Insurance" indicates the beneficiary has Part A—hospital benefits. "Medical Insurance" indicates the beneficiary has Part B—outpatient benefits

4. Effective dates. This defines the effective date for each benefit. Medicare will not pay for services before these dates

Common HICN Suffix Modifiers

A:	Wage earner	B:	Aged wife
B1:	Husband	C1:	Children
D:	Aged widow	D4:	Remarried widow
E:	Mother (widow)	F1:	Father
F2:	Mother		

Note: Railroad Medicare beneficiaries will have a letter *prefix* instead of a suffix.

Other Medicare Claim Submission Policies

- Physicians must submit professional service claims on behalf of beneficiaries treated on the HCFA-1500 form. Electronic submission can also be used. Failure to bill on behalf of beneficiaries may be subject to a civil monetary penalty of up to $10,000 per violation.

- Physicians may not charge for preparing or filing Medicare claims.

- Medicare-assigned claims must be filed within 1 year from the date of service or the payment will be reduced by 10%. If the date of service was in October, November, or December, a practice has until the following December to submit the claim without the 10% payment reduction.

- It is the responsibility of physicians to accurately report the level or type of service they provide to patients according to the coding guidelines and reimbursement rules of the AMA and HCFA. Always refer to the Medicare Part B bulletin for the latest coding changes and implementation dates.

How to File Primary Insurance if Not Medicare

- Bill all services, procedures, and supplies to the primary insurer and bill the full charge amount (standard rates).

- Identify Medicare as the secondary payer on the HCFA-1500 form.

- Items 11 a–d of the HCFA-1500 form: Enter primary insurance information.

- Items 9 a–d of the HCFA-1500 form: Enter Medicare as the secondary payer.

- Wait to receive primary explanation of benefits (EOB) with payments and/or denials before billing Medicare. In some instances electronic billing may benefit from tape-to-tape transfers.

How to File a Medicare Secondary Claim

- After receiving the EGHP primary insurance EOB for partial payment, full payment, or denials for services rendered, bill Medicare.

- If the primary insurer has not paid the bill in full, prepare a claim for Medicare showing the full charges for the services. (The full charge cannot exceed the limiting charge on a nonassigned claim to Medicare.)

- Attach a copy of the primary insurance EOB or a copy of the check. The documentation should reflect primary allowed and payment amounts.

- Mark or stamp "Medicare Secondary Payer." Note: Electronic billers must file a paper claim when Medicare is the MSP.

- Complete the HCFA-1500 form:

  — Items 11 a–d: Enter beneficiary's information.

  — Items 9 a–d: Enter primary insurer information.

  — Enter the amount paid by the primary insurer.

  — See Chapter 4 for detailed instructions on completing a HCFA-1500 form.

Medicare Relationship to Other Health Insurance Programs

- ***Commercial Insurance.*** Commercial insurance is always primary to any public program, including CHAMPUS and Medicare. Therefore, beneficiaries aged 65 or older who are covered by an employer health plan should use the commercial insurer as the primary insurer.

- *Medicaid.* As a general rule of thumb, a federal program supersedes a state program. So, if a person is eligible for Medicaid as well as Medicare, Medicare is usually the primary payer source. Further, all claims must be submitted assigned.

- *Workers' Compensation.* Expenses for medical care related to job-connected illness or injury are always paid by the workers' compensation program as primary.

- *Private Automobile Insurance.* Any claims arising out of an automobile accident or other personal injury claims are always payable as primary under a policy of automobile insurance and may be subject to recovery under the Federal Claims Collections Act.

When claims are filed to Medicare as the primary payer, a number of different RBRVS-related payment policies may alter the traditional 80/20 payment split. An overview of special RBRVS payment policies is discussed in the next section.

Medicare Managed Care (Part C)

The Balanced Budget Act of 1997 created new health care options called *Medicare + Choice* (or *Medicare Plus Choice*). Under Medicare + Choice, HCFA contracts with managed care plans or provider service organizations to provide Medicare benefits. When beneficiaries enroll in Medicare managed care plans, they select a doctor from the plan's list of primary care physicians, and their primary care physician is then responsible for coordinating all of their health care needs. An exception will be the first FFS Medicare Choice plan, Sterling Option I, available on a limited basis on July 1, 2000, which allows patients to see any traditional Medicare provider.

The managed care plans are reimbursed by HCFA, according to an "adjusted average per capita cost" (AAPCC). The AAPCC is the estimated average FFS cost of Medicare benefits for an individual by county of residence. It is based on the following factors: age, sex, institutional status, Medicaid, disability, and end-stage renal disease (ESRD) status. The AAPCC is the monthly capitation payment that will be made to the managed care plans. The provider is then at risk for all care of the patient. There may be some contractual exclusions, such as ESRD programs.

Medicare + Choice will increase the number of options beneficiaries can choose from to receive benefits. Provider groups include PPOs, provider-sponsored organizations (PSOs), medical savings account plans, and private FFS plans not otherwise available on traditional Medicare. Plans can expand benefits to include prescription drugs, routine eyewear, and worldwide emergency care.

How Medicare Managed Care Works   Medicare's managed care plans mostly work like traditional HMO plans; however, the first FFS plan started in 2000. Though committed to providing members with quality health care, managed care plans generally maintain some control over important health care decisions. They also can limit access to specialists and intervene in other medical decisions. Managed care plans contract with Medicare to provide all of Medicare's benefits.

Managed care plans generally cover more services and have fewer out-of-pocket costs than FFS. In addition to offering all statutory Medicare benefits, many plans promote preventive health care by providing extra benefits. Some of these benefits are eye examinations, hearing aids, routine physicals, and scheduled inoculations for little or no extra fee, as well as offering help with prescription drugs—and there is little or no paperwork in a managed care plan.

Each plan has its own network of hospitals, skilled nursing facilities, home health agencies, doctors, and other professionals. Depending on how the plan is organized, services are usually provided either at one or more centrally located health facilities, or in the private practice offices of the doctors and other health care professionals who are part of the plan.

Types of Medicare Managed Care Plans   Medicare offers two types of managed care contracts—"risk" or "cost" contracts. Here are some of the important differences:

- **Risk Plans.** These plans typically have "lock-in" requirements. This means that beneficiaries generally must receive all covered care through the plan or through referrals from the plan. If services that are not authorized by the plan are received, neither the plan nor Medicare will pay.

- **Cost Plans.** Cost plans do not have "lock-in" requirements. If beneficiaries enroll in a cost plan, they can either go to health care providers affiliated with the plan or go outside the plan. If beneficiaries go outside the plan, the plan probably will not pay but Medicare will.

If beneficiaries go outside of the plan, Medicare will pay its share of approved charges. Beneficiaries will be responsible for Medicare's coinsurance, deductibles, and other charges, just as if they were receiving care under the FFS system. Because of this flexibility, a cost plan may be a good choice for beneficiaries if they travel frequently, live in another state part of the year, or want to use a physician who is not affiliated with a plan.

Because Part C is relatively new, look for more details in the future. For more information, access the Medicare managed care comparison database, "Medicare Compare," at the HCFA web site (www.medicare.gov).

Medicare + Choice Program

In August 1997, the Balanced Budget Act of 1997 (BBA) created Medicare + Choice (Part C of the program), under which beneficiaries' health benefits may be delivered by managed care organizations, beginning in 1999. This change in Medicare is designed to reduce spending by encouraging free market competition. Under the traditional FFS system, a patient may choose almost any doctor, hospital, or other health care provider, and those providers are paid on the basis of each itemized service they provide.

The Medicare + Choice program also expanded managed care in rural areas by offering more attractive reimbursement rates to managed care organizations. The BBA added a 2% increase for all Medicare managed care plans and a special increase that raised rural areas to a "floor" payment rate. Citing financial pressures, a number of Medicare risk plans reduced their participation in Medicare or withdrew from the program entirely.

Congress created the Medicare + Choice program to give beneficiaries an expanded choice of private health plan options beyond the original Medicare and the previous Medicare managed care program. HCFA stopped accepting applications from managed care organizations under the previous contracting and payment methodology and now is only accepting Medicare + Choice–type plans. The federal and state governments dually administer the Medicare + Choice program. A Medicare + Choice organization must be licensed as a risk-bearing entity by each state in which it offers a Medicare + Choice plan.

Medicare beneficiaries may choose from Medicare + Choice plans that are available in the geographic area in which they live. Under the BBA, Medicare + Choice plans may take the following forms:

- *Coordinated Care Plans.* These include HMOs and PPOs that cover hospital care, physician's services, and other health care services for a monthly membership fee, and PSOs that provide a substantial proportion of health care items and services directly through affiliated providers who share substantial financial risk.

- *Private FFS Plans,* which reimburses providers at a rate determined by the plan on an FFS basis, without putting the provider at risk; does not vary reimbursement on the basis of utilization; and does not limit the selection of providers. The plans will be authorized to charge beneficiaries up to 115% of the plan's payment schedule, which differs from the Medicare fee schedule. The first FFS Choice plan, Sterling Option I, became available on a limited basis on July 1, 2000, which allows patients to see any traditional Medicare provider.

Beneficiaries have the option of remaining in the original FFS Medicare program. However, these Medicare + Choice plans generally have attracted beneficiaries by reducing their out-of-pocket expenses and eliminating the need for supplemental Medigap insurance. Some plans also provide benefits that are not covered under original Medicare, such as prescription drugs, eyeglasses, hearing aids, and dental care.

Beneficiaries who have been notified that their Medicare HMO will not continue to cover them have two options:

- They can enroll in another Medicare HMO, if one is available in their area and it has the capacity to take on more enrollees, or
- They can enroll in the original Medicare FFS program, with or without supplemental insurance.

Compliance Issues Concerning Medicare Billing

Because of the size and scope of the Medicare program, the government has several agencies and programs in place to identify and eliminate, fraud, abuse, and program waste. Medicare, like the health care industry as a whole, has focused on the use of "compliance" programs to police providers, who in turn, need to be policing themselves.

There have been laws and regulations that deal with fraud and abuse—the False Claims Act—since before Medicare's inception. However, the Justice Department has recently stated that health care fraud and abuse is their number two priority, second only to violent crime. As a result of this priority, the government has increased the number and severity of current laws that impact physicians and have added civil penalties that can cause billing errors to result in penalties of over $10,000 per claim.

While the topic of compliance is a book unto itself, the billing issues that practices need to be aware of when billing Medicare include, but are not limited to:

- Reassignment of payment
- Limiting charges (nonparticipating)
- Correct CPT code assignment and service utilization
- Diagnostic coding and medical necessity
- "Incident-to" billing for physician assistants, nurse practitioners, and other ancillary employees of the practice
- Evaluation and management and CPT documentation guidelines
- Ancillary orders and supervision requirements
- Teaching physician and resident billing
- Routine waiver of copayments, deductibles, or professional courtesy discounts

- Stark I and II antireferral and compensation regulations
- Credit balance refunds
- Correct coding initiative edits

Medicare Supplemental (Medigap) Insurance

While Medicare Part A and B cover many health care costs, beneficiaries will still have to pay Medicare's coinsurance and deductibles. There are also many medical services and items that Medicare does not cover.

Beneficiaries may purchase a Medicare supplemental insurance (Medigap) policy. Medigap is private insurance that is designed to help pay beneficiaries' Medicare cost-sharing amounts. There are 10 standard Medigap policies, and each offers a different combination of benefits.

The best time to buy a policy is during a Medigap open enrollment period. For a period of 6 months from the date beneficiaries are first enrolled in Medicare Part B and are aged 65 or older, beneficiaries have a right to buy the Medigap policy of their choice. That is the beneficiary's open enrollment period.

Beneficiaries cannot be turned down or charged higher premiums because of poor health if they buy a policy during this period. When the Medigap open enrollment period ends, beneficiaries may not be able to buy the policy of their choice. They may have to accept whatever Medigap policy an insurance company is willing to sell them.

If beneficiaries have Medicare Part B but are not yet 65, their 6-month Medigap open enrollment period begins when they turn 65. However, several states (Connecticut, Maine, Massachusetts, Minnesota, New Jersey, New York, Oklahoma, Oregon, Pennsylvania, Virginia, Washington, and Wisconsin) require at least a limited Medigap open enrollment period for Medicare beneficiaries under 65.

The beneficiary's state insurance counseling office can answer questions about Medicare and other health insurance information. They can also answer questions about Medicare SELECT, another type of Medicare supplemental health insurance that is sold by insurance companies and HMOs throughout most of the country.

Medicare SELECT

Medicare SELECT is the same as standard Medigap insurance in nearly all respects. The only difference between Medicare SELECT and standard Medigap insurance is that each insurer has specific hospitals, and in some cases specific doctors, that beneficiaries must use, except in an emergency, in order to be eligible for full benefits. Medicare SELECT policies generally have lower premiums than other Medigap policies because of this requirement.

Regional Carriers for DMEPOS Claims

HCFA has selected four regional Medicare contractors to be designated as durable medical equipment carriers (DMERCs). The DMERCs are responsible for processing all claims for durable medical equipment, prosthetics, orthotics, and supplies (DMEPOS). The address where the patient resides more than 6 months of the year defines the regional carrier where claims should be directed.

Medicaid

Title XIX of the Social Security Act is a federal/state entitlement program that pays for medical assistance for certain individuals and families with low incomes and resources. This program, known as Medicaid, became law in 1965 as a cooperative venture jointly funded by the federal and state governments (including the District of Columbia and the territories) to assist states in furnishing medical assistance to eligible needy persons. Medicaid is the largest source of funding for medical and health-related services for America's poorest people.

Within broad national guidelines established by federal statutes, regulations, and policies, each state (1) establishes its own eligibility standards; (2) determines the type, amount, duration, and scope of services; (3) sets the rate of payment for services; and (4) administers its own program. Medicaid policies for eligibility, services, and payment are complex and vary considerably, even among states of similar size or geographic proximity. Thus, a person who is eligible for Medicaid in one state may not be eligible in another state, and the services provided by one state may differ considerably in amount, duration, or scope from services provided in a similar or neighboring state. In addition, Medicaid eligibility and/or services within a state can change during the year

Medicaid was initially formulated as a medical care extension of federally funded programs providing cash income assistance for the poor, with an emphasis on dependent children and their mothers, the disabled, and the elderly. Over the years, however, Medicaid eligibility has been incrementally expanded beyond its original ties with eligibility for cash programs. Legislation in the late 1980s ensured Medicaid coverage to an expanded number of low-income pregnant women, poor children, and some Medicare beneficiaries who are not eligible for any cash assistance program. Legislative changes also focused on increased access, better quality of care, specific benefits, enhanced outreach programs, and fewer limits on services.

Cost of Program

Medicaid data as reported by the states indicate that more than 41.0 million persons received health care services through the Medicaid program in 1999. Total outlays for the Medicaid program in 1999 included direct payment to providers of $133.8 billion, payments for various premiums (for HMOs, Medicare, etc) of $31.2 billion, payments to the disproportionate share hospitals of $15.5 billion, and administrative costs of $9.5 billion. The total expenditure for the nation's Medicaid program in 1999, excluding administrative costs, was $180.9 billion ($102.5 billion in federal and $78.4 billion in state funds).

In most years since its inception, Medicaid has had very rapid growth in expenditures, although the rate of increase has subsided somewhat recently. This rapid growth in Medicaid expenditures has been due primarily to the following factors:

- The increase in size of the Medicaid-covered populations as a result of federal mandates, population growth, and the earlier economic recession. In recent years Medicaid enrollment has declined somewhat

- The expanded coverage and utilization of services

- The disproportionate share hospital (DSH) payment program, coupled with its inappropriate use to increase federal payments to states

- The increase in the number of very old and disabled persons requiring extensive acute and/or long-term health care and various related services

- The results of technological advances to keep a greater number of very-low-birth-weight babies and other critically ill or severely injured persons alive and in need of continued extensive and very costly care

- The increase in payment rates to providers of health care services, when compared to general inflation

The federal government pays a share of the medical assistance expenditures under each state's Medicaid program. That share, known as the federal medical assistance percentage (FMAP), is determined annually by a formula that compares the state's average per capita income level with the national income average. States with a higher per capita income level are reimbursed a smaller share of their costs. By law, the FMAP cannot be lower than 50% or higher than 83%. In 2000, the FMAPs varied from 50% in 10 states to 76.80% in Mississippi, and averaged 57% overall. The BBA also permanently raised the FMAP for the District of Columbia from 50% to 70% and raised the FMAP for Alaska from 50% to 59.8% only through 2000. For the children added to Medicaid through the State Children's Health Insurance Program (SCHIP), the FMAP average for all states is about 70%, compared to the general Medicaid average of 57%.

The federal government also reimburses states for 100% of the cost of services provided through facilities of the Indian Health Service, provides financial help to the 12 states that furnish the highest number of emergency services to undocumented aliens, and shares in each state's expenditures for the administration of the Medicaid program. Most administrative costs are matched at 50%, although higher percentages are paid for certain activities and functions, such as development of mechanized claims processing systems.

Except for the SCHIP and the Qualifying Individuals (QI) program (described later), federal payments to states for medical assistance have no set limit (cap). Rather, the federal government matches (at FMAP rates) state expenditures for the mandatory services, as well as for the optional services that the individual state decides to cover for eligible recipients, and matches (at the appropriate administrative rate) all necessary and proper administrative costs.

Within broad national guidelines that the federal government provides, each of the states: (1) establishes its own eligibility standards; (2) determines the type, amount, duration, and scope of services; (3) sets the rate of payment for services; and (4) administers its own program. Thus, Medicaid programs vary considerably from state to state, and within each state over time.

Eligibility for Medicaid

To be eligible for federal funds, states are required to provide Medicaid coverage for most individuals who receive federally assisted income-maintenance payments, as well as for related groups not receiving cash payments. The following displays the mandatory Medicaid eligibility groups:

- Recipients of Aid to Families With Dependent Children (AFDC)
- Children under age 6 who meet the state's AFDC financial requirements or whose family income is at or below 133% of the federal poverty level (FPL)
- Pregnant women whose family income is below 133% of the FPL (services to the women are limited to pregnancy, complications of pregnancy, delivery, and 3 months of postpartum care)
- Infants up to age 1 and pregnant women not covered under the mandatory rules whose family income is no more than 185% of the FPL (the percentage of FPL is set by each state)
- Supplemental Security Income (SSI) recipients (or aged, blind, and disabled individuals in states that apply more restrictive eligibility requirements)
- Special protected groups (typically, individuals who lose their cash assistance from AFDC or SSI because of earnings from work or increased Social Security benefits, but who may keep Medicaid for a period of time)

- Recipients of adoption assistance and foster care who are under Title IV-E of the Social Security Act
- Certain Medicare beneficiaries (described later)
- All children born after September 30, 1983, in families with incomes at or below the FPL (they must be given full Medicaid coverage until age 19; this phases in coverage, so that by the year 2002, all poor children under age 19 will be covered)

States also have the option to provide Medicaid coverage for other "categorically needy" groups. These optional groups share characteristics of the mandatory groups, but the eligibility criteria are somewhat more liberally defined. The broadest optional groups that states may cover (and for which they will receive federal matching funds) under the Medicaid program include:

- Children under age 21 who meet the AFDC income and resource requirements but who otherwise are not eligible for AFDC
- Recipients of state supplementary income payments
- Institutionalized individuals with income and resources below specified limits
- Certain aged, blind, or disabled adults who have incomes above those requiring mandatory coverage, but below the FPL
- Persons receiving care under home- and community-based waivers
- Tuberculosis-infected persons who would be financially eligible for Medicaid at the SSI level (but only for tuberculosis-related ambulatory services and for antituberculosis drugs)
- Federally sponsored Children's Health Insurance Programs
- "Medically needy" persons (described below)

The medically needy (MN) option allows states to extend Medicaid eligibility to additional persons. These persons would be eligible for Medicaid under one of the mandatory or optional groups, except that their income and/or resources are above the eligibility level set by their state. Persons may qualify immediately or may "spend down" by incurring medical expenses that reduce their income to or below their state's MN income level.

Medicaid eligibility and benefit provisions for the medically needy do not have to be as extensive as for the *categorically needy*, and may be quite restrictive. Federal matching funds are available for MN programs. However, if a state elects to have an MN program, there are federal requirements that certain *groups* and certain *services* must be included; that is, children under age 19 and pregnant women who are medically needy must be covered, and prenatal and delivery care for pregnant women, as well as ambulatory care for children, must be provided. A state may elect to provide MN eligibility to certain additional groups and may elect to provide certain additional services within its MN program. Currently, 38 states have elected to have an MN program and are providing at least some MN services to at least some MN recipients. All remaining states utilize the "special income level" option to extend Medicaid to the "near poor" in medical institutional settings.

Personal Responsibility and Work Opportunity Reconciliation Act of 1996

Public Law 104-193—known as the "welfare reform" bill—made restrictive changes regarding eligibility for SSI coverage that impacted the Medicaid program. For example, legal resident aliens and other qualified aliens who entered the United States on or after August 22, 1996, are ineligible for Medicaid for 5 years. Medicaid coverage for most aliens entering before that date and coverage for those eligible after the 5-year ban are state options; emergency services, however, are mandatory for both of these alien coverage groups. For aliens who lose SSI benefits because of the new restrictions regarding SSI coverage, Medicaid can continue only if these persons can be covered for Medicaid under some other eligibility status (again with the exception of emergency services, which are mandatory). Public Law 104-193 also affected a number of disabled children, who lost SSI as a result of the restrictive changes; however, their eligibility for Medicaid was reinstituted by Public Law 105-33, the BBA.

Temporary Assistance for Needy Families

In addition, welfare reform repealed the open-ended federal entitlement program known as Aid to Families With Dependent Children (AFDC) and replaced it with Temporary Assistance for Needy Families (TANF), which provides states with grants to be spent on time-limited cash assistance. TANF generally limits a family's lifetime cash welfare benefits to a maximum of 5 years and permits states to impose a wide range of other requirements as well—in particular, those related to employment. However, the impact on Medicaid eligibility is not expected to be significant. Under welfare reform, persons who would have been eligible for AFDC under the AFDC requirements in effect on July 16, 1996, generally will still be eligible for Medicaid. Although most persons covered by TANF will receive Medicaid, law does not require it.

Title XXI of the Social Security Act, known as the State Children's Health Insurance Program (SCHIP), is a new program initiated by the BBA. In addition to allowing states to craft or expand an existing state insurance program, SCHIP provides more federal funds for states to expand Medicaid eligibility to include a greater number of children who are currently uninsured. With certain exceptions, these are low-income children who would not qualify for Medicaid based on the plan that was in effect on April 15, 1997. Funds from SCHIP also may be used to provide medical assistance to children during a presumptive eligibility period for Medicaid. This is one of several options from which states may select to provide health care coverage for more children, as prescribed within the BBA's Title XXI program.

Medicaid coverage may begin as early as the third month prior to application—if the person would have been eligible for Medicaid had he or she applied during that time. Medicaid coverage generally stops at the end of the month in which a person no longer meets the criteria of any Medicaid eligibility group. The BBA allows states to provide 12 months of continuous Medicaid coverage (without reevaluation) for eligible children under the age of 19.

Medicaid does not provide medical assistance for all poor persons. Even under the broadest provisions of the federal statute, Medicaid does not provide health care services even for very poor persons unless they are in one of the groups designated above. Low income is only one test for Medicaid eligibility; assets and resources also are tested against established thresholds (as determined by each state, within federal guidelines).

Once eligibility for Medicaid is determined, coverage generally is retroactive to the third month prior to application. Medicaid coverage generally stops at the end of the month in which a person no longer meets the criteria of any Medicaid eligibility group. In addition to the Medicaid program, most states have additional "state-only" programs to provide medical assistance for specified poor persons who do not qualify for Medicaid. Federal matching funds are not provided for these state-only programs.

Scope of Medicaid Services

Title XIX of the Social Security Act requires that, in order to receive federal matching funds, a state must offer the following certain basic services to the categorically needy populations:

- Inpatient hospital services
- Outpatient hospital services
- Prenatal care
- Physician services
- Nursing facility services for people aged 21 or older
- Home health care for persons eligible for skilled nursing services
- Family planning services and supplies
- Rural health clinic services
- Laboratory and x-ray services

- Pediatric and family nurse practitioner services
- Nurse-midwife services
- Certain federally qualified ambulatory and health-center services
- Early and periodic screening, diagnostic, and treatment (EPSDT) services (under 21 years old)

States may also receive federal assistance for funding if they elect to provide other approved optional services. A few of the optional services under the Medicaid program include clinic services, nursing facility services for the aged and disabled, intermediate care facilities for the mentally retarded, optometrist services and eyeglasses, prescribed drugs, prosthetic devices, dental services, and tuberculosis-related ambulatory services and drugs for qualifying persons.

Physician Application and Participation

As with Medicare, physicians must apply to Medicaid and wait to receive a Medicaid physician ID number. Physicians who treat Medicaid patients must accept Medicaid's payment for services as payment in full. In most states, patients do not have a copayment, and physicians are not allowed to balance bill the patient.

Practices that provide services to Medicaid patients from more than one state, such as practices on state borders, need to know about the coverage policies of the applicable states, as they can vary significantly.

Medicaid is a recipient program, meaning that benefit and coverage information varies month by month. Because most state Medicaid programs issue eligibility cards on a monthly basis to patients, it is advisable to review Medicaid patients' current status before scheduling and providing services. Photocopying these cards at each visit helps verify the patient's status.

Medicaid Coordination of Benefits

Basically, Medicaid should be the payer of last resort in almost any situation. In the case of the patient with both Medicare and Medicaid, Medicaid will often pay the Medicare Part B deductible, coinsurance, and monthly premium amounts.

Relationship to Other Health Insurance Programs

- *Medicare.* Medicaid is always secondary to Medicare. All Medicare claims filed with Medicaid must be assigned. Medicaid will only fill the "Medigap" such that the total amount does not exceed the Medicaid fee schedule. Therefore, Medicaid may pay nothing if the payment received from Medicare exceeds Medicaid's fee for the same service.

- *Workers' Compensation.* Expenses for medical care related to job-connected illness or injury that are paid by the workers' compensation program as primary.

- *Private Automobile Insurance.* Any amounts paid by commercial insurance arising out of an automobile accident when the claims are also payable as primary under a policy of automobile insurance may be subject to recovery under the Federal Claims Collections Act.

Medicaid Claim Submission

While each state Medicaid program has its own coverage and payment policies, the billing requirements for Medicaid are the same as those for Medicare. Most Medicaid programs accept the HCFA-1500 for physician services. However, Medicaid coverage is limited, and the need to correctly code both CPT and ICD-9-CM codes is very important. Some state programs offer electronic claim submission.

Providers need to apply for enrollment into the Medicaid program before claims for services can be rendered. Once enrolled, be sure to obtain the most recent Medicaid *Physician Billing Guide* from the physicians' state Medicaid office.

Carefully review the billing guidelines and special coding requirements relative to the services physicians presently bill for.

Claims for services should be mailed within 4 to 6 days after the date of service. Some state programs start to deny services if the claim is submitted after 60 or 90 days from the date of service. Failure to meet this objective may indicate billing problems.

It is best to define Medicaid recipients as a separate financial class in billing software to assist in account follow-up with the physicians' Medicaid office. Be sure to identify contact names for reimbursement assistance.

Medicaid Managed Care Programs

A significant development in Medicaid is the growth in managed care as an alternative service delivery concept different from the traditional FFS system. Under managed care systems, HMOs, prepaid health plans, or comparable entities agree to provide a specific set of services to Medicaid enrollees, usually in return for a predetermined periodic payment per enrollee. Managed care programs seek to enhance access to quality care in a cost-effective manner. Waivers may provide the states with greater flexibility in the design and implementation of their Medicaid managed care programs. Waiver authority under sections 1915(b) and 1115 of the Social Security Act is an important part of the Medicaid program. Section 1915(b) waivers allow states to develop innovative health care delivery or reimbursement systems. Section 1115 waivers allow

Table 2.4   **States With Comprehensive Statewide Health Care Reform Demonstrations—June 30, 1999**

State	State Medicaid Enrollment	Expansion Enrollment	Managed Care Enrollment	Percent Enrolled in Managed Care
Arizona	401,066	0	363,662	90.67
Delaware	88,186	16,667	68,869	78.10
Hawaii	152,757	38,597	120,246	78.72
Kentucky	539,810	0	324,447	60.10
Maryland	501,000	0	347,937	69.45
Massachusetts	891,428	218,776	575,186	64.52
Minnesota	438,133	84,400	268,360	61.25
New York	2,225,694	0	659,569	29.24
Ohio	975,415	0	244,888	25.11
Oklahoma	372,501	0	193,902	52.05
Oregon	378,894	91,315	308,798	81.50
Rhode Island	134,018	7,925	85,900	64.10
Tennessee	1,312,969	485,495	1,312,969	100.00
Vermont	113,925	24,995	65,692	57.66
Wisconsin	395,336	0	187,543	47.44
Totals	8,951,132	968,170	5,127,968	57.29

Source: HCFA

statewide health care reform experimental demonstrations to cover uninsured populations and to test new delivery systems without increasing costs. Finally, the BBA provided states a new option to use managed care. The number of Medicaid beneficiaries enrolled in some form of managed care program is growing rapidly, from 14% of enrollees in 1993 to 54% in 1998.

Table 2.4 shows states with comprehensive statewide health care reform demonstrations, showing enrollment in managed care Medicaid in 1998.

Medicaid Coordination of Benefits

Basically, Medicaid should be the payer of last resort in almost any situation. In the case of the patient with both Medicare and Medicaid, Medicaid will often pay the Medicare Part B deductible, coinsurance, and monthly premium amounts.

The Medicaid-Medicare Relationship

Medicare beneficiaries who have low incomes and limited resources may also receive help from the Medicaid program. For such persons who are eligible for *full* Medicaid coverage, the Medicare health care coverage is supplemented by services that are available under their state's Medicaid program, according to eligibility category. These additional services may include, for example, nursing facility care beyond the 100-day limit covered by Medicare, prescription drugs, eyeglasses, and hearing aids. For persons enrolled in both programs, any services that are covered by Medicare are paid for by the Medicare program before any payments are made by the Medicaid program, since Medicaid is always the "payer of last resort."

Certain other Medicare beneficiaries may receive help with Medicare premium and cost-sharing payments through their state Medicaid program. Qualified Medicare beneficiaries (QMBs) and specified low-income Medicare beneficiaries (SLMBs) are the best-known categories and the largest in numbers. QMBs are those Medicare beneficiaries who have resources at or below twice the standard allowed under the SSI program and incomes at or below 100% of the FPL. For QMBs, Medicaid pays the hospital insurance (HI) and supplementary medical insurance (SMI) premiums and the Medicare coinsurance and deductibles, subject to limits that states may impose on payment rates. SLMBs are Medicare beneficiaries with resources like the QMBs, but with incomes that are higher, though still less than 120% of the FPL. For SLMBs, the Medicaid program pays only the SMI premiums. A third category of Medicare beneficiaries who may receive help consists of disabled-and-working individuals. According to the Medicare law, disabled-and-working individuals who previously qualified for Medicare because of disability, but who lost entitlement because of their return to work (despite the disability), are allowed to purchase Medicare HI and SMI coverage. If these persons have incomes below 200% of the FPL but do not meet any other Medicaid assistance category, they may qualify to have Medicaid pay their HI premiums as qualified disabled-and-working individuals (QDWIs). According to HCFA estimates, Medicaid currently provides some level of supplemental health coverage for 5 million Medicare beneficiaries within the above three categories.

For Medicare beneficiaries with incomes that are above 120% and less than 175% of the FPL, the BBA establishes a capped allocation to states, for each of the 5 years beginning January 1998, for payment of all or some of the Medicare SMI premiums. These beneficiaries are known as qualifying individuals (QIs). Unlike QMBs and SLMBs, who may be eligible for other Medicaid benefits in addition to their QMB/SLMB benefits, the QIs cannot be otherwise eligible for medical assistance under a state plan. The payment of this QI benefit is 100% federally funded, up to the state's allocation.

CHAMPUS/CHAMPVA/TRICARE

Background Information

CHAMPUS   The Civilian Health and Medical Program of the Uniformed Services (CHAMPUS) is a cost-sharing program for military families, retirees and their families, some former spouses, and survivors of deceased military members. The uniformed services include the Army, Navy, Air Force, Marine Corps, Coast Guard, Public Health Service, and the National Oceanic and Atmospheric Administration.

In the 1980s, in an effort to improve access to quality care, several "demonstration projects" were developed. The purpose of the projects was to offer service families a choice of ways to use their military health care benefits. These projects were very successful, and the decision was made to extend and improve the concept of CHAMPUS Reform Initiative (CRI). The new program was known as TRICARE.

CHAMPUS shares the cost of most medical services from civilian providers, when beneficiaries are not able to get care from a military hospital or clinic. Service families are eligible to receive inpatient and outpatient care from uniformed service hospitals and clinics. The types of medical services available at uniformed service hospitals vary by facility, and hospitals serve active-duty service members first.

There are four categories of eligibility: active duty, dependents of active duty, retired, and dependents of retired. All categories, except active duty, are afforded care in a uniformed service facility on a space-available basis.

The office of Civilian Health and Medical Program of the Uniformed Services (CHAMPUS), Aurora, CO 80045, administers the program.

CHAMPVA   The Civilian Health and Medical Program of the Veterans Affairs is a health benefit program for the families of veterans with 100% service-connected disability, or the surviving spouse or children of a veteran who died of a service-connected disability.

CHAMPUS   Now called *TRICARE Standard* in most of the country. TRICARE is the Defense Department's regional managed health care program for service families. It consists of three options: TRICARE Prime, TRICARE Extra, and TRICARE Standard.

TRICARE: The Basics

TRICARE is the Defense Department's regional managed health care program for service families. It is a combination of resources by the army, navy, and air force under a regional management. In the past, each service managed its resources independently under a central authority.

TRICARE offers families three choices: (1) TRICARE Prime, an HMO-type source of care that has very low costs; (2) TRICARE Extra, an expanded network of providers that offers reduced cost-sharing, does not require enrollment, and can be used on a case-by-case basis; and (3) TRICARE Standard, which is the same as CHAMPUS, with the same benefits and cost-sharing structure. For more information on CHAMPUS, see their web site at www.ochampus.mil. Following is a brief description of each option.

TRICARE Prime This is a voluntary enrollment option that is much like a civilian HMO. If members live in an area where TRICARE Prime is offered, they will enroll for a year at a time and normally receive care from within the Prime network of civilian and military providers.

Active-duty service members themselves will have automatic enrollment and will choose, or be assigned to, a primary care manager (PCM). Their families, and all others who are eligible, must take action if they want to enroll. Enrollment of newborns and newly adopted children in TRICARE Prime is automatic if another family member is enrolled (unless the sponsor specifies otherwise), but the children must be registered in the Defense Enrollment Eligibility Reporting System before their enrollment in TRICARE Prime becomes effective.

Active-duty families will not have to pay an annual enrollment fee. All others will, but there will be no annual deductibles, and the patient's share of the costs for services under Prime will be reduced. Members do not have to file claims when using TRICARE Prime network providers. Covered services will be like those of TRICARE Standard (formerly called CHAMPUS), plus additional preventive and primary care services. For example, physical screenings are covered at no charge under TRICARE Prime, but are not covered under the other two health care options, TRICARE Extra and TRICARE Standard. Members must choose, or will be assigned, a PCM from whom they will get most of their routine health care. TRICARE Prime enrollees also have a "point-of-service" (POS) option. This means that they can choose to obtain nonemergency services without a referral from their primary care physician. However, if they decide to get care under the POS option, there is an annual deductible of $300 for an individual, or $600 for a family. After the deductible is satisfied, cost-share for POS care will be 50% of the TRICARE allowable charge. Members may also have to pay any additional charges by nonnetwork providers—up to 15% above the allowable charge. They also may have to pay the entire bill when services are provided and, after a claim is filed, wait for reimbursement of the government's share of the costs.

TRICARE Extra Under this option, members do not have to enroll or pay an annual fee. They can seek care from a provider who is part of the TRICARE network, get a discount on services, and pay reduced cost-shares (5% below those of TRICARE Standard) in most cases. Members will not have to file any claims when using network providers. Members must meet the normal annual outpatient deductible ($50 for one person or $100 for a family for active-duty pay grades E-4 and below; or $150 for one person or $300 for a family for all other eligible persons), just as they would under TRICARE Standard.

TRICARE Standard   This option is what historically has been known as CHAMPUS. Just as under CHAMPUS, TRICARE Standard pays a share of the cost of covered health services that members obtain from a nonnetwork civilian health care provider. There is no enrollment in TRICARE Standard. The annual deductibles, cost-shares, and benefits are the same as for CHAMPUS.

Members have the freedom to choose their provider of care, but their costs will be higher than with the other two TRICARE options. Members must file their own claim forms, and perhaps pay a little more for the care (up to 15% more than the allowable charge), if the provider seen does not participate in TRICARE Standard. If the provider does participate, he or she agrees to accept the TRICARE Standard allowable charge as the full fee for the care received.

Continued Health Care Benefit Program (CHCBP)   CHCBP provides benefits similar to TRICARE Standard for a specific period of time (18 to 36 months) to eligible participants. Participants must enroll and pay monthly premiums.

Participants must enroll in CHCBP within 60 days after separation from active duty or loss of eligibility for military health care.

Members who leave active duty voluntarily and those who accept the lump-sum special separation benefit or voluntary separation incentive may also be entitled to CHCBP.

Claims Filing

For TRICARE Prime, the Prime provider files claims; for TRICARE Standard and TRICARE Extra, usually the patient is responsible for filing his or her own claim. Form DD2642-CHAMPUS should be used if the beneficiary files the claim. The HCFA-1500 form should be used if the provider files the claim

Timely Filing of Claims

Claims must be filed within 1 year from the date of service or within 1 year from the date of discharge. Claims received after the filing date will be denied. Some exceptions to the filing deadline are:

- Retroactive eligibility. Submit a copy of the determination with the claim
- Administrative error
- Mental incompetence when no one else is legally responsible for the patient
- Late adjudication of the primary carrier's processing of the claim

Eligibility

The categories of individuals eligible for CHAMPUS/CHAMPVA benefits are:

1. Spouses of active-duty members of the uniformed services

2. Children of active-duty members

3. Members of the uniformed services receiving or entitled to receive retired, retainer, or equivalent pay based on duty in the service

4. Spouses of retirees

5. Children of retirees

6. Widowers and widows of deceased active-duty members and deceased retirees who have not remarried

7. Children of deceased active-duty members and deceased retirees

8. Ex-spouses who have valid ID cards

Note: Family members of active-duty service members who died while on active duty, and who were on active duty for at least 30 days before death, will continue to be treated as active-duty family members for TRICARE Standard cost-sharing purposes for preexisting medical conditions for 1 year after their active-duty sponsor dies.

Note: To be eligible, children must be unmarried and under the age of 21 (age 18 for CHAMPVA). Financial dependence is not required except for students and disabled children who have passed their 18th or 21st birthday. Dependent student children are eligible if they are full-time students and have obtained a valid ID card.

The CHAMPVA sponsor (the active or retired military member) is not eligible for CHAMPVA benefits but is eligible for care from the VA.

When an individual reaches age 65 and becomes Medicare Part A eligible, CHAMPUS benefits cease. If Social Security eligibility is not met, CHAMPUS benefits will be extended indefinitely.

An individual under the age of 65 who becomes Medicare Part A eligible because of a disability and who elects Medicare Part B coverage retains CHAMPUS as a secondary payer effective October 1, 1991. Disabled spouse and dependent children of active-duty service members would have Medicare Part A and CHAMPUS without the Medicare Part B requirement.

TRICARE Standard does not cover:

- Active-duty service members
- Dependent parents and parents-in-law

Eligibility Verification

The Department of Defense maintains a worldwide database on military family enrollment and eligibility through the Defense Enrollment Eligibility Reporting System (DEERS). Both active and retired military sponsors and all family members must be entered in the DEERS computer data banks. This includes newborns, who must be enrolled in DEERS before claims for their care as TRICARE-eligible patients can be processed. It is the sponsor's responsibility to ensure that all participants are enrolled and keep the status of their family current. If the sponsor fails to notify DEERS of a change in status and ineligible participants receive care, the amount paid by TRICARE for that care must be returned. Patients and providers can verify eligibility by calling the appropriate center below:

> 800 334-4162 (California only)

> 800 527-5602 (Alaska and Hawaii only)

> 800 538-9552 (all other states)

A currently valid uniformed services identification card is required to establish eligibility. Children under age 10 are not issued ID cards except under unusual circumstances. Their eligibility is established on the basis of either parent's ID card. A "yes" in block 15b on the back of the card indicates eligibility.

CHAMPVA beneficiaries are issued a CHAMPVA ID card after the Veterans Affairs determines eligibility. A copy of a sample CHAMPUS ID card is shown in Exhibit 2.5. A copy of a sample CHAMPVA ID card is shown in Exhibit 2.6.

Exhibit 2.5   **Sample CHAMPUS ID Card**

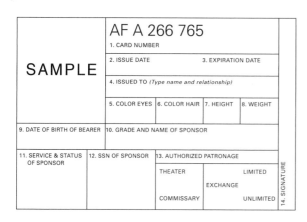
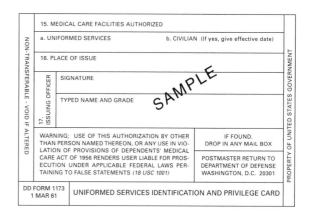

Exhibit 2.6 **Sample CHAMPVA ID Card**

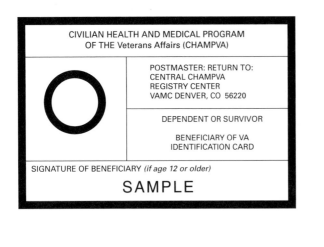

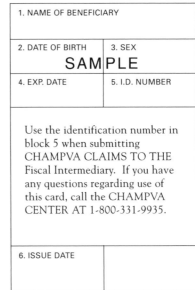

CHAMPUS Participation

As with Medicare, physicians must apply for and be approved by CHAMPUS in order for the patient to receive benefits for services. When the physician accepts assignment on a claim, he or she agrees to accept as payment the amount allowed by CHAMPUS, to write off the difference of the actual charge and the amount allowed by CHAMPUS, and to file the claim for the patient. The provider must collect any coinsurance amounts, noncovered items, or deductibles from the patient.

When the provider does not accept assignment, the practice may collect the full fee from the patient at the time service is rendered, is not bound by UCR agreements, and is not required to file claim forms.

Physicians who participate in the CHAMPUS program are expected to file insurance for the patient, write off the difference of the allowed amount (UCR) and the actual charge, and collect any outstanding copayments and deductibles for the patient.

CHAMPUS operates on a fiscal year instead of a calendar year. The fiscal year runs from October 1 to September 30. That means that, beginning each October, the deductible amount of $150 per individual and $300 per family must be met before CHAMPUS will begin paying on claims.

Only participating providers may file appeals and have right to information on participating claims.

Nonparticipating Providers

Federal law prohibits providers who do not accept assignment from billing TRICARE patients more than 115% of the allowable charge for any service.

Durable medical equipment and medical supply companies, ambulance companies, independent labs, pharmacies, mammography suppliers, and portable x-ray companies were exempt from billing limitations. However, as of January 1, 1999, these providers are no longer exempt and must adhere to federal law.

Covered Benefits

CHAMPUS provides coverage for most medical and surgical conditions; contagious diseases; and nervous, mental, and chronic disorders, such as alcoholism and certain obesity surgeries. The program will pay a coinsurance for drugs prescribed by physicians or dentists when obtained from a pharmacy by written prescription. Any service considered to be experimental is not a covered benefit of the program. There are some medication benefits programs available that require copayments and not coinsurance.

However, a few organ transplant operations are allowed, such as cornea, kidney, liver, and bone marrow, with some limitations imposed. Active-duty dependents only are eligible to receive one eye examination per year.

For psychiatric services, the provider should be aware that, for a certain number of visits (eg, 33 for Missouri, 22 for Illinois), regardless of the number of times he or she actually saw the patient, an ongoing treatment report must be completed. Otherwise, the patient will not receive further benefits or reimbursement from CHAMPUS.

Claims should be submitted on Form 501 or HCFA-1500. Because of the detailed information required for a CHAMPUS claim, it is best to use Form 501 whenever possible.

Nonavailability Statement

Any CHAMPUS beneficiary who lives within the zip code catchment area of a uniformed services hospital must obtain a nonavailability statement (NAS) before CHAMPUS will share the cost of nonemergency inpatient care from a civilian source. The zip code catchment area is based on approximately a 40-mile radius surrounding the military medical facility.

Obtaining the NAS waiver is the responsibility of the patient. Without the waiver, services could be denied for payment by CHAMPUS. All civilian hospital admissions require a nonavailability waiver from the military facility before admitting members who live within a catchment area surrounding a military medical facility.

There are 14 outpatient procedures that require an NAS before civilian care is rendered. These procedures are arthroscopy, breast mass or tumor excision, cataract removal, cystoscopy, dilation and curettage, gastrointestinal endoscopy, gynecologic laparoscopy, hernia repair, ligation or transection of fallopian tubes, myringotomy, neuroplasty, nose repair, strabismus repair, and tonsillectomy/adenoidectomy.

Services/Situations Requiring a Nonavailability Statement

1. When the patient has been receiving care from an outpatient civilian source and it is medically advisable that care continue from the civilian physician or source

2. When there is no space available at the military facility

3. When the military facility does not maintain the necessary medical facilities or personnel required for care or treatment

4. When the patient resides outside the catchment area

5. When the patient is covered by another insurance policy that is the primary payer

Inpatient Deductible and Coinsurance

For active-duty spouses and children, there is a coinsurance amount each time a patient is admitted to a civilian hospital. The amount is the total amount that would have been charged if the admission had been to a uniformed services medical facility. The charge for inpatient care at these facilities changes each year (typically October 1) and must be appropriately computed to determine the copayments. This includes CHAMPVA, whichever is less. There is no inpatient deductible.

Outpatient Deductible and Copayment

Effective April 1, 1991, family members of enlisted grades (E1–E4) and family members of CHAMPVA beneficiaries are responsible for the first $50 for coverage of outpatient services and supplies during any fiscal year (October 1 through September 30). For two or more members of the same family, the deductible is not to exceed $100 per fiscal year. For all other categories of CHAMPUS beneficiaries (ie, retirees and their family members and family members of active-duty sponsors in grade E5 or above), the outpatient deductible is $150, not to exceed $300 per fiscal year.

CHAMPUS pays 80% of the CHAMPUS-determined reasonable charges for covered services and supplies received by spouses and children of active-duty members after the deductible has been met. After the deductible has been met, CHAMPUS pays 75% for covered services received by retirees, spouses and children of retirees, spouses and children of deceased active-duty members and deceased retirees, and CHAMPVA beneficiaries. See Table 2.5 for TRICARE Prime vs Standard comparison.

Coordination of Benefits (or Double Coverage)

Section 779 of Public Law 97-377, the FY83 Department of Defense Appropriations Act, changed the procedure for determining the primary payer in a double-coverage situation. According to this law, *no CHAMPUS funds* "shall be available for the payment for any service or supply for persons enrolled in any other insurance, medical service, or health plan to the extent that the service or supply is a benefit under the other plan."

In other words, CHAMPUS is the secondary payer to *all* other insurance, medical service, or health plan. The exception to this rule is Medicaid and Indian Health Service. If the patient has Medicaid, then CHAMPUS is the primary payer. With Indian Health Service claims, if the patient was treated in a facility other than an Indian Health Service facility, then CHAMPUS is primary. This law was effective on December 21, 1982. Active-duty families no longer have the option to file with CHAMPUS first. The exclusionary clause for policies in effect before 1966 is no longer in existence, and private plans are also included as double-coverage situations. This includes HMOs and PPOs.

Relationship to Other Government Medical Programs

- *Medicare.* CHAMPUS-eligible dependents of active-duty sponsors with Medicare Part A maintain CHAMPUS as the secondary payer. Non–active-duty dependents under age 65 with a disability maintain CHAMPUS as the secondary payer if they have Medicare Parts A and B.

- *Medicaid.* If a person is eligible for Medicaid as well as CHAMPUS benefits, CHAMPUS always pays first.

- *Workers' Compensation.* Expenses for medical care related to job-connected illness or injury that are paid by the workers' compensation program, or can be paid by such a program, are not covered by CHAMPUS. Only if benefits are

Table 2.5   **TRICARE Prime vs Standard**

Benefit	Category	TRICARE Prime	Standard With Supplement	TRICARE Standard
Choice of care	All TRICARE eligibles	From approved network by primary care provider	Any hospital or authorized provider	Authorized provider
Annual enrollment	AD family members Retiree family	None $230 indiv/$460 fam	Varies	N/A N/A
Annual outpt deductible	E-4 and below E-5 and above Retirees & family	None None None	0	$50 indiv/$100 fam $150 indiv/$300 fam $150 indiv/$300 fam
Civilian outpatient copays	E-4 and below E-5 and above Retirees and family	$6 $12 $12	0	20% of allowable charges
Civilian inpatient copays	AD family members Retirees & family	$11 per day/ $25 minimum $11 per day/ $25 minimum	0	$10.8 5 per day/ $25 minimum Lesser of $390 per day or 25% of professional charges
Lab and x-ray services	E-4 and below E-5 and above Retirees and family	$8 $12 $12	0	20% 20% 25%
Ambulance service	E-4 and below E-5 and above Retirees and family	$10 $15 $20	0	20% 20% 25%
Emergency department visit	E-4 and below E-5 and above Retirees and family	$10 $30 $30	0	20% 20% 25%
Outpatient surgery	AD family members Retirees and family	$25 $25	0	25% 25%
Prescription drugs	AD family members Retirees and family	$5 $9	0	20% 25%
Pap smears	AD family members Retirees and family	None None	0	20% 25%
Home/family health	E-4 and below E-5 and above Retirees and family	$6 $12 $12	0	20% 20% 25%
Medical equipment/ supplies	E-4 and below E-5 and above Retirees and family	10% negotiated fee 15% negotiated fee 20% negotiated fee	0	20% 20% 25%

exhausted under the workers' compensation program would CHAMPUS then assume responsibility for the balance.

- *Private Insurance or Automobile Insurance.* Any amounts paid by CHAMPUS arising out of an automobile accident when these same amounts are also payable, in whole or in part, under a policy of automobile insurance may be subject to recovery under the Federal Claims Collections Act. Commercial insurance also supersedes CHAMPUS as primary except under certain coverage conditions.

- *Supplemental Insurance.* Supplemental insurance policies that pay for coinsurance and deductible and cost shares are secondary. CHAMPUS remains the primary payer.

CHAMPUS as Secondary Payer

Beneficiaries may not waive benefits due from their primary insurance. A claim must be filed with the primary carrier first. Failure to do so will result in denial of the claim by CHAMPUS.

Some limitations as secondary payer:

- Benefits will not be provided for services provided prior to coverage.

- Benefits will not be paid more as a secondary payer than would be paid in the absence of other coverage.

- Benefits will not exceed patient liability.

- Services must be covered.

Contacting CHAMPUS

CHAMPUS/CHAMPVA Billing Address

WPS—CHAMPUS/CHAMPVA
PO Box 7889
Madison, WI 53707-7891

CHAMPUS/CHAMPVA Correspondence Address

WPS—CHAMPUS/CHAMPVA Inquiry
PO Box 7927
Madison, WI 53707-7927

CHAMPUS/CHAMPVA Appeals

PO Box 8607
Madison, WI 53708-8607
The toll-free number for providers' use is 800 866-6337.

CHAMPVA

The Civilian Health and Medical Program of the Veterans Affairs (CHAMPVA) was created in 1973 to provide a medical benefits program for spouses and children of veterans with total, permanent, service-connected disabilities or for the surviving dependents of veterans who die as a result of service-connected disabilities. Members who receive CHAMPUS benefits do not qualify for coverage under CHAMPVA.

Dependent eligibility for benefits is determined by the Veterans Affairs (VA). The prospective recipient must go to the nearest VA hospital or clinic to be reviewed for eligibility in the program. If the person is eligible for CHAMPVA benefits, the VA will issue the recipient a CHAMPVA identification card.

CHAMPVA eligibility is impacted by a change in status such as marriage or divorce. Becoming eligible for Medicare or TRICARE also impacts coverage. Age and scholastic status or marriage of children will also change eligibility. Participants under 65 who are eligible for Medicare must be enrolled in Part A and Part B in order to be eligible for CHAMPVA. Those over 65 lose CHAMPVA eligibility if they are eligible for Medicare.

The benefits under the CHAMPVA program are similar to the benefits of members who are dependents of retired or deceased military personnel in the CHAMPUS program. CHAMPVA recipients have the same cost-sharing portions as retirees in the CHAMPUS program.

CHAMPVA covers most health care services and supplies that are medically necessary. Some general exclusions to coverage are:

- Services determined to be medically unnecessary
- Care as part of a grant, study, or research program
- Care considered experimental or investigational
- Care for persons eligible for benefits under other government programs, except Medicaid and State Victims of Crime Compensation programs
- Care for which the beneficiary is not obligated to pay
- Care provided by unqualified providers
- Custodial, domiciliary, or rest cures
- Dental care except treatment related to certain covered medical conditions
- Medications that do not require a prescription (insulin excluded)
- Personal comfort and convenience items
- Services rendered by providers suspended or sanctioned by other federal entities

CHAMPVA is always the secondary payer when other coverage is present except if the other coverage is Medicaid, State Victims of Crime Compensation, or a supplementing policy.

Beneficiaries will periodically be requested to complete an Other Health Insurance Certification questionnaire. The participant is responsible to report changes in coverage status. Changes may be reported by phone, but cancellation or termination of coverage must be in writing.

Provider Claims

When claims for CHAMPVA patients are submitted, the HCFA-1500 form should be used. Include a copy of any other explanation of benefits if applicable. Do not use the CHAMPVA claim form unless you are filing for the patient and payment is to go to the patient.

Claims must be submitted within 1 year of the date of service. Reconsideration of claims and appeals must also be submitted within 1 year from the date on the EOB.

CHAMPVA is administered through VA's Health Administration Center (HAC). Though information may be available through other VA facilities, only HAC is authorized to process CHAMPVA applications, determine eligibility, authorize benefits, and process claims. All inquires on CHAMPVA-related matters should be address to the HAC.

For new claims under 1 year old, send to:

VA Health Administration Center
CHAMPVA Claims
PO Box 65024
Denver CO 80206-9024

For inquiries, applications, appeals, and health care claims older than 1 year, use:

VA Health Administration Center
CHAMPVA Claims
PO Box 65024
Denver CO 80206-9024

The complete CHAMPVA handbook may be viewed at www.va.gov/hac/champva/handbook.htm.

Alternate Health Plans

In addition to the traditional plans discussed earlier, several alternative systems or managed care plans have come into prominence during the past few decades. These include health maintenance organizations (HMOs), preferred provider organizations (PPOs), independent practice associations (IPAs), physician/hospital organizations (PHOs), point-of-service plans (POSs), and self-funded plans. Most commercial and Blue Cross and Blue Shield programs offer one or more of these alternatives. Each is discussed below.

HMOs

HMOs provide comprehensive health care ranging from physician services to hospitalization. Patients enrolled in an HMO pay a fixed amount per month or other payment period. Enrollment entitles them to the full range of services offered by the HMO during the period of enrollment. An HMO can be viewed as a combination of a health insurer and a health care delivery system. Many commercial and Blue Cross and Blue Shield plans offer HMOs as an alternative to standard service contracts or indemnity plans.

HMO Operations/Patient Entitlements   Because HMOs are paid a fixed amount regardless of services provided, they generally attempt to reduce and control costs of health care delivery through utilization review, ambulatory surgery vs inpatient surgery, second opinions, and preventive medicine.

Enrollees are instructed to use only "panel" or "participating" physicians, hospitals, ancillary centers, etc, which the HMO has a contracted arrangement with. The patient may face financial responsibility for out-of-network charges. HMOs also save administrative costs through subcontracting key functions such as benefit communications management, physician enrollment and credentialing, claims processing, utilization review, and remittance management.

In an HMO program, the patient is usually responsible for a small copayment, ranging from $5 to $25, for visits to the physician. The patient has a selected group of physicians from which he or she may seek care. Should a patient elect to see a physician who does not participate in the HMO network, the patient may forfeit all benefits for those services. If the patient is not admitted to an HMO hospital, the patient may not receive any benefits for the hospital bill, nor will the physician receive payment even though he or she is an HMO provider of service. However, in an emergency situation, the patient will usually have 24 hours in which to transfer to an HMO facility unless it is a life-threatening situation.

While there are four different HMO types or "models," they share the common characteristic of operations, capitated reimbursement, and control over health care delivery and financing. The major differences between models involve the relationship between the HMO and its participating physicians. Each model type is discussed below.

Staff-Model HMOs   Staff-model HMOs employ physicians who are typically paid a fixed salary to provide services to HMO beneficiaries. Staff models are considered "closed-panel" HMOs because physicians must be members of the HMO. Staff models have a greater degree of control over the practice patterns of physicians, so the staff model may limit physician autonomy. As a result, HMOs can more easily manage and control utilization of health services.

Group-Model HMOs   Group-model HMOs primarily contract with larger, multispecialty physician groups; therefore, the physicians are employees of the group practice and not the HMO. Group models are also considered "closed panel" because physicians must be members of the group to gain access to HMO patients. The group model physician has more autonomy than does a staff model physician, but he or she must still adhere to internal utilization review and service cost goals set by the group practice to meet practice-wide goals.

There are two categories of group model HMOs—the captive group and the independent group. They are differentiated by the amount of non-HMO work provided by a contracted multispecialty practice.

Captive Group-Model HMO   The physician group exists solely to provide services to the HMO exclusively. The group does not service non-HMO clients. In most cases, these HMO models have formed the group practice to service its members, recruit physicians, and provide administrative support services to the physicians. The most prominent example of a captive group model is the Kaiser Foundation Health Plan, where the permanent medical groups provide all physician services to Kaiser's members.

Independent Group-Model HMO   The HMO contracts with an existing multispecialty group practice, and, in many cases, the group practice is the sponsor or owner of the HMO. An example of an independent group HMO is the Geisinger Health Plan of Danville, Pa, which is serviced by the Geisinger Clinics. Independent groups, as their name suggests, often service other contracts and patients in addition to the HMO members.

Individual Practice Association (IPA) Model   IPA models contract with independent physician groups for all specialties. The IPA is a separate legal entity that physicians are members of, but each practice retains its own office, staff, and physician identity. It also assumes risks associated with patient care.

IPA HMOs recruit physicians from all specialties so they can offer a complete package of services while minimizing the need to refer to out-of-plan physicians. While there may be more physician autonomy under IPAs, control over utilization and cost is much more difficult to manage. In addition, the IPA attempts to transfer financial risk back to the member practice and not the plan.

While the physician compensation arrangements vary from IPA to IPA, the HMO usually pays a fixed amount per subscriber (a capitation fee) to the IPA. The IPA in turn pays the member physicians, usually on an FFS basis, as services are rendered to the HMO patients. Some plans may pay the primary care physicians under a capitated arrangement and pay the specialists on a discounted FFS arrangement, or vice versa. Subcapitation is where the specialist is paid on a capitated basis. Since the specialists account for 80% of the costs, some programs have reversed capitation, where the specialist is capitated and the primary care physician receives a fee for service. The incentive is for the primary care physician to do more. HMOs have had to become more aggressive and creative in their compensation arrangements to recruit and maintain high quality of care and access to physicians of all specialties.

IPA physicians are paid from the pool of capitation funds. This provides them with an incentive to contain costs associated with the provision of care. That is, if the funds are exhausted, the IPA physicians may not get paid for all their services. On the other hand, if physicians provide services totaling less than the fund pool, the IPA physicians may profit.

Network or Direct-Contract Model HMOs   Network or direct-contract model HMOs contract with physicians at all levels and usually use a combination of each model type. The models contract directly with physicians to provide services to their members. A well-known example is US Healthcare of Bluebell, Pa.

Physician reimbursement may vary between capitation and discounted FFS, although capitation is more common. Direct-contract models retain more of the financial risk than do the IPA models, as well as the task of managing utilization and cost controls.

Physician Participation and General HMO Guidelines   Physicians must apply and sign contracts to become a participating provider with HMO groups. The contract defines the patient group to be covered, the physicians' scope of services, and method of reimbursement—either discounted FFS or capitation. The provider of services must file insurance claim forms, collect any deductible, coinsurance, or copayment amounts, and write off the difference of the actual billed charge and the allowed amount.

Exhibit 2.7 shows PPO and HMO enrollment through 1999. Although the number of HMO plans fluctuated during the past decade—primarily due to market consolidation—the increase in enrollment never wavered. Table 2.6 shows the percentage of HMOs penalizing physicians for not adhering to policies. Physician penalties for overutilization, excessive referrals, and violation of prescribing outside of the drug formulary have actually increased over the past year.

Exhibit 2.7 **PPO and HMO Enrollment**

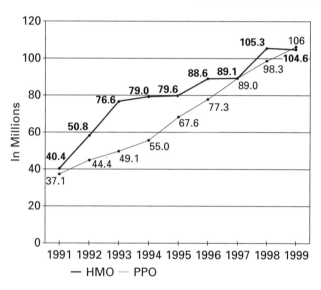

Note: PPO enrollment numbers reflect eligible employees. HMO enrollment numbers represent actual members.

©2000 SMG Marketing Group. Used with permission.

Table 2.6 **Percentage of HMOs Penalizing Physicians**

	Over-Utilization	Excessive Specialty Referrals	Violation of Prescription Prescribing	No Penalties
1999	30.40%	41.30%	38.60%	48.50%
1998	27.80%	36.20%	34.40%	53.90%

©2000 SMG Marketing Group.

The HMO plans offering fewer restrictions garner the higher market share as seen in Table 2.7 which shows the enrollment by type of HMO plan. Finally, Exhibit 2.8, shows the Medicare HMO enrollment growth rate through 1998.

PPOs

A PPO is generally defined as a group of health care providers, including physicians, hospitals, and allied institutions, that agree to provide services to a

Table 2.7 **Enrollment by Type of HMO Plan**

Plan Type	12/31/96	12/31/97	12/31/98	12/31/99	% Change 96–99	% Change 98–99
IPA	45,280,900	50,242,432	53,811,551	57,536,924	27.07%	6.92%
Network	8,361,900	15,233,840	21,539,232	23,753,198	184,06%	10.25%
Group	19,507,700	20,524,921	20,853,681	21,397,088	9.69%	2.61%
Staff	4,188,700	3,029,340	2,104,946	1,882,022	−55.07%	−10.59%
	77,339,200	89,030,200	98,309,410	104,569,232	35.21%	6.37%

©2000 SMG Marketing Group. Used with permission.

Exhibit 2.8 **Medicare HMO Enrollment Growth Rate**

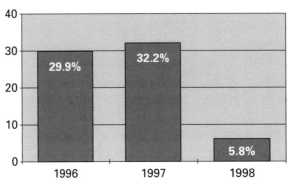

©2000 SMG Marketing Group. Used with permission.

specific pool of patients. PPOs have been offered by insurance carriers, groups of physicians, and groups of hospitals.

There are generally financial incentives offered to plan holders to use the "preferred" group of "closed-panel" or member providers for care. Participants using the preferred providers will benefit from lower deductibles, coinsurance, copayments, or other incentives. The physicians, in turn, benefit from access to new patients, increased patient utilization, and prompt FFS payment from the insurer. Under PPOs, the physician's reimbursement is based on a discounted fee schedule, and payment is based on traditional FFS billing.

Preferred provider organizations derive many of the cost-saving benefits from strict payment policies and discounted fee schedules. They also use some of the same techniques as HMOs to minimize utilization of services. Utilization review, second options, and ambulatory surgery options are often utilized to reduce costs.

Silent PPOs   One problem to be wary of when managing PPO discounts is what is referred to as a "silent PPO discount." This has become a very prevalent problem and can cost practices tens of thousands of dollars in due reimbursement that is improperly written off. Some insurance plans with which the practice

Exhibit 2.9   **PPO Eligible Employees***

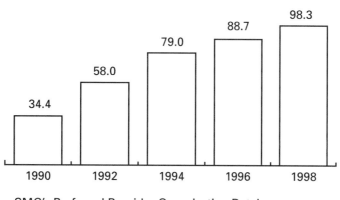

SMG's Preferred Provider Organization Database—
July 1999 Edition

*Excludes employees eligible for workers' compensation
and specialty plans

©2000 SMG Marketing Group. Used with permission.

does not have a signed contract will indicate on their EOB that they are taking their "contractual PPO discount." This is because they are part of a PPO that the practice has a signed contact with, but the plan really is not a part of the PPO network. Apparently traditional insurance plans can buy the fee schedules and physician listings of contracted provider from other insurance plan for which the practice does have a PPO contract. They use the data to reduce their payments and convince the practice staff that they must accept the "contractual PPO discount." Awareness of network health plans and PPO fee schedule amounts is critical for defeating this problem.

PPO Trends   According to the American Association of Preferred Provider Organizations (AAPPO) in their *Preferred Provider Organization Report: 1999 Edition* the number of PPO eligible employees rose from 34.4 million in 1990 to 98.3 million in 1998. Exhibit 2.9 depicts the significant increase in the PPO eligible employees since 1990. Exhibit 2.10 shows the grown of PPOs since 1987. Exhibit 2.11 shows the breakout of all PPOs by type as of 2000. Full service PPOs offer general medical/surgical, workers compensation, and at least two specialty services.

Current Market Events   As reported in the *1999 SMG Directory Report:*

- The *Mercer/Foster Higgins National Survey of Employer-sponsored Health Plans* revealed that PPOs gained five points of market share in 1998. A breakdown of the national employee enrollment gain reveals that 2% came from indemnity, 1% came from HMOs and another 2% came from POS plans. (See Exhibit 2.12.)

Exhibit 2.10   Growth Rate of PPOs

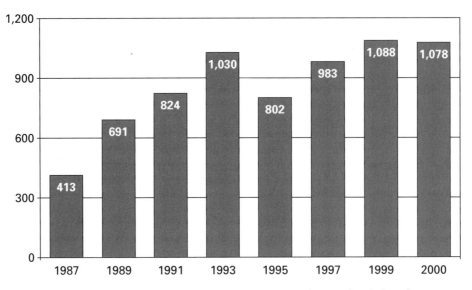

Note: The popularity of PPOs has risen due to consumer preference for choice of physicians versus more restrictive HMO models.

©2000 SMG Marketing Group. Used with permission.

Exhibit 2.11   Breakout of All PPOs by Type

PPO Service Types

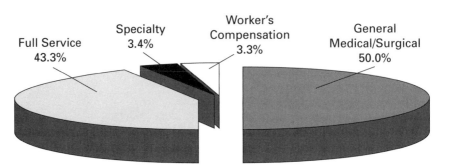

Note: The types of PPOs and the services they offer shifted slightly between 1998 and 1999. Currently 50% of the nation's PPOs are considered to be general medical/surgical types. This compares to 49.3% last year. Another 45.3% of all PPOs are considered to be full service PPOs. These were 47.2% of this type in 1998. The remainder of the PPO types are classified as specialty PPOs at 3.4% and workers' compensation PPOs at 3.3%.

©2000 SMG Marketing Group. Used with permission.

- PPOs are now in every one of the states and seven states (Texas, Florida, California, Illinois, Kentucky, Michigan and Nebraska) have more than 100 owned or leased PPOs.

- A significant consumer, patient and provider backlash to the HMO industry is creating expanded market opportunities for PPO products.

- Providers are helping to push PPO growth, as provider-sponsored PPOs now cover some 3.2 million of the 98.3 million PPO eligible employees, or about 3.3% of the national total.

Exhibit 2.12   National Employee Enrollment, 1993-1999

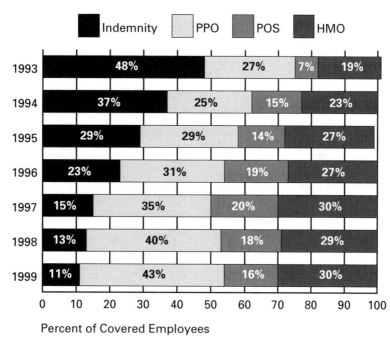

Percent of Covered Employees

©William M. Mercer, Inc. Used with permission.

- The PPO industry is consolidating with 17 PPO networks owning almost three-quarters of all PPOs nationwide.

- Although PPO enrollment historically cut into indemnity insurance enrollment, it is now cutting into HMO enrollment and HMOs are struggling to offer the same level of choice as PPOs.

- PPOs offer savings of 7% to 17% (average 12%) over traditional health plans with utilization review, according to a study by researchers at the University of Michigan. The source of cost savings is primarily discounts on physician fees and hospital per diem payments, with discounts ranging up to 20% off standard fees. But PPOs also experience 9.7% lower physician use, and a 9.3% lower rate of hospital admissions than the traditional health plan.

Conclusion   The growth of PPO enrollment and the evolution of hybrid PPO plans will continue in the coming years. Practices need to review each contract presented to them and be aware of the plan's discounted fee schedule, contract requirements, and potential risk incurred by the physician. As each PPO plan varies in coverage and benefit packages, the office staff needs to be aware of all PPO plans they participate in and their policies and procedures that must be maintained for successful claim submission.

POS Plans

Several commercial insurance plans have developed a new form of managed care that combines aspects of both PPOs and HMOs. This plan is called a point-of-service (POS) plan. Beneficiaries may select physicians and other health care providers who are members of the POS, or they may select providers outside of the POS. Financial incentives, usually in the form of lower fees, are offered to subscribers to encourage them to use member providers.

Self-funded Plans (Employee Retirement Income Security Act)

An increasing number of large corporations are dropping traditional health insurance from commercial carriers and insuring their employees through self-funded plans. To institute a self-funded plan, the corporation usually obtains an excess liability rider (reinsurance, stop-loss coverage) and then establishes a reserve fund to pay employee medical bills.

A third-party administrator (TPA) that establishes a PPO or similar type of arrangement with physicians, hospitals, and other health care providers frequently manages self-funded plans. Incentives are provided to employees to seek care from providers who have contracted with the corporation through the TPA to provide services at a discounted rate. These incentives may be in the form of first-dollar coverage or bonuses to employees who do not utilize health care services unnecessarily.

PSOs

A PSO is a Medicare + Choice organization that is a public or private entity and is organized and operated by a health care provider or group of affiliated health care providers. Recent legislation in the Balanced Budget Act of 1997 now legally defines PSOs as a public or private entity of affiliated providers, who provide a substantial portion (60% for rural PSOs, 70% for urban PSOs) of the care. They take a substantial portion of the risk to do this on the budget (capitation) the government provides for Medicare patients. The reserve needed by a PSO is less than that required for an HMO. The shortfall in reserves is usually covered by the state. PSOs can be formed by many types of entities, such as physician-hospital organizations (PHOs), which are an affiliate organization formed by physicians and hospitals that serve as collaborative providers.

It is anticipated by the Congressional Budget Office that 10 million people eligible by Medicare will be in PSOs during the next 4 years, compared with just under 5 million in HMOs after nearly 12 years of marketing. HCFA estimates that HMO membership will grow from 15% to 18% during the same period in which PSOs grow to serve more than 25% of the Medicare-eligible population.

Workers' Compensation and Disability

Workers' compensation programs offer benefits to workers who are injured on the job or contract a job-related illness. Claimants are entitled to benefit payments as well as having their medical cost for related services covered.

Workers' compensation is a state-required insurance plan in which employers make premium payments to a general fund. Each state may have different requirements that govern who is allowed to provide insurance. The level of benefits provided and types of injuries that are compensable are also subject to variation by state. Premiums depend on the type of work performed, the duration the insurance has been in place, and the number of claims. The amount of insurance an employer must carry depends on the risk of employee job-related injuries. Laws regulating workers' compensation programs vary from state to state.

Not all employees are covered by state-regulated programs. The federal government administers the Federal Employees Compensation Act, but the government has no role in the program. The Longshore and Harbor Workers' Compensation Act covers longshore, harbor, and other maritime workers. Railroad workers involved in interstate commerce are covered by health insurance and disability benefits instead of workers' compensation, as are the US Merchant Marines. The Federal Black Lung Program covers coal miners receiving benefits for black lung disease. Other occupations carry their own workers' compensation programs as well.

When an employee is injured on the job, the employee either must go to a designated physician or can select his or her own physician for an independent medical exam (IME). The physician conducting the IME is paid a predefined amount. When treating a patient covered under a workers' compensation program, be sure to obtain a "Statement of Injury" form from the patient's employer. In addition, some programs require special "medical report" forms to be completed for claims.

A commercial insurance carrier chosen by the employer may handle workers' compensation cases when allowed. Publicly funded state programs run others. Before admission, the carrier should be notified and verification of coverage obtained. The patient should have a written authorization form (possibly in the form of an incident report) signed by a representative of the employer. If not, this documentation should be requested of the employer. It should be established with the employer whether or not it recognizes responsibility for the injury. If so, a letter stating this obligation should be requested.

If the carrier denies a worker's compensation case, the patient has the right to appeal the denial to the state board and request a hearing. As long as the patient has an appeal pending, even though the claim may be previously denied, neither the hospital nor the physician can pursue payment from the patient. Inquiry regarding case status can be carried out either through the carrier or through the state board of workers' compensation. Additional forms and filing requirements may vary from state to state.

The level of compensation and benefits will vary depending on the term of the employee's disability. Some injuries do not result in time lost from work that exceeds the waiting period for cash benefits. The patient returns to work within a few days and only medical benefits are allowed.

In some cases the patient's injury results in time lost from work on a temporary basis. This results in a temporary total disability. In this case the employee is entitled to medical benefits as well as cash benefits for time lost from work. The employee eventually returns to work upon release by the physician. The employee may also return to work with the permission of the physician in a reduced capacity until full recovery is obtained.

An employee may be permanently disabled, but not totally disabled. This is called permanent partial disability. It involves an injury that is severe enough to impair the employee's function and is a permanent condition, but does not totally disable the employee. Medical benefits are paid until the employee obtains maximum improvement to the point that further medical care is not beneficial. The employee may also receive a disability payment based on the percentage of disability that has occurred.

Permanent total disability occurs when the injury is so severe that the employee cannot return to work. In this case the employee is entitled to medical coverage and cash benefits indefinitely.

3 Electronic Claims Processing

Objectives

After completing this chapter, you should be able to:

- Understand the background of electronic data interchange (EDI)

- Know the standards that must be developed under HIPAA

- Know the advantages projected for use of EDI

- Understand the shortcomings of EDI

- Understand privacy concerns regarding electronic transmission of confidential medical information

- Educate claims staff on patients' privacy

Introduction

In 1998, Medicare received and processed more than 700 million claims for Part A and Part B. More than 80% of these claims were submitted electronically by means of computer software developed for medical billing. Of these claims, Medicare received 149 million Part A claims in 1998, nearly all of which (more than 96%) were submitted electronically.

Companies, including medical practices, have historically relied on paper as the traditional medium for conducting their business. Records are maintained on paper, which are then mailed between companies to exchange information. Although the computer has become a staple of practically all offices, the use of mail to transmit paper information continues. Claims processors enter data into a form and mail the form to a third party, which then re-keys the data into another business application. Inherent in this process are delays, excessive paperwork, and the potential for errors as information is transcribed. However, beginning in the 1970s, certain industries such as banking and automotive have moved to electronic data interchange (EDI). In the medical community, paper records are now giving way to electronic medical records. Although recent reports indicate that no more than 5% of the physicians in the United States have moved to the use of electronic medical records, the trend to electronic medical records is predicted to follow the recent meteoric rise of EDI claim submission.

EDI has now become the preferred method of claims submission, especially by Medicare. Today, Medicare leads all other health care payers in electronic claims acceptance and processing. In the early 1980s, Medicare gave providers free or low-cost software so they could bill electronically. Initially, there were no national standards and each Medicare fiscal agent developed and distributed its own unique software. These different electronic formats hindered the development of affordable off-the-shelf medical billing software. Efforts by the Health Care Financing Administration (HCFA) that led to standardization of record layouts and other data processing elements has spurred the development, and medical community acceptance, of software for electronic claim preparation and submission. "Off-the-shelf" billing software in a wide price range is now readily available to the medical community. Even though Medicare provides free electronic billing software and support to assist providers, providers are not required to use Medicare's software. If they choose, a provider may purchase his or her own software from a public or commercial source. The producer of the software ensures that its product complies with Medicare requirements for electronic claim submission. HCFA has developed an electronic version of the HCFA-1500 claim form, which is on the Internet at www.hcfa.gov and which appears in Chapter 1 as Exhibit 1.1, and UB-92, which is also on the Internet at www.hcfa.gov and is attached as Exhibit 3.1. Physicians' use of claims that are filed electronically, however, still lags far behind that of hospitals.

Medical billing software helps providers manage financial information and reduces errors on claims submitted to Medicare and most other third-party payers. Medical billing software can be a stand-alone function or integrated with other aspects of a medical practice, such as patient medical records. It can be linked to the laboratory and other ancillary service areas and can interface with other software that will analyze claims for completeness, accuracy, and probability of being edited by Medicare.

Because of the simplicity of billing to all payers and the cash-flow benefits to the physician's practice, it is now highly recommended that they learn and start submitting EDI claims. The purpose of this chapter is to equip physicians and their staffs to do just this.

Advantages of EDI

- Paper claims are much slower to process.

- EDI can be almost error free, increasing claim acceptance rates. As an example, a private insurance carrier may require the use of procedure code 36145 when

Exhibit 3.1 UB-92 Form

billing for venipuncture. Medicare requires G0001 for the same service. The software automatically selects the right code for each insurer.

- The costs for EDI are far less, with savings recognized in both labor costs and materials, including postage.

- Billing of secondary payers will be faster, because the provider will more quickly learn what the primary payer will pay.

HCFA lists the following advantages of Medicare EDI on their web site at www.hcfa.gov:

- free electronic billing software and support for Medicare claims submission

- cost-effectiveness and less opportunity for error with electronic transactions

- lower administrative, postage, and handling costs than those associated with paper claim submissions.

- on-line receipt or acknowledgement.

- claim status and eligibility information in 24 hours or less

- delivery of electronic remittances to a provider-preferred location

- reduction of system costs by standardized electronic claims submission and coordination of benefits exchange and remittance receipt

- reduction of administrative costs by standardized formats, since one format will meet all current billing requirements and is accepted by all Medicare contractors as well as many third-party billers

- faster payment, with electronic claims generally being paid after 13 days, while paper claims cannot be paid for at least 27 days

- faster deposit of payments for accounts receivable through electronic funds transfer; payments can be in the provider's bank, drawing interest, in 2 working days after payment, while paper checks can take as long as a week to process

Key Questions to Ask About Your EDI System

- Which fields can be changed and by whom?

- How quickly are Medicare and other payer requirements and changes reflected in the EDI system?

- Are credit balances resolved in compliance with Medicare requirements and state laws?

- What are the limitations of the EDI system, and is there a manual process to fill the gaps?

- Are EDI system reports routinely reviewed by management, with documentation of corrective actions?

Options for Putting EDI Into Your Practice

- *EDI Service Bureaus.* By hiring another company to do EDI for you, this is the least involved service option.
- *Stand-Alone EDI.* This is a stand-alone, nonintegrated approach on a PC.
- *Integrated EDI.* This is a full-blown integrated EDI hands-off process that relies on computers to do all the work. This approach will integrate EDI with your other business applications.

Many firms offer simple terminals or data entry devices specifically for the purpose of submitting claims, and most provider practice management computer systems have capabilities for electronic claims submission. Computer vendors, Blue Cross and Blue Shield, Medicare, and other organizations can provide information about setting up an EDI system.

Medical Billing Software

Basic billing software relies heavily on user knowledge and entry skills. It is widely distributed by Medicare fiscal agents and the private sector. Users key most, if not all, claims information onto a claims facsimile. The software manipulates these entries to produce an electronic claim. Typical errors involve entry errors, incorrect or missing patient or provider information, incorrect or incomplete diagnosis codes, or invalid CPT® codes. Basic medical billing software, developed for mass markets, usually does not allow users to customize or override its programs. The greater risk of claim error is in data entry.

Informational software augments basic software capabilities. It uses databases and linked files to recall patient, provider, diagnostic, and service information. Invalid code combinations, missing diagnosis, and other errors that might prevent processing of a claim can be brought to the user's attention before the claim is submitted for payment. Informational software does not appear to generate erroneous claims. It provides tools to help providers code their claims accurately. Vulnerabilities are more likely to stem from improper software configuration and use. For example, limited procedure coding options for office visits may steer claim decisions to higher-valued procedure codes.

Interactive software combines and enhances basic billing and informational software capabilities. It can give the user options for correcting problems detected by the software. What distinguishes interactive software from other medical billing software is its ability to provide the user with information and the likely consequences (no pay, more pay, less pay) of their decision.

Proprietary software may present the greatest risk of misuse. This type of software is developed for a specific user. Inner workings of proprietary software may only be known to a single person or a select few. Hidden programs may add or modify claim information, producing erroneous or fraudulent claims. Unlike commercially available software packages, manufactured for a broad market, proprietary software is created to meet a specific, single customer's needs. Commercial software that produces inaccurate claims has a greater chance of detection and of being reported by honest medical providers. Proprietary software presents a vulnerability to Medicare because it is created for, and used by, a select few. Proprietary software, and not commercial software, possesses the greatest risk of being intentionally designed to produce improper or inaccurate claims.

EDI software is proliferating. Most EDI software contains claim-editing features that detect and report incomplete claims, invalid codes, or other problems that will cause the claim to be rejected. These basic edits flag or reject claims such as a prostatectomy in a female or a Pap smear in a male. These edit features force the practice to file cleaner claims.

Software companies point out that electronic software can easily assimilate the ever-changing regulations and reimbursement policies affecting providers. Edits, essential for correct coding, are now handled by software that allows for consistent accurate bills. New software is being developed that works with voice recognition software to permit the computer to read a medical record and correctly code it. Human error decreases as the use of software and electronics increases.

Most practices have found that EDI is far less expensive than processing paper claims. Third-party payers also realize cost savings through the receipt of electronic claims. Payment posting and reconciliation of claims is far superior with EDI, and EDI allows a tape-to-tape rollover, eg, Medicare to Medicaid, that cannot be accomplished with paper claims.

Shortcomings of EDI

While electronic claims are easier to submit, it should be noted that there are some risks of EDI: claims that require supplementary documentation must still be filed by the paper claim method. However, as EDI systems begin to accommodate the electronic transmission of reports, radiographs, and related information, claims may be generated in the future from an electronic medical record, which will enhance proper documentation. The potential for misuse of submitter numbers is a vulnerability not adequately addressed by Medicare. Also, startup costs for EDI may be significant. Billing companies, their employees, and employees of providers have access to patient and provider information needed to access the Medicare system. Clearinghouses or their employees can misuse this information to generate false claims (without the medical provider's knowledge).

Each time information changes hands or is acted upon outside an automated system, the risk of error increases. Source documents pass through the hands of many people before information is entered into a software program. Employees of the physician, or an outside billing agency, may misinterpret source document information, inadvertently incorrectly key information into the system, or add, delete, or modify information on source documents. Whether intentional or unintentional errors occur, the patient's medical record may not support the claim submitted to Medicare. The claim will be incorrect, resulting in an overpayment or underpayment. Because not all third-party payers accept electronic claims, even the most automated practices, clearinghouses, and service bureaus must still produce and mail a large number of paper claims. In most systems, a paper claim may be produced from the electronically stored data.

Be aware in particular of the following risks:

- An overreliance on computerized systems without a comprehensive knowledge of their limitations can result in major billing problems.

- Failure to have well-organized, clear documentation of the EDI system edits can leave the physician and practice open to increased compliance risks.

- If manual procedures are not implemented to fill the gap when the EDI system falls behind in changing edits as Medicare rules are changed, there is an increased risk of false claim allegations.

- By using less experienced personnel (a cost saving advantage touted by some EDI vendors), the physician's staff may not understand the underlying documentation requirements needed to support changing a diagnosis code when facing medical necessity denials.

- The mere presence or capability to print reports such as extensive management, productivity, and compliance monitoring is no assurance that the reports are read on a current basis and problems acted upon by responsible personnel. For example, multiple months of increasing frequency of claim denials could become a prosecutor's exhibit to support a False Claim Act allegation of reckless disregard.

- Anyone with access to a physician's electronic billing number and access to a telephone may be able to submit false claims for payment.

- Billing software that requires users to input extensive information increases the risk of claim error.

Pre-Claim Submission Operations

Before any type of claim can be generated and submitted for payment, your office staff needs to perform a number of preclaim tasks critical to ensure the validity and accuracy of the patient's billing data and submission of a clean claim. The basic objectives of office staff preclaim operations are to:

- Collect the patient's and responsible parties' information completely and accurately.

- Determine the appropriate financial class or account type (eg, commercial insurance, Medicare, Medicaid) and correctly assign primary and secondary insurance billing status when two insurance plans require coordination of benefits.

- Educate patients as to their ultimate financial responsibility for services rendered and obtain written waivers when necessary to support future collection efforts.

- Verify all data collected before rendering services or submitting claims and obtain updated profiles of insurance plan benefits by means of an insurance or employer verification form.

- Anticipate the need for collection through accounts receivable controls and quality data.

Privacy and Medical Records

The trade and lay press increasingly focus on privacy issues regarding the electronic transmission of medical data and records. Fears of private and confidential information are growing, fueled by well-publicized cases of the inadvertent release of confidential information that was stored or transmitted electronically.

In September 1997, the Secretary of Health and Human Services (HHS) issued five key principles that should underlie national health privacy legislation:

Consumer Control

Patients would have significant new rights to understand and control how their health information is used:

- Providers and health plans would be required to give patients a clear written explanation of how they will use, keep, and disclose information.

- Patients would be able to see and get copies of their records, and request corrections.

- A history of most disclosures would have to be maintained and be made accessible to patients.

- A patient's authorization to disclose information would have to meet specific requirements.

- A provider or payer generally would not be able to condition treatment, payment, or coverage on a patient's agreement to disclose health information for other purposes.

- Patients would have the right to restrict uses of their information.

Accountability

There would be punishment for covered entities that misuse personal health information. The statute provides the following penalties for misuse of health information:

- There would be federal criminal penalties for health plans, providers, and clearinghouses that knowingly and improperly disclose information or obtain information under false pretenses. Penalties would be higher for actions designed to generate monetary gain.

- Health plans, providers, and clearinghouses that violate these standards would be subject to civil liability.

- The statute includes new penalties for violations of a patient's right to privacy. These penalties include, for violations of the privacy standards by the persons subject to them, civil monetary penalties of up to $25,000 per person, per year, per standard. There are also substantial criminal penalties applicable to certain types of violations of the statute that are done knowingly: up to $50,000 and 1 year in prison for obtaining or disclosing protected health information; up to $100,000 and up to 5 years in prison for obtaining protected health information under "false pretenses"; and up to $250,000 and up to 10 years in prison for obtaining protected health information with the intent to sell, transfer, or use it for commercial advantage, personal gain, or malicious harm.

Public Responsibility

Some existing uses of information would not be affected at all, such as reporting of births and deaths and reporting of abuse such as child abuse. After balancing privacy and other social values, HHS is proposing rules that would permit disclosure of health information without individual authorization for the following national priority activities and for activities that allow the health care system to operate more smoothly:

- Oversight of the health care system, including quality assurance activities
- Public health
- Research

- Judicial and administrative proceedings
- Law enforcement
- Emergency circumstances
- To provide information to next of kin
- For identification of the body of a deceased person, or the cause of death
- As authorized for governmental health data systems
- For facility patient directories
- By banks and other financial institutions, to process health care payments and premiums
- For activities related to national defense and security

Boundaries

With few exceptions, an individual's health care information would be used for health purposes only. It would be easy to use health information for health purposes and difficult to use it for other purposes.

- Patient information could be used by a health plan, provider, or clearinghouse only for purposes of health care treatment, payment, operations, and some limited public policy priorities.
- All disclosures of information would be limited to the minimum necessary for the purpose of the disclosure.
- Disclosures with patient authorization would have to meet standards that would ensure that the authorization is truly informed and voluntary.
- The proposal would permit, but does not require, these types of disclosures. If there is no other law requiring that information be disclosed, physicians and hospitals will still have to make judgments about whether to disclose information, in light of their own policies and ethical principles.

Security

Covered entities that are entrusted with health information would be required to protect it against deliberate or inadvertent misuse or disclosure. Security measures would be required to establish policies to protect the information against improper use by employees or threats from outside. The following entities would be covered by the proposed rule:

- Health plans
- Health care providers that transmit health information electronically
- Health care clearinghouses

Impact on Existing Confidentiality Laws

The HHS proposal would not limit or reduce other stronger legal protections for confidentiality of health information. Stronger state laws (like those covering mental health and human immunodeficiency virus infection and information on acquired immunodeficiency syndrome) would continue to apply except for certain public health activities specified in the statute. The confidentiality protections would be cumulative, and the proposed rule would provide "floor preemption." The aim is to give individuals the benefit of all laws providing confidentiality protection.

In July 2000, the National Committee on Vital and Health Statistics (NCVHS) released its report and recommendations for uniform data standards for patient medical record information. The full report and their recommendations are available on the NCVHS Web site at www.ncvhs.hhs.gov/hipaa000706.

HIPAA and EDI

Standards to Be Developed Under HIPAA

The Health Insurance Portability and Accountability Act (HIPAA; Public Law 104-191), signed by President Clinton on August 21, 1996, aims to improve productivity of the American health care system. The law encourages development of information systems based on the exchange of standard management and financial data by means of EDI. It also requires organizations exchanging transactions for health care to follow national implementation guidelines for EDI established for this purpose. The Web site at aspe.os.dhhs.gov/admnsimp/ has more information on EDI efforts under HIPAA. The administrative simplification provisions under HIPAA are intended to reduce the costs and administrative burdens of health care by making possible the standardized, electronic transmission of many administrative and financial transactions that were previously carried out manually on paper.

These administrative simplification provisions require the Secretary of HHS to adopt standards for electronic transactions and data elements for those transactions; unique health identifiers for individuals, employers, health plans and health care providers; and security standards and safeguards for electronic information systems involved in those transactions. The Secretary of HHS is also responsible for standards for ensuring the privacy of electronic transactions.

HHS must develop and implement a plan to meet the law's mandate. With the exception of privacy standards, HCFA has been charged with the lead for coordinating the plan and its implementation. In May 2000, HHS announced that it expects to publish five final rules and two proposed rules for health data standards by the end of the year. These rules will include standards for electronic transactions, national provider and employee identifiers, and security and privacy standards for electronic transmission of protected health information.

What Is Protected Under the Proposed HIPAA Regulations?

"Protected health information" is:

- individually identifiable information
- that is or was at any time electronic and
- is in the hands of a covered entity.

Information becomes electronic when it is sent electronically or if it is maintained in a computer system. The fact that the information is later printed in "hard copy" will not eliminate its being considered "electronic" and thus covered under the HIPAA proposed regulations. Once information is electronic, it is forever covered under the regulations. HIPAA is clear that the information itself, rather than the record, is protected under the proposed regulations.

Who Is Covered Under the Proposed HIPAA Regulations?

The proposed regulations limits the breadth of the law to "covered entities," which are defined as health plans, health care clearinghouses, and any health care provider who transmits health information in an electronic form in connection with what are called "standard transactions." However, the law does not reach all individuals and companies that may receive, use, or disclose individually identified information. Thus, for example, an employer, workers' compensation company, or accountant who is provided the information for legitimate purposes will not come under these proposed regulations.

The AMA and EDI

Recent policies of the American Medical Association (AMA) on EDI include the following.

H-315.979 Electronic Data Interchange Status Report

The AMA will: (1) work to establish consensus on industry security guidelines for electronic storage and transmission of medical records as an important means of protecting patient privacy in a manner that avoids undue and nonproductive burdens on physician practices; (2) develop relevant educational tools or models in accordance with industry electronic security guidelines to assist physicians in compliance with state and federal regulations. (CMS Report 7, I-98)

H-190.992 Electronic Claims Submission

It is the policy of the AMA to: (1) support, assist and encourage the use of electronic data interchange (EDI) and electronic media claims (EMC) by physicians (amended: CMS Rep I-93-1); (2) support and continue its involvement in the development of uniform EMC format and technical requirements; (3) support the development of a minimum set of EMC services for use by Medicare carriers and other third party payers, with an emphasis on the transmission of explanation of benefits-type information to physicians; (4) continue to support the elimination of the Medicare 14-day payment delay regulation following Medicare carrier receipt of a claim; (5) oppose the development and implementation of a regulatory differential claims processing time standard for the payment of physician services by Medicare carriers based on method of claims submission; and (6) oppose the establishment, at this time, of any time tables or plans for mandatory EMC or EDI use by physicians. (Item 6 Amended: CMS Rep I-93-1) (BOT Rep W, A-90)

H-190.983 Submission of Electronic Claims Through Electronic Data Interchange

The AMA: (1) will take a leadership role in representing the interests of the medical profession in all major efforts to develop and implement EDI technologies related to electronic claims submission, claims payment, and the development of EDI standards that will affect the clinical, business, scientific, and educational components of medicine; (2) supports aggressive time tables for implementation of EDI as long as the implementation is voluntary, and as long as all payers are required to receive standard electronic claims and provide electronic reconciliation prior to physicians being required to transmit electronic claims; (3) supports the acceptance of the ANSI 837 standard as a uniform, but not exclusive, standard for those physicians who wish to bill electronically; and (4) will continue to monitor the cost-effectiveness of EDI participation with respect to rural physicians (CMS Rep 1-93-1).

H-190.980 Electronic Data Interchange and Telemedicine: Update

The AMA will continue to help create a uniform data set for electronic claims transmission to public and private payers, through its leadership of the National

Uniform Claim Committee, a committee chaired by the AMA that is comprised of key parties affected by health care electronic data interchange. (CMS Rep. 8, I-95)

H-190.978 National Clearinghouse for Health Care Claims

(1) The AMA adopts the following policy principles to encourage greater use of electronic data interchange (EDI) by physicians and improve the efficiency of electronic claims processing: (*a*) public and private payers who do not currently do so should cover the processing costs of physician electronic claims and remittance advice; (*b*) vendors, claims clearinghouses, and payers should offer physicians a full complement of EDI transactions (eg, claims submission; remittance advice; and eligibility, coverage, and benefit inquiry); (*c*) vendors, clearinghouses, and payers should adopt American National Standards Institute (ANSI) Accredited Standards Committee (ASC) Insurance Subcommittee (X12N) standards for electronic health care transactions and recommendations of the National Uniform Claim Committee (NUCC) on a uniform data set for a physician claim; (*d*) all clearinghouses should act as all-payer clearinghouses (ie, accept claims intended for all public and private payers); (*e*) practice management systems developers should incorporate EDI capabilities, including electronic claims submission; remittance advice; and eligibility, coverage and benefit inquiry into all of their physician office-based products; (*f*) states should be encouraged to adopt AMA model legislation concerning turnaround time for "clean" paper and electronic claims; and (*g*) federal legislation should call for the acceptance of the Medicare National Standard Format (NSF) and ANSI ASC X12N standards for electronic transactions and NUCC recommendations on a uniform data set for a physician claim. This legislation should also require that (i) any resulting conversions, including maintenance and technical updates, be fully clarified to physicians and their office staffs by vendors, billing agencies, or health insurers through educational demonstrations and (ii) that all costs for such services based on the NSF and ANSI formats, including educational efforts, be fully explained to physicians and/or their office staffs during negotiations for such contracted services. (2) The AMA continues to encourage physicians to develop electronic data interchange (EDI) capabilities and to contract with vendors and payers who accept American National Standards Institute (ANSI) standards and who provide electronic remittance advice as well as claims processing. (3) The AMA will continue to explore EDI-related business opportunities. (4) The AMA continues to facilitate the rapid development of uniform, industry-wide, easy-to-use, low-cost means for physicians to exchange electronically claims and eligibility information and remittance advice with payers and others in a manner that protects confidentiality of medical information and to

assist physicians in the transition to electronic data interchange. (5) The AMA will continue its leadership roles in the NUCC and WEDI. (BOT Rep 9, A-96; Amended by CMS Rep. 11, I-96)

H-190.977 Electronic Data Interchange Status Report

(1) Principles for development of a uniform data set for a noninstitutional electronic claim should: (*a*) build on, and seek needed improvements to, data elements in the existing HCFA-1500 paper form and Medicare electronic claims National Standard Format and relate directly to and conform to American National Standards Institute, Accredited Standards Committee, Insurance Subcommittee standards; (*b*) be equivalent across products, contracts, and government programs; (*c*) be as small as possible yet sufficient for use across the industry; (*d*) include data elements earmarked for one-time collection only, to avoid unnecessary duplication; (*e*) include data elements intended to serve as replacements for attachments; and (*f*) include standardization of optional or statutorily required elements. (2) The AMA will continue its dialogues with Community Health Information Networks and encourage sound, economic analyses of the costs and benefits to physicians of participating in these networks. (3) The AMA will continue to monitor and have input into the Medicare Transaction System (MTS), a unified Medicare claims processing system intended to consolidate and standardize operations. Public sector and proprietary review systems that may be used within MTS to detect fraud and abuse should adhere to AMA principles of medical review (eg, full disclosure of all payment and coding rules). (4) The AMA will encourage private payers to use all available technology to provide medical practices with up-to-date information (on deductibles and other payment elements) that eliminates erroneous claims and reduces administrative costs. Expanded information on health insurance cards is one of the options available to accomplish this objective. (5) The AMA will encourage the National Uniform Claim Committee to develop and seek implementation by all payers (including Medicare and Medicaid) of proposals acceptable to physicians to standardize third-party paper and electronic payment reporting methods, including remittance advices, explanations of benefits, "reason codes," and other explanations of third-party payment adjustment and actions. (CMS Rep 1, A-96)

H-190.976 Electronic Claims Submission

The AMA encourages insurance companies to adopt a standardized or open electronic claims submission protocol such as the National Standard Format (NSF) or American National Standard Institute (ANSI) such as utilized by Medicare, thus allowing physicians and other providers of health care to utilize electronic data interchange (EDI) efficiently and economically without needing redundant and proprietary standards and software for electronic claims submission; and encourages insurance companies to provide sufficient toll-free telephone lines in order to transmit this information, realizing the overall economies available to them from the conversion of paper claims to EDI. (Res 115, I-96)

H-190.974 Status Report on the National Uniform Claim Committee and Electronic Data Interchange

The AMA advocates use of the National Uniform Claim Committee standard claims/encounters data set for implementation of the administrative simplification provisions of the Health Insurance Portability and Accountability Act of 1996 (HIPAA); and strongly advocate that the CPT coding system be designated as the coding system to be used to report physician services under the HIPAA. (CMS Rep 2, A-97)

H-190.970 Status Report on the National Uniform Claim Committee and Electronic Data Interchange

The AMA advocates the following principles to improve the accuracy of claims and encounter-based measurement systems: (1) the development and implementation of uniform core data content standards (eg, National Uniform Claim Committee [NUCC] data set); (2) the use of standards that are continually modified and uniformly implemented; (3) the development of measures and techniques that are universal and applied to the entire health care system; (4) the use of standardized terminology and code sets (eg, CPT) for the collection of data for administrative, clinical, and research purposes; and (5) the development and integration of strategies for collecting and blending claims data with other data sources (eg, measuring the performance of physicians on a variety of parameters in a way that permits comparison with a peer group). (CMS Rep 2, I-97)

Provider Enrollment Chain and Ownership System (PECOS)

HCFA has developed a new computer system called PECOS, the Provider Enrollment Chain and Ownership System. HCFA recognizes the need to evaluate its electronic claim safeguards, and PECOS was developed to help ensure that only agencies authorized by a provider can submit claims. As further work is done in this area, HCFA may likely consider the following:

- Identifying and registering all clearinghouses and third-party billers. The Internal Revenue Service requires preparers of tax returns to identify themselves.

Medicare may require claim preparers to do the same. This would provide an easier audit trail and help ensure that claims enter the Medicare system from authorized sources.

- Improving safeguards to ensure that electronic claims are accepted only from authorized sites and terminals. Passwords and new technologies, such as caller identification, may be used to ensure that claims are received and processed only from known terminals.

- Educating the provider community concerning their liability for erroneous claims submitted to Medicare with the use of their provider number(s). HCFA currently relies on provider reviews of remittance notices to identify misuse of provider numbers. These notices can be rerouted to a billing company or another address, and providers may never see them. Providers should be made aware of their responsibility to review remittance notices.

Conclusion

The benefits of using EDI in your practice include speed, efficiency, improved cash flow, and decreased coding errors. As technology changes to address confidentiality and privacy concerns and more payers urge the use of EDI, the use of paper for claims processing will continue to decline. It appears that programs written for commercial distribution to a large audience pose little risk of producing erroneous or false claims. Proprietary software, by its nature, appears more likely to pose some risk of misuse or fraudulent use. As with paper claims, humans (and not software) may be the greatest cause of claim error.

4 The Coding Systems

Objectives

After completing this chapter, you should be able to:

- Identify the three volumes of *International Classification of Diseases–Ninth Revision, Clinical Modification* (ICD-9-CM) as they pertain to medical practices.

- Understand the general ICD-9-CM coding guidelines.

- Identify ICD-9-CM specific coding symbols, abbreviations, and notations.

- Understand the purpose of ICD-9-CM fourth and fifth digits.

- Understand the difference between V and E codes and the difference between *Includes* and *Excludes* notes.

- Locate the Neoplasm and Hypertension Tables in the index.

- Understand what the term *cross-reference* means.

- Describe how the three levels of HCPCS differ.

- Recognize the HCPCS coding guidelines and understand how CPT is organized.

- Recognize the format of CPT and CPT coding guidelines.

- Define evaluation and management services.

- Understand the rules that apply to surgery coding.

- Understand how CPT modifiers are used.

- Understand the Correct Coding Initiative.

Introduction

Practices use coding systems to communicate the procedures and services provided to patients and the reasons they were provided. Physician practices benefit from learning how to properly use the coding systems in two ways.

First, appropriate use of codes helps ensure proper payment from third-party payers and patients. Payers may reject or delay payment on claims without codes or with codes used incorrectly. Proper coding can enhance a practice's relationship with patients. When claims are coded accurately, patients who file their own claims will have fewer problems obtaining payment from their insurance company.

Second, appropriate use of codes reduces a practice's audit liability. When the reported codes do not accurately describe the procedures and services rendered, the physician may be accused of fraudulent billing, that is, billing for services and procedures other than those provided. Thus, learning how to code accurately and properly is in the practice's best interest.

The three coding systems most commonly used by physicians in the United States are CPT, HCPCS, and ICD-9. Each system is unique and serves a specific purpose in communicating to third-party payers what the physician did and why the physician did it. First, we give a brief overview of each system. The following sections give detailed information about each system.

1. *Current Procedural Terminology (CPT)®, Fourth Edition.* Created and maintained by the American Medical Association, CPT consists of more than 7000 codes used to report procedures and services. CPT codes communicate to third-party payers what the physician did. CPT codes are five-digit numbers accompanied by narrative descriptions. A two- or five-digit numeric modifier may also be used for additional modification of the CPT code description. All third-party payers accept CPT codes.

2. *HCFA's Common Procedure Coding System (HCPCS).* HCPCS (pronounced "hick-picks") was created by the Health Care Financing Administration (HCFA). HCPCS is a three-level coding system. Level I is the CPT code. Level II is a national alphanumeric code that begins with a letter followed by four numbers. Level II codes are usually thought of as the codes used to report supplies and injections to Medicare and other payers. Level III is a five-digit alphanumeric code applicable only within your state and is used by the state Medicare carrier for very unusual procedures for which there is no other level I or level II code available. These usually begin with the letters S and W through Z.

3. *International Classification of Diseases–Ninth Revision–Clinical Modification (ICD-9-CM).* This coding system is used to report patient illnesses, injuries, complaints, and/or symptoms, referred to as diagnoses. ICD-9-CM communicates to third-party payers the need for medical services, or why the physician performed the service. Like CPT, the ICD-9-CM system consists of code numbers and narrative descriptions. However, ICD-9-CM codes may range from three to five digits, depending on the level of specificity defined. The

physician (or coder) should code to the highest level of specificity. All ICD-9-CM codes are numeric except for E and V codes. E codes are used to report environmental events as the cause of an injury, poisoning, or other adverse effect and are used in addition to other ICD-9-CM codes (eg, E851 for accidental barbiturate poisoning). V codes are used for: health care encounters when the person is not sick (eg, V20.2 for a routine infant health check); person with a known disease obtaining a treatment for that disease (eg, V56.0 for extracorporeal dialysis for renal disease); and circumstances that influence a person's health status but is not itself a current injury or illness (eg, V10.07 for history liver cancer).

Other Coding Systems

Certain physicians use other coding systems, such as the *Diagnostic and Statistical Manual of Mental Disorders, Fourth Edition* (DSM-IV) for psychiatric and mental health services and CDT-3 for dental services. DSM-IV code books are available from the American Psychiatric Association at 800 368-5777. CDT-3 code books are available from the American Dental Association at 800 947-4746. Because of their focused nature, these other coding systems are not covered in this book.

CPT® Procedure Coding

CPT is the coding system used to describe services and procedures provided by physicians. Produced, published, and maintained by the American Medical Association, it is updated annually. A new publication is released each November, and the codes become effective on January 1.

Physicians should purchase the new CPT volume each year to ensure their use of the most current codes. The submission of deleted or incorrect CPT codes may result in reimbursement delay, denial, or audit liability. Copies of the CPT book are available from the American Medical Association.

CPT Organization

Codes in CPT are organized in six logical sections according to the types of services or procedures provided. These sections begin with guidelines that provide important coding rules and other information. It is important to be familiar with the six sections of CPT and the code number ranges in each section in order to better understand where to locate codes for different procedures or services. The six sections of CPT and their associated code ranges are as follows:

1. Evaluation and management services (codes 99201–99499). Physicians use codes from this section to report office, hospital, consultative, nursing home, and other related "visit" services. The book starts with this series of codes because they are the most frequently reported services by physicians.

2. Anesthesia (codes 00100–01999). The codes in this section describe anesthesia services any physician can use.

3. Surgery (codes 10040–69990). Surgery is the longest section in CPT. It includes codes that describe procedures ranging from simple wound repairs to organ transplants.

4. Radiology (codes 70010–79999). Diagnostic radiology, diagnostic ultrasound, radiation oncology, and nuclear medicine are covered in this section of codes.

5. Pathology and Laboratory (codes 80049–89399). These codes describe laboratory tests and pathology services.

6. Medicine (codes 90281–99199). This last section provides codes that describe a wide variety of medical services ranging from immunizations to electrocardiograms to psychotherapy.

CPT also provides information about the proper use and selection of codes. Specifically, you will find:

Introductions (roman numeral page numbers). These contain explanations of, and instructions for, the use of CPT.

Guidelines. Guidelines, which precede each section of CPT, contain important information specific to the section.

Appendices. Six appendices follow the Medicine section. Appendix A provides a complete list of the two-digit numeric modifiers for CPT codes and their descriptions. Appendix B summarizes code additions, deletions, and changes that occur for that year in the volume. Appendix C lists the short descriptions (28 characters or less) for each of the new, changed, or deleted codes. Appendices B and C are helpful to practices that use a computer to generate claims, as they provide a quick reference for updating the code databases. Appendix D contains clinical examples of the evaluation and management services and their corresponding CPT codes. Appendix E contains a summary of CPT add-on codes. Appendix F contains a summary of CPT codes exempt from modifier -51.

Index. The index follows Appendix F. Use it to locate the correct CPT code for a procedure. *Never* code directly from the index, as that can lead to coding errors. The index often lists a range of codes or multiple codes from which to choose. Read the complete descriptions, notes or parenthetic phrases, and guidelines of each code to ensure you select the correct one.

CPT Format

The CPT coding system utilizes an indented format, like that shown in the following example. This format is used to save space. You must be careful when reporting indented codes because the indented portion refers back to a common portion of the code above, which is not indented. The common portion is the portion printed before the semicolon (;). For example,

"Laryngoscopy, flexible fiberoptic;"

is common to codes 31575 through 31579. Thus, code 31576 is used to report:

"Laryngoscopy, flexible fiberoptic; with biopsy"

Following is an example of the indented format.

17106	Destruction of cutaneous vascular proliferative lesions (eg, laser technique); less than 10 sq cm
17107	10.0–50.0 sq cm
17108	Over 50.0 sq cm
17110*	Destruction by any method of flat warts or molluscum contagiosum, milia; up to 14 lesions
17111	15 or more lesions
11200*	Removal of skin tags, multiple fibrocutaneous tags, any area; up to and including 15 lesions
+11201	each additional ten lesions (List separately in addition to code for primary procedure)
	(use 11201 in conjunction with code 11200)
17250*	Chemical cauterization of granulation tissue (proud flesh, sinus, or fistula)
	(17250 is not to be used with removal or excision codes for the same lesion)

In addition to the indented format, the surgery section uses a consistent "universal" format that, like a road map, helps you locate codes. Surgery codes are first arranged by body system, such as integumentary, musculoskeletal, respiratory, and so on. As appropriate, codes within a body system are then arranged from the top of the system to the bottom, or from the outside to the inside of the body. Codes are further organized into types of procedures, such as incision, excision, repair, and the like.

CPT Symbols

CPT uses various symbols. These symbols and their meanings are described below.

- The solid circle (or bullet) appears to the left of codes new to CPT. "New" means the codes were not listed in the previous year's publication.

▲ A solid triangle (or delta) to the left of a code signifies that the code's narrative description has changed since last year's book. Description changes may be significant or relatively minor.

✱ Stars or asterisks appear to the right of several code numbers in the surgery section of CPT. The star signifies that because of the indefinite preoperative and postoperative services, the usual "package" concept for surgical services cannot be applied.

►◄ The two triangles facing each other are used to indicate new and revised text other than the procedure descriptors.

⤷ The arrow signifies that, in the Professional Edition of CPT, the code can be referenced to the CPT Assistant.

✚ The plus sign signifies "add-on codes"—some precedents are carried out in addition to the primary procedure performed. All add-on codes are exempt from the multiple procedure concept.

∅ This symbol indicates codes that are exempt from the use of modifier -51 but have not been designated as CPT add-on procedures/services.

The circle and triangle symbols are useful when referring to a specific code, because they identify the changes in each new volume of CPT. Symbols are a quick reference, saving the practice time from referencing Appendix B for each code it wishes to report.

CPT Notes

CPT contains several hundred notes and parenthetical remarks designed to assist with code selection. Notes precede groups of codes, follow a code(s) to which they apply, and, in at least one case, follow a section of codes. Parenthetical notes and remarks are typically provided to refer the coder to related procedures, or, in the case of deleted codes, to refer to codes that replace the deleted ones.

To code properly, review all notes pertaining to the code you are considering. Failure to read and understand notes can result in lower insurance reimbursements and audit liability.

CPT Index

The CPT index is an excellent starting point for locating codes. The page preceding the index gives instructions on how to use the index. Most codes can be located by looking under:

1. The name of the procedure or service (eg, incision, endoscopy).

2. The organ system or body area (eg, lung, genitourinary).

3. The patient's condition (eg, dislocation, pregnancy).

4. The use of synonyms (eg, renal for kidney), eponyms (eg, Abbe-Estlander), or abbreviations (eg, ECG, CAT scan).

Subterms, which follow most of the main terms in CPT, should be reviewed carefully as they may affect code assignments.

CPT Coding Guidelines

This section presents basic coding rules and special requirements that apply to frequently used sections of CPT.

Correct Coding Initiative (CCI) and HCFA Directives

In 1996, the National Correct Coding Council developed the Correct Coding Initiative (CCI) for HCFA as part of HCFA's effort to reduce coding errors and the inappropriate payments resulting from those errors. Medicare has since incorporated the edits, which are revised and updated quarterly, into their automated claims processing systems. Codes for services that are excluded by Medicare are not addressed by the CCI.

The CCI edits focus on multiple services billed for services to a patient on any particular day. Billing each of these services separately rather than globally is referred to as "unbundling" and may violate reimbursement regulations and leave a provider open to fraudulent billing charges. Most private insurance carriers also have similar edits in place with the same goal of identifying unbundled procedures. Understanding the CCI and proper coding will avoid these penalties and reduce delayed claim payments and unnecessary denials.

Black Box Edits In addition to the CCI edits, Medicare also uses commercial edits developed by McKesson HBOC, a health care information company. These edits, the intellectual property of McKesson HBOC, are often called "black box edits" because they are not released to the public.

Comparing the explanation of benefits (EOB) to the current CCI may identify these black box edits. Denials, which include notations such as "not paid separately," "incidental," or "bundled," are also indications of black box edits. If a service is denied but the code pair is not listed in the CCI, it is likely a black box edit. Medicare indicated in 2000 its intent to discontinue the use of these "black box edits."

General Rules Bundling or fragmented billing errors may occur in different ways, including:

- Fragmenting one service into separate component parts and billing each part separately
- Using several codes to describe a procedure when one comprehensive code will cover the entire procedure
- Using two codes for bilateral procedures when there is one specific code for the bilateral procedure
- Separating the surgical approach from the surgical procedure

To help ensure against improper coding and billing, it is important to always use the most current edition of the CCI. The CCI, available in hard copy, disk, or CD-ROM, may be obtained from the National Technical Information Services (800 553-6847 or http:www.ntis.gov).

How to Use the CCI Because the CCI comes in different formats, the exact method for identifying code pairs may differ. However, the basic principles remain the same:

- A comprehensive code is the principal code that describes a procedure. CCI looks for component or mutually exclusive codes for any comprehensive code.
- An incidental or component procedure is one that is performed at the same time as a more complex primary procedure. An incidental procedure requires little additional physician work and/or is clinically integral to the performance of the primary procedure.
- Medicare considers all services necessary to accomplish a given procedure as included in the description of that procedure.
- Mutually exclusive procedures are two or more procedures that are usually not performed during the same patient encounter on the same date of service.

In Exhibit 4.1, 17106 is the main procedure or comprehensive code. The codes in the second column are considered components of the main procedure, as they are necessary parts of the main procedure. The codes in column 3 are considered mutually exclusive to the main procedure because they cannot or normally are not performed at the same time on the same patient.

Exhibit 4.1   **Comprehensive, Component, and Mutually Exclusive Codes**

Comprehensive Code	Component Codes	Mutually Exclusive Codes
17106	11100, 11900 11901	17107, 17108

Comprehensive Code

17106	Destruction of cutaneous vascular proliferative lesions (eg, laser technique); less than 10 sq cm

Component Codes

11100	Biopsy of skin, subcutaneous tissue and/or mucous membrane (including simple closure), unless otherwise listed (separate procedure); single lesion
11900	Injection intralesional; up to and including seven lesions
11901	Injection intralesional; more than seven lesions

Mutually Exclusive Codes

17107	Destruction of cutaneous vascular proliferative lesions (eg, laser technique); 10.0–50.0 sq cm
17108	Destruction of cutaneous vascular proliferative lesions (eg, laser technique); over 50.0 sq cm

Medicare considers all the services necessary to accomplish a given procedure to be included (bundled) in the description of that procedure. In some cases, procedures normally denied as bundled may be paid separately by using the appropriate modifier. In the hard copy of the CCI, numerical indicators are listed next to the codes to indicate whether a modifier may be used with a particular code pair. The modifiers are:

- 0 = no modifier is allowed. The procedures will not be paid separately under any circumstance.

- 1 = modifier is allowed. The procedures may be paid separately with the appropriate modifier.

- 9 = use of modifier not specified. Use of the modifier may be permitted, depending on the circumstances.

In the absence of these modifiers, the following should be considered when determining if a modifier is appropriate:

- If the procedure was performed on different sites, such as a different body area, left or right, etc
- If the procedure was performed at a different time, such as a return to the operating room for an unstaged procedure
- If the procedure was performed with an evaluation and management visit for a different diagnosis
- If the procedure was performed with an evaluation and management visit for the same diagnosis if the decision to perform the surgery was determined during that same visit

Evaluation and Management (E&M) Services

Introduction   For each patient visit with a physician, medical record documentation is required to record pertinent facts, findings, and observations about an individual's health history, including past and present illnesses, examinations, tests, treatments, and outcomes. The medical record chronologically documents the care of the patient and is an important element contributing to high quality care. The medical record facilitates:

- The ability of the physician and other health care professionals to evaluate and plan the patient's immediate treatment, and to monitor his/her health care over time
- Communication and continuity of care among physicians and other health care professionals involved in the patient's care
- Accurate and timely claims review and payment
- Appropriate utilization review and quality of care evaluations; and
- Collection of data that may be useful for research and education

An appropriately documented medical record can reduce many of the difficulties associated with claims processing and may serve as a legal document to verify the care provided, if necessary.

What Do Payers Want and Why?   Because payers have a contractual obligation to enrollees, they may require reasonable documentation that services are consistent with the insurance coverage provided. They may request information to validate:

- The site of service

- The medical necessity and appropriateness of the diagnostic and/or therapeutic services provided; and/or

- That services provided have been accurately reported

To correctly document the services performed, specific requirements must be met to support the services rendered and to receive correct reimbursement for those services.

General Principles of Medical Record Documentation   The principles of documentation listed below are applicable to all types of medical and surgical services in all settings. For evaluation and management (E&M) services, the nature and amount of physician work and documentation vary by type of service, place of service, and the patient's status. The general principles listed below may be modified to account for these variable circumstances in providing E&M services.

1. The medical record should be complete and legible.

2. The documentation of each patient encounter should include:

    - The chief complaint and/or reason for the encounter and relevant history, physical examination findings and prior diagnostic test results

    - Assessment, clinical impression, or diagnosis

    - Plan for care

    - Date and a verifiable legible identity of the health care professional who provided the service

3. If not specifically documented, the rationale for ordering diagnostic and other ancillary services should be able to be easily inferred.

4. To the greatest extent possible, past and present diagnoses and conditions, including those in the prenatal and intrapartum period that affect the newborn, should be accessible to the treating and/or consulting physician.

5. Appropriate health risk factors should be identified.

6. The patient's progress, response to and changes in treatment, planned follow-up care and instructions, and diagnosis should be documented.

7. The CPT and ICD-9-CM codes reported on the health insurance claim form or billing statement should be supported by the documentation in the medical record.

8. An addendum to a medical record should be dated the day the information is added to the medical record, not the date the service was provided, and validated by signature.

9. A service should be documented during or as soon as practicable after it is provided in order to maintain an accurate medical record.

The confidentiality of the medical record should be fully maintained consistent with the requirements of medical ethics and of law.

1995 and 1997 E&M Guidelines   In 1995, HCFA issued guidelines to help establish standards for medical record documentation. These guidelines defined the documentation of the history, examination, and medical decision making in the medical record to support the level of service billed by the health care provider. HCFA revised these guidelines in 1997. These 1997 guidelines are more specific than those issued in 1995. HCFA also published proposed changes in June 2000, which are described briefly in this chapter.

At this time, the physician may use either the 1995 or 1997 guidelines. It should be noted that the changes in the guidelines from 1995 to 1997 affect the documentation of the history and the examination. The medical decision-making guidelines did not change. Once HCFA completes its pilot testing of the 2000 draft guidelines, it will further advise the physician community on implementation of any new guidelines.

Comparison of the 1995 and 1997 Guidelines   *History.* The 1995 and 1997 guidelines are very similar. A significant exception relates to the extended history of the presenting illness. Under the 1995 guidelines, the physician must document four elements of the history of the presenting illness in order to qualify for an extended history of the presenting illness. Under the 1997 guidelines, the physician may document either four elements or the presence of three or more chronic or inactive conditions.

Examination   The examination documentation requirements were greatly expanded under the 1997 guidelines. While the categories for the different levels of examination remained the same, the requirements to meet those levels of care changed.

The 1995 guidelines include the use of descriptors such as "limited," "extended," or "complete." However, these 1995 guidelines provide no specifics on the number of elements or body areas that must be examined to meet each level of care. Because of this nonspecificity of the descriptors, it may be difficult for an auditor and coder to agree on the level of care provided.

The 1997 examination guidelines are more quantifiable. In these guidelines, a specific number of elements must be documented in order to qualify for a specific level of service.

Examples:

> 1995 Expanded Problem Focused Examination: a limited examination of the affected body area or organ system and other symptomatic or related organ system(s)

> 1997 Expanded Problem Focused Examination: should include performance and documentation of at least six elements identified by a bullet (•) in one or more organ system(s) or body area(s).

The guidelines for single-organ exams may differ from those for the multisystem exam. The physician is not limited by specialty to use a specific type of exam. The nature of the presenting problem and the medical necessity will determine the type of examination that is performed.

Copies of the guidelines 1995 and 1997 E&M may be downloaded from the HCFA Web site at www.hcfa.gov.

Determining a Level of Care   The following criteria are presented in the proposed 2000 E&M coding guidelines.

There are seven components to consider in determining the level of care.

- History
- Examination
- Medical decision making
- Counseling
- Coordination of care
- Nature of presenting problem
- Time

The first three components, history, exam, and medical decision making, are the key components in determining a level of care. When time and counseling are a major factor of the E&M visit, different guidelines apply.

History   The history consists of four parts. Each part must be considered in determining a level of care. The four parts are:

- Chief complaint
- History of present illness
- Review of systems
- Past family and social history

A chief complaint is one sentence or phrase describing why the patient is seeing the provider at that instance. A chief complaint is indicated at all levels.

The history of present illness (HPI) is a narrative describing the symptoms and events leading to the provider encounter. Symptom description has eight possible elements:

- Location
- Quality
- Severity
- Duration
- Timing
- Context
- Modifying factors
- Associated signs and symptoms

There are two levels of HPI:

- Brief: requires one to three of these elements
- Extended: requires four or more elements, or three or more chronic or inactive conditions (the 1995 guidelines do not allow for the substitution of three or more conditions as an extended HPI)

The review of systems (ROS) is the response of the patient to specific questions about the different body systems. The recognized systems are:

- Constitutional symptoms (fever, weight loss, etc)
- Eyes
- Ears, nose, mouth, throat
- Cardiovascular
- Respiratory
- Gastrointestinal
- Genitourinary
- Musculoskeletal
- Integumentary (skin and/or breast)
- Neurologic
- Psychiatric
- Endocrine

- Hematologic/lymphatic
- Allergic/immunologic

There are three levels of the ROS.

Problem pertinent: requires documentation of the patient's positive responses and pertinent negatives for the system related to the problem

Extended: requires documentation of the patient's positive responses and pertinent negatives for two to nine systems

Complete: requires documentation of the patient's positive responses and pertinent negatives to 10 or more systems

For past family and social history (PFSH), three areas are considered:

- The patient's past medical history, including past provider visits, hospitalizations, surgeries, current medications, allergies, and other pertinent past data
- The patient's family history as it relates to health and hereditary issues
- The patient's social history (an age-appropriate review of past and current activities)

The two levels of PFSH are:

Pertinent: One specific item from any of the three areas

Complete: A review of two or all three of the PFSH history areas, depending on the category of the E&M service. A review of all three history areas is required for services that by their nature include a comprehensive assessment or reassessment of the patient. A review of two of the three history areas is sufficient for other services.

At least one specific item from two of the three history areas must be documented for a complete PFSH for the following categories of E&M services: office or other outpatient services, established patient; emergency department; domiciliary care, established patient; and home care, established patient.

At least one specific item from all of the three history areas must be documented for a complete PFSH for the following categories of E&M services:

- office or other outpatient services, new patient
- hospital observation services
- hospital inpatient services, initial care

- consultations
- comprehensive nursing facility assessments
- domiciliary care, new patient
- home care, new patient

Exam The second key component in determining the level of care is the examination. The requirements vary for the documentation of the exam, depending on which guidelines are being used. The 1997 guidelines are very specific and require the documentation of a certain number of elements for each level of care. The 1995 guidelines state the different levels of exam, without giving specifics on what documentation must be present.

The four levels of exam are as follows:

- Problem focused: requires the documentation of a limited examination of the affected body area or organ system.
- Expanded problem focused: requires the documentation of a limited exam of the affected body area or organ system and additional symptomatic or related systems.
- Detailed: requires the documentation of an extended examination of the affected area and other symptomatic or related organ systems.
- Comprehensive: requires the documentation of a general multisystem exam or a complete exam of a single organ system.

Medical Decision Making Medical decision making refers to the complexity of establishing a diagnosis and/or selecting a management option as measured by:

- the number of possible diagnoses and/or the number of management options that must be considered
- the amount and/or complexity of medical records, diagnostic tests, and/or other information that must be obtained, reviewed, and analyzed
- the risk of significant complications, morbidity and/or mortality, as well as comorbidities, associated with the patient's presenting problem(s), the diagnostic procedure(s), and/or the possible management options

There are four types of medical decision making:

- *Straightforward:* The problems addressed are straightforward and have minimal decision-making complexity.
- *Low complexity:* Typically, the problem(s) addressed will (1) be of low severity, low urgency, and low risk of clinical deterioration and complications, (2) have a

limited differential diagnosis and limited review of additional data, and (3) have straightforward diagnostic and/or therapeutic interventions and a straightforward treatment plan. For the purpose of documentation, two of these three elements must either meet or exceed the requirement for low complexity.

- *Moderate complexity:* Typically, the problem(s) addressed will (1) be of moderate severity with a low to moderate risk of clinical deterioration, (2) require review of a detailed amount of additional information with an extended differential diagnosis, and (3) require complicated diagnostic and/or therapeutic intervention, with a complicated treatment plan. For the purpose of documentation, two of these three elements must either meet or exceed the requirement for moderate complexity.

- *Highly complex:* Typically, the problem(s) addressed will (1) be of high severity with a high risk of complications and clinical deterioration, (2) require review of an extensive amount of additional information with an extensive differential diagnosis, and (3) require highly complex multiple diagnostic and/or therapeutic interventions, with a highly complex treatment plan. For the purpose of documentation, two of these three elements must either meet or exceed the requirement for highly complex medical decision making.

Table 4.1 shows the progression of the elements required for each level of medical decision making. To qualify for a given type of decision making, two of the three elements in the table must either meet or exceed the requirements for that type of decision making. Please refer to the HCFA guidelines at http:/www.hcfa.gov for more information and clarification regarding medical decision making.

Table 4.1   **Levels of Medical Decision Making**

Severity/ Urgency of Problem(s) and Risk of Complications and Deterioration	Differential Diagnoses and Amount/ Complexity of Data Reviewed	Treatment Plan Including Diagnostic and Therapeutic Tests, Procedures, and Interventions	Type of Decision Making
Low	Limited	Straightforward	Low
Moderate	Detailed	Complicated	Moderate
High	Extensive	Highly complex	High

Time   Time is calculated as either face-to-face or intraservice. Face-to-face time is the time the physician spends face-to-face with the patient or family. Use face-to-face time for office visits and other outpatient visits.

Intraservice time is for hospital and other inpatient visits. Intraservice time is calculated as the time spent both with the patient and on the floor.

In situations where an excessive amount of time is spent with a patient, prolonged service codes may be required. Prolonged service codes are used when the time spent with the patient exceeds the regular time by more than 30 minutes.

Time is not counted in emergency department levels of service. The nature of emergency department work does not allow for accurate estimates of the time spent on the floor or with the patient.

Counseling and Coordination of Care   In the case where counseling and/or coordination of care dominates (more than 50%) the physician-patient and/or family encounter (face-to-face time in the office or other outpatient setting or floor/unit time in the hospital or nursing facility), time is considered the key or controlling factor to qualify for a particular level of E&M services.

- DG: The total length of time of the encounter (face-to-face or floor time, as appropriate) and a full description/explanation of the counseling and/or activities coordinating care must be documented in the medical record.

- DG: Performance of a history and physical examination, although not required at each instance of counseling/coordination of care, should be referred to when appropriate.

- DG: Medical decision making associated with this service must be documented as part of the counseling and/or coordination of care.

     DG = Documentation guidelines

Nature of Presenting Problem   The nature of the presenting problem determines the type of care the patient will receive. Severely ill or injured patients may be admitted to the hospital, critical care unit, or emergency department. Patients with less severe problems may be admitted for observation or referred to a physician office.

Level of Care Determination   Determining the level of care documented requires first the consideration of all three key components and then the other four modifying factors. The procedure for new and established office visits in 2000 will be described here. Other E&M service levels are determined similarly. The reader should refer to the most current CPT manual or carrier manual for the most recent criteria.

New patient evaluations require at least all three of the key components: history, physical examination, and decision making (Table 4.2).

Table 4.2   **New Patient Evaluation**

Code	History	Physical	Decision Making	Typical Time
99201	Problem focused	Problem focused	Straightforward	10 min
99202	Expanded problem focused	Expanded problem focused	Straightforward	20 min
99203	Detailed	Detailed	Low complexity	30 min
99204	Comprehensive	Comprehensive	Moderate complexity	45 min
99205	Comprehensive	Comprehensive	High complexity	60 min

All three key components must be met or exceeded for new patients for office visits, domiciliary, home visits, office consultations, initial hospital care, initial inpatient consultations, hospital observation, emergency department services, confirmatory consultations, and comprehensive nursing facility assessments.

Established patient evaluations require at least two of the three key components (Table 4.3).

Table 4.3   **Established Patient Evaluation**

Code	History	Physical	Decision Making	Typical Time
99211	Minimal	Minimal	Minimal	5 min
99212	Problem focused	Problem focused	Straightforward	10 min
99213	Expanded problem focused	Expanded problem focused	Low complexity	15 min
99214	Detailed	Detailed	Moderate complexity	25 min
99215	Comprehensive	Comprehensive	High complexity	40 min

Two of the three key components must be met or exceeded for established patients in the office, home, domiciliary care, subsequent hospital care, nursing facility care, and follow-up inpatient consultations.

When counseling or coordination of care exceeds 50% of the patient visit, then time is the deciding factor in choosing a level of care. When more than 50% of the office visit involves counseling or coordination of care, the service can be coded based on the time element. In order to use time, the documentation in the chart must state the total length of time spent with the patient and the amount of time spent on counseling and coordination of care. Information on what was discussed with the patient should also be included. Table 4.4 shows a side-by-side comparison of E&M documentation guidelines.

Table 4.4   **Side-by-Side Comparison of E&M Documentation Guidelines**

Code Component	1995 Requirements	1997 Requirements	Draft Guidelines (June 2000)
History of present Illness (HPI)	Specific requirements	Specific requirements	Clearer requirements; explicit recognition of medication monitoring
Review of systems (ROS)	Specific body area or organ system requirements	Specific body area or organ system requirements	Less required; clearer examples are provided
Past, family, social history (PFSH)	Brief information required	Brief information required	No difference*
Physical exam	Specifically referenced general multisystem exam • Description of single-system exams inadequate • 4 levels • Requirements not clear	General multisystem exam and 10 single-system exams • 4 levels • Very descriptive Confusing shading & bullets format • Requirements often not relevant	Physician *tailors* documentation to exam • Only 3 levels • Vignette examples • No bullets • No shading • Minimal counting • No irrelevant facts to record
Medical decision making	4 levels • Laundry list of examples not reflective of clinical assessments & plans	4 levels • Laundry list of examples not reflective of clinical assessments & plans	Only 3 levels • Physician *tailors* documentation to assessment & plan of treatment • Vignette examples

Source: HCFA.

Summary   Understanding the requirements for documenting each level of service is critical to coding. Since undercoding and overcoding of services are primary areas related to investigation of fraud and abuse, knowing how to properly code and document services is no longer an option but a necessity.

Selecting the CPT Procedure Code

The CPT coding process involves six basic steps that, when followed, increase the likelihood of accurate code selection.

1. Identify the procedures and services provided. This entails reviewing the patient's record, operative report, radiology, laboratory reports, and so on. The first step in proper coding is identifying the procedures and services provided during the physician-patient encounter. Identification of routine services, such as office visits, is fairly straightforward. Identification of multiple services or complex procedures (especially surgeries) requires a higher-level understanding of CPT and of billing rules.

2. Consult the index to locate the code numbers. You must determine the main terms for each procedure to be coded and then identify that main term in the alphabetic index. Note any listed subterms below the main term and refer to cross-references provided in the index.

3. Locate the code(s) in the main body of the CPT book. Always refer to the code in the main body of the book, which may include notes or other important information that may affect code selection. Never code directly from the index.

4. Review the notes and parenthetical remarks associated with the codes. They may contain special rules or information that may affect your code selection. Also review the guidelines at the beginning of the section and subsection notes when included.

5. Code the billable procedures and services. After specific procedures and services have been identified, the next step is to code them.

6. Modify as necessary. Some situations will require adding appropriate modifiers to codes. Modifiers are discussed later in this chapter.

Note: Compare the final code description with the procedure or service provided to ensure that all components have been reported.

Selecting the E&M Services Code

Nearly one third of all services rendered by physicians nationwide are reported with codes from this section of CPT. Therefore, you must pay special attention to the rules related to coding E&M services. Rules for coding these services are in the E&M guidelines beginning on page 1 of the CPT book.

E&M services are coded according to the *content* of the service provided. The extent of the history taken by the physician, the extent of the examination, and the complexity of medical decision making involved are defined as *key components*. Four levels of history, four levels of examination, and four levels of decision making are defined. In most cases, code selection will depend on matching the levels of each key component provided with the levels specified in the codes. The four levels are problem focused, expanded problem focused, detailed, and comprehensive. These four clinical levels determine the numeric billing level that is forwarded to the carrier.

For example, if the physician saw an established patient in the office, took an expanded problem-focused history, performed an expanded problem-focused examination, and determined that medical decision making was of low complexity, code 99213 would be selected.

99213   Office or other outpatient visit for the evaluation and management of an established patient, which requires at least two of these three key components:

- an expanded problem-focused history
- an expanded problem-focused examination
- medical decision making of low complexity

Counseling and coordination of care with other providers or agencies are provided consistent with the nature of the problem(s) and the patient's and/or family's needs.

Usually, the presenting problems(s) are of low to moderate severity. Physicians typically spend 15 minutes face-to-face with the patient and/or family. However, time element is not used to determine service provided, unless 50% of the face-to-face time is spent counseling.

When a new patient is evaluated, all three key components are used for establishing the numeric level of billing. The lowest of the three levels of key components is used. When an established patient is evaluated, only two of three key components are used for billing purposes. The lower of the two levels determines the numeric level of billing.

Code selection for E&M services can be affected by other factors, called *contributing factors*. These include the nature of the patient's presenting problem(s), the provision of counseling and/or coordination of care services, and the amount of time the physician spends with the patient. While these factors are not key to choosing the E&M code, they can affect selection.

According to CPT E&M guidelines, time may become the controlling factor in selecting E&M codes only when more than 50% of the service rendered to the patient was related to counseling and/or coordination of care. Understanding how time is defined is important when time is used as the controlling factor in billing. For office E&M services, time is defined as time spent face-to-face with the patient; for hospital E&M services, time is defined as time spent on the patient's floor or unit.

All Medicare updates from local carriers should be read, as coding guidelines and documentation requirements change frequently.

E&M Documentation Guidelines

HCFA's revised documentation guidelines for E&M services have been indefinitely delayed. At this time, either the 1995 or 1997 guidelines may be used, whichever is most advantageous to the provider. As of June 2000, HCFA announced the pilot of a revised version of the 1995 guidelines. See HCFA's website at www.hcfa.gov/medicare for the most recent version of guidelines.

Surgery Coding

Special rules apply to the coding of surgical procedures. Three of the most important rules are discussed below.

Surgical Package Rules   Beginning coders often ask what services are included with surgical procedures. To address this issue, the CPT system provides the "surgical package" (or global surgery) definition. Shown in the surgery section guidelines, it specifies components assumed to be included in the surgery charge. The components are:

- The operation itself
- Local and topical anesthetics (if provided)
- Digital blocks (if provided)
- The normal, uncomplicated follow-up care related to the procedure

Thus, the physician should not bill separately for local or topical anesthetics, digital blocks, or hospital or office visits that are part of the normal follow-up. If the patient develops complications during follow-up, treatment of the complications may be coded. Preoperative services such as consultations, office visits, and initial hospital care are often billed separately by physicians. Payment for these services will depend on third-party payment policy.

The Medicare definition of the surgical package delineates the number of preoperative and postoperative days included as well as the types of services included in the package.

The Medicare global surgery package includes:

- A 1-day preoperative period. This includes all preoperative visits by the surgeon in or out of the hospital beginning the day before surgery.
- Intraoperative services that are a part of the procedure.
- A standard 90-day postoperative period (or follow-up) including any services the surgeon provided during that time, unless service was due to an unrelated condition. Minor surgical procedures include a 0- to 10-day postoperative period. There is no postoperative period for endoscopic diagnostic procedures performed through an existing body orifice.
- All medically necessary return trips to the operating room can be billed separately and will be paid at a reduced rate.

Several other payers also have surgical package definitions that may differ from the ones listed above. Physicians and staff need to be aware of the differences and code accordingly. Check with your local carriers for clarification of their policies.

Note: The global surgical package is very important in physician office claim submission. However, the surgical package is *not* applicable to hospital coding for the facility fee.

Separate Procedures   CPT codes were designed to combine several procedures that were often performed together, so reporting would use a minimum number of codes but still provide a complete picture of the service provided. In some cases, CPT has identified certain procedures as "separate procedures," which means these can be coded separately when performed independently and not in conjunction with the major or primary procedure.

Example:

52601   TURP, transurethral resection of the prostate, including control of postoperative bleeding, complete (vasectomy, meatotomy, cystourethroscopy, urethral calibration and/or dilation, and internal urethrotomy are included).

55250   Vasectomy, unilateral or bilateral (separate procedure), including postoperative semen examination(s).

In the above example, a transurethral resection of the prostate and a vasectomy were performed. Following the separate procedure guidelines, only code 52601 should be assigned because it incorporates both the resection of the prostate and the vasectomy. Code 55250 is identified as a separate procedure and can be reported separately when only the vasectomy is performed.

Starred Procedure Rules   A star appears to the right of several code numbers in the surgery section of CPT. The star signifies that the surgical package defined above does not apply to these codes and that special coding rules should be followed instead. Note that starred procedures are invariably minor surgeries that may or may not have associated preoperative and/or postoperative services. Thus, the surgical package does not logically apply. This means that, subject to the rules for coding starred procedures in the surgery section guidelines, preoperative and postoperative care can be billed separately from the procedure.

CPT Modifiers

CPT contains two-digit numeric modifiers that are used to report situations in which the service or procedure was altered by some specific circumstance. In such situations, the circumstance does not affect the selection of the CPT code.

For example, the physician performs a bilateral tympanostomy under general anesthesia.

Because code 69436 is a unilateral procedure code, the modifier -50 must be assigned to identify this procedure as bilateral, as shown in the example below:

69436-50   Tympanostomy (requiring insertion of ventilating tube), general anesthesia

The addition of the modifier indicates that the physician performed the procedure bilaterally.

All modifiers are listed in CPT's Appendix A. Modifiers relevant to each of the six sections of CPT are also provided in the section guidelines. Although CPT provides both two-digit (for example, -51) and five-digit (for example, 09951) modifiers, most payers accept, if not require, two-digit modifiers. Certain modifiers have specific uses (ie, -21, -24, -25 with E/M services). Some modifiers are commonly used with certain types of codes (ie, surgery, medicine), so as not to preclude or restrict their use to only one specialty. Use the modifier that depicts the circumstance most accurately.

Modifiers and Descriptors

-21 or 09921   Prolonged Evaluation and Management Services   This modifier is appropriate for use when service provided is prolonged and more than is usually required for the highest level of E&M service within a category. Appropriate documentation should also be sent with the claim to support the use of the modifier and the increase of payment requested. *This modifier should be used for E&M service code(s).*

-22 or 09922   Unusual Services   This modifier is appropriate when the service provided is greater than that usually required. A special report may be required to describe the unusual service provided. *This modifier is commonly used with anesthesia, surgery, radiology, and pathology/laboratory procedure code(s).*

-23 or 09923   Unusual Anesthesia   When a procedure that usually requires local or no anesthetic must be performed under a general anesthetic because of unusual circumstances, modifier -23 should be reported along with the procedure code. *This modifier should be used for anesthesia code(s).*

-24 or 09924   Unrelated Evaluation and Management Service by the Same Physician During a Postoperative Period   This modifier is appropriate to describe an E&M service provided to a patient during the postoperative period that is unrelated to the original procedure. *This modifier should be used for E&M service code(s).*

-25 or 09925   Significant, Separately Identifiable Evaluation and Management Service by the Same Physician   This modifier is appropriate to use when the physician needs to indicate, on the day a procedure or service identified by a CPT code was performed, that the patient's condition required a significant, separately identifiable E&M service above and beyond the other service provided or beyond the usual preoperative and postoperative care associated with the procedure. The symptom or condition for which the procedure and/or service was provided may prompt the E&M service. Different diagnoses are not required for reporting of the E&M services on the same date. Do not report this modifier for E&M services that result in the decision to do surgery. See modifier -57. *This modifier should be used for E&M service code(s).*

-26 or 09926   Professional Component   The majority of the procedures included in CPT include both the technical and professional component. This modifier is used to indicate that the physician provided only the professional component, not the technical. *This modifier is commonly used with surgery, radiology, medicine, and pathology/laboratory procedure code(s).*

-32 or 09932   Mandated Services   Mandated services refer to a confirmatory opinion conducted at the request of the payer, governmental, legislative, or regulatory requirement. *This modifier is commonly used with E&M services, anesthesia, surgery, radiology, pathology/laboratory, and medicine procedure code(s).*

-47 or 09947   Anesthesia by Surgeon   When the physician administers anesthesia in addition to performing the surgery, this modifier is reported. *This modifier should be used with surgery procedure code(s).*

-50 or 09950   Bilateral Procedure   There are only a few codes in CPT distinguishing between unilateral and bilateral procedures. This modifier is appropriate for use to describe a bilateral procedure. There are several ways to report the bilateral modifier. Coders should check with individual insurance carriers to determine their preference. *This modifier should be used with surgery procedure code(s).*

-51 or 09951   Multiple Procedures   When more than one procedure is performed on the same day during the same surgical episode, this modifier may be assigned. The first code listed should be the most resource intensive or the highest paying. Medicare reimbursement is reduced by 50% for the second procedure, 25% for the third procedure, etc. *This modifier is most commonly used with anesthesia, surgery, and radiology procedure code(s).*

-52 or 09952   Reduced Services   When the service documented in the medical record is less in time or effort than the descriptor in the CPT manual, this modifier may be reported to indicate that a lower level of service was provided. In addition, the charge should also be decreased. Note: For hospital outpatient reporting of a previously scheduled procedure/service that is partially reduced or canceled as a result of extenuating circumstances or those that threaten the well-being of the patient prior to or after administration of anesthesia, see modifiers -73 and -74. *This modifier is commonly used with E&M services, surgery, radiology, and pathology/laboratory procedure code(s).*

-53 or 09953   Discontinued Procedure   This modifier is used when the physician elects to terminate a surgical or diagnostic procedure because of extenuating circumstances or those that threaten the well-being of the patient. Note: This modifier is not used to report the elective cancellation of a procedure prior to the patient's anesthesia induction and/or surgical preparation in the operating suite. For outpatient hospital/ambulatory surgery center (ASC) reporting of a previously scheduled procedure/service that is partially reduced or canceled as a result of extenuating circumstances or those that threaten the well-being of the patient prior to or after administration of anesthesia, see modifiers -73 and -74. *This modifier is commonly used with anesthesia, surgery, radiology, and pathology/ laboratory procedure code(s).*

-54 or 09954   Surgical Care Only   As mentioned earlier, the surgical package includes the procedure and normal preoperative and postoperative care (excluding starred procedures). In some cases, however, the physician may perform only the surgical procedure. In these cases, modifier -54 or 09954 should be reported. In addition, the charges related to that code should be reduced. *This modifier should be used with surgery procedure code(s).*

-55 or 09955   Postoperative Management Only   When the physician provides only the postoperative management (not the preoperative or operative service) for a patient, modifier -55 or 09955 is reported. Again, the charges related to that code should be reduced to reflect the postoperative management fees only. *This modifier should be used with surgery procedure code(s).*

-56 or 09956   Preoperative Management Only   When the physician provides only the preoperative management (not the operative and postoperative service) for a patient, modifier -56 or 09956 is reported. Again, the charges related to that code should be reduced to reflect the preoperative management fees only. *This modifier should be used with surgery procedure code(s).*

-57 or 09957   Decision for Surgery   Adding the modifier -57 to the appropriate level of E&M service may identify an E&M service that resulted in the initial decision to perform the surgery, or the separate five-digit modifier 09957 may be used. *This modifier should be used with E&M service code(s).*

-58 or 09958   Staged or Related Procedure or Service by the Same Physician During the Postoperative Period   The physician may need to indicate that the performance of a procedure or service during the postoperative period was (*a*) planned prospectively at the time of the original procedure (staged); (*b*) more extensive than the original procedure; or (*c*) for therapy following a diagnostic surgical procedure. This circumstance may be reported by adding the modifier -58 to the staged or related procedure, or the separate five-digit modifier 09958 may be used. Note: This modifier is not used to report the treatment of a problem that requires a return to the operating room. *This modifier is commonly used with surgery, radiology, and medicine procedure code(s).*

-59 or 09959   Distinct Procedural Service   Under certain circumstances, the physician may need to indicate that a procedure or service was distinct or independent from other services performed on the same day. This may represent a different session or patient encounter, different procedure or surgery, different site or organ system, separate incision/excision, separate lesion, or separate injury (or area of injury in extensive injuries) not ordinarily performed on the same day by the same physician. However, when another already established modifier is appropriate, it should be used instead of modifier -59. Only if no more descriptive modifier is available, and the use of modifier -59 best explains the circumstances, should modifier -59 be used. *This modifier is commonly used with anesthesia, surgery, radiology, pathology/laboratory, and medicine procedure code(s).*

-62 or 09962   Two Surgeons (Co-surgery)   Although one surgeon performs most surgical procedures, there are some difficult surgeries requiring two surgeons. When two surgeons work together as primary surgeons performing distinct part(s) of a single reportable procedure, each surgeon should report his/her distinct operative work by adding the modifier -62 to the single definitive procedure code. Each surgeon should report the co-surgery once using the same procedure code. If additional procedure(s) (including add-on procedures) are performed during the same operative session, separate code(s) may be reported without the modifier -62 added. Modifier code 09962 may be used as an alternative to modifier -62. Note: If a co-surgeon acts as an assistant in the performance of additional procedure(s) during the same surgical session, those services may be reported by using separate procedure code(s) with the modifier -80 or modifier -81 added, as appropriate. *This modifier is commonly used with surgery and radiology procedure code(s).*

-66 or 09966   Surgical Team   Complex surgical procedures, such as heart and renal transplants, require a highly trained team of physicians and support staff to successfully conduct the procedure. Modifier -66 or 09966 should be reported indicating to the insurance carrier that more than one physician will be submitting claims for reimbursement. *This modifier is commonly used with surgery and radiology procedure code(s).*

-73 or 09973   Discontinued Outpatient Hospital/Ambulatory Surgery Center (ASC) Procedure Prior to the Administration of Anesthesia

Because of extenuating circumstances or those that threaten the well-being of the patient, the physician may cancel a surgical or diagnostic procedure subsequent to the patient's surgical preparation (including sedation when provided, and being taken to the room where the procedure is to be performed), but prior to the administration of anesthesia (local, regional block[s] or general). Modifier -73 or 09973 can be added to the procedure code for the intended service that is prepared for but canceled. Note: The elective cancellation of a service prior to the administration of anesthesia and/or surgical preparation of the patient should not be reported.

-74 or 09974   Discontinued Outpatient Hospital/Ambulatory Surgery Center (ASC) Procedure After Administration of Anesthesia

Because of extenuating circumstances or those that threaten the well-being of the patient, the physician may terminate a surgical or diagnostic procedure after the administration of anesthesia (local, regional block[s], general) or after the procedure was started (incision made, intubation started, scope inserted, etc). Modifier -74 or 09974 can be added to the procedure code when the procedure was started but terminated. Note: The elective cancellation of a service prior to the administration of anesthesia and/or surgical preparation of the patient should not be reported.

-76 or 09976   Repeat Procedure by Same Physician

Situations will exist where a procedure will need to be repeated by the same physician because of problems with the patient, equipment, emergencies, complications, etc. The repeat procedure is to be performed subsequent to the original procedure or service. In these situations, modifier -76 or 09976 should be reported. Documentation should include quite clearly why the surgery is being repeated. *This modifier is commonly used with surgery, radiology, pathology/laboratory, and medicine procedure code(s).*

-77 or 09977   Repeat Procedure by Another Physician

This modifier is similar to the previous modifier except that the physician performing the repeat surgery is not the same. As with the previous modifier, repeat procedures may be required because of problems with the patient, equipment, emergencies, complications, etc. The repeat procedure is to be performed during the same day as the original surgery. For instance, a physician may perform a percutaneous transluminal coronary angioplasty (PTCA) for a patient with acute coronary occlusion. Later in the day, the occlusion redevelops. If the original physician was not available to perform the PTCA, another doctor may perform it. The second doctor would report the PTCA code, as well as this modifier to alert the insurance carrier that the procedure was indeed performed two times in one day. Again, documentation should clearly state why the surgery was repeated and that a different physician is conducting the second procedure. *This modifier is commonly used with surgery, radiology, and medicine procedure code(s).*

-78 or 09978   Return to the Operating Room for a Related Procedure During the Postoperative Period   In some cases, a physician will be required to return to the operating room during the postoperative period of a procedure to address a condition that is related to the initial procedure. To report these situations, modifier -78 or 09978 should be assigned along with the procedure code. For instance, a patient having undergone abdominal surgery returns to the operating room 10 days after surgery for repair of abdominal wound dehiscence. The wound dehiscence repair, which is related to the original procedure, occurs during the postoperative period of that first procedure. Therefore, modifier -78 or 09978 should be reported along with the wound dehiscence repair code. Documentation in the medical record should clearly indicate the reason for the return visit to the operating room. *This modifier is commonly used with surgery, radiology, and medicine procedure code(s).*

-79 or 09979   Unrelated Procedure or Service by the Same Physician During the Postoperative Period   In other cases, a problem will arise requiring surgery or service by a physician who has recently performed surgery on the patient. If this service or second surgery is provided during the postoperative period of the first surgery, modifier -79 or 09979 is reported to explain the additional procedure or service. For instance, a patient may have had a cholecystectomy and is still in the postoperative period of that surgery and now is admitted to the hospital with multiple lacerations and contusions secondary to an automobile accident. Modifier -79 is applicable to describe the reason for the second admission while still in the postoperative period of the first procedure. Again, documentation should clearly include the diagnoses and services/procedures provided. *This modifier is commonly used with surgery, radiology, and medicine procedure code(s).*

-80 or 09980   Assistant Surgeon   When an assistant surgeon is required to help in performing a surgical procedure, the assisting surgeon should report modifier -80 or 09980 along with the appropriate surgery code. It is imperative that the assisting surgeon and primary surgeon submit the same code to the insurance carriers (with the assisting surgeon using modifier -80). Coders should note that the primary surgeon does not have to report modifier -80. The operative report should clearly state the reason for having an assistant surgeon, as well as his/her contribution to the surgery. *This modifier should be used with surgery and radiology procedure code(s).*

-81 or 09981   Minimum Assistant Surgeon   There may be a situation in which a physician requires some assistance in the operating room because of a minor problem encountered during the procedure. In these cases, modifier -81 or 09981 is reported to indicate that "minimum assistance" was provided. As with the previous modifier, the assisting surgeon reports the modifier along with the surgery code. Again, the surgery code submitted by the primary surgeon should be the same as the surgery code submitted by the assisting surgeon. Documentation in the record should provide the reason for requiring the minimum assistance. *This modifier should be used with surgery procedure code(s).*

-82 or 09982   Assistant Surgeon (When Qualified Resident Not Available)   In most teaching hospitals, residents are available to serve as assistant surgeon when the procedure requires an assistant. In these situations, if a resident is not available and another "nonresident" surgeon assists, modifier -82 is reported along with the surgery code by the assisting surgeon. The surgery code submitted by the assistant and the primary surgeon should be the same. Again, documentation in the record should indicate the fact that a qualified resident was not available and that an assistant was required for the procedure performed. *This modifier should be used with surgery procedure code(s).*

-90 or 09990   Reference (Outside) Laboratory   When the physician reports a procedure that was not done by his facility or office, this modifier should be assigned. *This modifier is commonly used with surgery, radiology, and pathology/laboratory procedure code(s).*

-91 or 09991   Repeat Clinical Diagnostic Lab   Report this modifier when a lab test is repeated on the same day for the same patient to obtain subsequent test results. Do not use this modifier when a lab test is repeated to rerun or confirm original results or because of testing problems.

-99 or 09999   Multiple Modifiers   When more than one modifier is appropriate to report the services provided to the patient, this modifier may be assigned to identify the use of multiple modifiers. The CPT code should be reported with modifier -99 with the other modifiers listed as part of the description of the service or as follows:

Example:	23931-99	Incision and drainage, upper arm or elbow area; infected bursa
	00947	Anesthesia provided by the surgeon
	00950	Bilateral procedure

This modifier is commonly used with surgery, radiology, and medicine procedure code(s).

HCPCS Procedure Coding

HCPCS is an abbreviation for the federal government's three-level coding system—the Health Care Financing Administration Common Procedure Coding System. CPT 2000 includes all level I and level II modifiers approved for physician and hospital outpatient use.

HCFA is the federal agency that administers the Medicare and Medicaid programs. In the 1980s, with the increasing use of electronic claims, the HCFA recognized the need for a nationwide standardized coding system. Because Medicare and Medicaid pay for physicians' services as well as other medical services and supplies, HCFA developed the following three levels of codes.

Level I—CPT

The American Medical Association (AMA) developed and first published CPT in 1966. It is used to report the procedures and services of physicians and services provided under the supervision of physicians, such as physical therapy. The *Current Procedural Terminology* manual, abbreviated CPT, is a five-digit coding system. In agreement with the AMA, HCFA adopted CPT as the first level of HCPCS coding. CPT, which is copyrighted by the AMA, includes more than 7000 numeric codes and represents approximately 90% of HCPCS.

Level II—National HCPCS Codes

Level II codes are for services and supplies not found in CPT, such as oral and injectable medications; durable medical equipment; prosthetics; orthotics; medical and surgical supplies; ambulance services; chiropractic, dental, and certain vision services and supplies; and temporary codes developed by HCFA. Level II codes are five digits and begin with the letters A through V. As implied in the name, level II national codes are used by all Medicare carriers (Part B) and intermediaries (Part A) and Medicaid in all states.

Level III—Local HCPCS Codes

Each Medicare carrier may use, on approval of HCFA, local codes intended for use only in its state or region. These five-digit codes begin with the letters S, W, Y, and Z. Very few level III codes remain in use because most codes needed now appear in level I (CPT) or level II. Level III local codes are usually issued each year in a bulletin or newsletter by the Medicare carrier for the state or region.

Modifiers Approved for Hospital Outpatient Use

Level I (CPT) Modifiers

-50   Bilateral Procedure

-52   Reduced Services

-59   Distinct Procedural Service

-73   Discontinued Outpatient Hospital/ASC Procedure Prior to the Administration of Anesthesia

-74   Discontinued Outpatient Hospital/ASC Procedure After the Administration of Anesthesia

-76   Repeat Procedure by Same Physician

-77   Repeat Procedure by Another Physician

Level II (HCPCS/National) Modifiers

-LT   Left side (used to identify procedures performed on the left side of the body)

-RT   Right side (used to identify procedures performed on the right side of the body)

-E1   Upper left eyelid

-E2   Lower left eyelid

-E3   Upper right eyelid

-E4   Lower right eyelid

-FA   Left hand, thumb

-F1   Left hand, second digit

-F2   Left hand, third digit

-F3   Left hand, fourth digit

-F4   Left hand, fifth digit

-F5   Right hand, thumb

-F6   Right hand, second digit

-F7   Right hand, third digit

-F8   Right hand, fourth digit

-F9   Right hand, fifth digit

-LC   Left circumflex coronary artery (Hospitals use with codes 92980-92984, 92995, 92996)

-LD   Left anterior descending coronary artery (Hospitals use with codes 92980-92984, 92995, 92996)

-RC   Right coronary artery (Hospitals use with codes 92980-92984, 92995, 92996)

-QM   Ambulance service provided under arrangement by a provider of services

-QN   Ambulance service furnished directly by a provider of services

-QR   Repeat laboratory test performed on the same day

-TA   Left foot, great toe

-T1   Left foot, second digit

-T2   Left foot, third digit

-T3   Left foot, fourth digit

-T4   Left foot, fifth digit

-T5   Right foot, great toe

-T6   Right foot, second digit

-T7   Right foot, third digit

-T8   Right foot, fourth digit

-T9   Right foot, fifth digit

HCPCS Coding Guidelines

HCPCS level II and level III codes are reported on claims in the same manner as level I (CPT) codes. Medicare requires that physicians and hospitals use certain level II codes instead of less specific CPT codes in certain circumstances. For example, covered and injectable medications must be submitted with the specific level II code that begins with "J," as well as the CPT code from the medicine section. The level II codes beginning with "A" must be used for billing covered supplies, such as surgical trays. Each Medicare carrier and intermediary can provide you with billing rules for level II and level III codes.

Codes Accepted by Your Carriers

Table 4.5 will help you determine the codes accepted by your carriers (CPT, HCPCS national and local, and ICD-9-CM). Defined by the type of payer, such as Blue Cross and Blue Shield or Medicaid, and by type of code, such as CPT or ICD-9-CM, the table provides an overview of standard policies of the listed types of carriers.

Table 4.5 — **Which Carriers Accept Which Codes**

Coding System	Insurance Carriers			
	Commercial Carriers	**Blue Cross and Blue Shield**	**Medicare**	**Medicaid**
CPT	Virtually all commercial carriers accept CPT codes	All Blue Cross and Blue Shield carriers accept CPT codes	All Medicare carriers accept CPT codes	All Medicaid Programs accept CPT codes or variations thereof
HCPCS National Codes	Many commercial carriers are starting to accept CPT codes	If Blue Cross and Blue Shield runs your Medicare program, they might accept HCPCS national codes	All Medicare carriers accept some HCPCS national codes (payment depends on coverage)	Most Medicaid programs accept HCPCS national codes
HCPCS Local Codes	Some commercial carriers will accept HCPCS local codes	If Blue Cross and Blue Shield runs Medicare program, they might accept HCPCS local codes	Your Medicare carrier will accept its own HCPCS local codes	Many Medicaid programs accept HCPCS local codes
ICD-9-CM Diagnosis Codes	Virtually all commercial carriers will accept ICD-9-CM codes	All Blue Cross and Blue Shield carriers accept ICD-9-CM codes	All Medicare carriers accept ICD-9-CM codes	Virtually all Medicaid programs accept ICD-9-CM codes

You can use the blank version of Table 4.6, which follows the completed Table 4.5, to list specific carriers in your area and their acceptance policies of the different coding systems.

Table 4.6 — **Codes Accepted by Your Carriers**

Coding System	Insurance Carriers			
	Commercial Carriers	**Blue Cross and Blue Shield**	**Medicare**	**Medicaid**
CPT				
HCPCS National Codes				
HCPCS Local Codes				
ICD-9-CM Diagnosis Codes				

ICD-9-CM

The *International Classification of Diseases, Ninth Revision–Clinical Modification* (ICD-9-CM) coding system was developed in 1978 by the US National Center for Health Statistics as a statistical classification system. It was created to replace the ICD-A system and to allow for better reporting of both inpatient and outpatient conditions. The ICD-A system, and now the ICD-9 system, were developed by the World Health Organization in Switzerland. The US National Center for Health Statistics added the "clinical modification" (CM) so that the ICD-9 system could be used for insurance reimbursement in the United States. ICD-9-CM is used by virtually all third-party payers in the United States as the coding system for describing patient conditions. It is updated annually in October. Physicians should use the most current ICD-9-CM coding books to ensure correct code assignment. It is expected that the next revision to ICD (ICD-10) will not be used by payers until after 2002.

The purpose of ICD-9-CM coding is threefold:

- To establish the medical necessity for the visit or service
- To provide statistics for morbidity and mortality rates
- To take the written description of a disease or state and translate that information into numbers, producing a common language

The complete ICD-9-CM coding system consists of three volumes:

> Volume 1. Diseases—Tabular List
>
> Volume 2. Diseases—Alphabetic Index
>
> Volume 3. Procedures—Tabular and Alphabetic Index

Physicians need only concern themselves with volume 1, the tabular list, and volume 2, the index. Volume 3, which contains codes and descriptions for procedures and an index to these codes, is used almost exclusively by hospitals. Volume 1, the tabular list, contains three-, four-, and five-digit codes and their associated descriptions. Volume 2 is the index to the codes in the tabular list.

The example below, taken from volume 1, demonstrates a four-digit ICD-9 code:

> 685.0   Pilonidal cyst w/abscess

In late 1991, the US Government Printing Office released the fourth edition of ICD-9-CM, which incorporates all the changes that were made to ICD-9-CM since the third edition was printed in 1980.

Requirements

A law requiring that all physicians use ICD-9-CM codes when reporting patient diagnoses to Medicare became effective on April 1, 1989. Lack of compliance on claims submitted to Medicare after June 1, 1989, can result in serious penalties ranging from nonpayment of assigned claims to fines of $2000 per occurrence on unassigned claims.

Although this law applies only to claims submitted to Medicare, the use of ICD-9-CM codes for reporting diagnoses to all third-party payers is advisable for several reasons. First, if diagnosis codes are not used, then payment may be denied or delayed. Second, when the codes are not used, the carrier's staff will locate an ICD-9-CM code based on the physician's description of the patient's problem. This coding is usually performed by individuals with either no or very limited medical background. As a result, the codes selected by the carrier may not logically match the procedure or service being reported, and the claim could be denied.

Finally, many third-party payers have purchased or developed software programs that compare the CPT code to the ICD-9-CM code. These programs test for logical relationships. They would, for example, reveal a mismatch between a procedure listed as the removal of a cyst and the diagnosis as hypertension. Such a claim would probably be automatically denied for lack of medical necessity or reasonableness.

In summary, the three reasons ICD-9-CM diagnosis codes must be reported on claims are as follows:

- Without diagnosis codes, the claim may be delayed or denied.
- The carrier's personnel may assign an incorrect code based on the limited information available to them.
- Computer programs automatically reject mismatched or illogical pairing of diagnosis and procedure codes.

For these reasons, it is becoming increasingly important that physicians become familiar with the ICD-9-CM coding system and its rules. ICD-9-CM code ranges from 001.0 through V82.9 are used to report the reason for treatment. The following sections discuss the organization of the ICD-9-CM coding manual; the use of abbreviations, symbols, and notes; and general coding rules important to physician practices. The discussion is not intended to be exhaustive.

Organization

Volume 1 of ICD-9-CM, the tabular list, contains codes and descriptions for diseases, illnesses, injuries, complaints, symptoms, signs, findings, and so on. It is organized into 17 chapters plus two supplementary sections. The supplementary sections are used for coding patients who are not being seen for a current illness ("V" codes) or when the patient's problem is due to an external cause related to injury or poisoning ("E" codes). Volume 2 of ICD-9-CM is an alphabetic listing of codes used as an index to the first volume.

Codes can be either third digit (category), fourth digit (subcategory), or fifth digit (subclassification). The additional fourth and fifth digits typically provide additional information to the category pertinent to the body area, site, or whether the patient did or did not present complications. An example of each level of code is shown below.

345	Epilepsy
345.0	Generalized nonconvulsive epilepsy
345.01	Generalized nonconvulsive epilepsy w/intractable epilepsy

In this example, 345 is the category. It is further defined by subcategory, in this case that the epilepsy is generalized nonconvulsive. The subcategory is further defined by a fifth-digit subclassification, in this case that the patient has intractable epilepsy with the generalized nonconvulsive epilepsy.

Note: Fifth-digit assignment is not optional—if available, you must always code to the greatest level of specificity.

Symbols, Abbreviations, and Notations

Two symbols are used throughout the first volume of ICD-9-CM. The first symbol, the *lozenge*, □, is used to show that the four-digit code is unique to ICD-9-CM. The second symbol, the section mark, §, is important because it alerts the coder to the presence of fifth digits that need to be added to the code for more specificity. In many instances, definitions for the fifth digits are found on pages preceding the code. The section mark also indicates that there is a footnote at the bottom of the page that applies to all subdivisions in that code.

There are two abbreviations in ICD-9-CM: NEC and NOS. Each has a specific meaning and importance to coding and reimbursement. NEC, which means "not elsewhere classified," is used when the coder lacks the information necessary to code the term to a more specific category. The ICD-9-CM index provides references to specific codes when such cases arise and uses the NEC abbreviation to help guide the coder. In other cases, there may not be a code that completely describes the patient's condition. NECs will also be used in these situations.

The NOS abbreviation, which means "not otherwise specified," appears throughout the tabular list and is frequently associated with the "unspecified" codes. In fact, "not otherwise specified" means the same as "unspecified." For example, suppose a patient is seen by his/her physician for ringworm, but the type is unknown. In this case, you would code as follows:

110.9   Dermatophytosis site NOS

When codes for unspecified conditions are reported to third-party payers, special attention may need to be given to the claim if reimbursement is expected. Many carriers will often suspend for review claims that list an unspecified diagnosis code. Therefore, a brief note with the claim explaining the patient's problem in more detail is prudent.

ICD-9-CM also uses notations to further assist the coder in selecting the appropriate code. Nonessential modifiers are one type of notation. In the index, main terms are shown in boldface type. The main term may be followed by a term or group of terms enclosed in parentheses. These terms are called *nonessential modifiers* because they may or may not appear in the diagnostic statement in order for the code to be used.

For example, under the main term "Encephalitis" in the index, seven nonessential modifiers are listed next to the main term, as shown below:

Encephalitis   (bacterial) (chronic) (hemorrhage) (idiopathic) (nonepidemic) (spurious) (subacute)

If the diagnostic statement contained one of these terms (eg, the patient has bacterial encephalitis), code 323.9 could be used. Conversely, if the diagnostic statement did not contain one of these terms, it could still be appropriate to use the code, depending on the circumstances. The nonessential modifiers give some examples of specific types of disorders that can be classified under this main term.

Essential modifiers, on the other hand, are indented line entries following the main term. They can represent differences in etiology, site, or other circumstances. For example, the main term "Burn" is followed by the subterm "arm(s)."

Another frequently used notation is the term *see also*. Found in the index and always printed in italics, this notation instructs the coder to refer to another category in addition to the one that the coder is referencing. For example, if you want to code toxic uninodular goiter, you might first look under "Toxic" in the Index. Under "Toxic" you will be instructed to "*see also* condition." So you would look under the entry for the condition (in this case, goiter) to begin locating the proper code.

Notes

ICD-9-CM uses notes to convey information. There are two types of notes—those appearing with groups of codes and those appearing with specific codes. Each type has a specific meaning in ICD-9-CM.

The first type of notes are "Includes" notes. These notes further define or give an example of the contents of a group of codes. Consider the following code from ICD-9-CM:

> 682   Other Cellulitis and Abscess
>
> > Includes: Abscess (acute), cellulitis (diffuse), lymphangitis, acute (with lymphangitis) except of finger or toe

These types of abscess or cellulitis could be coded by using listings from the 682 series.

The second type of notes, "Excludes" notes, means just the opposite of Includes notes. In ICD-9-CM, the term Excludes is always surrounded by a printed box so that it is easily noticed. Coders need to be aware of conditions that are excluded from groups of codes; therefore, they should take notice of the Excludes notes. Here is an example of an Excludes note:

> 737.0   Adolescent postural kyphosis
>
> > Excludes: Osteochondrosis of spine
> > (juvenile) (730.0);
> > Adult (732.8)

Thus, if a patient is suffering from adult postural kyphosis, codes from the 737 group would not be reported.

In addition to the Includes and Excludes notes, you may also find notes at the beginning of a section of codes and/or at the beginning of a chapter. These notes provide general coding guidance regarding the codes they precede. For example, five paragraphs of notes appear before the 369 group of codes for blindness and low vision. Referring to Chapter 2, Neoplasms, you will find extensive notes related to coding neoplasms. It is important to check for and read notes preceding codes as the notes may affect your code selection.

Tables

There are three tables the coder should be aware of in the index—the Hypertension Table, the Table of Neoplasms, and the Table of Drugs and Chemicals.

1. The Hypertension Table is found in the index by looking up the term *hypertension*. It is further broken down by concurrent disease or state, such as pregnancy. Note that there are three columns next to each entry that designate the hypertension state as:

   - Malignant

   - Benign

   - Unspecified

2. The Neoplasm Table is found in volume 2 and has a special listing for neoplasms. It is broken down into four main categories:

   - Malignant—a severe form of neoplasm possessing the property for destructive growth and metastasis

   - Benign—a nonmalignant neoplasm

   - Uncertain behavior—pathology has been unable to determine type of neoplasm on the basis of features that are present

   - Unspecified—physician has insufficient data to be able to categorize the neoplasm

   The malignant designation may be further classified by whether the neoplasm is primary, secondary, or cancer in situ.

3. The *Table of Drugs and Chemicals* is found in volume 2, section 2. This table contains a classification of drugs and other chemical substances to identify poisoning states and external causes of adverse effects.

Cross-reference Terms

Cross-reference terms are found in the alphabetic index and instruct the coder to search elsewhere in the ICD-9-CM manual before assigning a code. The three types of terms are *see*, *see also*, and *see category*. The *see* cross-reference directs the coder to an alternative term. The *see also* term directs the coder to look under another main term in the index, if all the information needed is not found under the first main term. The third type of cross-reference, *see category*, instructs the coder to a specific category in the tabular list. An important concept to remember is that, for these cross-referenced terms, one is directed to make a decision whether the referenced term applies or not. It does not necessarily mean to code that referenced term.

General ICD-9-CM Coding Guidelines

The process of coding with ICD-9-CM is much easier when the coder follows these steps:

1. Review the entire medical record. Do not code from just the face sheet with a list of diagnoses and procedures. Query the physician if the information in the medical record is not consistent.

2. Review all subterms and look first in the alphabetic index for the main term, and then refer to any applicable notes for the term, nonessential modifiers. Follow any cross-reference instructions.

3. Always verify the code numbers in the tabular list. Read and follow instructional terms and notes.

4. Code only three-digit codes for diseases if there are no fourth- or fifth-digit codes available.

5. Code only four-digit codes if there are no fifth-digit codes available.

6. Look for and be guided by the Includes and Excludes notes throughout the code book. These may appear after a particular code or under category section titles.

7. When assigning multiple diagnoses, always sequence the principal diagnosis first.

ICD-9-CM Codes Validate Medical Necessity for Procedures

Current requirements for medical necessity documentation include the substitution of the final diagnostic code when a symptom leads to the performance of a procedure. For example, if a patient undergoes a chest x-ray for "cough, sputum production, rales left lower lobe" and the study reveals "pneumonia," then pneumonia should be reported as the diagnosis on the billing form (if it is available at the time of billing).

On the other hand, should the study demonstrate no pathology or a diagnosis that is not considered to validate medical necessity, then the billing form should have a description of the indications or the clinical picture that led to the need for the study attended to it. For example, Colonoscopy 45378 (flexible, proximal to splenic flexure; diagnostic, with or without collection of specimen[s] by brushing or washing, with or without colon decompression) may be denied for payment if the only positive findings are internal hemorrhoids. If the patient underwent the procedure because of a strong family history of colon cancer, code G0105 might be more appropriate. Otherwise, an explanation describing the reason the diagnostic procedure was performed, such as "hematochezia not thought to be from rectal or perianal source," should be submitted along with the claim.

Fourth- and Fifth-Digit Codes

In many cases, there will be fourth- and fifth-digit ICD-9 codes from which to select. If there is a five-digit code, it must be used. If there is no five-digit code, but there is a four-digit code, use a four-digit code. Use a three-digit code only if there are no four- or five-digit codes.

Fourth-digit codes are expanded completely below the category to which they apply. For example, in the 556 series of codes for ulcerative colitis, four-digit codes are provided, such as:

556.5	Left-sided ulcerative (chronic) colitis
556.6	Universal ulcerative (chronic) colitis
556.8	Other ulcerative colitis
556.9	Ulcerative colitis, unspecified

In some cases, there are as many as 10 (0 through 9) fourth-digit codes provided; in others, there may be only one or two. Also, fourth-digit codes do not always follow strict numerical order.

Fifth-digit codes are presented in two different ways in ICD-9-CM. First, each fifth-digit code may be listed as found under the series 054.1 "Genital herpes." All possible fifth-digit codes are listed. (In this instance, there are five fifth-digit codes to choose from.) The second method involves printing the fifth digits themselves, with their definitions, immediately above the fourth-digit codes to which they apply, like this:

The following fifth-digit subclassification is for use with category 531:

0	without mention of obstruction
1	with obstruction

These are applied to the fourth-digit codes in the subcategory as appropriate. For example, if the patient has an acute gastric ulcer with perforation and obstruction, the correct code would be 531.11.

Many carriers' computer systems can identify claims containing ICD-9-CM codes that require fourth or fifth digits. Claims not listing fifth- or fourth-digit diagnosis codes when required may be denied.

Symptoms, Signs, and Ill-Defined Conditions

Some patients may present symptoms or signs that defy immediate diagnosis. Nonetheless, if a claim is filed, a diagnosis must be listed. Special codes can be used in such cases. Chapter 16 in ICD-9-CM provides codes for these types of conditions. For example, a physician is treating a patient who has burning and prickling sensations in his feet. Until a more definitive diagnosis is established, code 782.0, "Disturbance of skin sensation," can be listed.

It is important to understand that, in the absence of a definitive diagnosis, it is appropriate and preferable to list the symptom or other presenting problem. There can be legal consequences for those who list a code just to obtain payment, or for those who list a diagnosis when the diagnosis is not attested to or documented by the physician. Instead, list the code for the symptom. For example, the patient presents with pain during urination, blood in the urine, slight fever, and back pain. The physician suspects bladder tumors, but is unsure. Until he or she is sure of the diagnosis, the symptoms can be listed as the diagnosis, all of which will support the need for services, such as an office visit.

Observation Services

History   Observation status was established in 1986 by HCFA in order to allow an alternative method for physicians to oversee the care of patients in a hospital instead of the standard inpatient or outpatient modalities. The intent was to allow a patient to remain in a hospital environment and be observed for any insidious complications that a patient may have but are not be evident on initial examination by the emergency department and admitting physicians. This time period would allow certain clinical data and diagnostic exams to be performed to allow the physician to make or establish a more definitive diagnosis during this period of time.

Initially a time element was not established for how long a patient could be in observation, nor were specific diagnoses presented to give the physician a better picture of which patients would be appropriate for this service. On July 1, 1996, HFCA established a 48-hour maximum for Medicare, and they have provided a better picture of what type of patients should be admitted into the observation service.

Definition   According to HCFA guidelines, "Observation services are defined as services that are furnished on hospital premises and include the use of a bed and monitoring by nursing and ancillary staff. These services are to be reasonable and necessary to evaluate an outpatient's condition or to determine the need for a possible inpatient admission.

A physician's order must be given in order for such services to be covered. Another individual authorized by state law and hospital bylaws to admit patients to the hospital or to order other outpatient tests can order observation services.

Observation services are to be considered acute care services and handled accordingly.

These services typically do not exceed one day (24 hours), however; patients may require a second day (48 hours) for these services to take place. Observation services should not be substituted for a patient who meets criteria for a medically appropriate inpatient admission. Once the patient is admitted as an inpatient hospital admission, the patient should not be discharged to outpatient observation status."

General Guidelines for Outpatient Observation Services   Time begins for observation status when the patient is placed in an observation bed. No payment will be made after 48 hours unless medical documentation clearly dictates the need for continued observation status in which the patient did not qualify for inpatient care. Patients can be in a hospital for a 1-day inpatient stay, and this should not be substituted for outpatient observation services. The patient can be held liable for services beyond 48 hours; if this occurs; the patient needs to receive written notice of possible noncoverage of services that were provided.

One Day or Less Outpatient Observation Services   The patient is initially regarded as an outpatient if you have not formally admitted the patient as an inpatient. Many observation patients, in particular those in a surgical setting, recover sufficiently to be released or discharged on the same day that observation services began. These patients would be classified as outpatients. Patients whose condition worsens or who are determined after evaluation to require inpatient care are then formally admitted as inpatients on that particular day. This day will be considered their first inpatient day.

Second-Day Observation Services   Some patients will continue to required observation services overnight; they may be discharged or formally admitted on the following day. If not admitted or released on the following day, they are classified as outpatients. If formally admitted on the following day, this will be considered the patient's first inpatient day.

Services Denied on the Third Day of Observation Services   If the patient remains in observation status for a second night without a formal inpatient admission having occurred, further observation services are denied by Medicare (certain exceptional circumstances in a particular case may justify approval of an additional status).

Types of Services Not Covered

- Services that are not reasonable or necessary for the diagnosis or treatment of the patient but are provided for the convenience of the patient or physician

- Services that are covered under Part A or as part of another Part B benefit, such as services that are covered under ambulatory surgical center payment rates, outpatient diagnostic testing charges, or routine preparation services prior to the testing

- Standing orders for observation after outpatient surgery

- Services ordered as inpatient services but billed out as outpatient services

- Any substitution of an outpatient observation service for a medically appropriate inpatient admission

- Observation services provided for the convenience of the patient or the physician

- Observation services that exceed 48 hours, unless granted an exception by the fiscal intermediary

Billing Instructions   Although the physician will probably not have any direct exposure to the billing procedure, it is always prudent to have an understanding of what is involved in the process.

A HCFA billing form 1450, also known as the UB-92, is used when billing for observation services. Billing staff will use a revenue code of 762 for billing of observation services, which previously was subject to the ambulatory surgery center (ASC) payment limitation; this is no longer the case.

Payment for Hospital Observation Services   The physician's business office handles this information, but it is prudent to have an understanding of this information to give you a better idea of how the billing process works. There are four CPT codes that are to be used to report E&M services:

- 99217, Observation care discharge: this code is to be used for a patient on discharge from "observation status," be it a hospital discharge or change to inpatient status. This code cannot be used if the discharge is the same day as the initial date of "observation status."

- 99218, Initial observation care: this code is to be used to indicate that the problem for which the patient is admitted to "observation status" is of low severity.

- 99219, Initial observation care: this code is to be used to indicate that the problem for which the patient is admitted to "observation status" is of moderate severity.

- 99220, Initial observation care: this code is to be used to indicate that the problem for which the patient is admitted to "observation status" is of high severity.

Physician Billing for Observation Status After Admission to Observation
On the first day of admission to observation, the patient will be billed with an initial observation care code; if discharged this day; the 99217 code cannot be used.

On the second calendar day, with the expectation that the patient is to be discharged from observation status, the 99217 code should be used.

Admission to Inpatient Status From Observation   If the patient is admitted as an observation status case, but during the 24-hour period the patient is admitted as an inpatient, an initial hospital visit for E&M services should be billed. The observation discharge management code cannot be used if this patient is admitted to inpatient from observation status within the first 24 hours.

Hospital Observation During Global Surgical Period   According to HCFA guidelines, "The global surgical fee includes payment for hospital observation services, which includes the codes 99217-99220, unless the criteria for use of CPT modifiers 24, 25, or 57 are met. These services are paid for in addition to the global surgical fee only if both of the following requirements are met":

> Justification is seen in billing a hospital observation service with CPT modifiers 24, 25, or 57. The hospital observation service that is furnished by the surgeon meets all of the criteria.

An example of the decision for surgery during a hospital observation period is as follows:

> A patient is admitted to the hospital observation unit for observation by a neurosurgeon for a head injury. The surgeon decides during this observation period to perform surgery, and a -57 modifier is used to indicate that the decision was made for surgery. The surgeon would bill the appropriate level of hospital observation code along with the -57 modifier.

An example of hospital observation services during the postoperative period of a surgery is as follows:

> A patient at the 30th day after a Billroth II procedure is admitted to observation for abdominal pain by the surgeon who performed the surgery. The surgeon determines that the patient no longer requires surgery or observation and discharges the patient. The surgeon cannot bill for the observation services furnished during the global period because they were related to the previous surgery.

An example of a billable hospital observation service on the same day as the procedure is as follows:

> A patient has a laceration of the scalp repaired in the emergency department and is admitted to the observation unit for observation of a head injury by the physician who repaired the scalp. The physician would bill the observation code with a CPT modifier -25 and the procedure code.

The following examples are used for clarification of the proper use of observation status:

> A patient comes to a hospital's outpatient department to undergo a scheduled surgical procedure. The patient exhibits postoperative complications past the usual recovery period. The patient is then seen by the physician and placed on the observation unit. After a few hours the patient no longer exhibits any other postsurgical complications. The physician is made aware of this and orders the patient discharged. Outpatient observation services begin, in this case, when the patient is placed in the observation bed. The period of time that the patient is in the outpatient surgical suite and recovery room cannot be considered observation services.

> A patient is scheduled to have a rhinoplasty performed on an outpatient basis. The patient express a preference to spend the night in the hospital after the procedure despite the fact the procedure does not require the overnight stay. This stay cannot be billed as an observation status case as it is not medically necessary. The patient must be notified of the noncoverage and the possibility of being billed for these extra services. If the patient does have some unforeseen circumstances arise, then the patient can be admitted.

Observation or Inpatient Care Services   According to AMA's CPT 2000, "The following codes are used to report observation or inpatient hospital care services provided to patients admitted and discharged on the same date of service":

- 99234, Observation or inpatient hospital care: this code is used to indicate that the problem for which the patient was admitted to "observation status" or inpatient was of low severity.

- 99235, Observation or inpatient hospital care: this code is used to indicate that the problem for which the patient was admitted to "observation status" or inpatient was of moderate severity.

- 99236, Observation or inpatient hospital care: this code is used to indicate that the problem for which the patient was admitted to "observation status" or inpatient was of high severity.

V Codes

These codes, which begin with the letter "V," appear toward the end of volume 1 under the title "Supplementary Classification of Factors Influencing Health Status and Contact With Health Services." They are typically used when the patient is being seen for something other than a current illness or injury. A follow-up visit related to a history of major cardiovascular surgery that occurred 4 years ago would be an example.

E Codes

These codes are supplementary and are used to describe external causes of injuries, poisonings, or other adverse effects. They are never reported alone. E codes are located in volume 2 under Index to External Cause.

Coding Under Capitation

Coding is necessary under capitation because it drives cost management and cost centers. For example, all CPT codes or a list of all services included or excluded in the capitation rate must be in the contract. Practices can also use CPT codes to determine provider productivity and compensation under capitation arrangements.

In a managed care setting, codes can be used as a productivity measure for monetary rewards or continuing in the program. In many instances a relative value unit system is used.

5 Insurance Processing— Managing Insurance and Patient Accounts

Objectives

After completing this chapter, you should be able to:

- Explain the pre–claim submission operations process
- Recognize and describe the use of the different types of forms, including:
  - Patient information
  - Insurance coverage verification
  - Employer information
  - Assignment of benefits
  - Authorization to release medical-related information
  - Signature on file
  - Fact sheet
  - Medical cost estimate
  - Advance notice for elective surgery
  - Waivers of liability
- Recognize and describe the use of the different letters, such as:
  - Welcome
  - Filing supplemental claims
  - Deductible
- Understand the skills necessary for various front and back office positions
- Understand the importance of and how to improve the collection process

Introduction

With the knowledge of the different types of insurance and the ability to code services for reimbursement, the practice must now be able to report to the insurance plan the services provided so it receives appropriate reimbursement.

Unfortunately, this is often easier said than done. Because of the different types of health plans and changing reimbursement methods, the health insurance industry does not follow a set of "universal policies" that standardize or simplify the claim submission process. Each insurance plan usually has its own set of policies and procedures for claim adjudication, and medical practices are expected to understand and adhere to them if they are to receive payment for services rendered.

In this chapter we discuss the "preclaim" insurance processes necessary to manage insurance claim processing from collecting data to claim submission for appropriate payment. We also describe and present sample forms that will help simplify your data collection operations and report formats to increase your information management efficiency.

Unique Physician/Practitioner Identification Number

The Consolidated Omnibus Budget Reconciliation Act (COBRA) of 1985 mandated a unique identifier for each physician who provides services for Medicare patients and for which Medicare payment is issued. This identifier is known as the unique physician/practitioner identification number (UPIN). An identifier is to be issued regardless of the practice configuration (ie, group, solo, partnership). This number remains constant as long as the physician has a Medicare affiliation. The UPIN is established in a national Registry of Medicare Physician Identification and Eligibility Records (MPIER) and is described below. However, the National Provider Identification Number is expected to be implemented in the future, and HCFA's instruction for its use are described starting on page 187.

For the purpose of issuing a UPIN number, a physician is defined as a doctor of medicine or osteopathy, dental medicine, dental surgery, podiatric medicine, optometry, or chiropractic medicine legally authorized to practice by the state in which he/she performs.

A health practitioner includes, but is not limited to, physician assistant, certified nurse-midwife, qualified psychologist, nurse practitioner, clinical social worker, physical therapist, occupational therapist, respiratory therapist, certified registered nurse anesthetist, or any other practitioner as may be specified.

A group practice is defined by Medicare as a group of two or more physicians and nonphysician practitioners legally organized in a partnership, professional corporation, foundation, not-for-profit corporation, faculty practice plan, or similar association.

The Medicare manual states that a UPIN is to be assigned to all physicians, health care practitioners, and group practices that bill or perform services for

Medicare payment. The UPIN is a 10-character alphanumeric designation with two parts. The first part is alphanumeric and consists of 6 digits. The second part is numeric and is the location identifier. The five-digit location identifier is not released to the physician/practitioner.

Example:

A3456

The alpha digit identifies the configuration of the practice as follows:

Type of Practice	Identifier
Physician/health care practitioner in solo practice only	A
Physician/health care practitioner in group practice only	D
Physical therapist in group practice only	R
Group practice in multiple locations	W

Example

Dr Smith is a physician operating in both a solo and a group practice. His UPINs are:

Solo practice:	A1111 0001
Group practice:	W1111 0001

A1111 and W1111 are the physicians number, and 0001 is the location number.

If Dr Smith were in a multiple-location group practice, his numbers would be:

W1111 0001

W1111 0002

Transamerica Occidental Life Insurance Company (TOLIC) is the registry carrier that establishes and maintains the registry of physicians/health care practitioners/group practices receiving Part B Medicare payment. The mailing address is:

The Registry
Transamerica Occidental Life Insurance Company
PO Box 512575
Los Angeles, CA 90051-0575

All physicians, health care practitioners, and groups will receive a UPIN. The UPIN identifies each physician/health care practitioner/group for all billing and practice settings.

Every physician/health care practitioner/group practice must apply individually for a UPIN.

A physician or supplier that bills Medicare for a service or item must show the name of the ordering/referring physician on the HCFA-1500 claim form. If the ordering physician is also the performing physician, the name and number must be entered as the ordering physician.

If the ordering/referring physician is not assigned a UPIN, the biller must assign a surrogate UPIN until an application for a UPIN is processed.

The surrogate UPIN "NPP000" formerly used by nurse practitioners, certified nurse anesthetists, and physician assistants is no longer allowed. These individuals must obtain their own UPIN.

If any procedure codes associated with types of service for consultations, diagnostic radiology, diagnostic lab, or durable medical equipment, orthotics, and prosthetics are shown on the claim form, the name and UPIN of the ordering physician must be entered in fields 17 and 17a of the HCFA-1500. For electronic claims, the name and UPIN goes in record/field EAO-20.0, positions 80-94 of the electronic media claims format. The following guidelines apply:

- If the service is a diagnostic laboratory or radiology service, the assigned UPIN of the ordering/referring physician must be shown in item 17a on form HCFA-1500.

- If the performing physician is also the ordering physician, the physician must enter his/her name and UPIN in item 17 and 17a of form HCFA-1500, confirming that the service is not the result of a referral from another physician.

- If the ordering/referring physician is not assigned a UPIN, the biller may use OTH000 until a UPIN is assigned, or a surrogate may be used.

- If the service is a consultative service, the name and UPIN of the referring physician or other person meeting the statutory definition of a physician must be shown on form HCFA-1500 in items 17 and 17a.

- If the service was the result of a referral from a person not meeting the statutory definition of a physician or a limited licensed practitioner (pharmacist, midwife, psychologist), the billing physician must enter his or her name and UPIN in items 17 and 17a. In other words, the physician completes the form as if the patient initiated the service.

- If durable medical equipment, prosthetics, and orthotics are ordered, the name and UPIN of the ordering physician must be on form HCFA-1500 in items 17 and 17a.

Claims that require the physician name and UPIN, but do not have them, will be denied.

In some cases an individual UPIN is not issued, or may not have been issued at the time of service. In those cases the following UPINs may be used.

RES000   if a resident, intern, or fellow has not yet been issued a UPIN.

Physicians with the military, Department of Veterans Affairs, and Public Health Service who provide services to Medicare beneficiaries or refer beneficiaries for other services are to use the following surrogate UPINs until an individual UPIN is assigned.

VAD000   Physicians serving on active duty in the military of the United States and those employed by the Department of Veterans Affairs

PHS000   Physicians serving in the Public Health Service, including the Indian Health Service

RET000   Retired physicians

OTH000   For special situations that do not fall in the above categories

Incorrect use of surrogate UPIN is a violation of Medicare billing requirements. Suppliers will be notified they are in violation of the law, and continuation of this billing practice may result in referral to the Office of Inspector General (OIG).

Employee Job Descriptions

One of the keys to a successful practice is the assignment of responsibilities to various office personnel. To clearly state each employee's responsibilities and to eliminate miscommunications, all employees should have written descriptions of their job's duties. Job descriptions explain what is expected of employees and can be used as a tool to evaluate performance. Job descriptions can also be used to show employees why employment decisions were made in the event personnel discrimination charges are made. The following job descriptions are examples that should be modified to fit the unique requirements of each practice.

Office Manager

- Recruit, orient, train, supervise and evaluate all office personnel.
- Maintain confidential personnel records, including resumes, employment history, salary or wage history, paid days off, and vacation time.
- Respond to calls from patients regarding billing, balance due, and secondary insurance.
- Assist with patient registration, billing, and collections.

- Prepare checks for the payment of accounts payable and present with supporting invoices to authorized check signer.
- Prepare the month-end financial statements and management reports.
- Make sure the billing system's daily receipts agree with deposit slips and the patient registration log.
- Make sure all tax reports are prepared and filed on a timely basis.
- Prepare and file physicians' correspondence.
- Maintain and reconcile the petty cash fund monthly.
- Reconcile the bank accounts each month.
- Maintain all office equipment.
- Maintain appropriate quantities of business supplies.
- Ensure that all office employees are cross-trained.
- Provide financial counseling to patients as needed and regarding delinquent account balances.
- Perform routine internal control checks to identify potential problem areas.
- Manage billing and collection personnel to ensure compliance with office policies.

Billing and Collection Staff

- Know current Medicare rules and regulations applicable to the practice.
- Keep the Office Manager and Physicians informed of significant changes.
- Send out patient statements and insurance claims on a timely basis.
- Prepare and mail secondary insurance claim forms as soon as payments are received from primary insurance carriers.
- Respond to requests for medical records or other appropriate information by insurance carriers.
- Handle business and insurance carrier correspondence.
- Post and reconcile explanations of benefits (EOBs) promptly upon receipt.
- File all EOBs in billing business files.
- Age accounts receivable and follow up with timely phone calls and collection letters.
- Prepare and mail collection letters to patients each month.
- List patients' accounts to send to the practice's outside collection agency for follow-up, subject to office manager approval.
- Promptly prepare appeal letters with supporting documentation to Medicare and insurance carriers for denials.

- Follow up weekly on insurance claims not paid within 30 days.

- Post payments to patients accounts on a timely basis.

- Verify patient's insurance coverage in accordance with office policy.

- Obtain authorization numbers for insurance companies before service is provided.

- Prepare hospital inpatient summaries for use by the physicians when making rounds.

Reception and Patient Registration

- Answer all telephone calls and switch to/from answering service.

- Schedule daily appointments and instruct patients as to information needed.

- Keep reception room organized, neat, and ready for patients.

- Greet patients and visitors, determine needs, and respond accordingly.

- Obtain necessary new patient information.

- Copy the patients' insurance cards and drivers' licenses (if allowed by state law.).

- Remind patients of the office financial policy.

- Ask established patients upon arrival for their appointment about any change in insurance coverage since their last visit.

- Obtain new patients information sheet for all patients not seen within the last 12 months.

- Maintain appointment schedules and mail postcards or call patients to remind them of their appointments.

- Retrieve and file charts for each day's patients.

- Post charges; collect payments, copayments, or deductibles; post receipts.

- Collect accounts receivable from patients upon completion of or before their appointments.

- Refer patients with past-due accounts to the office manager for financial counseling.

- Contact patients who miss appointments with letters or phone calls.

- Retrieve and distribute the office mail each day.

Pre–Claim Submission Operations

Before any type of claim can be generated and submitted for payment, your office staff needs to perform a number of preclaim tasks critical to ensure the validity and accuracy of the patient's billing data and submission of a "clean claim."

The basic objectives of office staff preclaim operations are to:

1. Collect the patient's and responsible parties' information completely and accurately.

2. Determine the appropriate financial class or account type (eg, commercial insurance, Medicare, Medicaid, etc), and correctly assign primary and secondary insurance billing status when two insurance plans require coordination of benefits.

3. Educate the patient as to their ultimate financial responsibility for services rendered and obtain written waivers when necessary to support future collection efforts.

4. Verify all data collected prior to rendering services or submitting claims and obtain updated profiles of insurance plan benefits using an insurance/employer verification form.

5. Anticipate the need for collection through accounts receivable controls and quality data.

The basic pre–claim submission operations include:

- Appointments/preregistration
- Registration/patient demographic and insurance verification
- Patient education of payment policies and credit screening/financial arrangements
- Attainment of necessary preauthorizations
- Entry of patient data
- Capture of all billable services and transaction entry
- Claims processing and submission

The following sections in this chapter discuss each of these operations in detail.

Appointments/Preregistration

In most cases, new patients wishing to see a physician will call the physician group to make an appointment. This initial contact by the prospective patient is a perfect time to identify the reason for the visit, begin collecting patient demographic and insurance billing data, and schedule a convenient time for the physician and patient. It is also important to verify patient referral information and make arrangements to get necessary forms and authorizations completed, as applicable.

The need to identify the reason for the visit is important, as most practices have divided their appointment schedule to accommodate lengthy new patient history and physicals during a certain period, procedures during another time slot, and basic follow-up visits throughout the day. If the practice is at capacity, it may take 3 or more days to obtain an appointment; time that can be spent verifying the patient information.

The patient's demographic and insurance information should be obtained during the initial telephone contact through a polite telephone interview and recorded by means of a patient information form.

A good practice is to call the patient 1 or 2 days before the scheduled appointment, as a reminder. In some instances this will assist the patient who has forgotten or allow the practice to fill slots that may have gone unused. This is also a good time to gather information or remind them of the necessary information they will need to bring for their visit.

Patient Information Form

The patient information form is a vital document used to gather necessary demographic data about a patient, such as name, address, guardian or responsible party name, insurance company and health plan policy information, the name of the person or physician who referred the patient to the practice, and so on.

This form does not include any information related to medical conditions; it is usually only for insurance and payment-related information and/or for general marketing data. This form should be completed when a *patient first visits the practice, and at least once every year,* because approximately 20% of people move each year. In this way, the practice may keep its records current.

Typically, practices design the information form to fit on 8½″ × 11″ (standard size) paper with plenty of space allowed for patients to complete required information accurately. (See Exhibit 5.1.)

Not only is the patient information form valuable for gathering important insurance processing information, but it is also a way of tracking and finding patients who become delinquent in their payments. Additional information, such as secondary insurance coverage, and special circumstances, such as divorce, can also be gathered.

Give the patient information about the practice and collect as much patient information as possible on insurance coverage, including any toll-free numbers for eligibility verification and filing requirements. During the initial contact

Exhibit 5.1   New Patient's Information Sheet

PATIENT INFORMATION

Name: (First) _____ (MI) _____ (Last) _____

Date of Birth _____ Age _____ Sex: □ M □ F   Marital Status: □ S □ M □ W □ D

Address: (Street) _____

(City, State, ZIP) _____

Phone #: _____ Social Security #: _____ Driver License #: _____

Work #: _____ Employer: _____

Employer's Address: _____

Referring Physician: _____ If Student, School Name: _____ Full/Part Time _____

RESPONSIBLE PARTY OR SPOUSE INFORMATION

Name: _____ Relationship to Patient: _____

Address: (Street) _____

(City, State, ZIP) _____

Phone #: _____ Social Security #: _____ Driver License #: _____

Work #: _____ Employer: _____

Employer's Address: _____

Friend or Relative Not Living with You: _____ Phone #: _____

INSURANCE INFORMATION

Medicare #: _____ Medicaid #: _____

Insurance Co: _____ Phone #: _____

Insurance Address: _____

Group #: _____ Certificate or I.D. #: _____

Insured's Name: _____ Relationship to Patient: □ Self □ Spouse □ Dependent

Insured's Employer: _____ Phone #: _____

Employer's Address: _____

Insured's Social Security #: _____ Date of Birth: _____ Sex: □ M □ F

If the patient it covered by another insurance policy, please complete the following information for coordination of benefits. This information will enable your insurance company to process your claim more quickly. Thank you!

INSURANCE INFORMATION

Insurance Co: _____ Phone #: _____

Insurance Address: _____

Group #: _____ Certificate or I.D. #: _____

Insured's Name: _____ Relationship to Patient: □ Self □ Spouse □ Dependent

Insured's Employer: _____ Phone #: _____

Employer's Address: _____

Insured's Social Security #: _____ Date of Birth: _____ Sex: □ M □ F

I hereby assign, transfer, and set over to {Name of Practice} all of my rights, title, and interest to my medical reimbursement benefits under my insurance policy. I authorize the release of any medical information needed to determine these benefits. This authorization shall remain valid until written notice is given by me revoking said authorization. I understand that I am financially responsible for all charges whether or not they are covered by insurance.

Patient's Signature _____ Date _____

with the prospective patient, the office staff may want to communicate the following policies to the patient:

- Basic services for the condition and doctors' fees
- The patient's financial responsibility for services provided during the initial visit
- An estimate of the costs associated with a new-comprehensive history and physical examination
- Method of payment (health maintenance organization [HMO]/preferred provider organization [PPO]; copayment, cash, check, or credit card)
- Future visit payment policy
- Financial counseling available before the visit

A patient education brochure is an excellent way to communicate the policies and procedures of the practice.

After identifying the reason for the visit from the potential patient, a tentative patient care plan is developed so that all procedures and services planned for in the care plan (obstetrics, laboratory, surgery, injections, etc) can be verified for service coverage. All information obtained will be reviewed by the account manager/office manager to determine the prospective account's financial class, potential collectibility, creditworthiness, and the need for patient-related financial counseling.

Registration/Demographic and Insurance Coverage Verification

The importance of patient registration in capturing accurate information, including referring physician data and verifying all information provided by the patient, is an area often overlooked by staff responsible for billing because of time or perceived value. Demographic, financial, and referring physician information should be obtained. If a patient schedules an appointment at least 4 days in advance, mail a copy of your office brochure/financial policy, and new patient information sheet to the patient for completion at home.

Today, change is constant, so the need to obtain information for verification becomes more necessary. Insurance coverage or eligibility for public medical programs changes from one month to the next for thousands of Americans. Be alert for the use of forged health insurance ID cards for health care, and report any suspected occurrences to the payer immediately.

Practices must keep in mind that they are, in a broad sense, providers of "good-faith credit" for medical service rendered to patients. Too often, patients are extended "credit" without adequate review of their creditworthiness or a discussion of their ultimate financial responsibility.

The patient's registration information serves not only as the foundation for billing and collection, but also as a tool for credit-granting decisions made by the practice. The collectibility of each patient account, whether by insurance or self-pay, is only as strong as the information obtained from the patient, its verification for accuracy, and the patient's understanding of his or her financial obligations.

In most practices, the registration information provided by the patient on the demographic form is rarely verified for accuracy and completeness. The verification of all patient demographic and insurance information is a process that must be instituted to:

- Confirm patient insurance coverage for the service to be rendered and to determine primary and secondary coordination of benefit coverage, which allows for accurate billing of covered services.

- Serve as a quality assurance tool for correctly processing billing information (ultimately responsible for the success of collections).

- Serve as an indicator in identifying patients who need financial counseling or assistance with obtaining medical assistance for services rendered.

- Reduce unnecessary write-offs and negative adjustments for uncollectible charges due to denials, down-coding, or reduced payment because of nonverified coverage of services.

To reach the objectives listed above, all practices must implement a process of information/verification. We suggest that all patients undergo a thorough verification of all demographic, financial, and insurance coverage information they submit.

The verification coordinator must identify the primary carrier for proper coordination of benefits. Contact the primary insurance plan first to confirm coverage of the patient's services by means of the insurance coverage verification forms.

When verifying insurance coverage, remember that each category of physician (medicine, surgery, primary care) will ask about coverage and payment policies for services he or she performs relative to the patient's condition.

The office should verify all insurance information in each of the following situations:

- If the patient is to be admitted to the hospital or subject to an outpatient surgical procedure

- If the patient will have many visits to the office over an extended period of time

- If the patient will undergo a minor diagnostic or therapeutic procedure in the office

- If the office believes the patient may have deductible responsibilities
- If the office believes the patient's insurance may have changed or terminated
- For established patients, at least once a year, preferably between October and January

Employer Information/Insurance Verification Form

To be used in addition to the patient information form, this form provides specific information about the type and extent of insurance coverage the patient receives from his/her employer. This form is more discretionary. Some practices may find the additional information helpful, while others may find that the information gathered on the patient information form is adequate. Two different formats are shown in Exhibits 5.2 and 5.3.

How to Verify Insurance Coverage

The business support staff of a medical practice should be responsible for the verification of all patient demographics and insurance plan coverage for all services likely to be provided in the patient's care plan, before the initiation of such services. The process is explained below:

1. Before a patient is accepted as a new patient, and before the initiation of services, the patient registration staff will obtain:

   - Demographic and insurance information from the prospective patient using the patient demographic form. The patient demographic form should be filled out by (1) interviewing the patient over the phone, (2) having the patient fill out the form through the mail, or (3) having the patient complete it in the office, upon his or her arrival.

   - Copies of hospital admission and patient information (if applicable)

   - Copies of all insurance cards (front and back)

   - Copy of guarantor's driver's license (front only), if allowed by your state.

   - Insurance plan coverage and the order of benefit coordination (ie, primary, secondary, or tertiary) for multiple policies

2. From the above information, the patient registration or billing staff will verify all patient demographic and insurance policy coverage information electronically or manually through telephone contacts and cross-referencing information from different sources.

   - Patient and guarantor addresses are to be cross-referenced with telephone directories, postal addresses, driver's licenses, employment confirmation, and other sources of current information.

Exhibit 5.2   Employer/Insurance Verification Information Form

Date: _____

Employer Name: _____

Employer Address: _____

Benefits Coordinator: _____ Phone: _____

Insurance Carrier: _____ Plan Name: _____

Policy #: _____ Plan #: _____ Group #: _____

Type of Plan: ☐ Traditional ☐ 80/20 ☐ HMO ☐ PPO ☐ Other: _____

Mail Insurance Forms to: ☐ Carrier ☐ Employer

Billing Address: _____

Contact Person: _____ Phone Number: _____

Renewal Period – Medical Benefits and Limits Are Renewed on (M/D/Y): (Date): _____

Basic Coverage

Physician Payment Schedule: ☐ UCR ☐ RBRVS ☐ Other Data

Percentage of COB (ie, 80/20?): _____ % Insurance Coverage _____ % Patient Copayment

Annual Outpatient Deductible: _____ Amount of Deductible Remaining: _____

Maximum Benefit: _____

Noncovered Services: _____

Diagnostic Benefits

Percentage of COB (ie, 80/20?): _____ % Insurance Coverage _____ % Patient Copayment

Annual Outpatient Deductible: _____ Amount of Deductible Remaining: _____

Maximum Benefit: _____

Noncovered Services: _____

Major Medical Coverage

Annual Outpatient Deductible: _____

Amount of Deductible Remaining: _____

Maximum Benefit: _____

Noncovered Services: _____

Form Used: ☐ Company-Specific Form ☐ HCFA-1500

Notes: _____

_____

_____

Exhibit 5.3 **Patient/Insurance Coverage Verification Form**

Date: _____ Practice: _____ Verification By: _____

Patient Name: _____ Account #: _____

Date of Birth: _____ Social Security #: _____

Employer: _____ Phone/Contact: _____

Accident Date: _____ Accident Location: _____

Patient Care Plan

Dx: (1) _____ (2) _____

Dx: (3) _____ (4) _____

Patient Care Plans/Services: _____

Insurance Data

Insurance – 1

Billing Address: _____

Ins. Contact Name: _____ Phone: _____

Policy #: _____ Plan: _____ Group: _____

Coverage Effective Dates – (From) _____ (To) _____

Policyholder: _____ Relationship: _____

Insurance – 2

Billing Address: _____

Ins. Contact Name: _____ Phone: _____

Policy #: _____ Plan: _____ Group: _____

Coverage Effective Dates – (From) _____ (To) _____

Policyholder: _____ Relationship: _____

Basic Benefits	**Primary**	**Secondary**
1. Preexisting Wait Period		
2. Annual Deductible Amount	($)	
3. Deductible Paid to Date		
4. Out-of-Pocket Expenses:		
a. Coinsurance ($ or %)		
b. Copayment @ TOS?		
5. Calendar Year Maximum:	$ / days	$ / days
6. Lifetime Maximum:	$ / days	$ / days
7. Remaining Benefits:	$ / days	$ / days
8. Medical Records Required?	Y / N	Y / N
9. Coordinate Benefits (X-Over)?	Y / N	Y / N
10. 2nd Opinion Requirements?	Y / N	Y / N
11. Verified with (name):		
12. Phone # of Above:		
13. Date Verified:		

Procedures & Services	**Covered?**	**Coverage Details / Limits**
1. Office Services	Y / N	
2. Hospital	Y / N	
3. Consultations	Y / N	
4. ER Visits	Y / N	
5. Laboratory (Chem)	Y / N	
6. Procedures	Y / N	
7. Injections / Tx	Y / N	
8. Supplies	Y / N	
9. Drugs / Medications	Y / N	
10. Exclusions:		

- Each insurance plan identified by the patient is to be contacted to verify insurance coverage for patient services by means of one of the insurance coverage verification forms (ICVFs).

- Insurance plan coverage is to be verified one plan at a time, making sure to complete the insurance data section, benefits grid section, and the service coverage listing for all services pertinent to your practice that need to be verified for coverage.

3. Only confirmed and verified information is to be entered on the ICVF. Changes to the patient source document are to be made in red pen, initialed, and dated.

4. Insurance plan coverage(s) that cannot be verified must have the reason indicated on the ICVF report.

5. After all policy coverage(s) have been verified, the completed ICVF should be copied. The original is placed in the patient's chart. The copy should be stored in a three-ring binder labeled "Insurance/Employer Health Plan Profiles." Store the information alphabetically by insurance or employer name, and update the profiles for future reference.

Overview of the Patient ICVF

Basic Patient Demographic Data Section   The top section of the form is used to track the start and completion of the entire ICVF report for each new patient.

Date—Enter the date the verification process was initiated and completed.

Practice—Enter the practice name (helpful for multispecialty practices).

Verification by—Enter the name of the verification clerk.

Patient Name/Account Number—Enter patient's name and add practice account number later.

Date of Birth—Enter the patient's date of birth.

Social Security Number—Enter the patient's Social Security number.

Employer—Enter the name of the patient's employer.

Phone/Contact—Enter the contact name and phone number for benefits management.

Accident Date—If services are related to an accident (auto, workers' compensation, etc), enter the date of the accident.

Accident Location—Define where the injury occurred/location.

Patient Care Plan Section   This section maintains the clinical data needed to begin inquiry as to coverage and benefits. The patient's reason for the appointment or previously confirmed diagnoses from another physician for which the patient will be seen (as in the case of a consultation) should be entered here, as well as possible services—both diagnostic and therapeutic—that may/will be performed.

Dx: (1)—Enter the patient's primary diagnosis or complaint.

Dx: (2)—Enter the patient's secondary diagnosis or complaint.

Dx: (3)—Enter the patient's third diagnosis or complaint.

Dx: (4)—Enter the patient's fourth diagnosis or complaint.

Patient Care Plans/Services—List the possible services that may be reasonably expected to be performed on this patient.

Insurance Data Section   This section is used to record and then verify insurance plan information provided by the patient for future billing and coordination of the patient's benefits. All insurance plans submitted by the patient are to be verified individually. Note: It is extremely important to assign the proper order of multiple insurance plan coverages (ie, primary plan vs secondary plan).

Insurance–(1)—Enter the name of the carrier that has identified itself as the primary insurance plan.

Phone—Enter the carrier's phone number(s).

Billing Address—Enter the carrier's billing address.

Ins Contact Name—Enter the name of the insurance representative.

Phone—Enter the insurance contact's direct line and extension.

Policy Number—Enter the patient's verified policy number.

Plan—Enter the patient's verified plan number.

Group—Enter the patient's verified group number.

Coverage Effective Dates—Enter insurance plan effective dates of coverage, identifying (From) date and (To) date.

Policyholder—Enter verified policyholder's name.

Relationship—Verify relationship of patient to policyholder.

Note: After each insurance plan is verified one at a time, carefully complete the next section, the Benefits Section.

Basic Benefits Section   This section is developed like a grid to capture all insurance plan(s) information and for easy review of all plan benefits. The grid is divided into three columns, one for the insurance benefit question and one for each insurance plan—primary and secondary.

1. Preexisting Wait Period:

    Some policies do not provide benefits for certain conditions for a predetermined period of time. Example: A 12-month waiting period for maternity (ie, no benefits until plan is over 12 months into effect). Enter Y or N. *Note:* Some health plan policies do not provide benefits for certain conditions, diagnoses, or preexisting conditions regardless of the period of time. If this is the case, indicate "noncovered" on the space provided.

2. Annual Deductible Amount:

    What is the insurance plan's annual deductible amount (amount patient must pay out of pocket before insurance will start to cover services)? Enter the annual deductible dollar amount.

3. Deductible Paid to Date:

    How much has the patient paid toward the deductible to date (as of today)? Enter the deductible amount paid to date. Note: The difference is collectible at time of service.

4. Out-of-Pocket Expenses:

    Does the plan have a patient cost-sharing program that may include copayment or coinsurance provisions?

    a) Coinsurance = Dollar amount or percentage of patient financial responsibility, or

    b) Copayment @ TOS = The collection of a copayment at time of service, usually $5 to $20 per visit (see insurance card).

5. Calendar Year Maximum:

    The dollar amount and/or the number of days limited by the insurance policy as a total annual payable benefit, if applicable. Enter dollar amount and/or days limited.

6. Lifetime Maximum:

    The maximum dollar amount and/or the number of days allowed by the insurance policy as a total payable benefit, if applicable. Enter the maximum dollar amount and/or days allowed.

7. Remaining Benefits:

The dollar amount and/or the number of days available under the insurance policy for remaining payable benefits, if applicable. Enter dollar amount and/or days available.

8. Medical Records Required:

Are medical records or other supporting documents required for claim processing and receiving payment for services rendered? Enter Y or N. If yes, make note on expanded insurance information sheet (page 2, 3, or 4).

9. Coordinate Benefits (X-Over):

Will the primary policy coordinate or cross over the benefits with any secondary insurance? Enter Y or N.

10. Second Opinion Requirements:

Does the plan have second opinion requirements for specific conditions before payment of service benefits? Enter Y or N.

11. Verified with (name):

Enter the name of the person from the insurance plan to whom the verification clerk has been speaking to identify policy coverage.

12. Phone Number of Above:

Enter the phone number of the person from the insurance plan to whom the verification clerk has been speaking to identify policy coverage.

13. Date Verified:

Enter date the above information was verified.

Procedures and Services Section   This section is designed to capture individual insurance policy coverage information for all services that may be provided by your physicians and practice. Obviously, the services to be verified for coverage will vary by specialty, so think about the services your practice would need to verify most frequently.

Each insurance plan representative contacted should be asked to provide coverage information on anticipated service that potential patients will likely receive. When interviewing each insurance representative:

- Ask the questions listed below for each service.
- Indicate on the report if the policy provides coverage (Y or N).

- Indicate if the policy has limitations or maximum coverage amounts.
- Ask what code it requires for payment of the service—compare this to the CPT code to identify variations in coding requirements.
- Ask about any service limitations, coverage, or service exclusions.
- Ask what is the maximum reimbursement amount for each procedure.

Special coding or payment policies that may affect reimbursement should be inquired about as well, particularly for surgical-related practices. Some additional questions to ask include:

- Do they use the current CPT book?
- When must the new CPT codes be used (ie, effective date)?
- How is payment allowance based? (Ask payer to send copy of allowance data.)
- How does their plan define "global surgical package" and "global surgical periods"?
- Are complications from surgery bundled in postoperative care or can treatment be reported separately with appropriate modifiers?
- Are there any reductions in payment if performed in an outpatient hospital setting?
- How are multiple surgical procedures reimbursed? 1st__, 2nd__, 3rd__, 4th__, 5th+___
- What are their supply payment policies? Are HCPCS codes required or is 99070 acceptable?
- How are injectable drugs reimbursed and how should they be reported (J codes)?

Remember to document as much pertinent information about the policy coverage as possible, as the verification document serves as the ultimate quality assurance tool for billing and collections.

Only after a thorough verification of the patient's insurance plan coverage, the assignment of an unquestioned financial classification or account type, and having obtained signed agreements with the patient concerning financial obligation should a patient be admitted to your practice. All questionable information should be reviewed by the billing supervisor or office manager to determine the prospective patient's financial class, potential collectibility, creditworthiness, and the need for patient-related financial counseling and/or service deposit calculations.

The patient's demographic information on the patient and guarantor can be cross-referenced and verified through multiple reference sources, including:

1. Telephone directory or directory assistance

2. Social Security office

3. Post office

4. Annual city directory (ie, R. L. Polk directories cost approximately $120)

5. Personal bank

6. Employer

7. Driver's license—Contact Department of Motor Vehicles; requires name, date of birth, Social Security number, and driver's license number

8. County court offices—Legal or Auditor Department (all public records)

Patient Confidentiality and Registration

Concerns about patient confidentiality must be paramount in all office procedures. A breach of confidentiality is a disclosure to a third party, without patient consent or court order, of private information that the physician has learned within the patient-physician relationship. Disclosure can be oral or written, by telephone or fax, or electronically, for example, via e-mail or health information networks. The medium is irrelevant, although special security requirements may apply to the electronic transfer of information.

An area of potential concern involves the registration process. Routinely patients, as they arrive at your office, fill out a registration log indicating their name, time of appointment, time of arrival, and other basic information, such as whether their insurance information has changed since their last visit. These registration logs become the basis of the office visit for that day and are important in updating and verifying pertinent information. Questions of privacy, however, involve the information that is included on that log for all subsequent patients to view. Some physicians have addressed this by logs that have information on only one patient per sheet of paper. As each patient is checked in, the paperwork on that patient is removed from the log. Others, concerned that multiple pieces of paper will more likely get lost, limit the information on the log to the most basic facts, eg, name and time of appointment and a query as to whether any information has changed. An affirmative answer will result in the patient completing a form to update his or her information. It is most important to review your logs so that under no circumstances does the log ask for information related to the reason for the visit, the diagnosis, or any other information that is private or confidential.

Most physician offices have a sign-in sheet at the reception window. While some practices use pharmaceutical notepads to sign patients in, a formal sign-in sheet will provide the practice with a constant source of valuable information that will enhance practice operations. A sample sign-in sheet is shown in Exhibit 5.4.

Exhibit 5.4   Sample Sign-In Sheet

Date _____

Patient's Name _____

Has your address, phone number or insurance information changed since your last visit?
    yes ☐   no ☐

If yes, please complete the following:

Address _____
_____

Phone (home) _____
    (work) _____

Is this a new worker's compensation claim?
    yes ☐   no ☐

Time of Arrival _____

Time of Appointment _____

Physician's Name _____

Please indicate reason for appointment:
    ☐ Office Visit
    ☐ Laboratory only
    ☐ Injection only
    ☐ Blood pressure check only

The sample format of the sign-in sheet provides information about whether the patient is new or established; changes in address, employer, and insurance; and waiting time efficiency data based on appointment time and arrival data.

After the patient signs in, the receptionist should greet the patient and review the sign-in sheet. If the patient is a new patient, he or she should be given the patient demographic information form on a clipboard and asked to complete it. Some practices also give the patient a medical history form to complete, which is incorporated into the patient's medical record.

The receptionist or registration staff should ask to make photocopies of the patient's:

- Insurance card—front and back.
- Special billing forms.
- Driver's license, if allowed by state.

The patient information form shown in Exhibit 5.1 has a series of statements at the bottom. The patient must read, sign, and date it. The section states:

"I hereby assign, transfer, and set over to [Name of Practice] all of my rights, title, and interest to my medical reimbursement benefits under my insurance policy. I authorize the release of any medical information needed to determine these benefits. This authorization shall remain valid until written notice is given by me revoking said authorization. I understand that I am financially responsible for all charges whether or not they are covered by insurance."

This statement informs the patient that:

1. He or she has "assigned" or transferred the right of direct reimbursement from any health plan, including those that involve nonparticipating physicians, to the practice so the reimbursement can be mailed directly to the practice.

2. He or she has given authorization to release any medical record information needed to coordinate benefits and reimbursement.

3. The authorization is enforced unless he or she is otherwise notified.

4. He or she understands his/her financial responsibility for charges for services rendered.

While the patient information form serves the practice's internal needs, the practice should *obtain patient or guarantor signatures* on the following forms for the following insurance types:

From Patients With Commercial Insurance:

- Authorization to release medical-related information
- Assignment of benefits and payment to provider

From Patients With Medicare:

- Authorization to pay Medicare benefits (signature on file)
- Authorization to release medical-related information
- Assignment of benefits and payment to provider

From Patients With Blue Cross and Blue Shield/Managed Care Plans:

- Authorization to release medical-related information
- Assignment of benefits and payment to provider

Assignment of Benefits and Payment to Provider Form

The "assignment of benefits and payment to provider" form is used as authorization by patients to their insurance plan to send the check directly to the provider. This form is required when the providers are rendering services to patients with insurance plans that the provider(s) are not participating in. A sample is shown in Exhibit 5.5.

Exhibit 5.5   **Assignment and Instruction for
Direct Payment to Medical Providers**

Private – Group Accident – Health Insurance Authorization of Benefits

Patient: _____

Policyholder: _____

Employer: _____   Group #: _____

Social Security #: _____   Policy #: _____

I hereby authorize and instruct that _____ Insurance Company pay
authorized insurance benefits, on my behalf, by check made out and mailed to:

– or –

If my current policy prohibits direct payment to medical provider, then I hereby also instruct and direct you
to make out the check to me and mail it as follows:

c/o _____

for professional or medical expense benefits allowable, and otherwise payable to me under my current
insurance policy as payment toward the total charges for services rendered. *This is a direct assignment
of my rights and benefits under this policy.* This payment will not exceed my indebtedness to the above
mentioned assignee, and I have agreed to pay, in a current manner, any balance of said professional
service charges over and above this insurance payment amount. A photocopy of this Assignment shall be
considered as effective and valid as the original.

I also authorize the release of information pertinent to my case to any insurance company, adjuster, or
attorney involved in this case.

Signed and dated at the above named practice this _____ day of _____, 2____.

_____
Signature of Policyholder

_____
Witness

_____
Signature of Claimant, if other than Policyholder

When a provider is not participating in an insurer's plan, the checks are usually mailed to the patient or policyholder, making collection more difficult. It is also used if the patient's policy prohibits direct payment to the provider. Send this letter as a legal document to request direct payment.

The insurer will likely take one of three actions after receiving the authorization:

1. Send payment to the practice in the name of the practice.

2. Send payment to the practice in the name of the patient.

3. Refuse to send check to practice and continue sending the check(s) to the patient.

When to Use: The form should be filled out by the patient on his or her first visit to the practice, if the patient's insurance plan is one in which the provider(s) do not participate, or in cases where the checks are mailed to the patient.

What to Do: Complete the form and then have the patient and a witness sign the form. Make a copy and send it with the claim; retain the original in the patient's chart.

Authorization for Release of Medical-Related Information Form

Patient medical information is confidential and private. It cannot be released without the patient's consent. Because insurance companies sometimes need to refer to medical information before making a determination on a claim, you will need to have patients sign an authorization to release medical information, such as the "Authorization for Release of Medical-Related Information" form. See Exhibit 5.6.

Signature on File Form

Rather than having the patient sign each claim form being submitted, most practices have the patient sign a "blanket" statement, called a "signature on file" form. By obtaining the patient's signature on this form, the practice can enter the words "signature on file" in the appropriate block of the claim form (on the HCFA-1500, items 12 and 13). This form can also be used to obtain blanket authorization for assignment of benefits. A sample form, acceptable for Medicare and other patients, is shown in Exhibit 5.7.

Exhibit 5.6   **Authorization for Release of Medical-Related Information**

1.   I authorize Dr. _____ to disclose complete information to [name of insurance company] concerning his medical findings and treatment of the undersigned.

2.   Further, I authorize him to testify without limitation, as to all medical findings and the treatment administered to the undersigned, in any legal action, suit, or proceedings to which I am, or may become, a party; and I waive on behalf of myself and any persons who may have an interest in the matter all provisions of law relating to the disclosure of confidential medical information.

Signed,

_____   _____
Patient   Witness

_____   _____
Date   Place

Exhibit 5.7   **Signature on File Form**

I authorize any holder of medical or other information about me to release to [the Social Security Administration and Health Care Financing Administration or its intermediaries, carriers, and agents or name of insurance company], any information needed to determine the benefits for this or a related claim.

Also, I permit a copy of this authorization to be used in place of the original, and request payment of medical insurance benefits either to myself or to the party who accepts assignment. Regulations pertaining to Medicare assignment of benefits apply.

_____   _____
Signature   Date

Patient Education of Payment Policies

Each practice should have preestablished patient insurance policies and procedures for their office staff and should be able to consistently communicate, explain, and enforce the practice's payment policies to patients.

The goals of informing patients about the practice's financial and insurance policies are to make patients clearly aware of the following:

- In most cases, regardless of insurance status, patients are ultimately responsible for payment of all or some of their medical bills, and the amount due must be paid on demand as indicated by the practice.

- Unless the physician is under contract or has signed a participation agreement with a health insurance plan, the contract for the patient's health policy is *between the patient and the health insurer*. While the patient is ultimately financially responsible, the practice will submit the primary insurance on behalf of the patient.

- Insurance does not usually cover or pay for all medical charges, and the patient will almost always have some financial obligation for payment.

- Payment problems or the need for financial counseling to meet patient financial responsibilities must be brought to the attention of the billing staff before the rendering of service(s).

In addition, the billing staff should review some of the basic practice policies covering such issues as:

- Does the practice automatically produce a claim form (standard HCFA-1500) for all patients who have a primary insurance plan, or does the automatic claim generation only apply to Medicare or to Medicaid or to managed care plans, and so on?

- How is the coordination of benefits handled? Will the practice process primary payment and then automatically produce a claim form for patients who may have a supplemental insurance plan?

- At what point does the insurance balance overdue become the patient's responsibility? For example, when the office staff is having a difficult time with the collection of payment from third-party payers, the staff should contact the patient to inform him or her of the problem and enlist his or her assistance. Some practices give the patient's insurance 60 days, then the balance is transferred to the patient's responsibility for immediate payment.

Patient Communications

Many practices find it helpful to provide explanatory letters or pamphlets to their patients regarding insurance processing policies. Various sample letters are provided here as guides for your practice.

Welcome/Explanation Letter

Your practice may give a welcome letter to new patients that outlines your practice's insurance processing policies. The policies outlined in the sample letter shown in Exhibit 5.8 may not be appropriate for your practice, but this practice

Exhibit 5.8   Sample Welcome Letter

Family Medical Group   Lynn I. Hunt, MD

Seattle, Washington   Robert H. Squires, MD

Dear Patient:

If you have health insurance other than those specifically mentioned below, we ask that you pay us and then collect reimbursement from your insurance company. At the time of your clinic visit, you will be provided with a form that contains all the information necessary for you to file your claim with your insurance company. You will also receive a statement of current charges and any balance due each month. An additional copy of this is provided, which you may also use to bill your insurance company for current charges. If there is a problem or if you have a question, please feel free to discuss it with us. We are here to help you with this process.

Blue Cross and Blue Shield: If you have King County Blue Shield, we will bill King County Blue Shield for the entire amount of your charges. Any charges or balances not covered by King County Blue Shield will be billed directly to you.

Medicaid recipients must present a current, valid card prior to treatment. Any appropriate copayments or deductibles as determined by your Medicaid eligibility are due at the time of service. Please ask to speak to the bookkeeper regarding questions and payment arrangements.

Medicare patients are asked to pay for services at the time of their visit, unless prior payment arrangements have been made. We will submit your claim to Medicare, and you will receive payment directly from Medicare. If you require help with your billings or have difficulty paying the difference between what is charged and what Medicare pays, please ask to speak with the bookkeeper. Arrangements can be made for those with special needs.

Thank you for coming to our practice. Please tell us if you have any difficulty with your insurance claims.

Sincerely,

Lynn Hunt, MD

Robert Squires, MD

did a good job of explaining its policies to patients. You may want to copy this letter by using your practice's policies and guidelines.

Insurance Fact Sheet

An insurance fact sheet is another method of explaining insurance processing requirements to your patients. Considering the many different health insurance policies written today, it would be virtually impossible to create one insurance fact sheet that would serve all your patients. However, you can outline your patients' payment responsibilities and provide them with useful names and phone numbers. A sample of one practice's fact sheet is shown in Exhibit 5.9.

Medical Cost Estimate Form

Knowing what to plan for can lessen the burden of treatment of an illness or injury. Patients about to undergo medical treatment want to have some idea of what the costs will be so they can plan an appropriate budget. Also, by providing them with the required financial information, you increase the odds that the practice will receive prompt reimbursement.

The form shown in Exhibit 5.10 can help you provide them with this valuable information. You may want to contact the offices of other physicians involved in your patient's care, if necessary, to obtain an estimate of their charges.

Required Medicare Forms

In addition to the signature on file form, Medicare requires nonparticipating physicians to have the patient sign two additional forms. The first pertains to elective surgery.

When the nonparticipating physician plans to perform an elective surgery (one that can be scheduled in advance and for which a delay in performing the procedure does not cause serious damage to the patient), the physician does not accept assignment, and the fee is $500 or greater, the physician must notify the patient, in writing, of the anticipated cost and out-of-pocket expense. A notice for this purpose that is acceptable to Medicare is shown in Exhibit 5.11.

The second form pertains to services deemed by Medicare to be medically unnecessary or that are otherwise noncovered.

When the physician knows that a procedure or service may not be paid for by Medicare because it has been determined to be medically unnecessary to treat a specified condition, or when the physician has a legitimate reason to believe that Medicare will not cover the service, the physician must notify the patient,

Exhibit 5.9   **Insurance Fact Sheet**

At the time of your visit, you will be provided with a copy of our encounter form. The pink copy is to be attached to your insurance claim form and mailed to your insurance carrier.

You should follow these steps when completing your insurance claim form:

1. Be sure to fill out the top portion of the claim form.

2. It is not necessary for you to fill in the portions regarding diagnosis or procedures. That information is on the encounter form.

3. The physician's name, address, and provider number are also on the encounter form. You do not need to add this to the claim form.

4. If you have not already paid for your services, we will anticipate your forwarding the insurance check directly to our office so that we may credit your account. It is not necessary for you to deposit the check. You may simply endorse the back of the check as follows:

   Pay to the order of James Smith, MD

   and send it to our office in the enclosed envelope.

5. If you have a supplemental policy, fill out the top portion of the claim form, attach the Explanation of Medical Benefits (detach from your check), a copy of the encounter form, and mail them. Do not bill your supplemental policy before receiving an Explanation of Medical Benefits from your primary policy.

Helpful phone numbers:

Blue Cross and Blue Shield: _____

Travelers: _____

Medicaid: _____

Exhibit 5.10   Medical Cost Estimate Form

Patient Name: _____   Date: _____

Explanation of Procedure: _____

_____

	Fee	*% Covered by Insurance*
Surgery:	_____	_____
Assistant Surgeon:	_____	_____
Consultation:	_____	_____
Hospital Visits:	_____	_____
Other Professional Services:	_____	_____
*Anesthesiologist:	_____	_____
*Pathologist:	_____	_____
Total	_____	_____
Approximate Out-of-Pocket Cost	_____	_____

While you are in the hospital, there may be charges for laboratory tests, medications, transfusions, or special care that we are unable to estimate. Be assured that we are sensitive to the rising cost of medical services and will make every effort to deliver quality medical care in the most cost-efficient manner possible, without compromising your good health.

You may wish to contact the hospital business office at _____ for further information about hospital charges. Remember your health insurance card on the day of admittance!

[*You may want to explain that these are required by the hospital for certain surgeries, when applicable.]

Exhibit 5.11   Advance Notice Form for Elective Surgery Over $500

I do not plan to accept assignment for your surgery. The law requires that where assignment is not taken and the charge is $500 or more, the following information must be provided prior to surgery. These estimates assume that you have already met the $100 annual Medicare Part B deductible.

Type of Surgery : _____

_____

_____

Estimated Charge for Surgery $ _____

Estimated Medicare Allowable Charge $ _____

Your Estimated Out-of-Pocket Expense $ _____

_____
Patient Signature   Date

in writing, before providing the service. Therefore, the patient will be required to pay for the service.

The patient must sign this form for it to be considered valid by Medicare, and a new form must be completed for each situation. It is not to be used as a blanket statement. Both participating and nonparticipating physicians are required to provide this form in applicable circumstances (Exhibit 5.12).

Insurance Advanced Notice Service Waiver of Liability

Like the Medicare advanced notice, a similar form can be used to notify patients with other insurance plans. This reinforces the patient's understanding of his/her financial responsibility for services to be rendered. Have the patient complete the form and store it in the patient's file as shown in Exhibit 5.13.

Entry of Patient and Insurance Data

For practices that have a computerized billing system, the patient demographic and insurance information is usually entered into the system before the initial date of service encounter and the information has been verified before the encounter. While there are different software billing management programs, most have common data fields that are crucial for error-free insurance billing.

Because of the volume of data needed to process claims, most systems separate the entry of the patient information section from the responsible party section and from the insurance assignment section through separate screens. The patient data for each of these three sections need to be carefully reviewed and entered into the management system.

Probably the most important section in insurance billing is the assignment of primary and secondary insurance plan status. This is vital to ensuring proper coordination of benefits, clean claim processing, and appropriate reimbursement. To accomplish this, the data entry staff must understand coordination of benefit rules when more than one insurance plan is involved in a patient's account, and then translate that on the insurance data entry screen.

Be careful to place the correct numbers and letters in the respective fields for policy numbers, plan numbers, group numbers, authorization or precertification numbers, and extra insurance information such as accident-related data. Also be careful to fully review your insurance plan utility file before adding any new insurance plans to a patient file. Multiple insurance entries for a single insurance plan can easily complicate account follow-up and management.

Exhibit 5.12   Medicare Advanced Notice Service Waiver

Physician's Notice

Medicare will only pay for services that it determines to be "reasonable and necessary" under Section 1862(a)(1) of the Medicare law. If Medicare determines that a particular service, although it would otherwise be covered, is "not reasonable and necessary" under Medicare program standards, Medicare will deny payment for that service. I believe that, in your case, Medicare is likely to deny payment for the following reasons:

_____

_____

Note: On the above line, a specific procedure code and description of procedure *must* be listed here before the beneficiary signs the form.

Medicare does not usually pay:

1. For this many treatments/shots/visits.

2. For this service/drug/vaccine.

3. Because the treatment has yet to be proven effective.

4. For this office visit unless it was emergency care.

5. For like services by more than one doctor during the same time period.

6. For such an extensive procedure.

7. For this equipment or lab test.

8. Because the treatment is considered by Medicare to be "not reasonable or necessary."

Beneficiary Agreement

I, _____, have been informed on this date_____ by my physician (and/or staff) that he/she believes that Medicare is likely to deny payment for the service(s) identified above for the reasons stated. If Medicare denies payment, I agree to be personally and fully responsible for payment of the service(s) rendered.

Further, I will pay for these services on this date, understanding that the physician will bill my insurance(s) on my behalf. If the above physician is paid by my insurance, I will receive a refund for the portion of the bill covered by my insurance less any portion of the payment that is deemed my responsibility.

_____   _____
Beneficiary Signature   Staff/Witness Signature

**Exhibit 5.13   Insurance Coverage Advanced Notice
                    Service Waiver**

Physician's Notice

Some health insurance plans will only pay for services that they determine to be "reasonable and necessary."
If an insurance plan determines that a particular service, although it would otherwise be covered, is "not
reasonable and necessary," the insurance plan may deny payment for that service.

I believe that, in your case, your health plan is likely to deny payment for _____

_____

Policyholder/Patient Agreement

I, _____, have been informed on this date _____ by my physician (and/or staff)
that he believes that my health plan may deny payment for the service identified above for the reasons stated.
If the health plan denies payment, I agree to be personally and fully responsible for payment of the service(s)
rendered.

Further, I will pay for these services on this date, understanding that the physician will attempt to rebill
my insurance(s) on my behalf. If the above physician is paid by my insurance, I will receive a refund for the
portion of the bill covered by my insurance less any portion of the payment that is deemed my responsibility.

_____   _____
Policyholder/Patient Signature   Staff/Witness Signature

Another data field includes the patient's "financial" or "account type," which defines the primary account type for management and reporting purposes. The patient's account type is sometimes classified as a primary payer type (ie, Medicare, Medicaid, Blue Cross and Blue Shield, commercial, insurance only, self-pay, etc).

Capture of All Billable Services and Transaction Entry

Under fee-for-service, the traditional way to receive appropriate reimbursement is for the physician to report all pertinent services provided to the patient in the medical record and capture all billable services for transaction entry into the billing system.

We use the term *appropriate reimbursement* because, under most systems, CPT coding drives expected reimbursement. Accurate coding and reporting all services provided is the pre–claim processing area that makes or breaks a successful billing office. Yet, even under managed care plans that reimburse primary care physicians on a capitated rate, complete medical documentation and coding of all services rendered is just as important to review resource allocation and costs associated with care. Documentation is also used for physician productivity measurements that determine profit sharing and continuity as a plan provider.

To successfully capture all billable services, the following areas need to be addressed:

1. Comprehensive Medical Record Documentation

The medical record, while a clinical document, is also the ultimate medical billing document and is used by most health plans in adjudicating claims to support or deny reimbursements. Therefore, physicians need to develop detailed and qualitative notes of patient evaluation and management (E&M) encounters, diagnostic and therapeutic treatments, supplies, orders, and so on.

In December 1994, the American Medical Association (AMA) and Health Care Financing Administration (HCFA) jointly distributed *New E&M Documentation Guidelines,* which thoroughly defines all documentation components needed to meet and exceed level of service definition criteria. All practices should have received a copy of the guidelines from their Medicare carrier and should request a copy if not received. In 1997 new E&M guidelines were distributed; however, HCFA allows either the 1994 or 1997 criteria to be used, whichever is more appropriate for the provider. HCFA proposed revised E&M criteria in 2000, but implementation is not expected until 2001 or 2002.

2. Transfer of Clinical/Treatment Information to Appropriate CPT and ICD-9-CM Codes

From the medical record, all the physician services rendered and all medications and supplies provided need to be identified and coded. In addition, the patient's chief complaints, signs, symptoms, or qualified diagnosis(es) also need to be coded by means of valid *International Classification of Diseases, Ninth Revision–Clinical Modification* (ICD-9-CM) codes.

As coding serves as the basis for appropriate reimbursement, *the quality of the practice's coding skills is extremely important*. The coding staff should be encouraged to become certified procedural coders or become affiliated with associations that encourage certification and offer coding education programs. In-house code training systems are also helpful in fostering staff coding skills.

Key areas for coding skills include E&M level of service differentiation, *Current Procedural Terminology* (CPT) procedure and surgery coding, use of modifiers, supply and injectable drug billing, and the coding's potential impact on reimbursement. To properly coordinate insurance plan benefits between different physicians treating different diagnostic conditions, the assignment of the most appropriate level I and II HCFA's Common Procedure Coding System (HCPCS) codes (services and supplies) and ICD-9-CM diagnostic codes is needed to submit a clean claim and receive appropriate reimbursement.

To facilitate the charge capture process, most practices develop customized billing source documents, called encounter forms, to serve as internal charge forms.

Encounter Forms

Encounter forms or superbills, also referred to as charge tickets, are preprinted forms that list procedure codes and descriptions (and occasionally diagnostic codes) for services frequently rendered by the practice. The form also usually contains basic practice and patient information and serves as an internal charge form and patient invoice. It is usually prenumbered for internal controls.

The services and diagnoses are usually arranged by service classification—E&M services, injections, minor procedures, diagnostic tests, laboratory, and radiology services. Some forms are printed on two-ply carbonless paper—one copy for the practice, the other to serve as the patient's receipt. Others are printed with sequential numbers for tracking purposes. A sample encounter form is shown in Chapter 1.

Many practices rely on encounter forms because they are convenient. At the time of the visit, the physician or medical assistant simply checks off the services and patient diagnoses, the staff completes the charge information, and the charges are entered into the patient billing system. Unless filing a claim is required, as in the case of Medicare and many other carriers, a copy of the encounter form is provided to the patient to file with his or her insurance claim. In addition to their convenience, encounter forms save time, can be used with many third-party payers, and simplify paperwork and bookkeeping.

Encounter forms do, however, have significant drawbacks. First, it is impossible to list on the encounter form the complete range of procedure and diagnosis codes that are likely to be used by your practice. This can lead to miscoding of services and diagnoses, as most practices inappropriately select the closest code rather than take the time to refer to the code manual to locate the correct code. Second, encounter forms cannot be submitted to Medicare and many other carriers, nor are they useful when submitting claims for nonroutine or unusual services. It is important imperative to review and update the codes annually.

Finally, encounter forms are most often used with patients who pay at the time of the visit. Because the patient files his or her own claim, you may not know if the claim was denied or delayed because of improper codes listed on the encounter form. This lack of feedback can increase coding and other encounter form errors, which result in underpayments to patients and audit liability to physician practices.

The final assignment of the HCPCS and ICD-9-CM codes on the encounter form is often a shared responsibility between the physician, clinical support staff, and business office support staff. The physician knows best what service and supplies were provided to a patient and what was documented. Unfortunately, many physicians are not fond of coding, and some want to be totally free from the coding process. So, often the clinical support staff assists physicians in the assignment of HCPCS and ICD-9-CM. It is important to remember that, in cases of improper coding on fraudulent claims, the ultimate responsibility lies with the provider whose signature is on the claim.

Service Verification and Transaction Entry of Services Rendered

After the services and diagnoses have been marked on the encounter form, the encounter form is brought to the cashiering-discharge area. This is where the clinical assistant and the in-office coding staff first review the encounter form as a quality assurance check. They are responsible for:

- Reviewing the encounter form for complete charge capture and code assignment. They review the patient's chart against the encounter form for all supplies, drugs, and services provided.

- Proper assignment of E&M type of service (ie, is the patient a new or established patient? Is an encounter an office visit or a consultation?).

- The compatibility of the ICD-9-CM diagnoses codes with each CPT procedure code or E&M level of service.

- Assigning the ICD-9-CM diagnoses codes with fourth and fifth digits or to the highest specificity.

When the coding staff is satisfied with the code assignment, the patient's account is pulled up on the transaction entry screen of the computer system. Again, most billing management systems have standardized data fields for transaction entry and correspond to the HCFA-1500 claim form (to be discussed later).

The key data fields to complete per charge line item include the following:

- Date of service (DOS)—sometimes defined as "from and to dates"

- Place of service code—(ie, code 11 = office, 21 = hospital inpatient, 22 = hospital outpatient)

- Transaction codes—level I (CPT) and level II (HCPCS) codes

- Coding modifiers

- Attending practice physician code—defaults provider ID number

- Standard charge amount or special insurance charge default

- Number of units

- Definition of (1–4) diagnoses using ICD-9-CM codes

- Assignment of diagnosis codes to individual line items (1–4) cross-reference

The last data field for transaction entry on most billing systems is for indicating that the line item is to be billed to insurance. Some systems ask "bill insurance?" with a "Yes/No" field, while other systems allow the operator to bill a specific insurance plan through the assignment of insurance codes. After all line items have been coded, the transaction charges are added to the patient's account, and the patient's account is flagged by the system for generating a claim.

Filing Claims and Effect on Accounts Receivable

In the interest of keeping accounts receivable low, it generally is best to collect from the patient and have the patient file insurance claims for office visits if he or she has commercial insurance, unless special circumstances require that certain arrangements be made with the patient. Special circumstances include situations in which patients are clearly incapable of filing claims, when the law requires the office to file the claim, or when patients forget to bring their checkbooks or credit cards or have no other way of making a payment. Remember, billed services become accounts receivable, and it is always preferable to receive payment immediately.

To reemphasize the point, *if you collect up front, you avoid filing commercial insurance claims and maximize cash flow.* If an insurance claim is filed for commercial insurance, it becomes an account receivable to the practice and thus is subject to all the office policies and procedures necessary to obtain payment from the insurance company.

If the office collects payment for the visit, there is no account receivable for that transaction. The more money the office can collect at the front desk, the better the practice cash flow will be. The front desk should be able to collect some payment for at least 90% of visits, even if a patient pays only $5. In some instances practices accept charge cards to enhance collections and file the insurance for the patient. Although in many cases it is not mandatory for the practice to file the insurance claim, timing and proper filing of the form are enhanced when the practice completes the form.

Insurance Claims Processing and Submission

If a patient does not pay for the visit at the time of service, the office will need to prepare and file an insurance claim form with the patient's insurance company to receive payment. The manner in which the insurance claim form is completed and submitted will depend on the type of insurance. As was discussed before, some insurance companies only process paper claims, while others accept electronically submitted claims. So part of the insurance processing manager's responsibility is to organize which insurance claims need to be generated on paper and which can be sent electronically.

To receive appropriate payment from the insurance company, the office must prepare the insurance claim correctly, or produce what is referred to as a "clean claim." This means that every relevant box must be completed on the claim form for the insurance plan to process. Any error in the claim completion may cause payment to be delayed or denied. The most common form used to file insurance claims is the type mandated for use for Medicare claims, the HCFA-1500 form.

HCFA-1500 Universal Claim Form

The HCFA-1500 form is often called the universal claim form because virtually all third-party payers will accept it. In 1992 the HCFA-1500 form was changed so that it can be scanned by payers with the use of optical character recognition (OCR) equipment. As previously stated, Medicare requires that all physicians submit this form when providing services to Medicare patients.

In addition to using a special red ink for OCR purposes, the form was redesigned to allow for the reporting of additional information, such as the physician's UPIN, which is required by Medicare. These forms may be obtained from a variety of vendors and are relatively inexpensive. See Chapter 1.

Instructions for Completing a HCFA-1500 Form

Most insurance and managed care plans provide basic instructions for completing items on the claim form in the physician manual. If there are no special requirements, the item should be completed according to the requirements stated on the form. If the claim forms are not computer generated, it is best to type them. If they are handwritten, the staff should print the requirements with all capitals and black ink.

The claim form is divided into two major sections: patient information, items 1 through 13, and physician information, items 14 through 33. Refer to Exhibit 1.1 to see a HCFA-1500 form in its entirety.

Patient and Insured Information

Items 1 through 13 ask for information about the patient and the insured, and for a determination of whether the patient is a dependent. This is information that was completed on the registration form at the patient's initial office visit or at the hospital.

In practices that use computerized patient information–accounting systems, this information can be generated automatically by entering a single patient identification number assigned by the practice.

The following sections describe each of these 13 items; below the general explanation, where applicable, there are descriptions of the special requirements for Medicare, Medicaid, Civilian Health and Medical Program of the Uniformed Services (CHAMPUS), Civilian Health and Medical Program of the Veterans Affairs (CHAMPVA), and private plans.

Item 1: Type of Insurance   Indicate the type of insurance coverage applicable to a claim by checking the appropriate box. For example, if a Medicare claim is being submitted, check the Medicare box for the Federal Employment Compensation Act/Black Lung, FECA. For private plans such, as a Blue Shield claim, check OTHER.

Item 1a: Insured's ID Number   Enter the insured's primary identification number, including all letters. This is the number that appears on the plan identification card.

Medicare   Enter the health insurance claim number (HICN) from the Medicare card, including all the letters.

Medicaid   Enter the Medicaid number from the current Medicaid card. It is sometimes called the billing number or recipient number.

CHAMPUS   Enter the sponsor's Social Security number (SSN). Do not provide the patient's SSN unless the patient and sponsor are the same. If a sponsor is an active-duty security agent, enter "SECURITY." Additional information about sponsors is given in Chapter 9.

CHAMPVA   Provide the sponsor's SSN; add the number in item 5 of the CHAMPVA authorization card if there is no SSN.

Private Plans   Enter the insured's subscriber, enrollee, or member number. This may be the certificate number of the insured's number, and it is copied directly from the plan's identification number. Frequently, this number is the insured's SSN.

Item 2: Patient's Name   Enter the patient's last name, first name, and middle initial, if any, as shown on the identification card. The practice may know the patient by a nickname or the individual may want to be known by his or her middle name, but enter the name exactly as it appears on the card.

Item 3: Patient's Birth Date   Enter the patient's birth date and sex. Because many plans operated under different rules, providers will want to contact individual payers who they do business with to determine how that payer is handling date formats.

Medicare   Providers of services will be required as of October 1, 1998, to report eight-digit birth dates for items 3, 9b, and 11a on form HCFA-1500. This includes entering two-digit months (MM) and days (DD) and four-digit years (CCYY). The reporting requirement of eight-digit birthdates will not require a revision to form HCFA-1500. Eight-digit birthdates must be reported with a space between month, day, and year (ie, MM_DD_CCYY). On the form HCFA-1500, the space between month, day, and year is delineated by a dotted, vertical line.

Item 4: Insured's Name   Enter the full name of the insured.

Medicare   If there is a plan primary to Medicare, through the patient's or spouse's employment or any other source, list the name of the insured on that policy. When the insured and the patient are the same, enter the word "SAME". If Medicare is primary, leave blank.

Medicaid   Enter the full name of the insured.

Private Plans   Enter the full name of the insured if it is different from that of the patient.

Item 5: Patient's Address   Enter the patient's mailing address on the first line, the city and state on the second line, and the ZIP code and telephone number on the third line.

CHAMPUS   Do not provide a post office box number—enter the actual place of residence. If this is a rural address, the address must contain the route and box number. An APO/FPO address should not be used for a patient's mailing address unless that person is actually residing overseas.

Item 6: Patient Relationship to Insured   Check the appropriate box for the patient's relationship to the insured after item 4 has been completed.

Medicare   Enter the relationship of the individual whose coverage is the primary plan for the Medicare beneficiary.

CHAMPUS   If the patient is the sponsor, check the "self" block. If "other" is checked, indicate how the patient is related to the sponsor, for example, former spouse, parent. Parents, parents-in-law, stepparents, and parents by adoption are not CHAMPUS/CHAMPVA eligible. These categories of dependents may have ID cards with privileges for the military treatment facility, but not for CHAMPUS/CHAMPVA benefits. Grandchildren are not eligible unless they are legally adopted. Be certain that an ID card authorizes "CIVILIAN" medical benefits. Review the reverse side of the retiree's ID card (DD Form 2. Retired). An unnumbered block provides a date when civilian military care is no longer authorized. For example, the CHAMPUS beneficiary becomes eligible for Medicare. If the child is a stepchild, check the "child" box.

Private Plans   If the patient is the insured, check "self."

Item 7: Insured's Address   Enter the insured's address and telephone number. When this address is the same as the patient's address, enter the word "same." Complete this item only when items 4 and 11 have been completed.

CHAMPUS   Enter the address for the active duty sponsor's duty station or the retiree's mailing address. If the address is the same as the patient's address, enter "same." If the sponsor resides overseas, enter the APO/FPO address.

Private Plans   If the insured is the patient, enter "same."

Item 8: Patient Status   Check the appropriate box for the patient's marital status and indicate whether the patient is employed or is a full-time or part-time student.

Item 9: Other Insured's Policy or Group Number   Enter the insured's last name and his or her first name for a plan that is secondary to the patient's primary insurance plan listed in item 2.

Medicare   Enter the last name, first name, and middle initial of the enrollee in a Medigap policy if it is different from that shown in item 2. Otherwise, enter "same" or enrollee's name. If no Medigap benefits are assigned, leave this space blank.

Note: Only participating physicians are to complete items 9 and 9a-d and only when the beneficiary wishes to assign benefits under a Medigap policy.

Participating physicians and suppliers must enter the information required in item 9 and its divisions if the beneficiary requests this. A claim for which a beneficiary elects to assign benefits under a Medigap policy to a participating physician/supplier is called a *mandated Medigap transfer* or *crossover*.

Do not list other supplemental coverages that are not Medigap policies in item 9a-d when a Medicare claim is submitted. Other supplemental claims are forwarded automatically if the private plan contracts with a Medicare carrier to send Medicare claim information electronically. If there is no such contract, the beneficiary must file his or her own supplemental claim.

Medigap is medical insurance offered by a private plan to individuals covered by Medicare and is designed to supplement Medicare benefits. It fills in some of the gaps in Medicare coverage by providing payment for changes that Medicare does not cover, such as deductibles, coinsurance, and other limitations imposed by Medicare. It does not include limited benefit coverage available to Medicare beneficiaries such as a "specific disease," ie, cancer, or "hospital indemnity" per day coverage. Medigap excludes policies offered by an employer to employees or former employees, as well as policies offered by a labor union to members or former members.

CHAMPUS   Enter the name of the insured if it is different from that shown in item 2 (patient). For example, the patient may be covered under a plan held by a spouse, parent, or other person. (Items 11a-d should be used to report insurance plans covering the patient.) Note: Item 11d should be completed before the office staff determines the need for completing items 9a-d. If item 11d is checked, items 9a-d must be completed.

Private Plans Enter the name of the insured for secondary insurance plans to the patient's primary plan listed in item 2.

Item 9a: Other Insured's Policy or Group Number. Enter the plan ID number that is the policy or group number of the secondary insurance plan.

Medicare Enter the policy and/or group number of the Medigap insured preceded by MEDIGAP, MG, or MGAP. Note: Item 9d must be completed if you enter a policy and/or group number in item 9a.

CHAMPUS Enter the policy number of the other insured's plan.

Private Plans List the policy number of the secondary plan.

Item 9B: Other Insured's Date of Birth

Medicare Enter the Medigap insured's eight-digit birth date (MM\DD\CC\YY) and sex.

Because many plans operate under different rules, providers will want to contact individual payers whom they do business with to determine how that payer is handling date formats.

Item 9c: Employer's Name or School Name Enter the employer's name or school name for the secondary insurance plan.

Medicare Leave blank if a Medigap PAYERID is entered in item 9d. Enter the claims processing address for the Medigap insurer. Use an abbreviated street address, two-letter state postal code, and ZIP code copied from the Medigap enrollee's Medigap identification card. For example,

1257 Anywhere Street
Baltimore, MD 21204

is shown as

1257 Anywhere St. MD 21204.

CHAMPUS Enter the name of the employer or school.

Item 9d: Insurance Plan Name or Program Name Enter the name of the insurance program or plan that received the claim after the plan noted in item 1.

Medicare Enter the nine-digit PAYERID number of the Medigap insurer. If no PAYERID number exists, then enter the Medigap insurance program or plan name. If you are a participating provider and the beneficiary wants Medicare payment data forwarded to a Medigap insurer under a mandated Medigap transfer, all of the information in items 9, 9a, 9b, and 9d must be complete and accurate. Otherwise, the Medicare carrier cannot forward the claim information to the Medigap insurer.

CHAMPUS Enter the name of the insurance plan or the program name where the individual has other health insurance benefits. On an attached sheet, provide a complete mailing address for all other insurance information and enter the word "attachment."

Item 10: Is Patient Condition Related to: If the services listed on the claim form are for a work-related injury or accident-related injury, check the "yes" box.

Medicare Check "yes" or "no" to indicate whether employment, auto liability, or other accident involvement applies to one or more of the services described in item 24. Any item checked "yes" indicates that there may be subrogation primary to Medicare. Identify primary insurance information in item 11.

CHAMPUS Check "yes" or "no," but if this service was the result of an automobile accident, indicate the state where the accident occurred. The contractor will contact the patient for potential third-party liability information. When a third-party liability is involved, the beneficiary is required to complete DD Form 2527, Statement of Personal Injury—Possible Third Party Liability.

Private Plans Provide information concerning potential third-party liability.

Item 10d: Reserved for Local Use

Medicaid If the patient is entitled to Medicaid, enter the patient's number preceded by the letters MCD.

CHAMPUS Use this block to indicate that there is other health insurance.

Item 11: Insured's Policy Group or FECA Number Enter the insured's policy group or FECA number. If it is the same as in item 4, write "same."

Medicare THIS ITEM MUST BE COMPLETED BY THE PHYSICIAN, *who acknowledges having made a good faith effort to determine whether Medicare is the primary or secondary plan.* If there is insurance primary to Medicare, enter the insured's plan ID number and complete items 11a-c. If there is no insurance primary to Medicare, enter the word "none."

Insurance Primary to Medicare Circumstances under which Medicare payment may be secondary to other insurance:

- Group health plan coverage
  ⇒ Working aged

⇒ Disability

⇒ End-stage renal disease

- No-fault and/or other liability
- Work-related illness/injury

⇒ Workers' compensation

⇒ Black lung

⇒ Veterans' benefits

Note: For a paper claim to be considered for Medicare secondary payer benefits, a copy of the primary payer EOB must be forwarded along with the claim form.

CHAMPUS If the patient has other insurance, enter the plan ID number and indicate whether Medicare covers the patient. (Block 9a-d should be used to report another primary insurance plan.)

Item 11a: Insured's Date of Birth Enter the insured's eight-digit (MM\DD\CC\YY) birth date and sex if they are different from item 3.

CHAMPUS Complete the insured's eight-digit date of birth (MM/DD/CC/YY) and sex (check box). Enter the date of birth and sex if they are different from item 3.

Item 11b: Employer's Name or School Name

Medicare Enter the employer's name, if applicable,. If there is a change in the insured's insurance status, for example, retired, enter either a six-digit (MM\DD\YY) or eight-digit (MM\DD\CC\YY) retirement date preceded by the word "retired."

CHAMPUS Enter the employer's or school's name if applicable.

Item 11c: Insurance Plan Name or Program Name Enter the nine-digit PAYERID number of the primary insurer. If no PAYERID number exists, then enter the complete primary insurance plan or program name, such as Blue Shield of Illinois. If the primary payer's EOB does not contain the claims processing address, record the primary payer's claims processing address directly on the EOB.

CHAMPUS Enter the insurance plan or program name. If the patient has supplemental CHAMPUS coverage, it is not necessary to report a claim with that insurance first unless the insurance can be considered a primary plan. For CHAMPUS purposes, supplemental policies are those that are specifically designed to supplement CHAMPUS benefits, for example, payment of the beneficiary's cost share or deductible liability. Remember, CHAMPUS is secondary to all other medical insurance except Medicaid. When you submit the claim to the other insurer, attach a copy of the EOB from the primary insurance plan to the CHAMPUS claim.

Item 11d: Is There Another Health Benefit Plan?

Medicare   Leave blank. Not required by Medicare.

CHAMPUS   Check "yes" or "no" to indicate whether there is or is not another primary insurance plan. If secondary insurance, Medicare, or Medicaid covers the patient, enter that plan ID number. If Medicaid covers the patient, enter the word "Medicaid," followed by the Medicaid number.

Private Plans   Place an "X" in the "yes" box to indicate patient coverage by a third insurance plan. Enter the group number or group name if the patient is covered by an employer-paid medical insurance plan.

Item 12: Patient's or Authorized Person's Signature   The patient or
authorized representative must sign and enter either a six-digit date (MM\DD\YY), eight-digit date (MM\DD\CC\YY), or an alphanumeric date (ie, January 1, 1998) unless the signature is on file. The patient or authorized representative must sign the item unless the signature is on file in the practice or at the hospital. The signed authorization for the patient that is on file at the hospital should cover all inpatient and outpatient hospitalization services related to the services on the claim form. When the patient's representative signs, the relationship to the patient must be indicated. The patient's signature, authorizing the release of medical information, is necessary to process the claim. The patient's signature also authorizes payment of benefits to the provider of service when the provider accepts assignment on the claim.

Medicare   The program allows the obtaining of a lifetime authorization one time, which is kept on file. The registration form in Chapter 2 contains the terminology required by Medicare, and so a separate authorization is not necessary if the form is used. If a signature is obtained, enter "Signature on File" in item 12.

Signature by Mark (X)   When an illiterate or physically handicapped patient signs by mark, the patient's name and address must be entered next to the mark.

CHAMPUS   If a patient is under 18 years of age, either parent should sign unless the services are confidential. If the patient is 18 or older, but cannot sign the claim, the person who signs must be either the legal guardian or, in the absence of a legal guardian, the spouse or parent of the patient. The signer should write the patient's name in item 12, followed by the word "by" and his or her own signature. A statement must be attached to the claim giving the signer's full name and address, the signer's relationship to the patient, and the reason the patient is unable to sign. Also included must be documentation of the signer's appointment as a legal guardian, an indication of whether a power of attorney has been issued, or a statement that a legal guardian has not been appointed if such is the case.

Private Plans   It is very important to maintain current signatures for patients and/or insureds. Use the words "signature on file" if a valid signature is available. Most insurance and managed care plans will accept this, but have the right to request a copy of the actual signature.

Item 13: Insured's or Authorized Person's Signature   The signature in this item authorizes payment of medical benefits to the physician or provider for services listed on the claim.

Medicare   The signature in this item authorizes payment of mandated Medigap benefits to the participating physician or supplier if required Medigap information is included in item 9 and its subdivisions. The patient or his/her authorized representative signs this item, or the signature must be on file as a separate Medigap authorization. The Medigap assignment on file in the participating provider's office must be insurer specific. It may state that the authorization applies to all occasions of service until it is revoked.

Private Plans   If a plan has offered a contract for participation in its program and the doctor has not signed the contract, even though the signature is in item 13, payment may not be sent to the practice.

Physician or Supplier Information

These items describe diagnoses, procedures, and charges and give a history of the patient's condition. Most of this information is found on the patient's encounter form.

Item 14: Date of Current Illness, Injury, Pregnancy   Enter either a six-digit (MM\DD\YY) or eight-digit (MM\DD\CC\YY) date when the first symptoms began for the current illness, injury, or pregnancy (date of last menstrual period).

Medicare   For chiropractic services, enter either a six-digit (MM\DD\YY) or eight-digit (MM\DD\CC\YY) date of the initiation of the course of treatment and then enter either a six-digit (MM\DD\YY) or eight-digit (MM\DD\CC\YY) x-ray date in item 19.

Private Plans   This information is used in determining benefits or exclusions for preexisting conditions.

Item 15: If Patient Has Had Same or Similar Illness.

Medicare   Leave blank.

CHAMPUS   Enter the date when the patient first consulted the physician for a similar condition.

Private Plans   Enter the date when the patient first consulted the physician for a similar condition.

Item 16: Dates Patient Unable to Work in Current Occupation   Enter the dates the patient is employed and unable to work in his or her current occupation. Enter either six-digit (MM\DD\YY) or eight-digit (MM\DD\CC\YY) dates when the patient is unable to work. This is important if the patient has employment-related insurance coverage or workers' compensation.

Item 17: Name of the Referring Physician or Other Source

Medicare   Enter the name of the referring or ordering physician if the service or item was ordered or referred by a physician.

A *referring physician* is a physician who requests an item or service for the beneficiary for which payment may be made under the Medicare program. An *ordering physician* is a physician who orders nonphysician services for the patient, such as diagnostic laboratory tests, clinical laboratory tests, pharmaceutical services, and durable medical equipment.

The ordering/referring requirement became effective on January 1, 1992. *All* claims for Medicare covered services and items that result from a physician's order or referral must include the ordering/referring physician's name and *national provider identifier* (NPI). An NPI is a unique number assigned to each physician or other practitioner who bills the Medicare program. This includes parenteral and enteral nutrition, immunosuppressive drug claims, and the following:

- Diagnostic laboratory services
- Diagnostic radiology services
- Consultative services
- Durable medical equipment

Claims for other ordered/referred services that are not included in the preceding list must also show the ordering or referring physician's name and NPI. For example, a surgeon must complete items 17 and 17a when a physician sends a patient for a consultation. When the ordering physician is also the performing physician (as is often the case with in-office clinical laboratory tests), the performing physician's name and assigned NPI must appear in items 17 and 17a.

All physicians must obtain an NPI even though they may never bill Medicare directly. A physician who has not been assigned an NPI must contact the Medicare carrier. When a patient is referred to a physician who also orders and performs a diagnostic service, a separate claim is required for the diagnostic service.

- Enter the original ordering or referring physician's name and NPI in items 17 and 17a of the first claim form.

- Enter the ordering (performing) physician's name and NPI in items 17 and 17a of the second claim form.

CHAMPUS   Provide the name and address of the physician, institutional provider, or other source who referred the patient to the provider of the services identified on this claim. This is required for all consultation services. If your patient was referred from a military treatment facility (MTF), enter the name of the MTF and attach part DD2161 of SF 513, "Referral."

Item 17a: ID Number of Referring Physician

Medicare   Enter the HCFA-assigned NPI of the referring or ordering physician listed in item 17. Enter only the seven-digit base number and the one-digit check digit. When a claim involves multiple referring or ordering physicians, a separate HCFA-1500 must be used for each ordering or referring physician.

If the ordering or referring physician has not been assigned an NPI, one of the *surrogate* NPIs listed below must be used in item 17a. The surrogate NPI that is used depends on the circumstance and is used only until the physician is assigned an NPI. Enter the physician's name in item 17 and the surrogate NPI in item 17a. All surrogate NPIs, with the exception of retired physicians (RET000), are temporary and may be used only until an NPI is assigned.

Use the following surrogate NPIs for physicians who have not been assigned individual NPIs. Claims received with surrogate numbers will be tracked and may be audited:

- Residents who are issued an NPI in conjunction with activities outside their residency status must use that NPI. For interns and residents without NPIs, use the eight-character surrogate NPI RES00000.

- Retired physicians who were not issued an NPI may use the surrogate RET00000.

- Physicians serving in the Department of Veteran Affairs or the US Armed Services may use VAD00000.

- Physicians serving in the Public Health or Indian Health Services may use PHS00000.

Medicare extends coverage and direct payment in certain areas to practitioners who are state-licensed to order medical services including diagnostic tests or refer patients to Medicare providers without a supervising physician. Use the surrogate NPI NPP00000 on claims involving services ordered or referred by nurse practitioners, clinical nurse specialists, or any nonphysician practitioner who is state licensed to order clinical diagnostic tests.

When the ordering or referring physician has not been assigned an NPI and does not qualify to use one of the surrogate NPIs, use the surrogate NPI OTH00000 until an individual NPI is assigned.

Item 18: Hospitalization Dates Related to Current Services   Enter either a six-digit (MM\DD\YY) or eight-digit (MM\DD\CC\YY) date when a medical service is furnished as a result of, or subsequent to, a related hospitalization.

Item 19: Reserved for Local Use.

Medicare   Enter either a six-digit (MM\DD\YY) or eight-digit (MM\DD\CC\YY) date patient was last seen and the NPI of his/her attending physician when an independent physical or occupational therapist or physician providing routine foot care submits claims. For physical and occupational therapists, entering this information certifies that the required physician certification (or recertification) is being kept on file. Enter either a six-digit (MM\DD\YY) or eight-digit (MM\DD\CC\YY) x-ray date for chiropractor services. By entering an x-ray date and the initiation date for course of chiropractic treatment in item 14, you are certifying that all the relevant information requirements (including level of subluxation) are on file along with the appropriate x-ray and all are available for carrier review.

Enter the drug's name and dosage when submitting a claim for not otherwise classified (NOC) drugs.

Enter a concise description of an "unlisted procedure code" or an NOC code if one can be given within the confines of this box. Otherwise, an attachment must be submitted with the claim.

Enter all applicable modifiers when modifier -99 (multiple modifiers) is entered in item 24d. If modifier -99 is entered on multiple line items of a single claim form, all applicable modifiers for each line item containing a -99 modifier should be listed as follows: 1 = (mod), where the number 1 represents the line item and "mod" represents all modifiers applicable to the referenced line item.

Enter the statement "Homebound" when an independent laboratory renders an electrocardiogram tracing or obtains a specimen from a homebound or institutionalized patient.

Enter the statement "Patient refuses to assign benefits" when the beneficiary absolutely refuses to assign benefits to a participating provider. In this case, no payment may be made on the claim.

Enter the statement "Testing for hearing aid" when billing for services involving the testing of a hearing aid(s) is used to obtain intentional denials when other payers are involved.

When dental examinations are billed, enter the specific surgery for which the exam is being performed.

Enter the specific name and dosage amount when low-osmolar contrast material is billed, but only if HCPCS codes do not cover them.

Enter either a six-digit (MM\DD\YY) or eight-digit (MM\DD\CC\YY) assumed and/or relinquished date for a global surgery claim when providers share postoperative care.

Enter the statement "Attending physician, not hospice employee" when a physician renders services to a hospice patient but the hospice providing the patient's care (in which the patient resides) does not employ the attending physician.

Enter demonstration ID number "30" for all national emphysema treatment trial claims.

Item 20: Outside Lab

Medicare   Complete this item when billing for diagnostic tests subject to purchase price limitations. A "yes" check indicates that the diagnostic test was performed outside the entity billing for the service. When yes is annotated, item 32 must be completed. Enter the purchase price under charges (item 24f) if the "yes" block is marked. A "no" check indicates that "no purchased tests are included on this claim." When billing for multiple purchased diagnostic tests, each test must be submitted on a separate claim form.

Private Plans   Leave blank unless instructions are given by a specific plan.

Item 21: Diagnosis or Nature of Illness or Injury   Enter the patient's diagnosis and/or condition by using ICD-9-CM code numbers. Enter up to four codes in priority orders (primary condition, secondary condition, comorbid conditions, and complications). All narrative diagnoses for nonphysician specialties must be submitted on an attachment.

Item 22: Medicaid Resubmissions   Leave this blank. It is required by some Medicaid agencies if the agency is going to resubmit a claim. Show the resubmission code and the original claim reference number.

Item 23: Prior Authorization Number   Enter the professional review organization (PRO) prior authorization number for those procedures requiring PRO prior approval. Enter the investigational device exemption (IDE) number when an investigational device is used in a Food and Drug Administration (FDA)–approved clinical trial.

For physicians performing care plan oversight services, enter the six-digit Medicare provider number of the home health agency or hospice when CPT code 99375 or 99376 or HCPCS code G0064, G0065, or G0066 is billed.

Enter the 10-digit Clinical Laboratory Improvement Act certification number for laboratory services billed by a physician office laboratory.

CHAMPUS   Attach a copy of the authorization, for example, mental health preauthorization, heart-lung transplant authorization.

Private Plans   If required, enter the preauthorization number.

Item 24a: Dates of Service   Enter either the six-digit (MM\DD\YY) or eight-digit (MM\DD\CC\YY) date for each procedure, service, or supply. When "from" and "to" are shown for a series of identical services, enter the number of days or units in column 24g.

Item 24b: Place of Service   There are variations in the codes used for place of service (POS). The previous HCFA form (1-84) had specific codes printed on the reverse side for use in column 24b. HCFA (12-90) has no such codes printed. Some insurance plans still require the old (1-84) POS codes, and many require the new (12-90) ones.

Medicare   Use the new POS codes. Identify the location, using a place of service code, for each item used or service performed.

Note: When a service is rendered to a hospital inpatient, use the "inpatient hospital" code.

CHAMPUS   Use the new POS codes.

Private Plans   Check with the plan's billing instructions to determine which POS codes are required.

Item 24c: Type of Service   The type of service code is listed here when this is required.

Medicare   Providers are not required to complete this item.

Private Plans   Some plans require the use of type of service codes. Otherwise, leave it blank.

Item 24d: Procedures, Services, Supplies   Enter the five-digit CPT code or the HCPCS level II/III number for the service. Up to three modifiers can be used in the spaces next to the code. The first modifier is added between the solid line and the dotted line on the forms. If three modifiers are necessary, there should be two blank spaces between the second and third in the item to the right of the dotted line.

Medicare   Enter the procedures, services, or supplies, using the HCPCS codes. When applicable, show the HCPCS modifier with any procedure code.

Enter the specific code without a narrative description. However, when reporting an "unlisted procedure code" or an NOC code, include a narrative description in item 19, if a coherent description can be given within the confines of that box. Otherwise, an attachment must be submitted with the claim.

Private Plans   Not all modifiers are accepted. It is best to check with the individual plan to see which modifiers it recognizes.

Item 24e: Diagnosis Code   Enter the diagnosis code reference number as shown in item 21 to relate the date of service and the procedures performed to the appropriate diagnosis.

Medicare   Enter only one reference number per line item. When multiple services are performed, enter the primary reference number for each service: either a 1, a 2, a 3, or a 4. If a situation arises where two or more diagnoses are required for a procedure code (ie, Pap smears), you must reference only one of the diagnoses in item 21.

Item 24f: $Charges   Enter the charges for each listed service.

Item 24g: Days or Units   Enter the number of days or units. This field is most commonly used for multiple visits, units of supplies, anesthesia minutes, or oxygen volume. If only one service is performed, the numeral 1 must be entered.

Some services require that the actual number or quantity provided be clearly indicated on the claim form as units of service (eg, multiple ostomy or urinary supplies, medication dosages, or allergy testing procedures). When multiple services are provided, enter the actual number provided.

For anesthesia services, show the elapsed time in minutes in item 24g. Convert hours into minutes and enter the total minutes required for this procedure.

Item 24h: EPSDT Family Plan

Medicare   Leave blank. Not required by Medicare.

Medicaid   Use a checkmark or X if preventive services were provided under Medicaid.

Item 24i: EMG (Emergency)

Medicare   Leave blank. Not required by Medicare.

CHAMPUS   It is best to mark this block to indicate that the service was provided in a hospital emergency department.

Private Plans   Some plans may require that this item be marked to indicate the service was provided in a hospital emergency department.

Item 24j: COB (Coordination of Benefits)

Medicare   Enter the NPI of the performing provider of service/supplier if he or she is a member of a group practice.

Note: Enter the first two digits of the NPI in item 24j. Enter the remaining six digits of the NPI in item 24k, including the two-digit location identifier.

When several different providers of service or suppliers within a group are billing on the same form HCFA-1500, show the individual NPI in the corresponding line item.

Private Plans   Check this item if the patient is covered by one or more private plans. These plans are identified in items 11 and 11a-d.

Item 24k: Reserved for Local Use

Medicare   Enter the NPI of the performing provider of service/supplier if he or she is a member of a group practice.

Note: Enter the first two digits of the NPI in item 24j. Enter the remaining six digits of the NPI in item 24k, including the two-digit location identifier.

CHAMPUS   Enter the state license number of the provider.

Private Plans   Not required.

Item 25: Federal Tax ID Number   Enter the physician/supplier federal tax ID (employer identification number) or Social Security number.

Medicare   The participating physician or supplier's federal tax ID number is required for a mandated Medigap transfer.

Item 26: Patient's Account No.   Enter the patient's account number that was assigned by the practice's accounting system. This is an optional way to enhance patient identification by the physician. Some private plans, Medicaid, and some Medicare carriers include this information on their EOBs. It is easier to identify the patients and post the payments. As a service, any account numbers entered here will be returned to you.

Item 27: Accept Assignment?

Medicare   Check the appropriate box to indicate whether the physician accepts assignment of benefits. If Medigap is indicated in item 9 and Medigap payment authorization is given in item 13, the physician must also be a Medicare participating physician and must accept assignment of Medicare benefits for all covered charges for all patients.

The following services can be paid only on an assignment basis:

- Clinical diagnostic laboratory services
- Physician services provided to individuals entitled to both Medicare and Medicaid
- Participating physician/supplier services
- Services of physician assistants, nurse practitioners, clinical nurse specialists, nurse midwives, certified registered nurse anesthetists, clinical psychologists, and clinical social workers
- Ambulatory surgical center (ASC) services for covered ASC procedures
- Home dialysis supplies and equipment paid under method II

CHAMPUS   Check "yes" if you accept assignment—check "no" if you do not. Failure to complete this block results in nonacceptance of assignment. "Accept assignment" means that the provider has agreed to be a CHAMPUS participating provider on the claim and will accept the allowable amount as the total amount payable. When a provider accepts assignment, payment will be made to the provider. If the provider does not accept assignment, payment will be made to the patient or sponsor.

Private Plans   Not applicable to plans with which the doctor has a contract.

Item 28: Total Charge   Enter total charges for the services reported on the claim (ie, the total of all charges in item 24f).

Item 29: Amount Paid   Enter the total amount the patient paid on the covered services only.

CHAMPUS   Enter the amount received by the provider or supplier from the other plans or insurances. If the amount includes payment by any other insurance, the other insurance EOB, worksheet, or denial showing the amounts paid or denied must be attached to the CHAMPUS claim. Payment from the beneficiary should not be included.

Item 30: Balance Due   Enter the balance due (item 28 minus item 29).

Medicare   Leave blank—not required by Medicare.

Item 31: Signature of Physician or Supplier Including Degrees or Credentials   Enter the signature of the physician and/or his or her representative and either the six-digit (MM\DD\YY), eight-digit (MM\DD\CC\YY), or alphanumeric (ie, January 1, 1998) date the form was signed.

CHAMPUS   The signature of physician or supplier, including degree(s) or credentials and the date of the signature, is necessary unless other authorized signatures are on file with the contractor.

Item 32: Name and Address of Facility Where Services Were Rendered (If Other Than Home or Office)   Enter the name and address of the facility if services were furnished in a hospital, clinic, laboratory, or facility other than the patient's home or the physician's office.

Medicare   When the name and address of the facility where the services were furnished is the same as the biller's name and address shown in item 33, enter the word SAME. Providers of service (namely, physicians) must identify the supplier's name, address, and NPI when billing for purchased diagnostic tests. When more than one supplier is used, a separate HCFA-1500 should be used to bill each supplier.

This item is completed whether the supplier personnel performed the work at the physician's office or at another location.

If a QB or QU modifier is billed, indicating the service was rendered in a health professional shortage area (HPSA), the physical location where the service was rendered must be entered if other than home. However, if the address shown in item 33 is in an HPSA and is the same as where the services were rendered, enter the word "SAME."

If the supplier is a certified mammography-screening center, enter the six-digit FDA-approved certification number.

Complete this item for all laboratory work performed outside a physician's office. If an independent laboratory is billing, enter the place where the test was performed and the NPI, including the two-digit location identifier.

Item 33: Physician's, Supplier's Billing Name, Address, ZIP Code, and Telephone Number   Enter the physician and/or supplier's billing name, address, ZIP code, and telephone number.

Medicare   Enter the NPI, including the two-digit location identifier, for the performing physician who is not a member of a group practice. Enter the group NPI, including the two-digit location identifier, for the performing physician who is a member of a group practice.

CHAMPUS   Enter the provider number.

Private Plans   Enter the provider number for the plan.

Insurance Claim Processing Cycles

The number of claims generated will depend on the practice's volume of patients seen, type of services provided, and third-party payer mix. Based on the volume of claims, each practice will need to determine its individual "insurance claim billing cycles." Some practices generate claims at the end of each day, while others process claims only once a week. Always keep in mind that the sooner a claim is generated and submitted, the faster the insurance plan is likely to process it.

Filing Primary Insurance Claims

Insurance claims must be filed for patients covered by Medicare, Medicaid, workers' compensation, and almost all managed care plans, as required by law or the plan's contract with the physician. A medical office generally files primary insurance claims for all services provided as a courtesy to the patient.

To generate a claim form for all of the patient accounts that have been flagged to be billed to insurance, the insurance processing manager bills by account number, insurance plan, or patient last name using "from" and "to" data fields to define the range of patients to be billed. The computer system then generates claims one after another for patients meeting the selection criteria.

Once generated, the forms are separated and organized by insurance company name and address. Again, the way the claims are selected will have a great impact on the amount of manual sorting the office staff will need to perform to get the claims mailed out.

Before mailing insurance claims, the office should make sure all forms from the patients required by insurance companies have been completed and mailed. For example, some insurance plans have their own authorization statements that must be signed by the patients and submitted to the insurance companies before the physicians can be paid. If other physicians within HMOs or PPOs referred patients, make sure the appropriate referral forms have been completed and mailed, if applicable. Many managed care plans require primary care physicians to complete physician referral forms when patients are referred to specialists. To be paid, the specialists' offices must attach these forms to their own insurance claims.

Filing Secondary Insurance Claims

Most medical practices also file secondary insurance claims for their patients. Secondary insurance policies generally cover the services or patient responsibilities not covered by primary insurance plans. In almost all cases, these types of policies act as a supplement to Medicare coverage. Medicare supplemental insurance, or a Medigap policy, is a health insurance plan designed specifically to supplement Medicare's benefits by filling in some of the gaps in Medicare coverage. Not all supplemental policies provide the same benefits. Some pay for the Medicare deductible, while most pay the coinsurance amount. Some policies even cover a limited number of services not covered under the Medicare program.

It is crucial for an office to detect when a patient has a supplemental policy. If it does not, the office will often receive payment from Medicare and bill the patient for the coinsurance or deductible. After waiting a period of time, the office finds out the patient has not paid because he or she thought the office was filing the secondary insurance claim. This activity puts a strain on a practice's cash flow and creates older accounts receivable. The new patient information form must include a section that indicates whether a secondary insurance policy is in force. In addition, front desk personnel should be trained always to ask the patient if he or she has a supplemental policy, whether the patient is new or established.

The most important aspect of filing a patient's secondary insurance is timeliness. Because secondary insurance claims are for a relatively small amount of money, many practices do not pay strict attention to filing them. This delays the office's reimbursement and impedes its cash flow. It could also create inefficiencies because the collection personnel will have to spend time collecting a large number of small-balance accounts.

Secondary insurance claims are submitted on the patient's behalf *only after notification is received from the primary insurance company* as to the claim's disposition (ie, payment in full, partial payment, denials, etc). Usually within 30 days from claim receipt, insurance carriers send an EOB along with the payment to explain the way the claim was processed.

An EOB is an accompaniment to the check from the insurance company that indicates the services submitted on the claim and how much of the charged amount for each service was:

- Approved for payment (ie, the allowance or allowable amount)
- Disallowed or contractually adjusted (ie, amount of allowance that is unrecoverable)

- Applied to the patient's annual deductible
- Applied to the patient's copayment responsibilities
- Reduced or denied with explanation of determination
- Applied to other sources, such as "withhold" fees in managed care plans

EOBs provide the practice with essential information about the patient's financial responsibilities and the coordination of benefits between multiple insurance plans. A sample EOB is shown in Exhibit 5.14. While the actual EOB review process and payment posting will be discussed later, we will now finalize how to process secondary insurance claims.

After the primary insurance EOB data have been posted in the transaction entry payment screen, the practice processes all patient accounts with secondary insurance plans that continue to have an outstanding accounts receivable balance due. The billing system generates a claim that indicates the services provided and the amount paid by the other insurance plan. When submitting the secondary claim form, always attach a copy of the patient's EOB from the primary insurance company. The EOB assists the secondary payer in determining the coordination of benefits and ultimate patient responsibility.

Organizing Copies of Insurance Claim Forms

Depending on your billing system or whether your practice uses single-form or two-ply carbonless HCFA-1500 forms, the practice may need to file copies of the claim forms generated. Most practices file copies of unpaid insurance claim forms in a centralized location in the office so that anyone can go to that location and find the unpaid insurance claims. Centralizing the insurance claim forms allows for (a) easy access when performing insurance follow-up procedures, (b) a quick review of the claim forms if such a review is required, and (c) the easy tracking of the unpaid claims to other source documents in the office.

For example, the hard copies of the insurance claims should be tracked to the computer-generated unpaid insurance report to ensure the report's accuracy. The hard copy of the insurance claims can be used to track to the patient's ledger accounts for internal control purposes. In this situation, insurance claim amounts must always agree with the patient's accounts receivable on the account ledger.

One easy way to centralize the unpaid forms is to keep the office copies in an alphabetical or numerical expandable folder until payment is received. For insurance claims that are filed electronically, the electronic claim submission edit report, or a white paper printout of the actual insurance claim forms, should be maintained in the centralized file.

Exhibit 5.14   Explanation of Benefits

Participant Information:

Check #:   0123456789#

Participant: Last, First

SS #:   987-65-4321

Group #:   00000

To assist us in serving you, please include participant information and patient's name when you direct inquiries to:

Claims Office

P.O. Box 00000

Anywhere, USA 00000

Telephone (999) 888-9999

Explanation of Benefits

For services provided by: Iwill Fixit, MD

Patient/ Service	Service Date(s)	(A) Total – Charge	(B) Excluded – Amounts	(C) Not Payable – by Plan	(D) Co-insurance = Amount %		(E) Plan Paid Amount %	
Last, F								
Office visit	02/17/01	56.00	11.00 EM	10.00 CA			35.00	100%
X-ray	02/17/01	268.00		250.00 DD	3.60	20%	14.40	80%
Lab	02/17/01	20.00		15.00 CA			5.00	100%
Totals		**344.00**	**11.00**	**275.00**	**3.60**		**54.40**	

Payments made to:

03/04/01   Iwill Fixit, MD $54.40

Codes and Remarks

EM: This amount represents the discount that resulted from the patient using a preferred provider. The patient is not responsible for this amount.

CA: This is the patient's copayment amount for this charge. The patient is responsible for this amount.

DD: This amount was applied to the patient's deductible.

As practical as this sounds, it may prove impractical for some medical offices. This is especially true for practices that file a large number of claim forms and for offices that file most of their claims electronically. No matter how an office files its claims, an important practice management goal is to make sure all unpaid insurance claim forms are maintained in one centralized location.

Medicare Supplemental Insurance Policy Letters

Supplemental policies are separate health plans from another insurer that serve as a "secondary" source of coverage. Some supplemental insurance plans, referred to as "Medigap plans," are designed to supplement Medicare coinsurance, deductibles, and sometimes noncovered or unpaid services from Medicare. Many Medicare patients have these policies.

Supplemental plans are to be billed after Medicare has made its determination on a claim. In many states, the Medicare carrier will forward a claim to the supplemental carrier on behalf of the patient if the physician is participating with Medicare. This is commonly referred to as crossover claims processing.

In other states, the patient is responsible for filing the claim with the carrier for the supplemental policy. In some cases, the practice submits the claim on behalf of the patient; in other cases, the patient submits the claim.

If your practice does not accept assignment on Medicare claims and the patient has a supplemental policy, the following two sample letters (Exhibits 5.15 and 5.16) can be used to explain what the patient needs to do in each circumstance. Such letters can help to reduce the number of routine insurance calls to your office.

Deductible Letters

Often, patients are not sure whether they have met their annual deductible. The following letter can be used to inform patients about their deductible and the necessary payment they need to make to your practice. A sample letter is shown in Exhibit 5.17.

Handling Bad Debts

For the most part, medical practices grant credit and subsequently collect on accounts receivable. Unfortunately, every business (or practice) has customers (or patients) who will not keep their promise to pay. Proper management of this bad debt enhances the provider's professional practice and relieves financial and personal stress.

Exhibit 5.15   **Sample Letter for Filling a Supplemental Claim When the *Practice* Will File the Claim**

Dear Patient:

Supplemental policies are policies that pay for copayments, deductibles, and sometimes other services and procedures that are not paid by Medicare. They are billed for the part not paid for by your Medicare policy. This second billing may pay the majority, if not all, of the balance due our office after Medicare pays.

Should you have a supplemental insurance policy, we will be happy to submit a claim on your behalf once we receive your Explanation of Medicare Benefits and check. The Explanation of Medicare Benefits is the portion attached to your Medicare reimbursement check.

Any questions you have regarding payment of your claim should be directed to the Medicare office. Their toll-free number is 1-800-_____-_____, or you may call our office and speak with the billing supervisor.

After the supplemental policy has made a determination on the claim, we will notify you if there is a remaining balance due.

Thank you.

Sincerely,

[Name of Office Manager or Physician]

Exhibit 5.16   **Sample Letter for Filling a Supplemental Claim When the *Patient* Will File the Claim**

Dear Patient:

As required by law, we have submitted your Medicare insurance form for services we provided to you recently. In addition, you will find enclosed a completed insurance claim form for your supplemental policy. Upon receiving payment from Medicare, attach the Explanation of Medicare Benefits to the enclosed claim form before mailing it to your insurance carrier for processing.

Please do not send the form to the supplemental insurance company until you have been paid by Medicare and have attached the Explanation of Medicare Benefits to the form. Submitting the enclosed claim form without the Explanation of Medicare Benefits attached will result in a denied or delayed claim.

We are happy to provide our patients with this service. If you have any questions regarding this subject, please do not hesitate to call our office.

Sincerely,

[Name of Office Manager or Physician]

Exhibit 5.17   Sample Deductible Letter

Dear [Patient Name]:

Your insurance company has processed your claim in the amount of $_____ for services we provided to you on _____. A portion of the reimbursement was used to satisfy your annual deductible of $ _____.

This means you are responsible for paying the first $_____ each year before your insurance begins making payments. You need to pay this amount to our office. This is shown on the enclosed Explanation of Medical [Medicare] Benefits stating the reimbursement paid by your insurance carrier to our office.

We appreciate your prompt attention to this bill. For your convenience, a return envelope is enclosed.

Sincerely,

[Name of Office Manager]

Medical practices are very vulnerable to bad debts. Medicine has promoted itself to society as the caretaker and rescuer of the sick. Most physicians seek to please their patients; thus, they will ignore or suppress their collection processes to avoid patient complaint or anger. This "patient pleasing" is supported and promoted by society and within the profession itself. While physicians should not ignore or withhold necessary care from the underprivileged, they should be honest with themselves and their office staff as to how much can be given and yet remain financially viable. Likewise, patients who do have adequate financial resources should be held accountable for their agreed financial responsibility.

Medical practices sometimes enter into financially unhealthy business arrangements with third-party payers that increase bad debt. Physicians often sign contracts without reading them thoroughly or asking for appropriate advice and help. Examples of onerous contract provisions agreed to by physicians are 90-day filing clauses, "hold-harmless clauses" absolving the patient of financial liability in the event of insurance company insolvency, and burdensome "hassle factor" procedures. These contractual requirements can increase bad debts that must be written off by the practice.

Continued undisciplined provision of medical care to bad debt patients has detrimental consequences to the physician, the practice, the patient, and the profession. The physician loses income necessary to maintain professional growth, emotional health, and a balanced lifestyle. The practice loses revenue necessary to maintain professional employees, purchase needed equipment, and meet office expenses. Patients who do not pay can also develop a sense of entitlement that transfers to and disrupts other parts of the doctor-patient relationship. The profession suffers since it maintains higher charges than necessary to support this bad debt. These consequences can build fear, anger, and insecurity in the practice, inhibiting its operations and possibly leading to financial failure or ruin.

There are many reasons patients state that they will not pay their medical bills. Some are:

- Expense of medical care

- The patient's belief that the care rendered was inappropriate or ineffective

- Inaccurate mailing addresses or insurance billing addresses resulting in the bill never being received

- Misunderstanding of the level of reimbursement from third parties

- Personal financial problems

- Personal expectations that medical care should be rendered for free

Bad debts can be identified at any time. Accounts receivable more than 60 days old (or more than two billing cycles) should be considered bad unless a proper reason or communication has occurred. Since the collectibility of an account diminishes over time, past-due accounts should be addressed proactively.

The Collection Effort

The collection effort begins with the development of and adherence to the practice's collection policy. This policy defines to the patient the rules the practice will follow in collecting accounts. It must be written prospectively, agreed to by the providers, communicated to the staff, and implemented consistently for it to be effective. A sample collection policy is shown in Exhibit 5.18.

The best collection effort occurs while the patient is in the office. Many practices are afraid to ask their patients to pay their accounts. However, most patients will make some effort to pay their debt if asked to politely but firmly by the practice's staff. Exhibit 5.19 is a sample overdue letter.

Subsequent telephone calls and collection letters reminding patients of their debts and the practice's financial policy are important. Frequently, the patient will claim to have never received a bill or statement. Returned letters or disconnected telephone service confirm the inaccuracy of billing information within the practice. Excuses or reasons for nonpayment must be considered. In a polite but firm voice, the caller should develop an agreement by which the patient will pay his or her account, then document the agreement in the billing record and in a confirming letter to the patient. Consequences for noncompliance must be communicated to the patient at this time.

Collection efforts must follow all laws, federal, state, and local. For instance, there are "blackout" times when telephone calls cannot be made in most areas. Collection letters should be professionally written and use no abusive language. Failure to comply exposes the practice to lawsuit or ridicule.

The Collection Agency

If continued nonpayment occurs despite internal collection efforts, bad debts should be turned over to a collection agency. They should not be "written off," particularly if payment is still anticipated. A special account or some other subsidiary account of the accounts receivable should control these collections.

Since use of collection agencies has financial and emotional consequences to the patient, each collection account and medical record must be prospectively reviewed by the affected provider. There may be a valid medicolegal reason that the practice opts not to use a collection agency.

Exhibit 5.18   Sample Collection Policy

THE HOMETOWN CLINIC
Hometown, USA

PATIENT FINANCIAL POLICY AND PROCEDURE

Introduction:

The Hometown Clinic is a professional business providing health-related diagnostic and therapeutic services to its patients and clients with the expectation of making the profit needed to financially support its employees and their families, to pay its necessary expenses, and to develop future new services.

A professional relationship requires honest financial accountability. This document states the policy by which Hometown Clinic will hold itself and its patients and clients accountable.

Charges for Professional Services:

Every professional service and associated expense rendered will be charged to the patient according to a fee schedule prospectively determined by the clinic. Contractual discounts to third parties prospectively agreed to by the clinic will be honored in good faith. No fee or charge can be reduced or waived without the permission of only the administrator, billing manager, or his or her designee. An estimate of these fees can be requested prospectively.

A statement of charges will be given to the patient on the day of service or within one week of hospital discharge. Monthly statements of payment transactions and the total amount owed will be sent until the debt is totally satisfied.

Payment:

Payment for services rendered is due on the date of service and is part of the professional relationship. Hometown Clinic reserves the right to request payment of the total negotiated fee on the date due unless directed otherwise by contract. Cash, check, money order, and certain credit cards will be acceptable methods of payment.

All copayments and deductibles will be collected at the time of service. Unless insured patients can provide documentation that the deductible has been met, then payment for services will be based on the deductible having not been met. Unless insured patients can provide documentation of the copayment amount, then 20% of the fee will be due at the time of service.

Nonurgent professional services may be delayed or terminated within the guidelines of good medical practice for bad-faith patient noncompliance with this financial policy. Only the administrator, billing manager, or their designated representative can amend this policy.

Insurance:

Health insurance is primarily a contract between the patient and the insurance company; however, Hometown Clinic also has mutually agreed contractual obligations with certain private and government entities. The patient is primarily responsible for holding the insurance company accountable for claims reimbursement. Hometown Clinic will make available substantial resources to facilitate insurance payment and will dedicate its resources toward its own contractual obligations with these entities.

Credit:

Credit will be extended for 60 days to patients with valid insurance policies applicable to the charges for services after fulfillment of appropriate deductibles and copayments. After 60 days, this credit will be revoked and all payments will be immediately due.

Exhibit 5.18   Concluded

Collection Agencies

The Hometown Clinic will use all reasonable means to collect owed funds. Defaults in payment of agreed amounts will be automatically referred to a collection agency for payment.

Responsibilities of the Patient

The patient is to contact the insurance company and/or other third parties for necessary precertifications needed for insurance or third-party payment prior to the office visit. The patient likewise must familiarize himself or herself with the precertification requirements of the third-party payer for services rendered out of the office. A telephone number on the back of the insurance card can usually be used to obtain this information.

At each office visit or patient encounter, the patient will provide a current mailing address and telephone number as well as current third-party information necessary for billing purposes. This information must be given primarily to a billing representative or receptionist. The doctor or nurse will need to know the identity of the insurance company to make proper referrals under the managed care contract; thus, proper identification is mandatory.

After each office visit or within 1 week of hospital discharge, the patient will speak with a receptionist or billing representative to make payment arrangements for the services rendered.

The patient is to contact his or her insurance company if payment is not made within 60 days.

The patient is to immediately make total payment when the debt is due.

The patient is to proactively prospectively discuss extenuating circumstances with the Clinic.

Responsibilities of the Clinic

The Clinic will provide an accurate statement of charges on the day of office service or within 1 week of hospital discharge.

The Clinic will make a best effort to obtain necessary precertifications for requested procedures required by contracted third parties to facilitate approval for payment thereof. Failure to obtain precertifications or approval from the insurance company does not necessarily mean that the requested procedure is not medically necessary; in this circumstance, the patient may be financially responsible for services ordered or rendered.

Upon receiving accurate third party information, the clinic will file an appropriate AMA-approved claim to the appropriate entity (eg, insurance company, employer, workers' compensation plan). The Clinic will make a good-faith effort in concert with the patient to follow up these claims to facilitate payment.

The Clinic will uniformly and fairly enforce this policy and procedure upon all patients.

I attest that I have read this financial policy and procedure and have been given an opportunity to ask questions. I accept this policy and procedure and will comply with it as part of my professional relationship with the Clinic.

_____   _____

Patient or Responsible Party   Date

_____   _____

Witness   Patient's Name

Exhibit 5.19   Sample Overdue Letter

HOMETOWN CLINIC
111 Main Street
HOMETOWN, STATE 00000

To: Mr. Joe Patient
             121 Main Street
             Hometown, State 00000

Account: 00000

Dear Mr. Patient:

Review of our records shows that you have a seriously overdue account with our clinic of

$ _____. Please remit this balance to us immediately.

If you do not believe this amount is correct, please contact our office by telephone immediately so that this account can be reconciled.

Our collection policy states that if this account is not reconciled within thirty (30) days, we will employ a collection agency to assist in its collection.

Thank you for your prompt attention to this very important matter.

Sincerely,

Suzie B. Manager

Collection agencies are available in most communities. Local medical societies often endorse agencies that meet professional standards. Agencies should be chosen on the basis of their professional service, pricing, and sensitivity to health care issues. Often, practices use more than one agency according to their specific needs.

The Fair Credit Reporting Act

The Fair Credit Reporting Act [FCRA (15 USC §§ 1681-1681(u), *as amended*] is designed to protect the privacy of credit report information and to guarantee that information supplied by consumer reporting agencies (CRAs) is as accurate as possible. The FCRA requires that CRAs adopt reasonable procedures for meeting the needs of commerce for consumer credit, personnel, insurance, and other information in a manner that is fair and equitable to the consumer, with regard to the confidentiality, accuracy, relevancy, and proper utilization of such information. CRAs include many types of databases, eg, medical information services or credit bureaus that collect information to help businesses evaluate consumers. If you report information about consumers to a CRA, you are considered a "furnisher" of information under the FCRA, and the CRA must send you a notice of your responsibilities.

Your responsibilities under FCRA are summarized below. Items 2 and 5 apply only to furnishers who provide information to CRAs "regularly and in the ordinary course of their business." All information providers must comply with the other responsibilities.

1. *General Prohibition on Reporting Inaccurate Information.* You may not furnish information that you know, or consciously avoid knowing, is inaccurate. If you "clearly and conspicuously" provide consumers with an address for dispute notices, you are exempt from this obligation but subject to the duties discussed in item 3. What does "clear and conspicuous" mean? Reasonably easy to read and understand. For example, a notice buried in a mailing is not clear or conspicuous.

2. *Correcting and Updating Information.* If you discover you have supplied one or more CRAs with incomplete or inaccurate information, you must correct it, resubmit to each CRA, and report only the correct information in the future.

3. *Responsibilities After Notice of a Consumer Dispute From a Consumer.* If a consumer writes to the address you specify for disputes to challenge the accuracy of any information you furnished, and if the information is, in fact, inaccurate, you must report only the correct information to CRAs in the

future. If you are a regular furnisher, you also will have to satisfy the duties in item 2. Once a consumer has given notice that he or she disputes information, you may not give that information to any CRA without also telling the CRA that the information is in dispute.

4. ***Responsibilities After Receiving Notice From a Consumer Reporting.*** If a CRA notifies you that a consumer disputes information you provided:

   - You must investigate the dispute and review all relevant information provided by the CRA about the dispute.

   - You must report your findings to the CRA.

   - If your investigation shows the information to be incomplete or inaccurate, you must provide corrected information to all national CRAs that received the information.

   - You should complete these steps within the time period that the FCRA sets out for the CRA to resolve the dispute, normally 30 days after receipt of a dispute notice from the consumer. If the consumer provides additional relevant information during the 30-day period, the CRA has 15 days more. The CRA must give you all relevant information that it gets within 5 business days of receipt, and must promptly give you additional relevant information provided from the consumer. If you do not investigate and respond within the specified time periods, the CRA must delete the disputed information from its files.

5. ***Reporting Voluntary Account Closings.*** You must notify CRAs when consumers voluntarily close credit accounts. This is important because some information users may interpret a closed account as an indicator of bad credit unless it is clearly disclosed that the consumer—not the creditor—closed the account.

6. ***Reporting Delinquencies.*** If you report information about a delinquent account that is placed for collection, charged to profit or loss, or subject to any similar action, you must, within 90 days after you report the information, notify the CRA of the month and the year of the commencement of the delinquency that immediately preceded your action. This will ensure that CRAs use the correct date when computing how long derogatory information can be kept in a consumer's file.

How do you report accounts that you have charged off or placed for collection? For example:

- *A consumer becomes delinquent on March 15, 1998. The creditor places the account for collection on October 1, 1998.*

In this case, the delinquency began on March 15, 1998. The date that the creditor places the account for collection has no significance for calculating how long the account can stay on the consumer's credit report. In this case, the date that must be reported to CRAs within 90 days after you first report the collection action is "March 1998."

- *A consumer falls behind on monthly payments in January 1998, brings the account current in June 1998, pays on time and in full every month through October 1998, and thereafter makes no payments. The creditor charges off the account in December 1999.*

In this case, the most recent delinquency began when the consumer failed to make the payment due in November 1998. The earlier delinquency is irrelevant. The creditor must report the November 1998 date within 90 days of reporting the charge-off. For example, if the creditor charges off the account in December 1999 and reports this charge-off on December 31, 1999, the creditor must provide the month and year of the delinquency (ie, "November 1998") within 90 days of December 31, 1999.

- *A consumer's account becomes delinquent on December 15, 1997. The account is first placed for collection on April 1, 1998. Collection is not successful. The merchant places the account with a second collection agency on June 1, 1998.*

The date of the delinquency for reporting purposes is "December 1997." Repeatedly placing an account for collection does not change the date that the delinquency began.

- *A consumer's credit account becomes delinquent on April 15, 1998. The consumer makes partial payments for the next 5 months but never brings the account current. The merchant places the account for collection in May of 1999.*

Since the account was never brought current during the period that partial payments were made, the delinquency that immediately preceded the collection commenced in April 1998 when the consumer first became delinquent. See www.ftc.gov/ for more details.

Writing Off Bad Debt

Accounts more than 365 days old generally have only about a 10% chance of collection. Each provider and practice must decide what debt it should write off and whether it should continue to render professional service to patients with bad debt. This should follow local community professional standards.

6 After Submission of Claims

Objectives

After completing this chapter, you should be able to:

- Understand third-party reimbursements.

- Interpret EOBs and post payments.

- Improve management of accounts receivable.

- Understand how to handle difficult patient accounts.

Introduction

After claim submission, follow-up is necessary to ensure that the patient's insurance company has made proper payment and that the patient's account was reconciled. Managing patient accounts and receiving appropriate reimbursement for services rendered requires understanding third-party reimbursements, interpreting explanations of benefits (EOBs), posting payments, managing accounts receivable, and handling difficult patient accounts. These "back office" functions of insurance processing challenge even the most experienced physicians and their staff.

The success of most back office functions relies heavily on the success of the front office functions of patient and insurance data collection, information verification, and accurate coding and billing. It can be viewed that the account of a patient properly admitted is already half collected!

Understanding Third-Party Reimbursements

The amount a physician or patient is reimbursed for a service depends in part on the patient's insurance benefits. Traditional insurers often reimburse 80% of "reasonable charges," with the patient paying 20% and possibly more to fully satisfy the physician's charge. Under managed care plans, patients typically will pay fixed copayments of $5 to $20, with the remainder adjudicated by the insurance company. In almost all cases, required deductibles must be met for insurance payments. Should a provider be able to collect charges above the "approved amount," the process is termed "balance billing."

The reasonable charge or approved amount allowed for a service can vary from payer to payer, depending on the payer's reimbursement policy. For example, one payer may use a fee schedule, while another uses the usual, customary, and reasonable (UCR) system. Fees you receive from patients covered by a health maintenance organization (HMO), preferred provider organization (PPO), or independent practice association (IPA) may be based on a contract or on a capitation basis. Medicare has its own separate fee schedule based on the Resource-Based Relative Value Scale.

The following examples illustrate reimbursement of two payers—a commercial carrier and Medicare.

Commercial Payer Examples

1. Dr Smith charges $200 for a specific procedure. The patient's insurance company allows $187 and pays 80% of the allowable, or $149.60. Dr Smith does not have a negotiated contract with this insurance company. The patient has previously met his deductible and would thus be responsible for the difference (the copayment). Payment would be as follows:

Dr Smith's charge	$200.00		
Insurance payment	$149.60		
Patient coinsurance	$ 37.40	Amount due from patient	$50.40
Balance billing	$ 13.00		

   Dr Smith is obligated to collect the full amount of the $200 charge.

2. Dr Jones charges $50 for a service. He does have a discount contract with the insurance company requiring that he accept "reasonable charges." The patient has not met his $250 annual deductible. The payer allows $48 for the service and reimburses on the 80/20 basis. Payment would be as follows:

Dr Jones' charge	$50.00
Insurance payment	$ 0.00
Applied to deductible	$48.00
Contractual allowance	$ 2.00

Because the patient has not met his deductible and Dr Jones is contracted to accept "reasonable charges" as his full fee, the patient owes $48.00 and Dr Jones must "write off" $2.00.

3. Using example 2, if the patient had previously met his deductible, payments would be as follows:

Dr Jones' charge	$50.00
Insurance payment	$38.40
Patient coinsurance	$ 9.60 Patient responsibility is $9.60
Contractual adjustment	$ 2.00

    In this example, the insurance company pays $38.40, the patient pays $9.60, and the physician writes off $2.00.

    Note: The insurance company pays 80% of the allowed amount, or 80% of $48.00.

4. Dr Parsons provides a $100 service to a patient. Dr Parsons has a contract requiring that he accept the UCR amount minus 10% as his full fee. The patient's insurance states that $100 is UCR for this service and reimburses on the 80/20 basis. The patient has met her deductible. Payment would be as follows:

Dr Parsons' charge	$100.00
Approved charge	$ 90.00
Insurance payment	$ 72.00
Patient coinsurance	$ 18.00
Contractual adjustment	$ 10.00

    In this example, the amount allowed by the insurance company is the same as the physician's charge. The insurance company pays $72.00, the patient pays $18.00, and the physician writes off $10.00.

5. Dr Black charges $300.00 for a specific procedure performed in his office. The fee schedule with the insurance company for this procedure is $120.00. The patient's copayments for office visits are $20.00. Payment would be as follows:

Dr Black's charge	$300.00
Insurance payment	$100.00

Patient payment	$20.00
Contractual adjustment	$180.00

Note: Beware of insurance companies that pay discounted amounts without a contractual agreement authorizing the reduced payments. These "silent PPOs" should be challenged and reported to the state insurance commissioner.

Medicare Examples

Because Medicare reimburses on the basis of the Medicare Fee Schedule (MFS), charges and limits on charges are fixed. Physicians who participate in the Medicare program always accept assignment and agree to accept the MFS amounts for participating physicians minus deductibles and copayments as payment in full.

Nonparticipating physicians' MFS-allowed amounts are set at an amount 5% lower than those provided to participating physicians. If the nonparticipating physician does not accept assignment on a claim, the total charge is limited to 115% of Medicare's participating allowed amount. Fee schedules for participating and nonparticipating physicians, including limiting charges, are published annually and are available from the local carrier. If you have not yet obtained your fee schedule from Medicare, contact your Medicare carrier.

Patients covered by Medicare are responsible to meet an annual outpatient deductible of $100, after which Medicare pays 80% of the allowed fee schedule amount, and the beneficiary is responsible for the remaining 20%. Providers must contractually adjust or write off any amount above the approved charge. No balance billing above the approved charge is permitted.

1. Dr Jones is *participating* with Medicare. She bills $125 for a service provided to a Medicare patient. The patient has previously met her deductible, and the MFS amount for the service is $100. Payment would be as follows:

Dr Jones' charge	$125.00
Medicare payment	$ 80.00
Patient coinsurance	$ 20.00
Amount of write-off	$ 25.00

   Note: Dr Jones can collect a maximum of $100 between the patient and Medicare, as $100 is the MFS amount. The difference, $25, would be written off of Dr Jones' receivables as a contractual adjustment. Also note that participating physicians are allowed to charge more than the fee schedule amount even though they may only collect the amount specified by the fee schedule.

2. Dr Smith does *not participate* with Medicare, but is *accepting assignment* on this patient's claim. Although Dr Smith normally charges $325 to commercial carriers for the service provided to the patient, the MFS limiting charge amount that applies to nonparticipating physicians for the service is $267.65. Thus, Dr Smith can collect no more than $267.65 from the Medicare benefi-ciary. The patient has already met his Medicare deductible for the year. Payment would be as follows:

Dr Smith's charge	$267.65
Medicare's payment	$214.12
Patient coinsurance	$ 53.53
Remainder	$ 0.00

3. Dr Parsons is *not participating* with Medicare and *does not accept assignment* on a patient's claim. The patient has met her annual deductible. Dr Parsons must restrict his charge for the service to the limiting charge amount pro-vided on the MFS, $67.43. Medicare will allow for the service an amount equal to that given a nonparticipating physician who accepts assignment, or $58.63. Payments would be as follows:

Dr Parsons' charge	$67.43
Medicare's payment	$46.91
Patient coinsurance	$20.52
Remainder	$ 0.00

Medicare will pay 80% of the allowed MFS amount. In this example, the patient is responsible for the difference between Dr Parsons' charge and the amount of the Medicare payment. It is important to recall that Dr Parsons had to limit his charge to $67.43—the MFS amount that a nonparticipating physician is allowed to charge for the service when not accepting assignment.

Interpreting EOB and Payment Posting

When payments are received in your office either from insurance plans or from patients, they must be posted to the patient's account. Insurance payments received through the mail or electronically are typically accompanied by an

EOB. Payments from patients are received through the mail and at the time of their office visits. Payment posting is typically done on a computerized billing system or on the individual patient ledger cards if a pegboard system is used. A tracking system of accounts receivable (payments, contractual adjustments, write-offs), as well as carrier denials, needs to be maintained in order to monitor reimbursement patterns and trends.

Preposting Operations

Before posting an insurance payment to the patient's account, your practice should perform and document the following actions:

1. Compare the EOB with the original insurance claim, and review each carefully. All services reported on the claim form should be represented on the EOB. (*Note*: some insurance EOBs list services by line item, while others provide a single line-item determination for all services.) Look for changes in CPT coding by the insurance company (for example, determine if a service was down-coded). The goal is to identify charges that can be appealed or rebilled for payment.

2. Investigate all denied services, determine the reason for the service denial, and appeal them, if appropriate. (Denials are usually indicated with zeros in the allowed amount or amount paid data field on the EOBs.)

3. Appeal all payment reductions based on the insurance's UCR charge amount. Insurance companies utilize regional charge databases to inform a physician when the charge submitted exceeds the UCR norm. Unfortunately, the UCR data are often payer-specific, meaning that they are not the same for all insurers. Each insurance company has its own UCR. The insurer will send a UCR letter explaining why the insurance company reduced the physician's fee and why the company feels it is too high for the practice area. Do not bill at each insurance UCR. Uniform billing should be done for each service to all payers.

4. A payers request for additional information that appears on the EOB must be addressed immediately. The goal is to get paid as quickly as possible by the insurance company. Each insurer also has a time limit on claim rectification.

5. Trend denied services; look for billing errors that should be corrected.

The information contained on the EOB should be posted on the computer or manual patient ledger card promptly and carefully on receipt. An error in the posting process may cause the patient's account balance to be incorrect.

Tracking EOBs by carrier will help to monitor similar payments for similar procedures and diagnoses.

Contractual Adjustments

After the EOB has been carefully reviewed, the insurance payment should be posted to the patient's account. On the patient's account balance record, the office must account for the difference between the charge submitted on the claim and the amount allowed contractually, always specifically identifying in the patient record the type of adjustment made (for example, Medicaid, HMO or PPO, or a UCR reduction).

These types of adjustments generally are called *contractual adjustments*. A contractual adjustment is the difference between what a practice bills and what it is legally entitled to collect. For example, if a physician's normal fee were $1200 and he or she signs with a PPO that has a contractual reimbursement of only $1000 for the same service, the contractual adjustment would be $200. It is important to ensure that contractual adjustments shown on the EOB are in accordance with the contract. It is not uncommon to see contractual discounts taken in error by payers for which the physician has approved no previous discount agreement.

Note: Never let your practice lump all adjustments into an account called *credit adjustments*. Specifically identifying contractual adjustments and other write-offs is necessary to allow for analysis of trends and to more easily identify problems.

Specific identification of contractual adjustments by payer alerts a practice to which insurance programs are reducing charges the most. If the practice is writing off a large amount for a specific plan, the office should investigate and assess whether it makes sense to continue with the specific insurance plan. At the same time, the practice should determine if such write-offs are reasonable and, if so, whether they can be reduced. Specifically identifying write-offs is also a smart way to account for withholding adjustments made by managed care plans.

Withhold Adjustments

A withhold is an amount withheld from a physician's reimbursement that may or may not be reimbursed depending on the managed care plan's criteria for reimbursement. For example, if a physician's normal charge for a procedure is $1000 and he or she signs a managed care contract that will only reimburse $800 for the same procedure, the managed care plan will approve $800 for payment and may subtract another 10% as a withhold adjustment. Therefore, the practice receives a check for $720 instead of $800. The $80 withheld should be accounted for separately in your office's computer or by means of other documentation if the practice is on a manual system.

At the end of the year, the practice should review how much was withheld by each managed care plan and then appeal for reimbursement of the withhold. If a plan will not reimburse the withhold, the office should have a representative of the plan explain the plan's withhold policy. It is preferable to have written criteria that describe the withhold and indications for withhold at the beginning of the contractual period. Reconfirm that there is no change at the anniversary of each contract period. If a particular plan will not reimburse the withhold, the practice must know that the true discounted amount is not actually the approved amount but is also reduced by the plan withhold. An office should never write off the withhold amounts or any claim that has been denied by an insurance company until the issue has been fully investigated by the office manager.

Fractional Payment of the Allowed Charge

After taking into account contractual adjustments and other reductions, an insurance plan usually pays only a fraction of the allowed charge. Medicare, for example, pays 80% of the allowed amount. Some indemnity plans pay 90%. Your office should post the amount paid by the insurance plan to the patient's account in the computer or on a manual ledger account card. The balance of the account is the responsibility of the patient. The patient portion should be identified in their contract. It is important to know the patient responsibility before care is rendered.

If the balance is not paid, it should be billed in the next round of monthly statements. Therefore, your office needs to pay strict attention to the amount the patient is responsible for when posting insurance payments. This amount should be identified clearly when payment and contractual adjustments are posted in the computer or on the patient's manual ledger account card. If errors are made during the posting process, the aging of accounts will be unreliable. Also, when patients' statements are mailed, they may contain incorrect balances due, which is practically guaranteed to upset patients. In most cases, the patients' insurance plans will also send them their own copies of the EOB for the patients' records.

Filing the EOB

After the EOBs are posted, they should be filed with the respective copies of the insurance claim forms either in the patient's clinical file or in a separate business file set up for each patient. Some offices find it more efficient to maintain the EOBs in notebooks referenced by the insurance company. It is important for an office to keep the insurance claim forms and related EOBs together so that it can easily audit a patient's account history when such a need arises. In addition, a copy of the EOBs should be organized in a way that will allow the office manager or billing supervisor to review them for consistency in payment on a periodic basis.

7 Insurance Accounts Receivable Management

Objectives

After completing this chapter, you should be able to:

- Understand what is important for accurate accounts receivable report preparation.

- Recognize the use of the different types of accounts receivable follow-up letters to include:

  - Letter for claim inquiry on assigned claim

  - Letter for claim inquiry on unassigned claim

  - Letter to insurance commissioner

Introduction

While coding and billing are important to initiate the reimbursement process, tracking the amounts due your practice and payments received is critical to ensuring proper reimbursement. While verifying insurance information, determine if the deductible is met. Processing may be delayed in order to get other providers' (hospital) charges to apply to the deductible first. Having the ability to determine and separate accounts receivable (A/R) responsibility (ie, insurance and patient) will also help improve your practice's cash flow and overall A/R reduction.

Keeping in mind that the goal of the A/R process is to collect the greatest amount from the insurance plan and patient in the shortest time period. To efficiently manage the accounts receivable process, practices need to:

- Develop a systematic process that defines all A/R collection activities by priority parameters and defined policies and procedures that can be implemented to resolve balances due.

- Design A/R management reports using priority parameters for sorting reports, and provide relevant information for completing A/R tasks on the basis of staff member responsibility.

More simply put, reports must be defined so that the practice will receive the greatest benefit from their use in day-to-day A/R activities.

A/R Report Preparation

Most computer billing systems provide practices with powerful A/R reporting capabilities, giving the practice the ability to generate A/R reports based on different selection criteria such as account numbers, patient name, aging of accounts (30, 60, or 90 days), account or insurance type, and balance due amounts.

Unfortunately, some physician office staffs often underutilize the power of the reports themselves, making the follow-up and collections process even more difficult to manage. Either patient account number or patient last name, instead of a more effective priority parameter, sorts many practice A/R reports. Priority parameters represent the different categories or data fields available that can serve as the primary A/R sort specification.

Protocols should be determined for printing aging reports, and responsibilities should be assigned to appropriate staff members. Protocols for follow-up letters and collection agency referrals should also be established.

Instead of printing A/R reports by patient account number or name, practices should consider prioritizing accounts on the basis of a combination of the following:

- Balance due (highest to lowest)
- Aging of account
- Account type, payer type, or insurance plan
- Financial responsibility (insurance vs patient)
- Date of claim submission or date of service

The reasons for prioritizing accounts are quite important. First, all practices have limited staff and practice management resources; thus, the costs and benefits of all A/R activities must be considered. By focusing on the accounts with the highest outstanding balances as soon as possible, any problems with the claim can be identified and resolved through rebilling, thereby yielding a greater overall recovery. For example, some practices prioritize accounts in this way:

1. Greater than $3000

2. $2000 to $2999

3. $1000 to $1999

4. $500 to $999

5. $100 to $499

6. $50 to $99

7. $10 to $49

Second, the longer an account remains in A/R, the probability of collecting the full amount falls dramatically. According to industry collection studies, the collection recovery rate percentage by account aging is estimated as shown in Table 7.1.

Table 7.1   **Collection Recovery Percentages**

Current	60 days	90 days	180 days	220 days	Over 1 year
100%	90%	50%	30%	19%	11%

By sorting the A/R reports by account aging "buckets" (ie, 30, 60, 90, 120, etc), the practice can focus on the account with the most outstanding days in aging. Some practices print separate A/R reports by aging category, such as those accounts for more than 120 days, or from the "oldest" to "youngest" aging bucket.

Third, A/R problems are frequently based on similar circumstances caused by the type of account. For example, if the practice billed a wrong CPT code to Medicare for all patients, all beneficiary accounts affected will have A/R problems. So, to efficiently follow up with A/R problems and to follow up with as many similar account types as possible when communicating with a certain insurance type, the staff may want to organize the accounts into similar categories, account types, payer types, or specific insurance plans.

Fourth, identifying the reason for the A/R problem(s) may become more difficult because the practice cannot separate the patient responsibility from the insurance responsibility. This often occurs because insurance verification was not performed before services were rendered. If your A/R system can track and separate out insurance and patient responsibility by A/R report, seriously consider this option.

Fifth, A/R reports and staff's A/R activities can be enhanced by simply resorting the way the A/R reports are printed, using the criteria listed above.

Most A/R report formats can be reprogrammed by either the office staff or software technical support group, to facilitate the practice's desire to recover more A/R. Large A/R balances may result in the need to borrow money to cover a cash flow deficit. The "time value" of money (how much it actually costs the practice) can be calculated by multiplying the amount owed by the days owed divided by 365, multiplied by the interest rate of a money market account. For example, if $100.00 is owed for 120 days at a interest rate of 3% annually, the amount you have lost, if collected today, is:

$$\$100 \times \frac{120}{365} \times 0.03 = \$0.99 \text{ or } 1\% \text{ of the total amount of the bill.}$$

If a practice grosses $300,000 annually, that is a giveaway of about $3000 annually.

Follow-up of Unpaid Insurance Claims

The following general system can be used to collect on unpaid insurance claims.

Identifying Unpaid Claims

At least once a week the office should identify unpaid insurance claims that are at least 25 days old. The reason for starting at 25 days is that the office must find out as soon as possible whether claim forms were received by the insurance companies and entered into their computers. A chronic problem for many offices is that insurance companies will say they have no record of receiving claims.

By starting at 25 days, the office can refile claims early. Also, the sooner you start the follow-up process, the more quickly claims will be paid on balance. *A major goal of every medical practice is to obtain payment consistently within 30 to 45 days for all insurance claim forms filed.* Many insurance contracts also require that claims be filed within 90 days; thus, starting early prevents nonpayment for this reason.

This is where the revised A/R report will help. Practices may also want to use the copy of the claims, which should have a centralized location, usually an alphabetized expandable file, for unpaid claims. Some offices may keep the office copies in patients' charts. Unless the office has access to a list of the unpaid claims, however, keeping the forms in the charts will often create inefficiencies. This is because the collection personnel will have to pull charts in order to follow up on accounts and will not know at any one time which claims are 25 days old.

Telephone Calls

For each claim at least 25 days old, the office should make an inquiry to each insurance company. Some insurance companies, including Medicare, have automated response units that facilitate the process. This inquiry must always be documented in the billing record. The name of the contact at the insurance company, the reason the claim has not been paid, and the date payment can be expected should be documented. If made on paper, the documentation should be attached to each office copy of the unpaid claim until payment is received. If the office files a large number of claims electronically, the forms can be attached to the computer edit report that lists the electronically filed claims.

Whether telephone calls should be made to every insurance company that has billings more than 25 days old depends on how many claims are filed each week, how large the balances are, and the capabilities of the office's collection personnel. The goal of any office should be to try to make the phone calls.

"Tracer" Claims

If calls cannot be made or if communications with the insurance company fail, practices may want to use the tracer method. Tracer claims are a copy of the original claim form with the word "TRACER" stamped on it. (Do not stamp in red, as the red will not be seen when microfilming. Blue, purple, green, etc, are okay.) The date of the tracer should also be written on the claim. These claims are then refiled with the respective insurance companies. A tracer designation indicates to most insurance companies that the office is inquiring about the status of an unpaid claim.

Refiling Claims—Rebilling

Depending on the follow-up call, the office should refile claims (via facsimile, if possible) or do whatever is necessary to get claims paid as quickly as possible. The practice's staff member who makes the calls must document whom he or she talked to at the insurance companies. That way, the employee will have names of people to call back if the claims continue to be delinquent. Duplicate billing is a concern of the OIG. When resubmitting an unpaid claim, be sure to write: "This is not a duplicate bill. We have not been paid on the original claim submitted."

Insurance A/R Process Overview

As a summary of the insurance A/R process, the following steps may be taken to follow up with previously submitted claims:

1. Contact the insurance company by telephone (claims submitted at least 25 days ago).

2. Send tracer claim or claim inquiry letter to insurance company (assigned or unassigned).

3. After 40 days, contact the patient to inform him or her of problems and enlist his or her assistance.

4. Make second telephone contact to insurance company (claims submitted at least 50 days ago).

5. Patient becomes financially responsible for charges at 60 days. Some contracts will not allow patient to be billed. When billing the patient after 60 days, inform him or her of what and with whom contact has been made with the insurer.

6. Request a review and insurance appeal with documentation.

Sample Insurance A/R Follow-up Letters

Occasionally, insurance companies are slow to pay a claim. In these situations, you may want to consider inquiring about the status of the claim. For assigned claims, the practice may send a letter, similar to the sample letter shown in Exhibit 7.1.

In cases where an unassigned claim has been filed, the patient must make an inquiry to the insurance company. A letter from the patient to the slow-paying insurance company may help speed payment to the patient, which will in turn speed payment to your office. You may want to provide a letter, similar to the one shown in Exhibit 7.2, to the patient to send to the insurance company.

Appeals to the Insurance Commissioner

When all reasonable efforts to collect from an insurance company have failed, a formal complaint may be filed with one's state department of insurance. Each state has its own laws and protocols to follow; thus, inquiry should be made prior to the complaint. *Some states require the patient to file the complaint, whereas others allow the physician or both to file.* See Exhibit 7.3 for a sample letter to the insurance commissioner.

**Exhibit 7.1   Sample Letter for Claim Inquiry
on *Assigned* Claim**

Physician or Group Name

Address

Phone

Applicable Identification Number(s)

Insurance Carrier

Claims Processing Department

Address

RE: Patient's Name

        Policyholder's Name

        Policy Number

        Patient's Identification Number

Dear Sir or Madam:

On [date], a claim was filed on behalf of the patient named above. To date, no payment has been received for this claim. We are requesting information regarding the following:

☐   Please verify amount of payment made to patient.

☐   Please review reimbursement due to under/overpayment of $_____ .
       Other: _____

Insurance Company Reply:

☐   Payment was made to patient in the amount of $_____ on _____ .
       Correct reimbursement should be $_____ .

☐   Payment was made to your office on _____ for $_____ .

☐   Other:

_____   _____   _____

Signature   Title   Date

Exhibit 7.2 **Sample Letter for Claim Inquiry on *Unassigned* Claim**

Patient's Name
Address
Phone Number

Insurance Company Name
Address

Attention: Supervisor of Claims Department

RE: Patient's Name
        Policyholder's Name
        Policy Number
        Patient's Identification Number

Dear Sir or Madam:

On [date] Dr [physician's name] of [include group or practice name, address, and applicable identification number], who is my physician, submitted an insurance claim for me in the amount of $_____ for my medical treatment. _____ weeks have passed and payment has not been received by me or my physician. Please check your records and contact me or Dr [physician's name] office immediately regarding this claim. I am anxious to settle this matter.

Yours truly,

Patient's Name

Exhibit 7.3   Sample Letter to the Insurance Commissioner

Date

State Insurance Commissioner
Address
City, State, Zip Code

Dear Insurance Commissioner:

My physician filed the attached insurance claim form over thirty (30) days ago. Even after repeated attempts by my physician's office to contact the insurance company regarding the payment status of this claim, to this date my insurance company has not paid this claim and has provided no explanation to my physician for its nonpayment.

Please accept this letter as a formal written complaint against the insurance company. Your prompt attention to this matter would be greatly appreciated.

I am providing the insurance company and my physician with a copy of this notice.

Sincerely,

[Patient's Name]

pc: Practice Name
    Address

 # Requests for Review and Appeals

Objectives

After completing this chapter, you should be able to:

● **Understand the purpose of appeals to insurance companies.**

● **Understand the process of requesting a Medicare review.**

● **Recognize the use of a letter to request a review.**

Appeals to Insurance Companies

It is essential that a medical practice's appeals to insurance companies be handled correctly. For Medicare and Medicaid plans, the carriers in each state have a specific methodology for appealing insurance claims. For other insurance carriers, appeals should be submitted in writing. Your appeal letter should state clearly why the charge should be allowed and the medical necessity, if applicable. Attach documents that support your claim.

Periodically review a sample of your appeal letters to see how often and how quickly your office is paid after your appeals are filed. If reimbursements have taken a long time, the cause could be a poorly drafted appeal letter or your failure to include supporting documents. Never send an appeal letter that simply asks for a review of the denied or reduced charge. The letter must explain to the insurance company why the amount should be paid. Otherwise, the insurance company will assume it was correct in the first place in denying or reducing the charge. A letter asking only for a review is a waste of time; it will not result in a paid claim.

Requests for Review

Medicare has a formal administrative appeals process in which physicians and patients may challenge the determination of a claim. Most other insurance companies also allow for a review. Requesting a review is a simple process and very often results in a more favorable determination on a claim.

Some reasons why you may want to request a review are:

- The services were denied

- The services were down-coded to a lower level and paid at the lower level

- The allowed amount seems unreasonable or too low

- Other reasons, as appropriate

To request a review, a letter needs to be sent to the carrier or insurance payer requesting a review. Your letter should identify the claim to be reviewed, and it should clearly state your reasons why you feel the determination should be changed. Include supporting documents you feel will help the reviewer see why the determination should be changed. Include information or explanations that were not included with the claim the first time it was submitted. This will help the reviewer see more clearly why the determination was incorrect the first time.

Medicare Part B Appeal Rights

If you are dissatisfied with the carrier's initial determination and the determination is subject to appeal, a review may be requested.

A review is an independent reexamination of the entire claim. This is the first level of appeal following a denial. Because a review does not require the presence of oral testimony, it is a less costly procedure and a more expeditious device for handling complaints.

If a provider requests the review, only the contested services will be considered, not the entire claim.

The request for a review must be made within 6 months of the initial determination as indicated on the explanation of Medicare benefits (EOMB). You may receive an extension to the 6-month filing requirement if good cause is shown. The following are examples of good cause:

- Circumstances beyond your control, including mental or physical impairment, or communication difficulty

- Death of an individual or advanced age (advanced age is met automatically if the individual is 75 before the date services under dispute began)

- Incorrect or incomplete information about the subject claim furnished by official sources (Health Care Financing Administration [HCFA], intermediary, or Social Security office) to the individual

- Delay resulting from efforts to secure supporting evidence, where the individual did not realize that the evidence could be submitted after filing a request

- Unusual or unavoidable circumstances that demonstrate that the individual could not reasonably be expected to have been aware of the need to file on a timely basis

- When destruction or other damage of the individual's records was responsible for the delay in filing

As a provider of services to Medicare beneficiaries, you may appeal (request a review of) an initial claim determination if you:

- Accepted assignment on the claim; or

- Did not accept assignment on the claim, the claim was denied as not reasonable and necessary, and no waiver of liability was obtained from the beneficiary, thus requiring you to return to the beneficiary any money you had collected for that service; or

- Are a nonparticipating physician, practitioner, or supplier taking assignment for a specific service; or

- Are acting as the duly authorized representative of the beneficiary.

Before a review is requested, the EOMB should be checked to determine (1) if the allowed amount shown for that procedure is the proper allowance for that service and (2) if rebundling and/or global surgery edits have been correctly applied. *The appeals process cannot resolve complaints with the Medicare Fee Schedule or with national policy decisions.* Appeals should be filed only on those claims in which you feel an error has been made or extenuating circumstances were overlooked.

A request for an explanation of the denial is not sufficient to open the review process. The request must be in writing and should include:

- Name
- Provider number
- Fiscal year of appeal
- Name of carrier
- Identification of the issue in dispute
- A copy of the denial and request for adjustment if applicable. Facsimile transmissions are not acceptable. Be sure to state that a review is requested.

If you remain dissatisfied after the review determination, and the amount in controversy is at least $100, a "fair hearing" may be requested.

The purpose of the hearing process is to give you an opportunity to present the reason for your dissatisfaction and receive a new determination based on the information developed at the hearing level. The individual requesting a hearing has the right to be represented by a qualified individual of choice. Claims may be added together to meet the $100 requirement.

There are two types of hearings.

1. *In-Person Hearing.* This is the traditional type of hearing in which you (or your representative) is offered the opportunity to present both oral testimony and written evidence to support your complaint. You will also be given the chance to dispute the information used to deny the claim.

2. *Telephone Hearing.* Telephone hearings are more convenient and less costly than in-person hearings. The same opportunities exist for stating your position. You do not have to travel to the hearing site. You may call in from any location.

Another option exists for those who wish to dispute the findings of the review, but who do not wish to present an oral argument. This option is called an on-the-record (OTR) decision. OTR decisions are the same as the above options without the oral testimony. The decision is based on the facts that are in the file, including any information that has been presented to the hearing officer (HO). These hearings may be used to determine issues concerning Part B only. Part A issues must be resolved by HCFA.

Examples of some issues that cannot be determined at the hearing are:

- Entitlement to coverage

- The qualification of an independent laboratory or portable x-ray supplier to meet coverage conditions

- Issues related to hospital insurance benefits under Part A.

The HO must handle a request for a hearing in one of the following ways:

- Dismiss the request

- Remand the claim for payment

- Accept a withdrawal of the complaint by the claimant or representative

- Transfer the request for the hearing if out-of-area jurisdiction applies

- Transfer to the appropriate party if the issues are outside of the HO's responsibility

Requests for fair hearings must be filed in writing and signed by you or your representative. The request must be filed within 6 months of the date of the review determination. You must specify the desire to appeal the matter further. These requests should be addressed to the attention of the Hearing Department, with indication of the type of hearing preferred.

If your request for a hearing has not been acknowledged in writing within 3 weeks, a second request should be sent. The regulations require that the carrier acknowledge receipt of hearing requests within 10 days. If you do not receive a timely acknowledgment, the carrier may not have received your request.

(If your request for a hearing is not acted upon within 60 calendar days from the day it is received, you have the right to a hearing regardless of the amount in controversy.)

The parties to the hearing are any person(s) who was a proper party to the review and any other person(s) whose rights to benefits may be prejudiced by the hearing decision. This includes members of the beneficiary's immediate family or the executor or heirs of a decedent's estate.

Waiver of Right to Appear

If you decide to waive your right to appear at the hearing either in person or by telephone, the HO will make a decision based on the record. The waiver must be in writing and may be withdrawn at any time prior to the rendering of a decision.

Disability or Death of Party

If a party cannot execute his or her request because of a mental or physical condition, the chosen representative may represent the deceased or disabled party. A physician cannot represent a deceased patient without written permission from a legal representative of the beneficiary's estate.

The hearing officer should render his or her decision no later than 30 days after the hearing. A copy of the decision indicating the results of the hearing will be mailed to the last known address of each party and authorized representative.

Administrative Law Judge Appeals

If the determination made by the hearing officer remains unsatisfactory and the amount in controversy is at least $100 for home health claims and $500 for all other Part B claims, you may request a hearing before an administrative law judge (ALJ) of the Social Security Administration.

An ALJ is a hearing official assigned to the Office of Hearings and Appeals. The ALJ conducts evidentiary hearings on appeals from Medicare Part A and B determinations. The ALJ hearing is a quasi-judicial administrative hearing conducted by a federal ALJ. It results in a new decision by an independent reviewer.

Claims may be added together to satisfy the $500 requirement. The request must be in writing and filed within 60 days of the date of the carrier's fair hearing decision of record.

Appeals Council

If the decision of the ADL is still unsatisfactory and the amount in controversy is at least $1000, an appeal may be made to the Appeals Council. The Appeals Council can decide to turn down a case, or it can decide to take up a case on its own. This is the highest level of administrative review before judicial review is initiated.

For individual claims submitted by providers, physicians, and others who furnish items and services to Medicare beneficiaries, the responsibility for gathering and submitting documentation that supports claims and appeals rests with the provider. Consultants may offer guidance and assistance as necessary, but the responsibility for identifying what is needed and where it is located falls to the practice or provider. Be specific in stating the reason for the appeal and send any supporting documentation.

Table 8.1 shows the number of cases sent for appeal in 1997. It also indicates the number of cases completed, and the percentage of cases that were decided in the appellant's favor. For instance, on the initial hearing level for physician appeals, 3,868,160 cases were received; 3,337,592 cases were completed and 70% of those cases were decided in the appellant's favor.

Table 8.1   **Appeals Statistics for Fiscal Year 1997**

Part B appeals for services for hospital outpatient and home health:

	Received Cases	Completed Cases	Appellant Won
Contractors	152,521	160,082	44%
Hearing officers	20,514	14,988	40%
ALJ	3,120	1,321	59%

Part B appeals for services related to physician and other services:

	Received Cases	Completed Cases	Appellant Won
Contractors	3,868,160	3,337,592	70%
Hearing officers	86,746	86,898	45%
ALJ	8,412	4,701	51%

Source: Michael Hash, Deputy Administrator, HCFA, before the Subcommittee on Health, House Committee on Ways and Means, April 23, 1998.

As you can see, it is to the provider's advantage to challenge denials not prohibited from appeal when merited. Denials typically come from computer edits and claims processors. Computer edits do not always allow for modifiers or different diagnoses for different procedures, or other modifying factors, thus causing claims to be denied in error. Claims processors may lack experience or make errors in keystrokes during data entry, causing a denial to be generated.

Below is a list of documentation sources that have proven useful as support for providers during the appeal process.

- X-ray reports
- Test results
- Medical history
- Documentation of severity or acute onset
- Consultation reports
- Billing forms
- Referrals
- Plan of treatment
- Nurses' notes
- Ambulance trip sheets
- Operative reports
- Hospital progress notes
- Copies of communications between physician and/or beneficiary, hospital, carrier, laboratory, etc

A sample letter that you may use to request a review is shown in Exhibit 8.1.

Exhibit 8.1   Sample Letter to Request a Review

Insurance Company Name
Review Appeals Department
Address

RE: Patient's Name
     Policyholder's Name
     Contract or Policy Number
     Claim Number
     Submission Date

Dear Madam or Sir:

We are requesting a review of the above-identified claim on behalf of your beneficiary. A signed authorization for release of information is enclosed, allowing you to correspond directly with our office regarding this claim.

In reviewing this claim, please consider the following facts and circumstances:

1.

2.

3.

4.

5.

(Etc)

The enclosed [consultation, laboratory, operative, etc] report(s) support our position. We appreciate your prompt attention to this review.

Sincerely,

[Name of Physician]
[Identification Number(s)]

9 Compliance Programs and the Office of Inspector General

Objectives

After completing this chapter, you should be able to:

- Understand the history of compliance programs
- Understand why compliance programs are important for health care providers
- Understand the seven core elements of an effective compliance program

Introduction

This chapter focuses on compliance programs—a concept virtually unheard of before the passage on August 21, 1996, of the Health Insurance Portability and Accountability Act of 1996 (commonly called "HIPAA"), Public Law 104-191. This law launched a new effort by the federal government, joined in part by the individual states, to eliminate fraud, abuse, and waste in the United States health care system.

The Office of Inspector General (OIG) and the Department of Health and Human Services (HHS) routinely report to Congress their findings on fraud and abuse. Exhibit 9.1 shows the estimated improper payments by type of error for Medicare. Note that physician documentation controls the two largest causes: lack of medical necessity and unsupported charges. Since the inception of compliance programs, their direct value to health care providers has been the subject of myriad trade journal articles, seminars, and speeches. With the issuance to date of nine "model" compliance plans by the OIG of the HHS covering providers from large hospital systems to small physician groups, it would be impossible to be ignorant of the government's strong encouragement that all health care providers establish compliance programs.

Nevertheless, many physicians and other providers continue without them, perhaps in the belief that the costs of such programs outweigh their advantages, or that they themselves are honest and will not be the object of a government investigation. This chapter reviews the history and reasoning behind the

Exhibit 9.1   Estimated Improper Payments by Type of Error

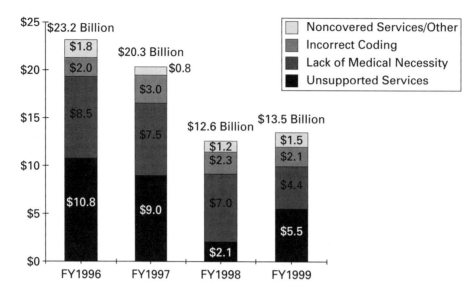

Courtesy: Healthcare Management Advisors, 2000.

concept of compliance programs, the seven core elements that must be included for a program to be effective (and thus worthwhile to the provider), the role of the compliance officer, and the risks to providers for failure to implement a compliance program *before* they become the target of a government investigation or whistle-blower suit under the False Claims Act. See Table 9.1 for a summary of *qui tam* or whistle-blower cases.

Table 9.1   Qui Tam Explosion Since 1987

- 33 cases in 1987 vs 486 cases in 1999
- $3.5 billion recovered since 1987
    - Department of Justice intervened in $3.3 billion
- Better chance of success in "private" actions
- $500 million paid out to whistle-blowers
- Several billion dollar sized cases are reported to be in the works

Courtesy: Healthcare Management Advisors, 2000.

The Goldilocks Quality of Care Standard

One of the most difficult compliance issues facing physicians and health care providers involves the quality of patient care. Failure to provide adequate diagnoses and treatments can result in charges of substandard care. However, providing tests or services not generally accepted by certain health care standards may result in charges that the physician is providing medically unnecessary services. This has resulted in what Healthcare Management Advisors calls the Goldilocks quality of care standard (see Exhibit 9.2). With fee-based payers alleging medically unnecessary services and capitated payers alleging substandard care, the "range of reasonableness" is being squeezed. Only those physicians providing not too much and not too little will be found to be promoting "just the right" amount of service.

Exhibit 9.2   **The Goldilocks Quality of Care Standard**

Courtesy: Healthcare Management Advisors, 2000.

It is not an exaggeration to say, with the intense focus on government regulation and the ever-increasing scrutiny of health care providers, that the development and implementation of a compliance program has become important if not vital for all health care providers. While the OIG has not made a compliance program mandatory, the failure to develop an effective compliance program leaves physicians and other providers at risk for significant fines and penalties including, but not limited to, exclusion from the federal Medicare and Medicaid programs and imprisonment. These penalties and fines are not illusory, and the number of cases investigated by the government is increasing.

The value of a compliance program begins when it is implemented—only a compliance program developed and implemented before any government investigation will be considered as a mitigating factor in an investigation of a provider. The government typically writes their own style of a compliance program (usually referred to as Corporate Integrity Agreements) for providers after an investigation, with little input from the provider. Having a "voluntary" compliance program is definitely preferred.

The OIG's model or "Compliance Program Guidance for Individual and Small Group Physician Practices" (See Appendix C for a complete copy) was issued in its final form in September 2000. The AMA and many other professional groups had filed comments and objections to the OIG's draft guidance originally issued in 1999. This final compliance program guidance addresses many of those comments and concerns raised by physicians who have long believed that compliance programs were too expensive and too complex for their practices. Prior model programs have been released by the OIG for nursing facilities; Medicare + Choice programs; hospices; the durable medical equipment, prosthetics, orthotics, and supply industry; home health agencies; clinical laboratories; and hospitals.

The OIG's model compliance program for physicians identifies these four basic compliance risks for physician practices: (a) accurate coding and billing, (b) reasonable and necessary services, (c) adequate clinical and HCFA 1500 documentation, and (d) avoiding improper inducements, kickbacks and self-referrals. Thirteen additional risk areas are specified in Appendix A of the OIG's guidance document, including for example gainsharing arrangements, professional courtesy discounts, unlawful advertising and third party billing services. Physicians are reminded that they remain responsible for billing errors or false claims submitted by third party billing services, even if the physician had no knowledge of the impropriety (see page 34 of the OIG model).

HHS Inspector General June Gibbs Brown has said, "Adopting a voluntary compliance program is a lot like practicing preventive medicine; it helps identify and treat small problems before they become big problems." A well-developed and effective compliance program should reduce the number of claims rejected because of improper coding and billing. The risk of allegations of fraud, abuse, and waste should be decreased by the creation of an audit trail that documents the provider's efforts and commitment to follow all applicable rules and guidelines.

Seven Steps to Have an Effective Compliance Program

The OIG modified its more legalistic style used in previous model programs released for other types of providers and in this model for physicians has used a more straight forward list of recommended sequential "steps," which are summarized following.

1. Start an ongoing program of monitoring and auditing claims with internal personnel or external sources.

2. Establish written practice standards and procedures for compliance risk areas.

3. Designate a compliance officer or multiple employees to assigned specific compliance monitoring efforts, or retain an outsourced compliance officer.

4. Provide internal or external employee training and education at least annually on the compliance program, proper coding and billing procedures,

and specifically on any problem areas identified from monitoring and auditing.

5. Respond to detected offenses and develop corrective action plans, using the compliance officer, legal counsel or outside assistance if needed.

6. Develop open, accessible lines of communication that encourage reporting of suspected violations, such as an anonymous drop box or hotline.

7. Enforce disciplinary standards through well-publicized guidelines, making it clear that compliance is treated seriously and that violations will be dealt with consistently and uniformly.

Written Standards of Conduct and Policies

The development and distribution of written standards of conduct, as well as written policies and procedures that promote the provider's commitment to compliance, are vital for an effective compliance program. An initial step is the development of a code of conduct. This code should reflect the provider's philosophy as to coding, billing, patient care, and documentation. Additionally, the provider should develop a policies and procedure manual. This manual should include all internal policies including, but not limited to, those on office procedures, billing, coding, documentation, collections and adjustments, patient quality of care, marketing, patient outreach, and employee hiring and firing. A description, including the individual (by job title) responsible for each process, what training is required, the method for completing each procedure, the documentation and process for reporting misconduct and the steps for correction of misconduct, should be detailed. The policies and procedures manual may be developed from information available from other groups, but must be customized to reflect the unique characteristics of the practice. Additionally, providers should review and include publications from the government and other sources that apply to their practice. Importantly, the policy and procedures manual must be updated as changes occur in law or policy—a manual that sits on a shelf with no changes, modifications, or revisions will not meet the spirit and intent of the OIG and will not provide the protection to the provider that a well-maintained manual gives.

The policy and procedures manual must be readily available to all employees. If individual copies are not provided to each employee, employees must know where the information is located. As noted below in the section on training, all new employees should be trained on the information contained in the policies and procedures manual.

If the provider's resources are limited, the OIG recommends focusing on those areas at highest risk. A review of the policies and procedures currently in place, analysis of frequent rejections of claims, and an evaluation of employee and patient complaints are good starting points to identify likely high-risk areas.

The Compliance Officer

The provider must designate a chief compliance officer and other appropriate people charged with the responsibility of operating and monitoring the compliance program and who report directly to the chief executive officer and the governing body. It is generally the compliance officer's duty to:

- Oversee and enforce the compliance program
- Ensure that all reports of possible misconduct are promptly investigated
- Monitor the compliance program to ensure its effectiveness
- Maintain records of all reports made to or by the compliance officer, including the resolution of the problem and the response to the reporting party
- Maintain documentation of all compliance training and orientation of employees
- Create and distribute a periodic and regular report of all activity, problems, responses, and the general effectiveness of the compliance program
- Develop a method to revise and improve the compliance program and provide training as needed

The selection of the compliance officer is key to the success of the compliance program. Optimally, the compliance officer should have background and experience in billing and coding, have effective communication skills, and be careful with details. If this function is performed internally, the compliance officer should be a high-ranking officer or employee. The compliance officer should report directly to the Board of Directors/Trustees and the chief executive officer.

Alternatives to an internal compliance officer, especially for smaller physician practices and other health care providers, may include the selection of an outsourced consultant, billing company, or other entity that acts as the compliance officer, or the division of the responsibilities of the compliance officer among the staff who may be designated as "compliance contacts."

The Education and Training Program

The compliance program must include mandatory training of all employees, including the providers themselves as well as all staff. Each employee must be made aware of his or her individual obligations to uphold the standards as outlined in the code of conduct and the adverse consequences, including legal sanctions, that may be imposed if the standards are not met. Periodic meetings should be held to inform staff of any regulatory and policy changes, including, but not limited to, changes in Medicare and Medicaid.

The level of training may vary depending on the job function of the individual. For example, while it is imperative that all coders and billers understand in detail correct coding rules, regulations, and procedures, a receptionist may instead need understand only the importance of compliance with all laws without the same specificity as one responsible for coding and billing. Periodic tests for all employees, to determine the understanding of their particular training, should be given.

Documentation of all training is imperative. Details and records including the schedule and content of all training must be kept. Sign-in sheets for attendees must be included and maintained in the training records. A description of all material distributed, including policy and procedure manuals, checklists, and any other compliance-related information along with the periodic tests and their results, should be included in the compliance officer's documentation. In addition, the personnel files should detail information of all conferences, in-services, and other training for each employee.

Educational and reference material should be available to employees at all times. The compliance library should include current information from Medicare and Medicaid publications and bulletins, current editions of the *International Classification of Diseases, Ninth Revision (ICD-9)*, *Current Procedural Terminology* (CPT), the Health Care Financing Administration's Common Procedure Coding System (HCPCS), and Correct Coding Initiative (CCI), and all other materials the compliance officer determines necessary for the provider's particular practice. For the smaller practice, the use of an office bulletin board to post and update compliance information might also be a way to make sure everyone in the practice has access to up-to-date compliance information.

Internet-based education has emerged as viable, effective means to meet the training component of the OIG "elements of an effective compliance program." This is due to several important, genuine advantages inherent in the Internet delivery mechanism:

- Internet-based training and education is available 24 hours a day, 7 days a week, so it is available for use by all shifts and can be accessed anywhere there is an Internet connection.

- Internet-based training and education is well suited to the health care market, because the same program can be utilized across all geographic locations operated by the provider.

- The Internet affords features and functionality well suited to effective training, such as interactive quizzing, case studies, and benchmark testing. With reporting and tracking capabilities, compliance staff have instant records of who has been trained and who requires further training.

- Content can be added to the Internet platform as soon as it is created, allowing providers access to a constantly expanding curriculum responsive to new trends and developments.

Compliance training tools take full advantage of the benefits of the Internet platform with lessons on functional compliance, integrated with legal and regulatory requirements. An online demo can be found at www.complianceedge.com where the viewer will be able to access some of the various menu items shown in Exhibit 9.3.

Process for Reporting Complaints

A compliance program cannot be effective without a clearly delineated procedure for reporting possible problems or violations. Each employee must be aware of his or her individual responsibility to immediately report any possible problems. The overall process must be user-friendly and allow for the prompt resolution of reported problems. Hotlines or e-mail that allow for anonymous communication may be advisable. For providers with a small number of employees, the use of suggestion boxes, an "open-door policy," or the use of an outside

---

Exhibit 9.3   Sample Compliance Training and Education Tool

Internet-based tool featuring self-paced lessons, grouped in suggested courses representing major functional areas within provider settings. Lesson takes approximately 60 minutes to complete. Each lesson includes:

• Pretest	• Pop-up windows
• Purpose of lesson	• Job-specific applications
• Lesson objectives	• Summary
• Setting the stage	• Posttest
• Laws/regulations	• Reporting features
• Case studies/examples	

EXAMPLES OF SPECIFIC LESSONS MAY INCLUDE

Advance notification of Medicare Non-Coverage	Compliance with outpatient technical modifiers
Medical necessity certification	Physician recruitment: Anti-Kickback and Start Law
Physician compliance: The Stark Law	Physician billing at teaching hospitals (PATH)
Physician False Claims and Anti-Kickback Law	Physician recruitment and tax-exempt status
Patient Rights: privacy, Confidentiality, & Care Participation	Related party transactions

Courtesy: Ernst & Young LLP, and CCH INCORPORATED.

"hotline" service contractor to which reports are made may be considered. Whatever approach is taken, the development of a log to record the reported problem and actions taken will be strong evidence of the provider's commitment to compliance.

All employees must understand that:

- Reporting fraud or abuse is required

- Failure to report fraudulent or abusive activity is a violation of policy and procedure

- There will be no retribution for reporting fraudulent or abusive activity when done in good faith

A periodic report to employees with information as to the problems discovered through the compliance efforts (without violation of confidentiality) and their resolution will help encourage employees in their vigilance.

Disciplinary Procedures and Guidelines

The compliance program must include the development of a system to respond to allegations of improper and illegal activities and the enforcement of appropriate disciplinary action against employees who have violated internal compliance policies, applicable statutes, regulations, or federal health care program requirements. The compliance officer must respond quickly to any violations or problems. A thorough investigation and immediate and appropriate corrective and disciplinary actions are key. Discipline must be consistent for infractions and violations. Ignoring problems, including failure to properly discipline the employee, may expose the provider to criminal and civil prosecution. Quick and decisive action sends a message that the provider will not tolerate inappropriate behavior.

Compliance Monitoring and Audits

Periodic monitoring and audits are an effective method to ensure that proper billing and coding procedures are in place and followed. Employees, if qualified and with sufficient time, may perform this function, or the provider may contract with an experienced consultant for these services. Whether audits are conducted by an employee or a contractor, a baseline must be established to determine the level of accuracy of the coding and billing process. The number of errors found in the baseline audit will also determine how often repeat audits should be performed, eg, monthly, quarterly, or yearly.

Retrospective audits are often used to discover how the organization has been managing the coding and billing processes. However, before a retrospective audit is performed, a procedure should be established for the refund of overpayments if errors are found in the claims process. It may also be advisable to consult counsel on the refund process. Statistically valid random samples for retrospective audits should not be selected without approval by legal counsel, as carriers or other payers can easily use the results of such audits and may extrapolate the results to all prior claims.

Many audits reveal services provided that were not previously billed, as well as undercoded claims, the correction of which offsets overcoded claims.

For the most comprehensive coverage, an independent compliance risk assessment or audit may be performed by or under the supervision of legal counsel. This audit should include a review of all contracts, compliance with federal and state laws and regulations, and operating procedures. While a smaller organization may be reluctant to expend the funds for this audit, it can be an excellent tool for discovering compliance risks that can be corrected before they become major problems.

Examples of reports available from an outsourced monitoring service for evaluation and management and CPT procedure coding for an ear, nose, and throat (ENT) physician are shown in Exhibits 9.4 and 9.5. These show that the ENT physician's use of levels 4 and 5 for established patient visits is significantly less than that of his peers and that septoplasty and nasal endoscopy procedures are significantly higher in volume than for most other ENTs. These comparisons can

Exhibit 9.4   Physician Benchmarking—E & M Distribution

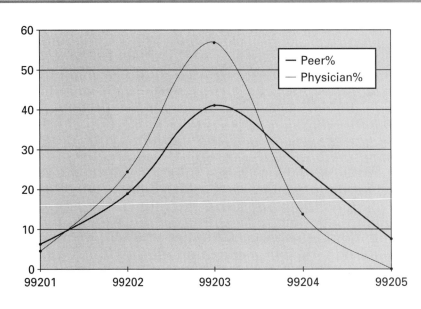

Courtesy: Healthcare Management Advisors, 2000.

Exhibit 9.5 **Physician Benchmarking—Variances from National Peers, Top 10 HCPCS Procedures**

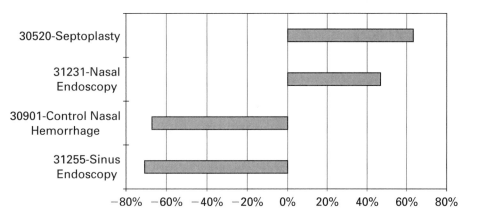

Courtesy: Healthcare Management Advisors, 2000.

identify practice profiles that may be targeted for investigation by carriers or other payers.

Most physician practice billing systems provide reports that compare the current month's volume by HCPCS/CPT code to that of prior months, quarters, or years. These comparisons can be used to identify unexplained variations that could be the result of improper coding or billing practices.

The compliance monitoring process can be manually performed or computerized. Typically the manual process is limited to certain specific claims that may be targeted on the basis of prior experience, professional judgment, or random selection.

Computerized compliance monitoring systems offer the advantages of monitoring 100% of claims, automation of the process, and continuous coverage (regardless of vacations, illness, etc). The most advanced computerized compliance monitoring systems include:

- Ability to easily interface with virtually any billing system
- All Medicare CCI, local medical review policy (LMRP), and Medicaid edits
- Edits for all CPT and ICD coding rules
- Ability to sort edit results and other reports by date of service, account, payer, ICD-9 or HCPCS/CPT codes, age, sex, case length, etc
- Peer comparisons to Medicare and other payer normal distributions
- Summary graphs and detailed, drill-down reports
- Ability to monitor productivity, revenue, patterns of care, and significant variations from other peer norms and/or prior trends

An example of such a computerized compliance monitoring system can be seen at www.EMDsolutions.net.

Investigation and Remediation of Systemic Problems and Nonemployment or Retention of Sanctioned Individuals

Systemic, rather than isolated, problems are of most concern to the OIG. Because of this, the OIG has stressed the importance of the compliance officer looking for trends and patterns of abuse. The compliance officer must initiate prompt steps to investigate all reports or indications of suspected noncompliance to determine whether a material violation of applicable law or the requirements of the compliance program has occurred. If a material problem is found, the compliance officer must immediately take all steps necessary to correct the problem. This may include an immediate refund of overpayments, termination of the employee responsible, and/or report to the government. However, it is advisable to consult with legal counsel prior to reporting to the government.

The OIG also encourages the compliance officer to determine whether the presence of individuals under investigation may hinder the process. If so, such individuals may be moved away from their normal work until the investigation is completed. At the same time, the compliance officer should take all necessary steps to prevent the destruction of records or other evidence that may in any way be pertinent to the investigation. All such information and evidence should be secured by the compliance officer in a safe location.

The OIG has also established an affirmative duty on providers to verify that all employees and contractors have been checked to ensure that they are not under sanctions. The Cumulative Sanction Report is an OIG-produced report available on the Internet at www.dhhs.gov/progorg/oig/cumsan/index.htm. The Cumulative Sanction Report is updated on a regular basis to reflect the status of health care providers who have been excluded from participation in the Medicare and Medicaid programs. The General Services Administration also maintains a monthly listing of debarred contractors on the Internet at www.epls.arnet.gov/.

To learn more about the potential Medicare issues to be investigated by the OIG, review the Annual OIG Work Plan at www.dhhs.gov/prog.org/OIG/wrkplan/index.htm for a complete listing of the projects the OIG plans to conduct. See Tables 9.3 and 9.4 for a summary of selected OIG Work Plan projects for 2001 involving physician services.

Table 9.3 | **OIG Projects for Physicians**

- Physicians at teaching hospitals (PATH)
- Critical care codes
- Reassignment of benefits to clinics
- Podiatry services
- Nonphysician practitioners
- Advance beneficiary notices by physicians
- Services and supplies incident to physicians' services

Courtesy: Healthcare Management Advisors, 2000.

Table 9.4 | **Other OIG Projects**

- CLIA certifications and proficiency testing
- Duplicate billing for DME and HHA
- Appropriateness of home equipment
- Separately billed ESRD services
- Medical necessity and coding of orthotics
- Blood glucose test strips
- Appropriate use of J9999 for chemotherapy
- C/ORF medical necessity and eligibility

Courtesy: Healthcare Management Advisors, 2000.

Compliance and Internal Controls

It is management's responsibility to establish effective internal controls. These are checks and balances to reduce the risks of transactions being recorded improperly or not being recorded at all. Effective internal controls also reduce the risk of embezzlement. Table 9.5 shows an example of a basic internal control checklist.

Management should review its practice's internal controls with this checklist to identify major deficiencies. Deficiencies should then be addressed by changing the assignments of tasks to improve the separation of duties by using an external accountant or consultant to provide additional independent control.

The Value a Compliance Program Brings to the Provider

The purpose of compliance programs is manifold: to establish an atmosphere in which commitment to proper coding, billing, and adherence to all rules and

Table 9.5 | **Basic Internal Control Checklist**

1. The person preparing and making deposits is not authorized to sign checks.

2. A person other than the check signer can review bank statements, canceled checks, and endorsements of canceled checks for any irregularities.

3. Bank accounts are reconciled monthly and reviewed by a person other than a check signer.

4. Patient encounter forms are prenumbered and accounted for on a daily basis.

5. The person posting payments to patient accounts does not open the mail or prepare deposits.

6. Patients on the sign-in sheet are reconciled to the daily report of charges.

7. Daily reports of payments received are reviewed for unposted patient charges.

8. The contractual adjustments for the month and year to date appear reasonable on the basis of the practice's payer mix and payer contracts.

9. A sample of patient charges is traced from the explanation of benefits (EOB) to each individual patient account and payments are traced to deposit slips.

10. Write-offs of patient accounts are reviewed monthly for appropriateness.

11. Individual passwords are required for access to the computer system and are not shared.

12. All practice employees have reference checks and names compared to Medicare exclusion lists before hiring and are bonded.

Courtesy: Healthcare Management Advisors, 2000.

regulations is clearly articulated; to promote policies and procedures for ferreting out problems and reporting them when they are found; to set out rules for the consistent and even-handed discipline of wrong-doers; and to self-report to the government if overpayments or other material errors have been made. The provider who meets the standards of an "effective" compliance program may minimize the potential cost and disruption of a full-scale government audit and investigation, be permitted to negotiate a fair monetary settlement, and avoid an OIG exclusion preventing the entity from doing business with the federal health care programs.

Conclusion

The OIG is committed to its stated goal of combating fraud, abuse, and waste in the health care system. An active compliance program is strong evidence of a provider's equal commitment to this goal.

Developing and implementing a compliance program can appear to be a daunting task. The resources and time need to commit to the project are substantial. However, the rewards are even greater. Increased revenue, streamlined procedures, and well-educated and understanding staff are all benefits of a good compliance program.

There are many resources available to help develop a compliance program. Whether a provider chooses to create his or her own program, or enlist the services of an outside firm, having a compliance program is the best way to protect the provider, both financially and legally.

10 Privacy, Confidentiality, and the Health Insurance Portability and Accountability Act

Objectives

After completing this chapter, you should be able to:

- Understand the law today on medical record privacy

- Understand the changes proposed under HIPAA

- Know the five key principles of the proposed HIPAA legislation

- Appreciate the practical changes that will affect the health care provider

Introduction

Changes are coming to health care privacy issues. Although the requirements of the Health Care Portability and Accountability Act (HIPAA) are not yet in effect, substantial changes are inevitable and will result in significant modifications in the way health care providers collect, maintain, secure, and distribute health information about their patients.

Background

The use of computer and telecommunications has forever changed the way health information is viewed and the steps necessary to protect its confidentiality. Information is now easily transmitted in electronic form. Providers communicate with each other by means of modems; payers require electronic submission of claim information; state lines mean nothing in cyberspace. These rapid changes require a federal approach to health care information to help avoid the problems that arise from relying solely on a patchwork of state laws. States, however, continue to have an important role in privacy laws. Rules of preemption will apply, meaning simply that a state may regulate in areas in which the federal government has not regulated or where a state's laws are more stringent than the federal government's.

Concerns about privacy are also exacerbated by the rapid changes in medical devices, pharmaceuticals, and genetics. Look into a crystal ball at the human genome project and see the use of genetic testing to determine one's susceptibility to disease as marked in one's genetic code, allowing the person to be proactively treated years, if not decades, before the disease surfaces. This leads to questions of privacy of such genetic information, denial of insurance coverage on the basis of genetic codes, and limitations on medical research because of the reluctance of individuals to be tested and chance the inadvertent release of their most personal genetic information.

Complete and accurate medical records have been, and remain, vital to the care of the patient. However, as technology changes how physicians provide care, requirements for confidentiality have also changed. The laws, adjusting to keep up with technology and the proposed rules under HIPAA, discussed below, mean simply that what was formerly understood to be "confidential" may no longer be so. The laws in the area of medical records, confidentiality, and privacy have never been completely clear. While some laws mandate the *absolute privacy* of the medical record unless there has been a specific authorization to release data, other laws mandate that a provider *must disclose* medical information, even in the face of an objection from the patient. The health care provider must carefully review each planned disclosure to prevent an inadvertent error. Specific statutory provisions, such as those relating to drug and alcohol or psychiatric records, must be considered. Release of information is an area fraught with danger for a provider, payer, employer, or any other organization or person who has access to patient records and confidential information. Liability for the improper release of information is not an idle threat, and given the increasing focus in the lay press on these issues, it is likely to be the subject of much attention in the future.

The attention centered on patient records lies, in part, on the many uses of what was once considered private and confidential information. In addition to being the fundamental documentation upon which the patient receives treatment, the record is the cornerstone of payment by third-party payers (including Medicare, Medicaid, the Civilian Health and Medical Program of the Uniformed Services, and federal employee health plans). Without review of records, which may be prospective, concurrent, and retrospective, managed care companies may not authorize and/or pay for services sought and rendered. Access to patient records to these third-party payers is allowed except for the self-pay patient, and even those records are subject to review by government regulators and hospital or physician representatives as part of programs such as quality assurance and utilization review.

The Family Medical Leave Act (FMLA) bases its very law on the medical needs of a member of an employee's family. Release of records to an employer of an employee's family member may be required to receive FMLA benefits. The FMLA requires that any such medical records be kept separate from personnel files of the employee and be maintained in confidence. Employers must now be the keepers of sensitive and private information regarding people with whom they have a relationship only through the employment of another family member. Under the Americans With Disabilities Act (ADA), employees may be required to release their own medical information to their employer. As with the FMLA, the employer will now be entrusted with confidential medical information that it must ensure remains confidential and private.

Recently, the use of medical records has also been the basis for investigations of fraud, abuse, and waste in the medical system. Review of medical records and the services provided, for example, may be compared for discrepancies with the coding and amount billed for these services. As part of their investigation, these records may be reviewed and analyzed by members of the Federal Bureau of Investigation, Department of Justice, state Medicaid fraud units, and a multitude of other government agents, all without the patient's consent or even knowledge.

The American Medical Association (AMA) and other organizations have issued policy statements on the issue of privacy of medical records (see "AMA Policies Related to Computer-Based Patient Records and Electronic Medical Records" at www.ama-assn.org/med-sci/cpt/emrpolicy). Also see, for example, a May 2000 article in the *American Medical News* regarding researchers and their concerns over restriction of access to medical records, at www.ama-assn.org/sci-pubs/amnews/pick_00/gvsa0508.

Consumers are increasingly concerned about the privacy of their medical records. Just one example of potential misuse and concern is the proposed merger of banks and insurance companies. The potential of a loan denial based on the borrower's insurance health records has resulted in proposed privacy reforms to prevent such use of medical records. The use of the Internet, with the well-publicized failure to ensure privacy and the threat of hackers, has resulted in a growing and often warranted fear among Americans that information posted on the Internet is not protected. Polls show that a vast majority of Americans believe they have lost control over how companies use their private information. In 1999 to 2000 it was reported that more than 2000 privacy bills were being considered by state legislatures, addressing everything from medical records to privacy of bank accounts and criminal convictions.

Connection Between HIPAA and Privacy Regulations

Into this maelstrom, the US Department of Health and Human Services (HHS) has issued proposed regulations that specifically address some of the areas raised by the growth of technology. HIPAA, Public Law 104-191, enacted August 21, 1996, required that HHS issue final regulations no later than February 21, 2000. However, there have been delays in the issuance of these final regulations, and at the time of this writing, the final regulations are anticipated to be released no earlier than fall of 2000.

In November 1999, HHS did publish its proposed privacy rules under HIPAA. These were developed as a result of HHS working with an interagency team including members of the Departments of Labor, Defense, Justice, and Commerce, the Social Security Administration, the Office of Personnel Management, the Department of Veterans Affairs, and the Office of Management and Budget. During the public comment period after their publication, HHS received more than 40,000 comments on these proposed rules.

What Is Protected Under the Proposed HIPAA Regulations?

"Protected health information" is:

- individually identifiable information,

- which is or was at any time electronic, and

- is in the hands of a covered entity.

Information becomes electronic when it is sent electronically or if it is maintained in a computer system. The fact that the information is later printed in "hard copy" will not eliminate its being considered "electronic" and thus covered under the HIPAA proposed regulations. Once information is electronic, it is forever covered under the regulations. HIPAA is clear that the information itself, rather than the record, is protected under the proposed regulations.

"Individually identifiable information" is defined as any information from which an individual could be identified and includes a list of data that may trigger this definition, including name, Social Security number, or zip code.

The Five Principles of Privacy Legislation Under HIPAA

1. *Boundaries.* Personally identifiable health information is to be used, with very few exceptions, only for health purposes. The proposed rules would

apply the HIPAA privacy legislation to providers, payers, and any other person or entity who receives this health information from a provider or payer.

2. *Security.* Health information provided by an individual should not be used or given out unless (*a*) the patient authorizes it or (*b*) there is a clear legal basis for doing so. Each organization will be required to establish rules and procedures for safeguarding health information, including discipline and sanctions for employees who violate these rules.

3. *Consumer Control.* Individuals must have the right to (*a*) know what is contained in their records, (*b*) know who has looked at them, (*c*) inspect and copy their records, and (*d*) correct their records if necessary. All individuals must be given clear explanations of their rights, including an understanding of how their health information will be used.

4. *Accountability.* Under the proposed HIPAA privacy rules, there may be criminal felony penalties if an individual knowingly obtains or uses health care information in violation of the legislation. If the violation was for monetary gain, it is proposed that the penalties increase. Civil money penalties would be imposed if it were proven that there was a pattern or practice of illegal disclosures. Additionally, the individual whose health information was illegally disclosed should have the right to bring an action for actual damages and equitable relief.

5. *Public Responsibility.* The right of the individual to privacy of his or her own health information must be balanced against the public interests, including combating disease; rooting out fraud, abuse, and waste in the health care system; providing quality care; and conducting effective research. These areas of public interest might, under specific circumstances, allow disclosure of health information without the authorization of the individual.

Who Is Covered Under the Proposed HIPAA Regulations?

The proposed regulations limit the breadth of the law to "covered entities," which are defined as health plans, health care clearinghouses, and any health care provider who transmits health information in an electronic form in connection with what are called "standard transactions." However, the law does not reach all individuals and companies that may receive, use, or disclose individually identified information. Thus, for example, an employer, workers' compensation company, or accountant who is provided the information for legitimate purposes will not come under these proposed regulations.

To deal with this concern, at least in part, the regulations address the issue of "business partners." Covered entities would be allowed to disclose health information, that would otherwise not be permitted to be disclosed, to their "business partners," including individuals and companies (but not their own employees) hired to perform a business function for the covered entity. However, such disclosure would be permitted only if it were necessary for the business partner to perform its job, and, further, the covered entity must enter into a contract with each business partner. In each contract, the covered entity must establish rules for the disclosure of health information to the business partner and limit the redisclosure by the business partner to another individual or entity.

When Information May Be Used and Disclosed Without Authorization

Under certain conditions, covered entities could use and disclose protected health information, without authorization, for treatment, payment, and health care operations. This would include purposes such as quality assurance, utilization review, credentialing, and other activities that are part of ensuring appropriate treatment and payment. Also, individuals may ask a covered entity to restrict the further use and disclosure of protected health information for treatment, payment, or health care operations with the exception of uses or disclosures required by law. The covered entity would not be required to agree to such a request but, if the covered entity and the individual agree to a restriction, would be bound by the agreement.

Practice Administrative Requirements for the Health Care Provider and Payer

The proposed rule would require providers and payers to develop and implement basic administrative procedures to protect health information and the rights of individuals with respect to that information. These would include:

- Documentation of policies and procedures for complying with the requirements of the proposed rule. The documentation must include a statement of the entity's practices regarding (*a*) who would have access to protected health information and (*b*) how that information would or would not be disclosed to other entities.

- Administrative systems that enable covered entities to protect health information in accordance with the proposed rule. Specifically, all covered entities would be required to:

  — Designate a privacy official

  — Provide privacy training to members of its workforce

  — Implement safeguards to protect health information from intentional accidental misuse

  — Provide a means for individuals to lodge complaints about the entity's information practices and maintain a record of any complaint

  — Develop a system of sanctions for members of the workforce and business partners who violate the entity's policies.

The proposed rules discuss the "scalability" and flexibility of these privacy standards. Recognizing the differences in the business, size, and resources between and among covered entities, the proposed rules leave the detailed policies and procedures for meeting these privacy standards to the discretion of each covered entity. Each covered entity is to assess its own needs and implement privacy policies appropriate to its information practices and business requirements.

Time Schedule for Implementation of Privacy Regulations

HIPAA requires implementation and compliance with any privacy regulations 2 years after the final regulations are effective. "Small health plans" will be given 3 years for compliance.

Conclusion

The only certainty is that federal and state laws will continue to change to attempt to keep up with technology and concerns of privacy and confidentiality. However, the law is always slower to react than the changes in the marketplace, and each individual, whether a consumer of medical care or a physician providing such care, must be aware of the potential for danger and take all reasonable steps to try and protect this confidential and extremely personal information. Table 10.1 shows 10 steps to prepare for HIPAA

Table 10.1   **10 Steps to Prepare for HIPAA**

1. Determine whether you are a **covered entity**. If you transmit patient information in an electronic form or maintain information in a computer system you are probably a covered entity and subject to all HIPAA privacy regulations.

2. Determine whether you **contract with a covered entity**. If you receive information from a covered entity, then the information is subject to the HIPAA regulations.

3. Define what information is **individually identifiable information** protected under HIPAA. Recognize that once information is protected under HIPAA it is always protected.

4. Establish a **compliance program** that sets accountability for meeting the HIPAA requirements. This can become part of an overall **corporate compliance program** that also addresses issues of fraud, abuse and waste.

5. Designate a **privacy official** with responsibility for establishing policies and procedures to comply with HIPAA. This may be the **corporate compliance officer**.

6. Establish **policies and procedures** to safeguard the privacy and confidentiality of the protected information.

7. **Train** all members of your workforce. Incorporate this into your annual training under your corporate compliance program.

8. Establish a method for employees to report misuse of any confidential information. Consider having this as part of your **corporate compliance hotline**. Make sure that you maintain a **log** of all complaints. Detail any **corrective actions** taken in response to these complaints.

9. Develop and uniformly implement **discipline and sanctions** for misuse of confidential information.

10. Remain vigilant. Continuously **monitor legislation and regulations** and alert employees to any significant changes. **Update policies and procedures** as necessary to reflect changes in the law. **Monitor the log of complaints** to identify trends. Ensure that all complaints have been properly addressed.

Source: Healthcare Management Advisors. *HMA Strategy Advisor.* April 21, 2000.

Appendix A

Glossary of Terms

Health care and insurance have their own "language." The following glossary includes terms commonly used in the industry. Learning these terms will increase your understanding of the claims management process.

Accreditation—Certification that an organization meets the reviewing organization's standards. Examples: accreditation of health maintenance organizations by the National Committee for Quality Assurance (NCQA) or accreditation of preferred provider organizations by the American Accreditation Health care Commission/URAC.

Activities of daily living (ADLs)—Measures, used in an index or scale, of an individual's degree of independence in bathing, dressing, using the toilet, eating, transferring (moving from a bed to a chair), and moving across a small room.

Adjudicate—To process an insurance claim for coverage determination by an insurance company or agent.

Adjusted average per-capita cost (AAPCC)—The estimated average fee-for-service cost of Medicare benefits for an individual by county of residence. It is based on the following factors: age, sex, institutional status, Medicaid, disability, and end-stage renal disease (ESRD) status. The Health Care Financing Administration (HCFA) uses the AAPCC as a basis for making monthly payments to managed care plans.

Adjustments to payment rates—Payment systems usually include adjustments to the base payment rates designed to allow for differences in providers' circumstances that are expected to affect their costs of furnishing care. Payment rates may be adjusted, for instance, to accommodate differences in local prices for inputs, which may account for more than 50% of the observed variation in providers' costs for a given product or service. Other adjustments may be made to reflect unusual circumstances, such as delivery of specialized types of care or atypical characteristics of beneficiaries.

Allowable—The fee (the "approved amount") the third-party payer decides the physician should be paid for the services provided to a patient. The amount is usually the same as or lower than the physician's fee and serves as a payment baseline for adjudicating the claim.

Ambulatory patient groups (APGs)—A prospective payment system for the facility component of ambulatory care rendered in hospital ambulatory surgery, emergency department, and outpatient clinic settings. Used by Medicaid and Blue Cross in some states

Ambulatory Payment Classifications (APCs)—Medicare's Outpatient Prospective Payment System (OPPS) for the vast majority of hospital outpatient services effective August 1, 2000.

Ancillary—A term used to describe additional services performed related to care, such as lab work, x-ray, and anesthesia.

Appeal—The request for review by a physician or other provider who questions the correctness of a health plan's reimbursement for services rendered. The physician usually appeals by sending additional information in the form of clinical or demographic information to clarify to the health plan and to receive appropriate reimbursement.

Assignment—An arrangement in which the policyholder designates that the physician receive the benefits (payment) for a claim. This differs from the usual procedure in which the person who has the insurance policy is the person who is to receive the benefits (payment) from that policy. Under assignment, in return for receiving direct payment from most third-party payers, the physician agrees to accept the third-party payer's allowable as the maximum amount that may be collected from the payer and patient for that claim.

Balance bill—The amount the physician collects from the patient, which is the difference between the physician's fee (the amount billed) for a service and the amount paid by a third-party payer. In some cases, the balance bill is limited to the difference between the third-party payer's allowable fee and the amount paid by the payer. If the physician accepts assignment of benefits, he or she may not bill the patient for the balance. Instead, the balance difference is not collected; the physician writes it off the books, and the patient is billed only for the amount of the copayment, deductible, or coinsurance, as applicable.

Base payment amount—In a payment system, the amount that a purchaser commits to pay providers for a standard unit of service or product furnished to a covered beneficiary. The base payment amount corresponds to a payment system's unit of payment, which may be individual services, bundles of services (such as hospital stays), episodes of care, or specified periods of time. Providers' payment rates for individual services or products are determined by applying two types of adjustments to the base payment amount. One is based on a relative weight designed to measure the expected relative costliness of each distinct service or product, compared with the cost of the average unit. The other type of adjustment is designed to reflect differences in providers' circumstances that are likely to affect their costs of furnishing care. The base payment amount (sometimes called a conversion factor) thus determines the level of the payment rates in the payment system.

Beneficiary—The person who "benefits" from having the insurance policy. Typically, this person is the patient, but it can also be a spouse or the parent or guardian of a child. Persons enrolled in the Medicare program are commonly referred to as beneficiaries.

Beneficiary appeal—A request by a Medicare beneficiary to have a health care decision altered or reversed.

Benefits—The amount payable by a plan to a provider, group, or hospital, as stated in the policy, toward the cost of a medical service.

Benefits package—A term informally used to refer to the employer's benefit plan or to the benefit plan options from which the employee can choose. "Benefits package" highlights the fact a health benefits plan is a compilation of specific benefits.

Board certified (Boarded, Diplomate)—Designation given a physician who has passed a written and oral examination given by a medical specialty board and who has been certified as a specialist in that area.

Bundling—A payment method that combines minor medical services or surgeries and principal procedures when performed together or within a specific period of time. Some governmental programs and insurance plans "bundle" the payment of the lesser service into the payment for the principal procedure.

Cap rate—The fixed prepaid amount of payment under capitation. Also known as capitation rate.

Capitation—A method of insurance reimbursement for professional services performed in which a provider is paid a fixed amount per patient for a defined time period (month or year) rather than a fee-for-service payment.

Case management— A method of coordinating services patients receive to ensure they seek and receive appropriate and necessary care to minimize duplication of services, tests, and costs.

Case mix—The mix of patients treated within a particular institutional setting, such as a hospital or nursing home. Patient classification systems—such as diagnosis related groups and Resource Utilization Groups, Version III—can be used to measure hospital and nursing home case mix, respectively.

Case-mix index (CMI)—A measure of the average expected relative costliness of the mix of services or products furnished by a provider or group of providers. The average is calculated by multiplying the number of units supplied in each classification category by the relative weight for the category, adding the results across all categories, and dividing by the total number of units across all categories.

Certificate of coverage—A description of the benefits included in an insurance plan. The certificate of coverage is required by state insurance laws and represents the coverage provided under the policy issued to the contract holder. The certificate is provided to subscribers via the certificate booklet.

CHAMPUS/CHAMPVA—Civilian Health and Medical Programs of the Uniformed Services/Veterans Affairs, a government-sponsored health program for active-duty and retired personnel and their eligible dependents, and veterans.

Claim—The request for payment of a health care provider's fees for services provided to patients.

Classification system—A system that provides the foundation for payment systems by identifying distinct services or products that will be priced separately because they are expected to require different amounts of providers' resources. Each payment system has a classification system that corresponds to the payment system's unit of payment (services, episodes of care, and so on). Examples include the Health Care Financing Administration's Common Procedure Coding System used in the physician fee schedule and the diagnosis related groups patient classification system used in the hospital inpatient prospective payment system.

Clinical Laboratory Improvement Act (CLIA)—This act regulates all laboratories that examine human specimens to provide information to assess, diagnose, prevent, or treat any disease or impairment. CLIA mandates that virtually all laboratories meet applicable federal requirements and have a CLIA certificate in order to receive reimbursement from federal programs.

Coding—The process of communicating to the third-party payers the services performed (*Current Procedural Terminology*, Fourth Edition) and the diagnostic conditions (*International Classification of Diseases, Ninth Revision, Clinical Modification*) treated by means of a standardized listing of alphanumeric codes.

Conditions of participation (COPs)—Requirements that health care facilities and organizations must meet to be eligible to receive Medicare payments.

Consultation—A type of physician evaluation in which one physician requests the opinion and advice of another physician in diagnosing or treating a patient condition. The consulting physician must communicate his or her findings to the requesting or attending physician. The Health Care Financing Administration has established definitive criteria that define the parameters of a consultation.

Contract capitation—A per-member, monthly payment to a provider that covers contracted services and is paid in advance of the delivery of the service.

Contractual disallowance—The amount of a health care provider's charge that exceeds the contracted amount a health insurance plan has agreed to pay (allowance) that must be contractually adjusted from the patient's financial responsibility.

Conversion factor—A dollar amount that is multiplied by a measure of relative resource use to determine a payment rate. Conversion factors, such as those used to pay physicians and hospitals (under diagnosis related groups and Ambulatory Payment Classifications), serve the same purpose as the base payment amounts in other payment systems.

Coordination of benefits—An insurance policy clause that defines how the plan will reimburse for services when more than one insurance plan is applied to the claim for physician services; the process of adjudicating claims between two or more health insurance plans.

Coinsurance—A type of cost sharing in which beneficiaries and insurers share liability in a specified ratio for the established payment to a provider for a covered service. For example, Medicare beneficiaries pay coinsurance equal to 20% of the program's physician fee schedule amount for physician's services.

Copayment—The fixed portion of a visit that the patient is responsible for paying to the physician or other provider for each service provided, commonly used in managed care plans. There may be a $5 to $10 copayment for primary care visits, $10 to $15 copayment for specialty visits, and a $5 to $15 copayment for pharmacy, lab, or x-ray procedures. The copayment is a fixed fee per visit, while the coinsurance varies with the cost of the procedure and is a percentage.

Cost sharing—Payments that health insurance enrollees make for covered services. Examples of cost sharing include coinsurance, copayments, deductibles, and premiums.

Cost-based reimbursement—The method Medicare initially used to pay health care facilities for services furnished to beneficiaries. Payment was based on providers' costs as reported on annual cost reports, which identified incurred costs by type of service, separated allowable costs reasonably related to the provision of patient care from those attributable to unrelated activities, and distinguished costs related to services furnished to Medicare patients from those incurred for others.

Coverage—The type and range of benefits—services, procedures, medical items, and so on—for which an insurance policy will pay. Coverage varies from payer to payer. It may include surgery or medical treatment of illnesses or injuries, emergency department care, and hospital services.

CPT®—*Physicians' Current Procedural Terminology*, a systematic listing and coding of procedures and services performed by physicians. Each procedure or service is identified with a five-digit code.

Deductible—The amount the patient must pay "out of pocket" before insurance reimbursement starts. Usually calculated on an annual basis, the deductible can range from $100 to $5000, depending on the insurance policy.

Dependent—A covered person's spouse, not legally separated from the insured, and unmarried child(ren) who meet eligibility requirements.

Diagnosis—The physician's classification of a patient's condition, sign, or symptom. Diagnoses are defined by the *International Classification of Diseases, Ninth Revision, Clinical Modification* (ICD-9-CM) coding system, volumes 1 and 2.

Diagnosis related groups (DRGs)—A patient classification system used to identify distinct types of hospital inpatient cases that should be priced separately because they are expected to require different amounts or types of providers' resources. The DRGs are the foundation of Medicare's hospital inpatient prospective payment system. Each DRG is intended to distinguish patients with similar clinical conditions who are treated with common medical or surgical treatment strategies. For example, patients with blocked coronary arteries treated with coronary bypass surgery with cardiac catheterization are distinguished from those who do not have catheterization.

Disallowance—The amount of a health care provider's charge that exceeds a health insurance plan's maximum allowable payment (allowance) or contracted payment as a percentage of provider-billed amount. Also referred to as disallowed amount, nonallowed amount, or contractual disallowance.

Drug formulary—A listing of prescription medications that are approved for coverage by a payer. The list is subject to periodic review and modification by the payer.

Durable medical equipment (DME)—Medical equipment that has a long duration of usefulness. Durable medical equipment is covered under Medicare Part B and includes, but is not limited to, oxygen tents, hospital beds, and wheelchairs used in patients' homes.

Eligibility—The provisions of a group policy or insurance contract that state requirements that applicants must satisfy to become insured with respect to themselves or their dependents.

Emergency—A condition of recent onset and sufficient severity, including but not limited to severe pain, that would lead a prudent layperson, possessing average knowledge of medicine and health, to believe that his or her condition, sickness, or injury is of such a nature that failure to obtain immediate medical care could result in:
- Placing the member's health in serious jeopardy;
- Serious impairment to bodily functions;
- Serious dysfunction of any bodily organ or part; or
- Other serious medical consequences.

Such conditions include but are NOT limited to chest pain, stroke, poisoning, serious breathing difficulty, unconsciousness, severe burns or cuts, uncontrolled bleeding, or convulsions and other acute conditions.

Employer group—A group of eligible employees to whom health care benefits are extended through a benefits plan provider. The relationship is formalized through a contract. For the employer group to be recognized, a true employee-employer relationship must exist. Examples of groups that would not qualify include social clubs and independent contractors.

Encounter form—An itemized billing statement listing *Current Procedural Terminology* and *International Classification of Diseases, Ninth Revision, Clinical Modification* codes most often used by physicians to note diagnosis and treatment and related fees.

End-stage renal disease (ESRD)—A medical condition in which a person's kidneys have stopped functioning on a permanent basis, leading to the need for long-term dialysis and other medical services. Medicare beneficiaries with ESRD are not allowed to join managed care plans. If a Medicare managed care plan member later develops ESRD, he or she is allowed to stay in the plan.

Exclusive provider organization (EPO)—A health insurance plan similar to a health maintenance organization (HMO), but in which the member must stay within the provider network in order to receive benefits. EPOs are regulated under insurance statutes, not HMO legislation.

Employee Retirement Income Security Act (ERISA)—An act that places regulations on employee benefit plans, including health insurance. One of the provisions requires payers to send the member an explanation of benefits when a claim is denied. ERISA plan regulations supersede state plan regulations.

Established patient—A patient who has received professional services within the past 3 years from a physician or another physician of the same specialty (with the same billing number) who belongs to the same group practice.

Exclusion—A health insurance contract clause that defines conditions or treatments not covered by a health policy. Policy exclusions require practices to make patients aware of their financial responsibility for noncovered services through waiver of liability statements. Also called exceptions.

Explanation of medical benefits (EOMB)—The third-party payer report that explains the coverage and reimbursement determination for a claim or group of claims. Also referred to as EOB.

Federal Medicaid Managed Care Waiver Program—The process used by states to receive permission to implement managed care programs for their Medicaid or other categorically eligible beneficiaries.

Federal qualification—A status defined by the Tax Equity and Fiscal Responsibility Act (TEFRA), conferred by the Health Care Financing Administration (HCFA) after conducting an extensive evaluation of the managed care organization's structure and operations. An organization must be federally qualified or be designated as a health maintenance organization (HMO) or a competitive medical plan (CMP) to be eligible to participate in Medicare cost and risk contracts. Likewise, a managed care organization must be federally qualified or state plan defined to participate in the Medicaid managed care program.

Fee-for-service (FFS)—A billing and reimbursement method in which physicians charge for each medical service or unit provided to a patient.

Fee schedule—A list of charges or payments coded by procedure. Physicians have internal practice charge fee schedules, while Medicare has a payment fee schedule.

Fiscal soundness—The requirement that managed care organizations have sufficient operating funds on hand or available in reserve to cover all expenses associated with services for which they have assumed financial risk.

Flexible benefit option—An option that some Medicare managed care plans may offer that allows members to select additional benefits with a different payment structure.

Formulary—A list of selected pharmaceuticals and their appropriate dosages. In some managed care plans, providers are required to prescribe only from the formulary.

Gatekeeper—A primary care physician who serves as the patient's agent and arranges for and coordinates appropriate medical care and other necessary and appropriate referrals.

Global period—A defined period of time during which all medical services related to a similar condition or diagnosis are included in the payment for the initial surgery or treatment. Medicare sets global surgical periods (GSPs) from 0 to 90 days postoperatively.

Graduate medical education—The period of medical training that follows graduation from medical school; it is commonly referred to as internship, residency, and fellowship training. Medicare provides payments to hospitals to support its share of the direct costs related to these training programs and to support the higher patient care costs associated with the training of residents.

Group health coverage—A health benefits plan that covers a group of people as permitted by state and federal law.

Group or network model—A managed care organization model in which the managed care organization contracts with more than one physician group, and may contract with single and multispecialty groups that work out of their own office facility. The network may or may not provide care exclusively for the managed care organization's members.

Health Care Financing Administration (HCFA)—The administration that governs the financial affairs and operations of the Medicare and Medicaid systems for all health care providers.

HCPCS—The Health Care Financing Administration's Common Procedure Coding System, a national coding system that provides a uniform method for health care providers to report professional services and supplies.

Health insurance claim form—The HCFA-1500 is the most commonly used claim form for processing physician service billing, while UB92 forms are used primarily by hospitals. These claim forms are accepted by most insurance plans for processing claims, and include demographic patient information, coded clinical information, and charges.

Health maintenance organization (HMO)—A type of health insurance plan in which the physician is paid a capitated or fixed rate per month per patient enrolled in the practice. HMOs emphasize providing quality services while reducing utilization of specialists and increasing control of patient care by primary care gatekeepers.

Health Plan Employer Data and Information Set (HEDIS)—A set of standardized measures of health plan performance. HEDIS allows comparisons among plans on quality, access, and patient satisfaction; membership and use; financial information; and management. Employers, health maintenance organizations, and the National Committee for Quality Assurance developed HEDIS.

Health plan—An organization that acts as insurer for an enrolled population.

HIPAA—The Health Insurance Portability and Accountability Act of 1996, an extensive law that provides funding and direction for investigations of fraud, abuse, and waste in the health care system. Also mandates policies and protections for confidentiality of electronically transmitted medical information.

Home health care—Skilled nursing care, physical therapy, speech therapy, occupational therapy, medical social services, or home health aide services provided in Medicare beneficiaries' homes. The first 100 visits following an acute-care hospital stay or a skilled nursing facility stay are covered under Medicare Part A. Subsequent postacute visits and those not preceded by a hospitalization or a stay in a skilled nursing facility are covered under Medicare Part B. There is no beneficiary cost sharing for home health services.

Hospice—A medical and psychosocial program designed to provide for and relieve the suffering of terminally ill people. Medicare beneficiaries already enrolled in Medicare-certified hospice programs are not allowed to enroll in managed care plans. If a Medicare managed care plan member needs hospice care once already enrolled, he or she will be allowed to stay in the plan.

Hospital insurance trust fund—The trust fund that finances services covered under Medicare Part A. Its primary source of income is payroll taxes paid by employees and employers.

ICD-9-CM—A diagnostic code system based on the *International Classification of Diseases, Ninth Revision, Clinical Modification* (ICD-9-CM), volumes 1 and 2, used in the United States. The ICD-9-CM coding system is maintained by the National Center on Vital and Health Statistics and the Health Care Financing Administration. It differentiates diagnostic conditions and reflects care practiced, and is used by hospitals, governments, health insurance plans, and health care providers in the United States.

Indemnity plan—A traditional health insurance plan that reimburses the policyholder a defined amount or percentage for expenses from illness or accidents through fee-for-service. The most common indemnity plans pay 80% of total charges, leaving policyholders with a 20% coinsurance.

Indirect medical education adjustment—An adjustment applied to payments under the prospective payment system for hospitals that operate approved graduate medical education programs. For operating costs, the adjustment is based on the hospital's ratio of interns and residents to the number of beds. For capital costs, it is based on the hospital's ratio of interns and residents to average daily occupancy.

Individual practice association (IPA)—A type of health maintenance organization that provides services through an association of self-employed physicians or physician groups who provide services in their offices, but negotiate contracts as a group of providers.

In-network—Seeing a provider who has contracted with a managed care provider to participate in the network of physicians and hospitals.

Inpatient—A person admitted to the hospital as a bed patient for more than a specific number of hours.

Insurance claim form—A reprinted form filed with a health insurance carrier that details the services provided and other pertinent data to receive benefit (payment).

Instrumental activities of daily living (IADLs)—Measures, used in an index or scale, of an individual's degree of independence in aspects of cognitive and social functioning, such as shopping, cooking, doing housework, managing money, and using the telephone. (See activities of daily living.)

Insurance claim form—A reprinted form filed with a health insurance carrier that details the services provided and other pertinent data to receive benefit (payment).

***International Classification of Diseases, Ninth Revision, Clinical Modification* (ICD-9-CM)**—A system for classifying and coding diagnoses and procedures. This system is used to facilitate the collection of uniform and comparable health information.

Lifetime reserve days—A benefit under which, if hospitalized more than 90 days for a single spell of illness, beneficiaries may draw upon a reserve of 60 days, which require a daily copayment ($384 in 1999). Each lifetime reserve day used is nonrenewable.

Limiting charge—The maximum amount a nonparticipating physician can charge for services to a Medicare patient.

Long-term care—Services that support, treat, and physically rehabilitate people with functional limitations or chronic conditions who need ongoing health care or assistance with activities of daily living.

Major teaching hospital—A hospital with an approved graduate medical education program and a ratio of interns and residents to beds of 25% or greater.

Managed care—A controlled method of delivering health care services in the most appropriate and cost-effective way. All care is managed, from managed indemnity to at-risk health maintenance organization (HMO) care. The lower the premium, the more strictly the plan is managed. Many define this as preferred provider organization or HMO care. The purest definition is at-risk capitated care.

Managed care organization (MCO)—An entity that integrates financing and management with the delivery of health care services to an enrolled population. An MCO provides, offers, or arranges for coverage of designated health services needed by members for a fixed, prepaid amount. There are three basic models of MCOs: group or network model, individual practice association, and staff model.

Management services organization (MSO)—A management entity owned by a hospital physician organization or third party. The MSO contracts with payers, hospitals, and physicians to provide services such as negotiating fee schedules, handling administrative functions, billing, and collections.

Market basket index—A price index designed to measure prices for the typical mix of goods and services providers purchase to produce a specific product or set of products relative to a base year. Generally, these indexes contain three elements: a set of input categories, such as labor, supplies, and purchased services; a set of price proxies representing the price levels for the input categories; and a fixed set of weights (proportions) representing the relative importance of each input category in providers' input expenditures for the base year. The actual or projected values of the price proxies for a year are multiplied by the category weights and summed to obtain the overall market basket index value for the year. The rate of change in input prices can be calculated by comparing index values over time. The Health Care Financing Administration computes separate market basket indexes for most facilities; it also calculates a similar measure, called the Medicare Economic Index, for physicians' office practices.

Medicaid—A federal and state funded medical assistance program administered by each state that provides basic health benefits for persons who cannot pay for them or are otherwise indigent.

Medical necessity—A term of a contract under which payers pay only the cost of covered services considered medically necessary. Payers generally reserve the right to determine whether a service or supply is medically necessary. The fact that a physician has prescribed, ordered, recommended, or approved a service or supply does not, in itself, make it medically necessary and a covered service. A service is generally considered medically necessary if it is:
- Appropriate and consistent with the diagnosis and could not have been omitted without adversely affecting the patient's condition or the quality of medical care rendered
- Compatible with the standards of acceptable medical practice in the United States
- Provided not solely for a member's convenience or the convenience of the physician or hospital
- Not primarily custodial care
- The least costly level of service that can be safely provided; for example, a hospital stay is necessary when treatment cannot be safely provided on an outpatient basis

Medicare—A federal health care program for people 65 years old or older and for people with conditions such as end-stage renal disease. Coverage includes Part A inpatient hospital and Part B outpatient physician services.

Medicare Part A—Also called hospital insurance, the part of the Medicare program that covers the cost of hospital inpatient care and related posthospital services, including some care provided by skilled nursing facilities and home health agencies. Eligibility is normally based on prior payment of payroll taxes. Beneficiaries are responsible for an initial hospital deductible per spell of illness and for copayments for some services.

Medicare Part B—Also called supplementary medical insurance, the part of the Medicare program that covers the cost of physicians' services, outpatient laboratory and x-ray tests, durable medical equipment, outpatient hospital care, some home health care, and certain other services. The voluntary program requires payment of a monthly premium, which covers approximately 25% of program costs, with general tax revenues covering the rest. Beneficiaries are responsible for an annual deductible and coinsurance payments for most covered services.

Medicare carrier—A health insurance company that has been awarded a contract to serve as the government's administrative contractor to process and adjudicate claims under the Medicare Part B outpatient health program for beneficiaries in a defined geographic location, usually by state.

Medicare HMO—A managed care approach to Medicare. These plans use a limited network of health care providers and require prior approval from a primary care physician. When a person enrolls in a Medicare managed care plan, he or she selects a physician from the plan's list of primary care physicians. This primary care physician is then responsible for coordinating all of the beneficiary's health care needs.

Medicare intermediary—A health insurance company that has been awarded a contract to serve as the government's administrative contractor to process and adjudicate claims under the Medicare Part A inpatient health program for beneficiaries in a defined geographic location, usually by state.

Medicare Physician Fee Schedule—The resource-based fee schedule Medicare uses to pay for physicians' services.

Medicare risk contract—A contract between Medicare and a health plan under which the plan receives monthly capitated payments to provide Medicare-covered services for enrollees and thereby assumes insurance risk for those enrollees.

Medicare + Choice—A program created by the Balanced Budget Act of 1997 to replace the methods Medicare previously used to pay health maintenance organizations (HMOs). Beneficiaries have the choice to enroll in a Medicare + Choice plan or to remain in the traditional Medicare program. Medicare + Choice plans may include coordinated care plans (HMOs, preferred provider organizations, or plans offered by provider-sponsored organizations), private fee-for-service plans, or high-deductible plans with medical savings accounts.

Medigap insurance—Privately purchased individual or group health insurance policies designed to supplement Medicare coverage. Benefits may include payment of Medicare deductibles and coinsurance, as well as payment for services not covered by Medicare. Medigap insurance policies must conform to one of 10 federally standardized benefit packages.

Modifier—A two-digit alpha or numeric code used with procedure codes to provide additional clarification of the circumstances related to the provision of health care services. For example, CPT modifier -51—multiple surgical procedure is used with secondary surgical procedure codes to indicate that more than one procedure was performed by the same surgeon on the same day as another procedure.

National Committee for Quality Assurance (NCQA)—A nonprofit organization that evaluates and accredits managed care plans. It is also responsible for implementing the Health Employer Data and Information Set (HEDIS) data reporting system, which provides standardized performance measures for managed care plans.

New patient—A patient who has not received any professional services within the past 3 years from a physician or another physician of the specialty who belongs to the same group practice or uses the same billing number.

Nonparticipating provider—A physician, hospital, or other medical provider that has not entered into a service agreement with a particular payer to provide benefits upon certain terms including specified rates.

Nursing facility (NF)—An institution that provides skilled nursing care and rehabilitation services to injured, functionally disabled, or sick persons; or regularly provides health-related services to individuals who, because of their mental or physical condition, require care and services that can be made available to them only through institutional facilities. In the past, certification distinctions were made between a skilled nursing facility and an intermediate care facility (the latter was certified only to furnish less-intensive care to Medicaid recipients). The Omnibus Budget Reconciliation Act of 1987 eliminated that distinction by requiring all nursing facilities to meet skilled nursing facility certification requirements for Medicare purposes.

Open enrollment—A period during which eligible persons can enroll in a health benefits plan.

Other teaching hospital—A hospital with an approved graduate medical education program and a ratio of interns and residents to beds of less than 25%.

Outliers—Cases that substantially differ from the rest of the population of cases. With regard to hospital payment, outliers are identified as cases with extremely high costs compared with the prospective payment rate in the diagnosis related group. Hospitals receive additional payments for these cases under the prospective payment system.

Out-of-pocket expenses—Costs borne by the member that are not covered by the health care plan.

Outpatient—A patient who visits a clinic or hospital to receive medical diagnosis or treatment, but does not occupy a hospital bed for a specified minimum stay.

Part B premium—A monthly premium paid (usually deducted from a person's Social Security check) to cover Part B services in fee-for-service Medicare. Members of Medicare managed care plans must also pay this premium to receive full coverage and be eligible to join and stay in a managed care plan.

Participation—A contract between a physician and a third-party payer under which the physician agrees to accept assignment on all claims submitted to that payer. Participation contracts are often for a limited period of time, such as a year.

Peer review—Evaluation of the quality of the total health care provided by plan providers by equivalently trained medical personnel.

Peer review organization (PRO)—A state-based organization, also known as a quality improvement organization, that undertakes Medicare quality improvement and peer review activities under contract to the Health Care Financing Administration (HCFA). *Quality improvement organization* is the term preferred by the organizations themselves, although *peer review organization* is the term used in legislation, regulations, and publications by HCFA.

Per diem reimbursement—Reimbursement to an institution based on a fixed rate per day rather than on a charge-by-charge basis. There may be separate categories of per diem, for example, medical, surgical, intensive care unit, etc, each with a different reimbursement.

Per member per month (PM/PM)—The unit of measure related to each effective member for each month the member was effective. The calculation is number of units divided by member months.

Physician's Current Procedural Terminology (CPT®)—A list of medical services and procedures performed by physicians and other providers. Each service and/or procedure is identified by its own unique five-digit code. CPT has become the health care industry's standard for reporting physician procedures and services, thereby providing an effective method of nationwide communication.

Physician-hospital organization (PHO)—Hospital and medical staff (or an independent practice organization) that provide services to patients and negotiate and obtain managed care contracts.

Place of service code—A series of standardized codes used by physicians to report the location where the health care services were provided (office, hospital, home, etc).

Physician organization (PO)—A group of physicians banded together, usually for the purpose of contracting with managed care entities or to represent the physician component in a physician-hospital organization.

Point of service (POS)—A plan in which members do not have to choose services (health maintenance organization vs traditional) until they need them.

Preadmission certification—A component of a utilization management program that reviews an inpatient hospital stay prospectively to determine coverage.

Preauthorization—A prospective process to verify coverage of proposed care, to establish covered length of stay, and to set a date for concurrent review.

Precertification—A method for preapproving all elective hospital admissions, surgeries, and other provider services as required by insurance carriers. Approval is essential before payment for services is received.

Preexisting condition—A physical condition that existed prior to the issuance of an insurance policy or enrollment in a managed care plan.

Preferred provider organization (PPO)—A managed care plan that contracts with networks or panels of providers to furnish services and be paid on a negotiated fee schedule. Enrollees are offered a financial incentive to use providers on the preferred list but may use nonnetwork providers as well.

Premium—The periodic payment (usually monthly) made by a policyholder to an insurance company to subscribe to a health insurance plan.

Preventive health care—Health care that seeks to prevent the occurrence of conditions by fostering early detection of disease and morbidity and that focuses on keeping patients well in addition to healing them when they are sick.

Primary care physician (PCP)—The physician who serves as the initial contact between the member and the medical care system. The PCP is usually a physician, selected by the member upon enrollment, who is trained in one of the primary care specialties, and who treats and is responsible for coordinating the treatment of members assigned to his or her panel.

Primary carrier/payer—The insurance carrier that pays benefits first when the patient has more than one insurance plan. The primary carrier is billed first.

Principal inpatient diagnosis–diagnostic cost group (PIP-DCGs)—A risk adjustment method that is the basis for the interim risk adjustment system for Medicare + Choice payment rates. Beneficiaries' relative health status is measured by means of the principal diagnoses of inpatient hospitalizations. The model is prospective, meaning that payments in a year are based on inpatient hospitalizations during the previous year.

Prior authorization number—The number assigned by a health insurance plan after the precertification approval process for treatment is completed.

Private contracting—A physician payment option created by the Balanced Budget Act of 1997. Under private contracts, beneficiaries agree to pay full charges directly to physicians, and no bills are submitted to Medicare. Physicians who enter into these contracts cannot submit bills to Medicare for any patient for a period of 2 years.

Productivity—A measurement of the quantity of resources used to produce a unit of output. Productivity increases when an organization produces more output with the same resources or the same output with fewer resources.

Prospective payment system (PPS)—A system under which a provider's payment is based on predetermined rates and is unaffected by its incurred costs or posted charges. Examples of prospective payment systems include the one Medicare uses to pay hospitals for inpatient care and the physician fee schedule.

Provider—The person or entity providing health care–related services, such as a physician or a hospital.

Provider number—A unique physician identification number (UPIN) assigned to a health care provider by insurance carriers and the government for accounting and tracking purposes.

Provider-sponsored organization (PSO)—A Medicare + Choice organization that is a public or private entity and is established or organized and operated by a health care provider or group of affiliated health care providers.

Qualified Medicare Beneficiary (QMB)—A Medicaid program that pays for Medicare premiums, deductibles, and coinsurance for beneficiaries with incomes at or below the federal poverty level. Some beneficiaries may also qualify for full Medicaid benefits under state laws.

Quality Improvement System for Managed Care (QISMC)—Health care quality measurement, reporting, and improvement requirements for health plans participating in Medicare + Choice.

Quality assurance—A process or system designed to identify problems in health care delivery, take action to address the problems, and assess the effectiveness of corrective actions.

Quality improvement—A process or system designed to improve the processes of delivering health care so as to increase the likelihood of achieving desired outcomes.

Quality improvement organization (QIO)—A state-based organization, also known as a peer review organization, that undertakes Medicare quality improvement and peer review activities under contract to the Health Care Financing Administration (HCFA). *Quality improvement organization* is the term preferred by the organizations themselves, although *peer review organization* is the term used in legislation, regulations, and publications by HCFA.

Referral—The introduction or transfer of a patient's care from one physician to another or to another health care provider.

Reimbursement—Money paid by a third-party payer for a patient's medical bills.

Reinsurance—An insurance arrangement whereby the managed care organization or provider is reimbursed by a third party for costs exceeding a preset limit, usually an annual maximum. This is also called *stop-loss coverage*.

Relative weights—A value used with product classification systems in payment systems to adjust payment rates to reflect the expected relative costliness of each service or product, compared with the cost of the average service unit. Relative weights may be based on providers' national average charges or costs for cases in each product category. When charge or cost data are unavailable, weights may be based on judgments by clinicians or other experts, as are the relative values for the professional component of the Medicare physician fee schedule.

Resource Utilization Groups, Version III (RUG-III)—A system for determining case mix in nursing facilities. The RUG-III system classifies patients on the basis of functional status (as measured by an index of activities of daily living) and the number and types of services used. Each RUG has a nursing index or weight indicating the average level of resources needed to provide nursing services to patients in the group. Rehabilitation RUGs also have indexes indicating the average levels of resources required to furnish therapy services.

Risk adjustment—A system of adjusting rates paid to managed care providers to account for differences in beneficiary demographics, such as age, gender, race, ethnicity, medical condition, geographic location, at-risk populations (for example, homeless), etc.

Risk contract—A contract payment methodology between the Health Care Financing Administration (HCFA) and a managed care organization (health maintenance organization or competitive medical plan). This requires the delivery of at least all Medicare-covered services to members, as medically necessary, in return for a fixed monthly payment from the government and sometimes an additional fee paid by the enrollee. The managed care organization is then liable for those contractually offered services without regard to cost. (Note: Medicaid beneficiaries enrolled in risk contracts are not required to pay premiums.) Risk contracts may occur between any insurer and provider group. The group at risk accepts prepayment and is responsible for all contracted care.

Risk score—A measure of the expected costliness of a beneficiary with specific characteristics, compared with the cost of caring for the average beneficiary. For example, if the average cost of caring for beneficiaries is represented by a risk score of 1, then a beneficiary with a risk score of 1.2 would be expected to cost 20% more than average.

Risk selection—Any situation in which health plans differ in the average health risk associated with their enrollees because of enrollment choices made by the plans or enrollees. When risk selection occurs, health plans' expected costs differ because of underlying differences in their enrolled populations.

Risk sharing—A method of providing additional payment amounts for high-cost patients or to offset plan losses, for example, stop-loss policies that provide additional payments once a spending threshold has been reached.

Secondary carrier/payer—The insurance carrier that pays benefits after the primary insurance plan has paid first when a patient has more than one health plan.

Skilled nursing facility (SNF)—An institution that has a transfer agreement with at least one hospital that provides primarily inpatient skilled nursing care and rehabilitative services, and that meets other specific certification requirements.

Specialist physician—A physician who is certified to practice in a specific field, other than general or family practice, for example, cardiologist.

Specified Low-Income Medicare Beneficiary (SLMB)—A Medicaid program that pays the Medicare Part B premium for Medicare beneficiaries with incomes between 100% and 120% of the federal poverty level.

Staff model—A managed care organization model that employs physicians to provide health care to its members. All premiums and other revenues accrue to the managed care organization, which compensates physicians by salary.

Standardization—A process of adjusting charges or costs for particular services or bundles of services to remove differences that result from geographic variation in price levels, demographic characteristics, beneficiary health risk, and other factors. Standardization is intended to make charges or costs more comparable among providers, plans, and geographic areas.

Supplemental insurance—Health insurance held by Medicare beneficiaries that covers part or all of the program's cost-sharing requirements and some services not covered by traditional Medicare. Beneficiaries may obtain these policies as a retirement benefit from a former employer or by individual purchase.

Third-party payer—An entity, such as an insurance company, that has agreed via a contract (that is, the insurance policy) to pay for medical care provided to the patient. "Third-party" refers to the involvement of another entity besides the two parties directly involved in medical care, the patient and the physician. Third-party payer is frequently used interchangeably with insurance company, insurer, or payer.

Type of service code (TOS)—A code to be entered in block 24C of the HCFA-1500 form that defines the type of service provided—medical care, surgery, and so on.

UCR payment—An abbreviation for "usual, customary, and reasonable" payment, an amount paid by a health plan based on a combination of the physician's usual fee, the customary fee charged by physicians in a specific locality, and the reasonable fee for the service.

UPIN—The unique physician identification number used by Medicare for accounting and tracking physician services.

Uncompensated care—Care provided by hospitals or other providers that is not paid for directly (by the patient or by a government or private insurance program). It includes charity care, which is furnished without the expectation of payment, and bad debts, for which the provider has made an unsuccessful effort to collect payment due.

Update—A periodic adjustment (usually annual) designed to raise or lower a base payment amount to account for the effects of anticipated changes in factors that affect the costs that efficient providers would be expected to incur in providing care.

Utilization management—A process that measures the use of available resources to determine medical necessity, cost-effectiveness, and conformity to criteria for optimal use.

Utilization review—The process of examining health care services to measure medical necessity, quality of patient care, and the appropriateness of care to identify overuse or ineffective outcomes.

Wellness programs—A broad range of employer-sponsored facilities and activities designed to promote safety and good health among employees. Its purpose is to reduce the costs of accidents, sickness, absenteeism, lower productivity, and health care costs.

Withhold incentive—The percentage of payment held back by the insurer for a "risk account" in managed care health maintenance organization plans to cover unforeseen expenses. Withhold arrangements are used as an incentive for physicians to manage their utilization of higher-priced diagnostics and treatments with the potential for sharing profits (or losses).

Appendix B

Internet Resources

Coding Resources

American Medical Association [www.ama-assn.org/]

The AMA is a voluntary membership organization of physicians that is the patient's advocate and the physician's voice. It sets standards for the profession of medicine. The AMA is also the developer of the *Current Procedural Terminology* (CPT). The current fourth edition is a listing of descriptive terms and identifying codes for reporting medical services and procedures. The purpose of CPT is to provide a uniform language that accurately describes medical, surgical, and diagnostic services, and thereby serves as an effective means for reliable nationwide communication among physicians, patients, and third parties. For direct information on AMA's CPT products and services including AMA's new CPT Information Services, which allows AMA members to have their CPT coding questions answered by phone or by written response, visit www.ama-assn.org/med-sci/cpt/cpt.htm

American Academy of Professional Coders (AAPC) [www.aapcnatl.org/]

The AAPC is the largest professional network of CPT, ICD-9-CM, and HCPCS coders in the nation who share a common interest in procedural and diagnostic coding issues. Physicians and other employers often require CPC or CPC-H certified employees, recognizing the level of coding knowledge represented by these accreditations.

Central Office on ICD-9-CM [www.icd-9-cm.org/]

Created through a written memorandum of understanding between the AHA, World Health Organization, and National Center for Health Statistics in 1963, the Central Office on ICD-9-CM serves as a clearinghouse for issues related to the use of ICD-9-CM, maintains the integrity of the classification system, recommends revisions to the system as needed, and develops educational material and programs on ICD-9-CM. The public-private partnership now also includes HCFA and AHIMA. This site offers access to education information and products of the Central Office.

Medicare Online Training [www.medicaretraining.com/]

This site specializes in self-paced Medicare training provided by the Health Care Financing Administration (HCFA), the government agency that runs Medicare nationwide.

National Correct Coding Initiative (CCI) Reference Tools [www.ntis.gov/product/correct-coding.htm]

Now you can have just the correct coding reference tool you need to ensure that your Part B claims will not be disallowed. NTIS, in cooperation with HCFA, offers a series of lookup references that will show you which codes cannot be used together in your reimbursement claims.

Outpatient Code Editor [www.ntis.gov/product/hcfa-outpatient-code-editor.htm]

Hospitals or other facilities with outpatient billing will find this software an important tool. It combines CCI edits with the new Ambulatory Payment Classifications (APC) assignment program designed to meet mandated Medicare outpatient prospective payment system (OPPS) implementation.

Compliance Resources

EMTALA [www.emtala.com/]

A resource for current information about the Federal Emergency Medical Treatment and Active Labor Act, also known as COBRA or the Patient Anti-Dumping Law.

Federal Trade Commission Telemarketing Fraud Web site [www.ftc.gov/bcp/conline/edcams/telemarketing/index.html]

Telemarketing fraud robs Americans of at least $40 billion a year. This web site provides information for consumers about telemarketing fraud as well as resource materials for educators, providers, and community organizations.

Health Care Compliance Association [www.hcca-info.org/]

The Health Care Compliance Association is the only nonprofit organization solely dedicated to improving the quality of health care compliance. The HCCA Web site includes information on education and conferences, compliance resources, health care compliance news, and links to government compliance guidance.

Health Hippo [hippo.findlaw.com/]

Health Hippo is a collection of policy and regulatory materials related to health care, with some graphics sprinkled in.

healthfinder [www.healthfinder.gov/]

healthfinder® is a free gateway to reliable consumer health and human services information developed by the US Department of Health and Human Services.

healthfinder® can lead you to selected online publications, clearinghouses, databases, Web sites, and support and self-help groups, as well as the government agencies and not-for-profit organizations that produce reliable information for the public.

National Healthcare Anti-Fraud Association [www.nhcaa.org/]

Founded in 1985 by several private health insurers and federal/state law enforcement officials, the National Health Care Anti-Fraud Association (NHCAA) is a unique, issue-based organization comprising private- and public-sector organizations and individuals responsible for the detection, investigation, prosecution, and prevention of health care fraud.

Government Resources and Agencies

Agency for Healthcare Research Quality [www.ahrq.gov]

Practical health care information, research findings, and data to help consumers, health providers, health insurers, researchers, and policymakers make informed decisions about health care issues.

Department of Health and Human Services [www.hhs.gov]

Top level site on HHS Agencies on the Internet, News & Public Affairs, What's New, Research Data, Policy, Topic Index.

Health Care Financing Administration [www.hcfa.gov/]

The federal agency that administers Medicare, Medicaid, and the State Children's Health Insurance Program (SCHIP).

Government Printing Office (GPO) Access on the Web [www.access.gpo.gov/su_docs/aces/aaces002.html]

Federal Register, congressional bills, congressional record, public laws, and US code.

Medicare Payment Advisory Commission [www.medpac.gov/]

The Medicare Payment Advisory Commission (MedPAC) is an independent federal body that advises the US Congress on issues affecting the Medicare program. It was established by the Balanced Budget Act of 1997 (Public Law 105-33), which merged the Prospective Payment Assessment Commission (ProPAC) and the Physician Payment Review Commission (PPRC).

National Practitioner Data Bank and the Healthcare Integrity and Protection Data Bank [www.npdb-hipdb.com/]

The NPDB and the HIPDB are part of the government's efforts to improve health care quality and alleviate the financial burden that health care fraud and abuse impose on the nation.

OSHA Bloodborne Pathogen Directive
[www.osha.gov/media/oshnews/nov99/national-19991105.html]
The Occupational Safety and Health Administration expects health care providers to minimize serious health risks faced by workers exposed to blood and other potentially infectious materials, such as human immunodeficiency virus (HIV), hepatitis B, and hepatitis C.

The Public Health Data Standards Consortium
[www.cdc.gov/nchs/otheract/phdsc/phdsc.htm]
The consortium will expand public health involvement in existing health data standards and content organizations and facilitate the development of new public health data standards. The consortium will also help educate the public health and health services research communities about HIPAA and health data standards issues.

White House Federal Briefing Room: Health Statistics
[www.whitehouse.gov/fsbr/health.html]
This site contains statistical health information updated on a monthly basis. Topics include vital statistics, use of health services, prevention and risk, health status, reportable diseases, and health care expenditures.

Medical Ethics Resources

American Society of Law, Medicine and Ethics
[www.lawlib.slu.edu/aslme/]
The mission of the American Society of Law, Medicine and Ethics (ASLME) is to provide high-quality scholarship, debate, and critical thought to the community of professionals at the intersection of law, health care, policy, and ethics.

APA Ethics Information [www.apa.org/ethics/ethics.html]
From the American Psychological Association, links to ethical principles, statements, and guidelines for psychologists, online services, and guidelines for the care of animals.

Bioethical Services of Virginia
[www.members.aol.com/bsvinc/bsvpage.html]
This site offers an array of medical ethics programming functions for community hospitals, state facilities for individuals with mental retardation, mental health institutes, and community services boards.

Bioethics [www.gen.emory.edu/MEDWEB/keyword/Bioethics.html]
A fairly complete list of bioethics resources from MedWeb.

Bioethics Online Service [www.mcw.edu/bioethics/]

A list of bioethics resources from the Medical College of Wisconsin.

Dental Ethics [www.cpmcnet.columbia.edu/health.sci/dental.toc/ Dental_Educational_Software/Dental-Ethics/ethics-welcome.html]

Ethical questions and answer in dentistry from the Columbia-Presbyterian Medical Center.

Genetics & Ethics [www.ethics.ubc.ca/brynw/]

Links on this Web site include the Human Genome Project, journals, public action groups, genetics and the law, and general philosophy resources.

Human subjects and research ethics [www.psych.bangor.ac.uk/deptpsych/Ethics/HumanResearch.html]

A pointer to information about the ethical aspects of research involving human subjects as participants.

MacLean Center for Clinical Ethics [www.ccme-mac4.bsd.uchicago.edu/CCME.html]

This site consists of interdisciplinary-based resources on practical ethical concerns confronting patients and health professionals. The center's core faculty of physicians, nurses, legal scholars, philosophers, and social scientists directs medical ethics education at the University of Chicago.

Medical Ethics Exhibit [www.learner.org/exhibits/medicalethics/]

Is assisted suicide legal? What are the potential benefits—and dangers—of human cloning research? Should patients be entitled to any medical treatment they want? These and other questions are explored through the Annenberg/CPB Project, "Medical Ethics."

National Reference Center for Bioethics Literature [www.adminweb.georgetown.edu/nrcbl/]

The National Reference Center for Bioethics Literature (NRCBL) is a specialized collection of books, journals, newspaper articles, legal materials, regulations, codes, government publications, and other relevant documents concerned with issues in biomedical and professional ethics.

Professional Associations and Other Resources

American Academy of Physician Assistants (AAPA) [www.aapa.org/]

The American Academy of Physician Assistants (AAPA) is the only national organization that represents physician assistants (PAs) in all specialties and all employment settings. Its membership also includes physician assistant students and supporters of the profession.

American Association of Retired Persons [www.aarp.org/]

AARP is the nation's leading organization for people age 50 and older. It serves their needs and interests through information and education, advocacy, and community services that are provided by a network of local chapters and experienced volunteers throughout the country.

American College of Emergency Physicians [www.acep.org/]

The American College of Emergency Physicians is a medical specialty society that was formed in 1969 to improve emergency care by setting high standards for emergency medical education and practice.

American College of Healthcare Executives (ACHE) [www.ache.org/]

The American College of Healthcare Executives is an international professional society of nearly 30,000 health care executives. ACHEís publishing division, Health Administration Press, is a major publisher of books and journals on all aspects of health services management in addition to textbooks for use in college and university courses.

American College of Nurse Practitioners (ACNP) [www.nurse.org/acnp/]

Founded in 1993, the American College of Nurse Practitioners (ACNP) is a national nonprofit membership organization focused on keeping NPs current on legislative, regulatory, and clinical practice issues.

American College of Physician Executives (ACPE) [www.acpe.org/]

Founded in 1975 as the American Academy of Medical Directors, the American College of Physician Executives has grown to more than 12,000 physician members with management or administrative responsibilities in hospitals, group practices, managed care, government, universities, the military, and industry.

American Health Information Management Association [www.ahima.org/]

The American Health Information Management Association (AHIMA) is the professional association that represents more than 40,000 specially educated health information management professionals managing, analyzing, and utilizing data vital for patient care—and making it accessible to health care providers when it is needed most. The site provides a variety of information on reimbursement resources.

American Health Lawyers Association [www.healthlawyers.org/]

This site is focused on leading health law to excellence through education, information, and dialogue. The American Health Lawyers Association (Health Lawyers) is the nation's largest, nonpartisan, 501(c)(3) educational organization devoted to legal issues in the health care field.

American Hospital Association [www.aha.org/default.asp]

The American Hospital Association (AHA) is the national organization that represents and serves all types of hospitals, health care networks, and their patients and communities. Close to 5000 institutional, 600 associate, and 40,000 personal members come together to form the AHA.

Association of American Medical Colleges [www.aamc.org/]

The AAMC is a nonprofit association comprising the 125 accredited US medical schools; the 16 accredited Canadian medical schools; more than 400 major teaching hospitals and health systems, including 70 Department of Veterans Affairs medical centers; nearly 90 academic and professional societies representing 75,000 faculty members; and the nation's medical students and residents.

Catholic Health Association of the United States [www.chausa.org/]

The Catholic Health Association of the United States represents the combined strength of its members, more than 2000 Catholic health care sponsors, systems, facilities, and related organizations. Founded in 1915, CHA unites members to advance selected strategic issues that are best addressed together rather than as individual organizations.

Doctors Guide to the Internet—Medical Conferences & Meetings [www.pslgroup.com/confdate.htm]

The Congress Resource Centre (CRC) is a one-stop site of organized links and information designed to facilitate planning and scheduling for a featured congress.

Healthcare Billing and Management Association (HBMA) [www.hbma.com/]

Founded in 1993, the Healthcare Billing and Management Association (HBMA) is the only trade association representing third-party medical billers. HBMA members process physician and other provider claims integral to the health care delivery system.

Healthcare Conventions [www.healthopps.com/health11.html]

Provides a searchable database of health care–related conventions and job fairs.

Healthcare Financial Management Association [www.hfma.org/]

HFMA is the nation's leading personal membership organization for more than 33,000 financial management professionals employed by hospitals, integrated delivery systems, long-term and ambulatory care facilities, managed care organizations, medical group practices, public accounting and consulting firms, insurance companies, government agencies, and other health care organizations.

Healthcare Management Advisors, Inc [www.HMA.com]

One of the nation's leading compliance and data quality consulting firms supplies the analysis, training, ongoing education, and technical support needed by hospitals and physicians to remain competitive and on top of increasingly complex billing, coding, and compliance regulations. Provides APC, HIPAA, Self-disclosure & SNF/HHA Resource Centers.

healthgrades.com physician report cards [www.healthgrades.com/prc/index.cfm?ct=1]

A searchable database that provides a list of physicians in the specialty and geographic area specified. In addition, detailed physician profiles, maps and driving directions, and links to physician Web sites are provided. Other pages provide information on hospitals, health plans, nursing homes, home health agencies, hospice programs, fertility clinics, chiropractors, dentists, and more health care–related facilities.

Medical Group Management Association [www.mgma.com/]

Founded in 1926, MGMA is the leading organization representing medical group practice nationwide. More than 7100 health care organizations and nearly 20,000 individuals are MGMA members, representing more than 185,000 physicians.

Modern Physician Magazine [www.modernphysician.com/]

Modern Physician is a monthly business news magazine written for physician executives who are key players in the effort to reshape America's major medical institutions.

National Association of Insurance Commissioners [www.naic.org/]

The NAIC is the organization of insurance regulators from the 50 states, the District of Columbia and the four U.S. territories. The NAIC provides a forum for the development of uniform policy when uniformity is appropriate. With offices in Kansas City, New York and Washington, DC, the NAIC staff provides invaluable support the insurance commissioners. The site includes access to information on Committee Activities, Insurance Regulators, Upcoming Events, State Regulations and more.

National Association of Psychiatric Health Systems
[www.naphs.org/]
Created in 1933, the National Association of Psychiatric Health Systems today
represents delivery systems working to coordinate a full spectrum of treatment
services, including inpatient, residential, partial hospitalization, and outpatient
programs as well as prevention and management services.

National Association of Public Hospitals and Health Systems
[www.naph.org/]
The National Association of Public Hospitals and Health Systems has represented the nation's urban safety net health systems, and the people they serve,
since 1981. NAPH members provide the full range of services to their patients
and communities, from primary care and public health services to highly specialized services.

National Association of State Medicaid Directors
[www.medicaid.aphsa.org/NASMD.htm]
The NASMD is a bipartisan, professional, nonprofit organization of representatives of state Medicaid agencies. The primary purposes of NASMD are to serve
as a focal point of communication between the states and the federal government and to provide an information network among the states on issues pertinent to the Medicaid program.

National Committee for Quality Assurance (NCQA)
[www.ncqa.org/]
The National Committee for Quality Assurance (NCQA) is a private, not-for-
profit organization dedicated to improving the quality of health care. The organization's primary activities are assessing and reporting on the quality of the
nation's managed care plans.

National IPA Coalition [www.nipac.org/]
NIPAC is the leading resource for physician organizations that manage risk contracts. Their mission is "to enhance physician-directed managed healthcare."

National Practitioner Data Bank [www.npdb.com/]
The NPDB and the HIPDB are part of the government's efforts to improve
health care quality and alleviate the financial burden that health care fraud and
abuse impose on the nation.

The *New England Journal of Medicine* [www.nejm.org/]
The *New England Journal of Medicine On-line* now offers subscribers access to full
text plus several additional features. The *Journal On-line* continues to offer to all

users many selections from the *Journal*, including abstracts of all scientific articles.

Professional Association of Healthcare Office Managers (PAHCOM) [www.pahcom.com/]

PAHCOM is a nationwide organization dedicated to providing a strong professional network for physician practice managers, and includes salary surveys.

WebDoctor [www.gretmar.com/webdoctor/journals.html]

Index to on-line medical journals.

State Medical Boards

State	URL
AK	www.dced.state.ak.us/occ/pmed.htm
AL	www.bmedixon.home.mindspring.com/
AZ	www.docboard.org/bomex/index.htm
CA	www.medbd.ca.gov
CO	www.dora.state.co.us/medical
CT	www.state.ct.us/dph
DC	www.dchealth.com/lra/news.stm
FL	www.doh.state.fl.us/mqa
GA	www.sos.state.ga.us/ebd-medical/
IA	www.docboard.org/ia/ia_home.htm
ID	www.idacare.org
IL	www.state.il.us/dpr
IN	www.ai.org/serv/hpb_lookup_ia
KS	www.ink.org/public/boha/
KY	www.state.ky.us/agencies/kbml
MA	www.massmedboard.org/
MD	www.docboard.org/md/default.htm
ME	www.docboard.org/me/me_home.htm
MI	www.commerce.state.mi.us/bhser/home.htm
MN	www.bmp.state.mn.us/
MO	www.ecodev.state.mo.us/pr/healarts/
MS	www.msbml.state.ms.us

MT	www.com.state.mt.us/license/pol/pol_boards/med_board/board_page.htm
NC	www.docboard.org/nc
NE	www.hhs.state.ne.us/
NH	www.state.nh.us/medicine
NJ	www.state.nj.us/lps/ca/medical.htm
NV	www.state.nv.us./medical/
NY	www.health.state.ny.us/nysdoh/opmc/main.htm
OH	www.state.oh.us/med/
OK	www.osbmls.state.ok.us/
OR	www.bme.state.or.us/
PA	www.dos.state.pa.us/bpoa/medbd.htm
RI	www.docboard.org/ri/main.htm
SC	www.llr.state.sc.us./me.htm
SD	www.state.sd.us/dcr/medical/med-hom.htm
TN	www.state.tn.us/health
TX	www.tsbme.state.tx.us/
UT	www.commerce.state.ut.us/dopl/disc.htm
VA	Licensing at www.dhp.state.va.us Board at www.dhp.state.va.us/levelone/med.htm
VT	www.docboard.org/vt/vermont.htm
WA	Press releases at www.doh.wa.gov/publicat/Publications.htm MQAC at www.doh.wa.gov/hsqa/hpqad/MQAC
WI	www.badger.state.wi.us/agencies/drl/
WV	www.wvdhhr.org/wvbom/

Appendix C

OIG Compliance Program Guidance for Individual and Small Group Physician Practices—Final Guidelines

Appendix C includes the OIG Compliance Program Guidance for Individual and Small Group Physician Practices and the press release announcing its publication.

In addition to compliance guidance, the document also discusses some of the areas of fraud and abuse that are of concern to the OIG.

Office of Inspector General
Public Affairs
330 Independence Ave., SW
Washington, DC 20201

NEWS RELEASE

FOR IMMEDIATE RELEASE

Monday, September 25, 2000
Contact: Judy Holtz (202) 619-0260
or Ben St. John (202) 619-1028

Inspector General Issues Voluntary Compliance
Program Guidance for Physician Practices

The Department of Health and Human Services' Office of Inspector General ("OIG") today issued final guidance to help physicians in individual and small group practices design voluntary compliance programs.

"The intent of the guidance is to provide a roadmap to develop a voluntary compliance program that best fits the needs of that individual practice. The guidance itself provides great flexibility as to how a physician practice could implement compliance efforts in a manner that fits with the practice's existing operations and resources," Inspector General June Gibbs Brown said.

The final guidance—Compliance Program Guidance for Individual and Small Group Physician Practices—is scheduled for publication this week as a Federal Register notice and is being posted today on the OIG website. Inspector General Brown further commented, "We are encouraging physician practices to adopt the active application of compliance principles in their practice, rather than implement rigid, costly, formal procedures. Our goal in issuing this final guidance was to show physician practices that compliance can become a part of the practice culture without the practice having to expend substantial monetary or time resources."

The OIG believes the great majority of physicians are honest and committed to providing high quality medical care to Medicare beneficiaries.

Under the law, physicians are not subject to civil, administrative or criminal penalties for innocent errors, or even negligence. The Government's primary enforcement tool, the civil False Claims Act, covers only offenses that are committed with actual knowledge of the falsity of the claim, reckless disregard or deliberate ignorance of the truth or falsity of a claim. The False Claims Act does not cover mistakes, errors or negligence. The OIG is very mindful of the difference between innocent errors ("erroneous claims") and reckless or intentional conduct ("fraudulent claims").

A voluntary compliance program can help physicians identify both erroneous and fraudulent claims and help ensure that submitted claims are true and accurate. It can also help the practice by speeding up and optimizing proper payment of claims, minimizing billing mistakes and avoiding conflicts with the self-referral and anti-kickback statutes.

Unlike other guidance previously issued by the OIG, the final physician guidance does not suggest that physician practices implement all seven standard components of a full scale compliance program. While the seven components provide a solid basis upon which a physician practice can create a compliance program, the OIG acknowledges that full implementation of all components may not be feasible for smaller physician practices. Instead, the guidance emphasizes a step by step approach for those practices to follow in developing and implementing a voluntary compliance program. As a first step, physician practices can begin by identifying risk areas which, based on a practice's specific history with billing problems and other compliance issues, might benefit from closer scrutiny and corrective/educational measures.

The step by step approach is as follows: 1) conducting internal monitoring and auditing through the performance of periodic audits; 2) implementing compliance and practice standards through the development of written standards and procedures; 3) designating a compliance officer or contact(s) to monitor compliance efforts and enforce practice standards; 4) conducting appropriate training and education on practice standards and procedures; 5) responding appropriately to detected violations through the investigation of allegations and the disclosure of incidents to appropriate Government entities; 6) developing open lines of communication, such as discussions at staff meetings regarding erroneous or fraudulent conduct issues and community bulletin boards, to keep practice employees updated regarding compliance activities; and 7) enforcing disciplinary standards through well-publicized guidelines.

The final guidance identifies four specific compliance risk areas for physicians: 1) proper coding and billing; 2) ensuring that services are reasonable and necessary; 3) proper documentation; and 4) avoiding improper inducements, kickbacks and self-referrals. These risk areas reflect areas in which the OIG has focused its investigations and audits related to physician practices.

Recognizing the financial and staffing resource constraints faced by physician practices, the final guidance stresses flexibility in the manner a practice implements voluntary compliance measures. The OIG encourages physician practices to participate in the compliance programs of other providers, such as hospitals or other settings in which the physicians practice. A physician practice's participation in such compliance programs could be a way, at least partly, to augment the practice's own compliance efforts.

The final guidance also provides direction to larger practices in developing compliance programs by recommending that they use both the physician guidance and previously issued guidance, such as the Third-Party Medical Billing Company Compliance Program Guidance or the Clinical Laboratory Compliance Program Guidance, to create a compliance program that meets the needs of the larger practice.

The final guidance includes several appendices outlining additional risk areas about which various physicians expressed interest, as well as information about criminal, civil and administrative statutes related to the Federal health care programs. There is also information about the OIG's provider self-disclosure protocol and Internet resources that may be useful to physician practices.

Note: The final physician guidance is available on the Office of Inspector General Web site at http://www.hhs.gov/oig/new.html

OIG Compliance Program Guidance for Individual and Small Group Physician Practices

The compliance program guidance below is available at the OIG Web site http://www.hhs.gov/oig/new.html.

The Office of Inspector General Compliance Program Guidance for Individual and Small Group Physician Practices

September 2000

Table of Contents

3. Format of the Training Program

4. Continuing Education on Compliance Issues

Step Five: Responding to Detected Offenses and Developing Corrective Action Initiatives

Step Six: Developing Open Lines of Communication

Step Seven: Enforcing Disciplinary Standards Through Well-Publicized Guidelines

    C. Assessing a Voluntary Compliance Program

III. Conclusion

Appendix A: Additional Risk Areas

I. Reasonable and Necessary Services

    A. Local Medical Review Policy

    B. Advance Beneficiary Notices

    C. Physician Liability for Certifications in the Provision of Medical Equipment and Supplies and Home Health Services

    D. Billing for Non-covered Services as if Covered

II. Physician Relationships with Hospitals

    A. The Physician Role in EMTALA

    B. Teaching Physicians

    C. Gainsharing Arrangements and Civil Monetary Penalties for Hospital Payments to Physicians to Reduce or Limit Services to Beneficiaries

    D. Physician Incentive Arrangements

III. Physician Billing Practices

    A. Third-Party Billing Services

    B. Billing Practices by Non-Participating Physicians

    C. Professional Courtesy

IV. Other Risk Areas

    A. Rental of Space in Physician Offices by Persons or Entities to which Physicians Refer

    B. Unlawful Advertising

Appendix B: Criminal Statutes

I. Health Care Fraud (18 U.S.C. 1347)

II. Theft or Embezzlement in Connection with Health Care (18 U.S.C. 669)

III. False Statements Relating to Health Care Matters (18 U.S.C. 1035)

I. Introduction

This compliance program guidance is intended to assist individual and small group physician practices ("physician practices")[1] in developing a voluntary compliance program that promotes adherence to statutes and regulations applicable to the Federal health care programs ("Federal health care program requirements"). The goal of voluntary compliance programs is to provide a tool to strengthen the efforts of health care providers to prevent and reduce improper conduct. These programs can also benefit physician practices[2] by helping to streamline business operations.

Many physicians have expressed an interest in better protecting their practices from the potential for erroneous or fraudulent conduct through the implementation of voluntary compliance programs. The Office of Inspector General (OIG) believes that the great majority of physicians are honest and share our goal of protecting the integrity of Medicare and other Federal health care programs. To that end, all health care providers have a duty to ensure that the claims submitted to Federal health care programs are true and accurate. The development of voluntary compliance programs and the active application of compliance principles in physician practices will go a long way toward achieving this goal.

Through this document, the OIG provides its views on the fundamental components of physician practice compliance programs, as well as the principles that a physician practice might consider when developing and implementing a voluntary compliance program. While this document presents basic procedural and structural guidance for designing a voluntary compliance program, it is not in and of itself a compliance program. Indeed, as recognized by the OIG and the health care industry, there is no "one size fits all" compliance program, especially for physician practices. Rather, it is a set of guidelines that physician practices can consider if they choose to develop and implement a compliance program.

As with the OIG's previous guidance,[3] these guidelines are not mandatory. Nor do they represent an all-inclusive document containing all components of a compliance program. Other OIG outreach efforts, as well as other Federal agency efforts to promote compliance,[4] can also be used in developing a compliance program. However, as explained later, if a physician practice adopts a voluntary and active compliance program, it may well lead to benefits for the physician practice.

A. Scope of the Voluntary Compliance Program Guidance

This guidance focuses on voluntary compliance measures related to claims submitted to the Federal health care programs. Issues related to private payor claims may also be covered by a compliance plan if the physician practice so desires.

The guidance is also limited in scope by focusing on the development of voluntary compliance programs for individual and small group physician practices. The difference between a small practice and a large practice cannot be determined by stating a particular number of physicians. Instead, our intent in narrowing the guidance to the small practices subset was to provide guidance to those physician practices whose financial or staffing resources would not allow them to implement a full scale, institutionally structured compliance program as set forth in the Third Party Medical Billing Guidance or other previously released OIG guidance. A compliance program can be an important tool for physician practices of all sizes and does not have to be costly, resource-intensive or time-intensive.

B. Benefits of a Voluntary Compliance Program

The OIG acknowledges that patient care is, and should be, the first priority of a physician practice. However, a practice's focus on patient care can be enhanced by the adoption of a voluntary compliance program. For example, the increased accuracy of documentation that may result from a compliance program will actually assist in enhancing patient care. The OIG believes that physician practices can realize numerous other benefits by implementing a compliance program. A well-designed compliance program can:

- speed and optimize proper payment of claims;

- minimize billing mistakes;

- reduce the chances that an audit will be conducted by HCFA or the OIG; and

- avoid conflicts with the self-referral and anti-kickback statutes.

The incorporation of compliance measures into a physician practice should not be at the expense of patient care, but instead should augment the ability of the physician practice to provide quality patient care.

Voluntary compliance programs also provide benefits by not only helping to prevent erroneous or fraudulent claims, but also by showing that the physician practice is making additional good faith efforts to submit claims appropriately. Physicians should view compliance programs as analogous to practicing preventive medicine for their practice. Practices that embrace the active application of compliance principles in their practice culture and put efforts towards compliance on a continued basis can help to prevent problems from occurring in the future.

A compliance program also sends an important message to a physician practice's employees that while the practice recognizes that mistakes will occur, employees have an affirmative, ethical duty to come forward and report erroneous or fraudulent conduct, so that it may be corrected.

C. Application of Voluntary Compliance Program Guidance

The applicability of these recommendations will depend on the circumstances and resources of the particular physician practice. Each physician practice can undertake reasonable steps to implement compliance measures, depending on the size and resources of that practice. Physician practices can rely, at least in part, upon standard protocols and current practice procedures to develop an appropriate compliance program for that practice. In fact, many physician practices already have established the framework of a compliance program without referring to it as such.

D. The Difference Between "Erroneous" and "Fraudulent" Claims to Federal Health Programs

There appear to be significant misunderstandings within the physician community regarding the critical differences between what the government views as innocent "erroneous" claims on the one hand and "fraudulent" (intentionally or recklessly false) health care claims on the other. Some physicians feel that Federal law enforcement agencies have maligned medical professionals, in part, by a perceived focus on innocent billing errors. These physicians are under the impression that innocent billing errors can subject them to civil penalties, or even jail. These impressions are mistaken.

To address these concerns, the OIG would like to emphasize the following points. First, the OIG does not disparage physicians, other medical professionals or medical enterprises. In our view, the great majority of physicians are working ethically to render high quality medical care and to submit proper claims.

Second, under the law, physicians are not subject to criminal, civil or administrative penalties for innocent errors, or even negligence. The Government's primary enforcement tool, the civil False Claims Act, covers only offenses that are committed with actual knowledge of the falsity of the claim, reckless disregard, or deliberate ignorance of the falsity of the claim.[5] The False Claims Act does not encompass mistakes, errors, or negligence. The Civil Monetary Penalties Law, an administrative remedy, similar in scope and effect to the False Claims Act, has exactly the same standard of proof.[6] The OIG is very mindful of the difference between innocent errors ("erroneous claims") on one hand, and reckless or intentional conduct ("fraudulent claims") on the other. For criminal penalties, the standard is even higher — criminal intent to defraud must be proved beyond a reasonable doubt.

Third, even ethical physicians (and their staffs) make billing mistakes and errors through inadvertence or negligence. When physicians discover that their billing errors, honest mistakes, or negligence result in erroneous claims, the physician practice should return the funds erroneously claimed, but without penalties. In other words, absent a violation of a civil, criminal or administrative law, erroneous claims result only in the return of funds claimed in error.

Fourth, innocent billing errors are a significant drain on the Federal health care programs. All parties (physicians, providers, carriers, fiscal intermediaries, Government agencies, and beneficiaries) need to work cooperatively to reduce the overall error rate.

Finally, it is reasonable for physicians (and other providers) to ask: what duty do they owe the Federal health care programs? The answer is that all health care providers have a duty to reasonably ensure that the claims submitted to Medicare and other Federal health care programs are true and accurate. The OIG continues to engage the provider community in an extensive, good faith effort to work cooperatively on voluntary compliance to minimize errors and to prevent potential penalties for improper billings before they occur. We encourage all physicians and other providers to join in this effort.

II. Developing a Voluntary Compliance Program

A. The Seven Basic Components of a Voluntary Compliance Program

The OIG believes that a basic framework for any voluntary compliance program begins with a review of the seven basic components of an effective compliance program. A review of these components provides physician practices with an overview of the scope of a fully developed and implemented compliance program. The following list of components, as set forth in previous OIG compliance program guidances, can form the basis of a voluntary compliance program for a physician practice:

- conducting internal monitoring and auditing through the performance of periodic audits;

- implementing compliance and practice standards through the development of written standards and procedures;

- designating a compliance officer or contact(s) to monitor compliance efforts and enforce practice standards;

- conducting appropriate training and education on practice standards and procedures;

- responding appropriately to detected violations through the investigation of allegations and the disclosure of incidents to appropriate Government entities;

- developing open lines of communication, such as (1) discussions at staff meetings regarding how to avoid erroneous or fraudulent conduct and (2) community bulletin boards, to keep practice employees updated regarding compliance activities; and

- enforcing disciplinary standards through well-publicized guidelines.

These seven components provide a solid basis upon which a physician practice can create a compliance program. The OIG acknowledges that full implementation of all components may not be feasible for all physician practices. Some physician practices may never fully implement all of the components. However, as a first step, physician practices can begin by adopting only those components which, based on a practice's specific history with billing problems and other compliance issues, are most likely to provide an identifiable benefit.

The extent of implementation will depend on the size and resources of the practice. Smaller physician practices may incorporate each of the components in a manner that best suits the practice. By contrast, larger physician practices often have the means to incorporate the components in a more systematic manner. For example, larger physician practices can use both this guidance and the Third-Party Medical Billing Compliance Program Guidance, which provides a more detailed compliance program structure, to create a compliance program unique to the practice.

The OIG recognizes that physician practices need to find the best way to achieve compliance for their given circumstances. Specifically, the OIG encourages physician practices to participate in other provider's compliance programs, such as the compliance programs of the hospitals or other settings in which the physicians practice. Physician Practice Management companies also may serve as a source of compliance program guidance. A physician practice's participation in such compliance programs could be a way, at least partly, to augment the practice's own compliance efforts.

The opportunities for collaborative compliance efforts could include participating in training and education programs or using another entity's policies and procedures as a template from which the physician practice creates its own version. The OIG encourages this type of collaborative effort, where the content is appropriate to the setting involved (i.e., the training is relevant to physician practices as well as the sponsoring provider), because it provides a means to promote the desired objective without imposing excessive burdens on the practice or requiring physicians to undertake duplicative action. However, to prevent possible anti-kickback or self-referral issues, the OIG recommends that physicians consider limiting their participation in a sponsoring provider's compliance program to the areas of training and education or policies and procedures.

The key to avoiding possible conflicts is to ensure that the entity providing compliance services to a physician practice (its referral source) is not perceived as nor is it operating the practice compliance program at no charge. For example, if the sponsoring entity conducted claims review for the physician practice as part of a compliance program or provided compliance oversight without charging the practice fair market value for those services, the anti-kickback and Stark self-referral laws would be implicated. The payment of fair market value by referral sources for compliance services will generally address these concerns.

B. Steps for Implementing a Voluntary Compliance Program

As previously discussed, implementing a voluntary compliance program can be a multi-tiered process. Initial development of the compliance program can be focused on practice risk areas that have been problematic for the practice such as coding and billing. Within this area, the practice should examine its claims denial history or claims that have resulted in repeated overpayments, and identify and correct the most frequent sources of those denials or overpayments. A review of claim denials will help the practice scrutinize a significant risk area and improve its cash flow by submitting correct claims that will be paid the first time they are submitted. As this example illustrates, a compliance program for a physician practice often makes sound business sense.

The following is a suggested order of the steps a practice could take to begin the development of a compliance program. The steps outlined below articulate all seven components of a compliance program and there are numerous suggestions for implementation within each component. Physician practices should keep in mind, as stated earlier, that it is up to the practice to determine the manner in which and the extent to which the practice chooses to implement these voluntary measures.

Step One: Auditing and Monitoring

An ongoing evaluation process is important to a successful compliance program. This ongoing evaluation includes not only whether the physician practice's standards and procedures are in fact current and accurate, but also whether the compliance program is working, i.e., whether individuals are properly carrying out their responsibilities and claims are submitted appropriately. Therefore, an audit is an excellent way for a physician practice to ascertain what, if any, problem areas exist and focus on the risk areas that are associated with those problems. There are two types of reviews that can be performed as part of this evaluation: (1) a standards and procedures review; and (2) a claims submission audit.

1. Standards and procedures

It is recommended that an individual(s) in the physician practice be charged with the responsibility of periodically reviewing the practice's standards and procedures to determine if they are current and complete. If the standards and procedures are found to be ineffective or outdated, they should be updated to reflect changes in Government regulations or compendiums generally relied upon by physicians and insurers (i.e., changes in Current Procedural Terminology (CPT) and ICD-9-CM codes).

2. Claims Submission Audit

In addition to the standards and procedures themselves, it is advisable that bills and medical records be reviewed for compliance with applicable coding, billing and documentation requirements. The individuals from the physician practice involved in these self-audits would ideally include the person in charge of billing (if the practice has such a person) and a medically trained person (e.g., registered nurse or preferably a physician (physicians can rotate in this position)). Each physician practice needs to decide for itself whether to review claims retrospectively or concurrently with the claims submission. In the Third-Party Medical Billing Compliance Program Guidance, the OIG recommended that a baseline, or "snapshot," be used to enable a practice to judge over time its progress in reducing or eliminating potential areas of vulnerability. This practice, known as "benchmarking," allows a practice to chart its compliance efforts by showing a reduction or increase in the number of claims paid and denied. The practice's self-audits can be used to determine whether:

- bills are accurately coded and accurately reflect the services provided (as documented in the medical records);
- documentation is being completed correctly;
- services or items provided are reasonable and necessary; and
- any incentives for unnecessary services exist.

A baseline audit examines the claim development and submission process, from patient intake through claim submission and payment, and identifies elements within this process that may contribute to non-compliance or that may need to be the focus for improving execution.[7] This audit will establish a consistent methodology for selecting and examining records, and this methodology will then serve as a basis for future audits.

There are many ways to conduct a baseline audit. The OIG recommends that claims/services that were submitted and paid during the initial three months after implementation of the education and training program be examined, so as to give the physician practice a benchmark against which to measure future compliance effectiveness.

Following the baseline audit, a general recommendation is that periodic audits be conducted at least once each year to ensure that the compliance program is being followed. Optimally, a randomly selected number of medical records could be reviewed to ensure that the coding was performed accurately. Although there is no set formula to how many medical records should be reviewed, a basic guide is five or more medical records per Federal payor (i.e., Medicare, Medicaid), or five to ten medical records per physician. The OIG realizes that physician practices receive reimbursement from a number of different payors, and we would encourage a physician practice's auditing/monitoring process to consist of a review of claims from all Federal payors from which the practice receives reimbursement. Of course, the larger the sample size, the larger the comfort level the physician practice will have about the results. However, the OIG is aware that this may be burdensome for some physician practices, so, at a minimum, we would encourage the physician practice to conduct a review of claims that have been reimbursed by Federal health care programs. If problems are identified, the physician practice will need to determine whether a focused review should be conducted on a more frequent basis. When audit results reveal areas needing additional information or education of employees and physicians, the physician practice will need to analyze whether these areas should be incorporated into the training and educational system.

There are many ways to identify the claims/services from which to draw the random sample of claims to be audited. One methodology is to choose a random sample of claims/services from either all of the claims/services a physician has received reimbursement for or all claims/services from a particular payor. Another method is to identify risk areas or potential billing vulnerabilities. The codes associated with these risk areas may become the universe of claims/services from which to select the sample. The OIG recommends that the physician practice evaluate claims/services selected to determine if the codes billed and reimbursed were accurately ordered, performed, and reasonable and necessary for the treatment of the patient.

One of the most important components of a successful compliance audit protocol is an appropriate response when the physician practice identifies a problem. This action should be taken as soon as possible after the date the problem is identified. The specific action a physician practice takes should depend on the circumstances of the situation. In some cases, the response can be as straight forward as generating a repayment with appropriate explanation to Medicare or the appropriate payor from which the overpayment was received. In others, the physician practice may want to consult with a coding/ billing expert to determine the next best course of action. There is no boilerplate solution to how to handle problems that are identified.

It is a good business practice to create a system to address how physician practices will respond to and report potential problems. In addition, preserving information relating to identification of the problem is as important as preserving information that tracks the physician practice's reaction to, and solution for, the issue.

Step Two: Establish Practice Standards and Procedures

After the internal audit identifies the practice's risk areas, the next step is to develop a method for dealing with those risk areas through the practice's standards and procedures. Written standards and procedures are a central component of any compliance program. Those standards and procedures help to reduce the prospect of erroneous claims and fraudulent activity by identifying risk areas for the practice and establishing tighter internal controls to counter those risks, while also helping to identify any aberrant billing practices. Many physician practices already have something similar to this called "practice standards" that include practice policy statements regarding patient care, personnel matters and practice standards and procedures on complying with Federal and State law.

The OIG believes that written standards and procedures can be helpful to all physician practices, regardless of size and capability. If a lack of resources to develop such standards and procedures is genuinely an issue, the OIG recommends that a physician practice focus first on those risk areas most likely to arise in its particular practice.[8] Additionally, if the physician practice works with a physician practice management company (PPMC), independent practice association (IPA), physician-hospital organization, management services organization (MSO) or third-party billing company, the practice can incorporate the compliance standards and procedures of those entities, if appropriate, into its own standards and procedures. Many physician practices have found that the adoption of a third party's compliance standards and procedures, as appropriate, has many benefits and the result is a consistent set of standards and procedures for a community of physicians as well as having just one entity that can then monitor and refine the process as needed. This sharing of compliance responsibilities assists physician practices in rural areas that do not have the staff to perform these functions, but do belong to a group that does have the resources. Physician practices using another entity's compliance materials will need to tailor those materials to the physician practice where they will be applied.

Physician practices that do not have standards or procedures in place can develop them by: (1) developing a written standards and procedures manual; and (2) updating clinical forms periodically to make sure they facilitate and encourage clear and complete documentation of patient care. A practice's standards could also identify the clinical protocol(s), pathway(s), and other treatment guidelines followed by the practice.

Creating a resource manual from publicly available information may be a cost-effective approach for developing additional standards and procedures. For example, the practice can develop a "binder" that contains the practice's written standards and procedures, relevant HCFA directives and carrier bulletins, and summaries of informative OIG documents (e.g., Special Fraud Alerts, Advisory Opinions, inspection and audit reports).[9] If the practice chooses to adopt this idea, the binder should be updated as appropriate and located in a readily accessible location.

If updates to the standards and procedures are necessary, those updates should be communicated to employees to keep them informed regarding the practice's operations. New employees can be made aware of the standards and procedures when hired and can be trained on their contents as part of their orientation to the practice. The OIG recommends that the communication of updates and training of new employees occur as soon as possible after either the issuance of a new update or the hiring of a new employee.

1. Specific Risk Areas

The OIG recognizes that many physician practices may not have in place standards and procedures to prevent erroneous or fraudulent conduct in their practices. In order to develop standards and procedures, the physician practice may consider what types of fraud and abuse related topics need to be addressed based on its specific needs. One of the most important things in making that determination is a listing of risk areas where the practice may be vulnerable.

To assist physician practices in performing this initial assessment, the OIG has developed a list of four potential risk areas affecting physician practices. These risk areas include: (a) coding and billing; (b) reasonable and necessary services; (c) documentation; and (d) improper inducements, kickbacks and self-referrals. This list of risk areas is not exhaustive, or all-encompassing. Rather, it should be viewed as a starting point for an internal review of potential vulnerabilities within the physician practice.[10] The objective of such an assessment is to ensure that key personnel in the physician practice are aware of these major risk areas and that steps are taken to minimize, to the extent possible, the types of problems identified. While there are many ways to accomplish this objective, clear written standards and procedures that are communicated to all employees are important to ensure the effectiveness of a compliance program. Specifically, the following are discussions of risk areas for physician practices:[11]

a. Coding and Billing

A major part of any physician practice's compliance program is the identification of risk areas associated with coding and billing. The following risk areas associated with billing have been among the most frequent subjects of investigations and audits by the OIG:

- billing for items or services not rendered or not provided as claimed;[12]
- submitting claims for equipment, medical supplies and services that are not reasonable and necessary;[13]
- double billing resulting in duplicate payment;[14]
- billing for non-covered services as if covered;[15]

- knowing misuse of provider identification numbers, which results in improper billing;[16]

- unbundling (billing for each component of the service instead of billing or using an all-inclusive code);[17]

- failure to properly use coding modifiers;[18]

- clustering;[19] and

- upcoding the level of service provided.20

The physician practice written standards and procedures concerning proper coding reflect the current reimbursement principles set forth in applicable statutes, regulations[21] and Federal, State or private payor health care program requirements and should be developed in tandem with coding and billing standards used in the physician practice. Furthermore, written standards and procedures should ensure that coding and billing are based on medical record documentation. Particular attention should be paid to issues of appropriate diagnosis codes and individual Medicare Part B claims (including documentation guidelines for evaluation and management services).[22] A physician practice can also institute a policy that the coder and/or physician review all rejected claims pertaining to diagnosis and procedure codes. This step can facilitate a reduction in similar errors.

b. Reasonable and Necessary Services

A practice's compliance program may provide guidance that claims are to be submitted only for services that the physician practice finds to be reasonable and necessary in the particular case. The OIG recognizes that physicians should be able to order any tests, including screening tests, they believe are appropriate for the treatment of their patients. However, a physician practice should be aware that Medicare will only pay for services that meet the Medicare definition of reasonable and necessary.[23]

Medicare (and many insurance plans) may deny payment for a service that is not reasonable and necessary according to the Medicare reimbursement rules. Thus, when a physician provides services to a Medicare beneficiary, he or she should only bill those services that meet the Medicare standard of being reasonable and necessary for the diagnosis and treatment of a patient. A physician practice can bill in order to receive a denial for services, but only if the denial is needed for reimbursement from the secondary payor. Upon request, the physician practice should be able to provide documentation, such as a patient's medical records and physician's orders, to support the appropriateness of a service that the physician has provided.

c. Documentation

Timely, accurate and complete documentation is important to clinical patient care. This same documentation serves as a second function when a bill is submitted for payment, namely, as verification that the bill is accurate as submitted. Therefore, one of the most important physician practice compliance issues is the appropriate documentation of diagnosis and treatment. Physician documentation is necessary to determine the appropriate medical treatment for the patient and is the basis for coding and billing determinations. Thorough and accurate documentation also helps to ensure accurate recording and timely transmission of information.

i. Medical Record Documentation

In addition to facilitating high quality patient care, a properly documented medical record verifies and documents precisely what services were actually provided. The medical record may be used to validate: (a) the site of the service; (b) the appropriateness of the services provided; (c) the accuracy of the billing; and (d) the identity of the care giver (service provider). Examples of internal documentation guidelines a practice might use to ensure accurate medical record documentation include the following:[24]

- The medical record is complete and legible;

- The documentation of each patient encounter includes the reason for the encounter; any relevant history; physical examination findings; prior diagnostic test results; assessment, clinical impression, or diagnosis; plan of care; and date and legible identity of the observer;

- If not documented, the rationale for ordering diagnostic and other ancillary services can be easily inferred by an independent reviewer or third party who has appropriate medical training;

- CPT and ICD-9-CM codes used for claims submission are supported by documentation and the medical record; and

- Appropriate health risk factors are identified. The patient's progress, his or her response to, and any changes in, treatment, and any revision in diagnosis is documented. The CPT and ICD-9-CM codes reported on the health insurance claims form should be supported by documentation in the medical record and the medical chart should contain all necessary information. Additionally, HCFA and the local carriers should be able to determine the person who provided the services. These issues can be the root of investigations of inappropriate or erroneous conduct, and have been identified by HCFA and the OIG as a leading cause of improper payments.

One method for improving quality in documentation is for a physician practice to compare the practice's claim denial rate to the rates of other practices in the same specialty to the extent that the practice can obtain that information from the carrier. Physician coding and diagnosis distribution can be compared for each physician within the same specialty to identify variances.

ii. HCFA 1500 Form

Another documentation area for physician practices to monitor closely is the proper completion of the HCFA 1500 form. The following practices will help ensure that the form has been properly completed:

- link the diagnosis code with the reason for the visit or service;

- use modifiers appropriately;

- provide Medicare with all information about a beneficiary's other insurance coverage under the Medicare Secondary Payor (MSP) policy, if the practice is aware of a beneficiary's additional coverage.

d. Improper Inducements, Kickbacks and Self-Referrals

A physician practice would be well advised to have standards and procedures that encourage compliance with the anti-kickback statute[25] and the physician self-referral law.[26] Remuneration for referrals is illegal because it can distort medical decision-making, cause overutilization of services or supplies, increase costs to Federal health care programs, and result in unfair competition by shutting out competitors who are unwilling to pay for referrals. Remuneration for referrals can also affect the quality of patient care by encouraging physicians to order services or supplies based on profit rather than the patients' best medical interests.[27]

In particular, arrangements with hospitals, hospices, nursing facilities, home health agencies, durable medical equipment suppliers, pharmaceutical manufacturers and vendors are areas of potential concern. In general the anti-kickback statute prohibits knowingly and willfully giving or receiving anything of value to induce referrals of Federal health care program business. It is generally recommended that all business arrangements wherein physician practices refer business to, or order services or items from, an outside entity should be on a fair market value basis.[28] Whenever a physician practice intends to enter into a business arrangement that involves making referrals, the arrangement should be reviewed by legal counsel familiar with the anti-kickback statute and physician self-referral statute.

In addition to developing standards and procedures to address arrangements with other health care providers and suppliers, physician practices should also consider implementing measures to avoid offering inappropriate inducements to patients.[29] Examples of such inducements include routinely waiving coinsurance or deductible amounts without a good faith determination that the patient is in financial need or failing to make reasonable efforts to collect the cost-sharing amount.[30]

Possible risk factors relating to this risk area that could be addressed in the practice's standards and procedures include:

- financial arrangements with outside entities to whom the practice may refer Federal health care program business;[31]

- joint ventures with entities supplying goods or services to the physician practice or its patients;[32]

- consulting contracts or medical directorships;

- office and equipment leases with entities to which the physician refers; and

- soliciting, accepting or offering any gift or gratuity of more than nominal value to or from those who may benefit from a physician practice's referral of Federal health care program business.[33]

In order to keep current with this area of the law, a physician practice may obtain copies, available on the OIG web site or in hard copy from the OIG, of all relevant OIG Special Fraud Alerts and Advisory Opinions that address the application of the anti-kickback and physician self-referral laws to ensure that the standards and procedures reflect current positions and opinions.

2. Retention of Records

In light of the documentation requirements faced by physician practices, it would be to the practice's benefit if its standards and procedures contained a section on the retention of compliance, business and medical records. These records primarily include documents relating to patient care and the practice's business activities. A physician practice's designated compliance contact could keep an updated binder or record of these documents, including information relating to compliance activities. The primary compliance documents that a practice would want to retain are those that relate to educational activities, internal investigations and internal audit results. We suggest that particular attention should be paid to documenting investigations of potential violations uncovered by the compliance program and the resulting remedial action. Although there is no requirement that the practice retain its compliance records, having all the relevant documentation relating to the practice's compliance efforts or handling of a particular problem can benefit the practice should it ever be questioned regarding those activities.

Physician practices that implement a compliance program might also want to provide for the development and implementation of a records retention system. This system would establish standards and procedures regarding the creation, distribution, retention, and destruction of documents. If the practice decides to design a record system, privacy concerns and Federal or State regulatory requirements should be taken into consideration.[34]

While conducting its compliance activities, as well as its daily operations, a physician practice would be well advised, to the extent it is possible, to document its efforts to comply with applicable Federal health care program requirements. For example, if a physician practice requests advice from a Government agency (including a Medicare carrier) charged with administering a Federal health care program, it is to the benefit of the practice to document and retain a record of the request and any written or oral response (or nonresponse). This step is extremely important if the practice intends to rely on that response to guide it in future decisions, actions, or claim reimbursement requests or appeals.

In short, it is in the best interest of all physician practices, regardless of size, to have procedures to create and retain appropriate documentation. The following record retention guidelines are suggested:

- The length of time that a practice's records are to be retained can be specified in the physician practice's standards and procedures (Federal and State statutes should be consulted for specific time frames, if applicable);

- Medical records (if in the possession of the physician practice) need to be secured against loss, destruction, unauthorized access, unauthorized reproduction, corruption, or damage; and

- Standards and procedures can stipulate the disposition of medical records in the event the practice is sold or closed.

Step Three: Designation of a Compliance Officer/Contact(s)

After the audits have been completed and the risk areas identified, ideally one member of the physician practice staff needs to accept the responsibility of developing a corrective action plan, if necessary, and oversee the practice's adherence to that plan. This person can either be in charge of all compliance activities for the practice or play a limited role merely to resolve the current issue. In a formalized institutional compliance program there is a compliance officer who is responsible for overseeing the implementation and day-to-day operations of the compliance program. However, the resource constraints of physician practices make it so that it is often impossible to designate one person to be in charge of compliance functions.

It is acceptable for a physician practice to designate more than one employee with compliance monitoring responsibility. In lieu of having a designated compliance officer, the physician practice could instead describe in its standards and procedures the compliance functions for which designated employees, known as "compliance contacts," would be responsible. For example, one employee could be responsible for preparing written standards and procedures, while another could be responsible for conducting or arranging for periodic audits and ensuring that billing questions are answered. Therefore, the compliance-related responsibilities of the designated person or persons may be only a portion of his or her duties.

Another possibility is that one individual could serve as compliance officer for more than one entity. In situations where staffing limitations mandate that the practice cannot afford to designate a person(s) to oversee compliance activities, the practice could outsource all or part of the functions of a compliance officer to a third party, such as a consultant, PPMC, MSO, IPA or third-party billing company. However, if this role is outsourced, it is beneficial for the compliance officer to have sufficient interaction with the physician practice to be able to effectively understand the inner workings of the practice. For example, consultants that are not in close geographic proximity to a practice may not be effective compliance officers for the practice.

One suggestion for how to maintain continual interaction is for the practice to designate someone to serve as a liaison with the outsourced compliance officer. This would help ensure a strong tie between the compliance officer and the practice's daily operations. Outsourced compliance officers, who spend most of their time offsite, have certain limitations that a physician practice should consider before making such a critical decision. These limitations can include lack of understanding as to the inner workings of the practice, accessibility and possible conflicts of interest when one compliance officer is serving several practices.

If the physician practice decides to designate a particular person(s) to oversee all compliance activities, not just those in conjunction with the audit-related issue, the following is a list of suggested duties that the practice may want to assign to that person(s):

- overseeing and monitoring the implementation of the compliance program;
- establishing methods, such as periodic audits, to improve the practice's efficiency and quality of services, and to reduce the practice's vulnerability to fraud and abuse;

- periodically revising the compliance program in light of changes in the needs of the practice or changes in the law and in the standards and procedures of Government and private payor health plans;

- developing, coordinating and participating in a training program that focuses on the components of the compliance program, and seeks to ensure that training materials are appropriate;

- ensuring that the HHS-OIG's List of Excluded Individuals and Entities, and the General Services Administration's (GSA's) List of Parties Debarred from Federal Programs have been checked with respect to all employees, medical staff and independent contractors;[35] and

- investigating any report or allegation concerning possible unethical or improper business practices, and monitoring subsequent corrective action and/or compliance.

Each physician practice needs to assess its own practice situation and determine what best suits that practice in terms of compliance oversight.

Step Four: Conducting Appropriate Training and Education

Education is an important part of any compliance program and is the logical next step after problems have been identified and the practice has designated a person to oversee educational training. Ideally, education programs will be tailored to the physician practice's needs, specialty and size and will include both compliance and specific training.

There are three basic steps for setting up educational objectives:

- determining who needs training (both in coding and billing and in compliance);

- determining the type of training that best suits the practice's needs (e.g., seminars, in-service training, self-study or other programs); and

- determining when and how often education is needed and how much each person should receive.

Training may be accomplished through a variety of means, including in-person training sessions (i.e., either on site or at outside seminars), distribution of newsletters,[36] or even a readily accessible office bulletin board. Regardless of the training modality used, a physician practice should ensure that the necessary education is communicated effectively and that the practice's employees come away from the training with a better understanding of the issues covered.

1. Compliance Training

Under the direction of the designated compliance officer/contact, both initial and recurrent training in compliance is advisable, both with respect to the compliance program itself and applicable statutes and regulations. Suggestions for items to include in compliance training are: the operation and importance of the compliance program; the consequences of violating the standards and procedures set forth in the program; and the role of each employee in the operation of the compliance program.

There are two goals a practice should strive for when conducting compliance training: (1) all employees will receive training on how to perform their jobs in compliance with the standards of the practice and any applicable regulations; and (2) each employee will understand that compliance is a condition of continued employment. Compliance training focuses on explaining why the practice is developing and establishing a compliance program. The training should emphasize that following the standards and procedures will not get a practice employee in trouble, but violating the standards and procedures may subject the employee to disciplinary measures. It is advisable that new employees be trained on the compliance program as soon as possible after their start date and employees should receive refresher training on an annual basis or as appropriate.

2. Coding and Billing Training

Coding and billing training on the Federal health care program requirements may be necessary for certain members of the physician practice staff depending on their respective responsibilities. The OIG understands that most physician practices do not employ a professional coder and that the physician is often primarily responsible for all coding and billing. However, it is in the practice's best interest to ensure that individuals who are directly involved with billing, coding or other aspects of the Federal health care programs receive extensive education specific to that individual's responsibilities. Some examples of items that could be covered in coding and billing training include:

- coding requirements;
- claim development and submission processes;
- signing a form for a physician without the physician's authorization;
- proper documentation of services rendered;
- proper billing standards and procedures and submission of accurate bills for services or items rendered to Federal health care program beneficiaries; and
- the legal sanctions for submitting deliberately false or reckless billings.

3. Format of the Training Program

Training may be conducted either in-house or by an outside source.[37] Training at outside seminars, instead of internal programs and in-service sessions, may be an effective way to achieve the practice's training goals. In fact, many community colleges offer certificate or associate degree programs in billing and coding, and professional associations provide various kinds of continuing education and certification programs. Many carriers also offer billing training.

The physician practice may work with its third-party billing company, if one is used, to ensure that documentation is of a level that is adequate for the billing company to submit accurate claims on behalf of the physician practice. If it is not, these problem areas should also be covered in the training. In addition to the billing training, it is advisable for physician practices to maintain updated ICD-9, HCPCS and CPT manuals (in addition to the carrier bulletins construing those sources) and make them available to all employees involved in the billing process. Physician practices can also provide a source of continuous updates on current billing standards and procedures by making publications or Government documents that describe current billing policies available to its employees.[38]

Physician practices do not have to provide separate education and training programs for the compliance and coding and billing training. All in-service training and continuing education can integrate compliance issues, as well as other core values adopted by the practice, such as quality improvement and improved patient service, into their curriculum.

4. Continuing Education on Compliance Issues

There is no set formula for determining how often training sessions should occur. The OIG recommends that there be at least an annual training program for all individuals involved in the coding and billing aspects of the practice. Ideally, new billing and coding employees will be trained as soon as possible after assuming their duties and will work under an experienced employee until their training has been completed.

Step Five: Responding to Detected Offenses and Developing Corrective Action Initiatives

When a practice determines it has detected a possible violation, the next step is to develop a corrective action plan and determine how to respond to the problem. Violations of a physician practice's compliance program, significant failures to comply with applicable Federal or State law, and other types of misconduct threaten a practice's status as a reliable, honest, and trustworthy provider of health care. Consequently, upon receipt of reports or reasonable indications of suspected noncompliance, it is important that the compliance contact or other practice employee look into the allegations to determine whether a significant violation of applicable law or the requirements of the compliance program has indeed occurred, and, if so, take decisive steps to correct the problem.[40] As appropriate, such steps may involve a corrective action plan,[41] the return of any overpayments, a report to the Government,[42] and/or a referral to law enforcement authorities.

One suggestion is that the practice, in developing its compliance program, develop its own set of monitors and warning indicators. These might include: significant changes in the number and/or types of claim rejections and/or reductions; correspondence from the carriers and insurers challenging the medical necessity or validity of claims; illogical patterns or unusual changes in the pattern of CPT-4, HCPCS or ICD-9 code utilization; and high volumes of unusual charge or payment adjustment transactions. If any of these warning indicators become apparent, then it is recommended that the practice follow up on the issues. Subsequently, as appropriate, the compliance procedures of the practice may need to be changed to prevent the problem from recurring.

For potential criminal violations, a physician practice would be well advised in its compliance program procedures to include steps for prompt referral or disclosure to an appropriate Government authority or law enforcement agency. In regard to overpayment issues, it is advised that the physician practice take appropriate corrective action, including prompt identification and repayment of any overpayment to the affected payor.

It is also recommended that the compliance program provide for a full internal assessment of all reports of detected violations. If the physician practice ignores reports of possible fraudulent activity, it is undermining the very purpose it hoped to achieve by implementing a compliance program.

It is advised that the compliance program standards and procedures include provisions to ensure that a violation is not compounded once discovered. In instances involving individual misconduct, the standards and procedures might also advise as to whether the individuals involved in the violation either be retrained, disciplined, or, if appropriate, terminated. The physician practice may also prevent the compounding of the violation by conducting a review of all confirmed violations, and, if appropriate, self-reporting the violations to the applicable authority.

The physician practice may consider the fact that if a violation occurred and was not detected, its compliance program may require modification. Physician practices that detect violations could analyze the situation to determine whether a flaw in their compliance program failed to anticipate the detected problem, or whether the compliance program's procedures failed to prevent the violation. In any event, it is prudent, even absent the detection of any violations, for physician practices to periodically review and modify their compliance programs.

Step Six: Developing Open Lines of Communication

In order to prevent problems from occurring and to have a frank discussion of why the problem happened in the first place, physician practices need to have open lines of communication. Especially in a smaller practice, an open line of communication is an integral part of implementing a compliance program. Guidance previously issued by the OIG has encouraged the use of several forms of communication between the compliance officer/committee and provider personnel, many of which focus on formal processes and are more costly to implement (e.g., hotlines and e-mail). However, the OIG recognizes that the nature of some physician practices is not as conducive to implementing these types of measures. The nature of a small physician practice dictates that such communication and information exchanges need to be conducted through a less formalized process than that which has been envisioned by prior OIG guidance.

In the small physician practice setting, the communication element may be met by implementing a clear "open door" policy between the physicians and compliance personnel and practice employees. This policy can be implemented in conjunction with less formal communication techniques, such as conspicuous notices posted in common areas and/or the development and placement of a compliance bulletin board where everyone in the practice can receive up-to-date compliance information.[43]

A compliance program's system for meaningful and open communication can include the following:

- the requirement that employees report conduct that a reasonable person would, in good faith, believe to be erroneous or fraudulent;

- the creation of a user-friendly process (such as an anonymous drop box for larger practices) for effectively reporting erroneous or fraudulent conduct;

- provisions in the standards and procedures that state that a failure to report erroneous or fraudulent conduct is a violation of the compliance program;

- the development of a simple and readily accessible procedure to process reports of erroneous or fraudulent conduct;

- if a billing company is used, communication to and from the billing company's compliance officer/contact and other responsible staff to coordinate billing and compliance activities of the practice and the billing company, respectively. Communication can include, as appropriate, lists of reported or identified concerns, initiation and the results of internal assessments, training needs, regulatory changes, and other operational and compliance matters;

- the utilization of a process that maintains the anonymity of the persons involved in the reported possible erroneous or fraudulent conduct and the person reporting the concern; and

- provisions in the standards and procedures that there will be no retribution for reporting conduct that a reasonable person acting in good faith would have believed to be erroneous or fraudulent.

The OIG recognizes that protecting anonymity may not be feasible for small physician practices. However, the OIG believes all practice employees, when seeking answers to questions or reporting potential instances of erroneous or fraudulent conduct, should know to whom to turn for assistance in these matters and should be able to do so without fear of retribution. While the physician practice may strive to maintain the anonymity of an employee's identity, it also needs to make clear that there may be a point at which the individual's identity may become known or may have to be revealed in certain instances.

Step Seven: Enforcing Disciplinary Standards Through Well-Publicized Guidelines

Finally, the last step that a physician practice may wish to take is to incorporate measures into its practice to ensure that practice employees understand the consequences if they behave in a non-compliant manner. An effective physician practice compliance program includes procedures for enforcing and disciplining individuals who violate the practice's compliance or other practice standards. Enforcement and disciplinary provisions are necessary to add credibility and integrity to a compliance program.

The OIG recommends that a physician practice's enforcement and disciplinary mechanisms ensure that violations of the practice's compliance policies will result in consistent and appropriate sanctions, including the possibility of termination, against the offending individual. At the same time, it is advisable that the practice's enforcement and disciplinary procedures be flexible enough to account for mitigating or aggravating circumstances. The procedures might also stipulate that individuals who fail to detect or report violations of the compliance program may also be subject to discipline. Disciplinary actions could include: warnings (oral); reprimands (written); probation; demotion; temporary suspension; termination; restitution of damages; and referral for criminal prosecution. Inclusion of disciplinary guidelines in in-house training and procedure manuals is sufficient to meet the "well publicized" standard of this element.

It is suggested that any communication resulting in the finding of non-compliant conduct be documented in the compliance files by including the date of incident, name of the reporting party, name of the person responsible for taking action, and the follow-up action taken. Another suggestion is for physician practices to conduct checks to make sure all current and potential practice employees are not listed on the OIG or GSA lists of individuals excluded from participation in Federal health care or Government procurement programs.[44]

C. Assessing a Voluntary Compliance Program

A practice's commitment to compliance can best be assessed by the active application of compliance principles in the day-to-day operations of the practice. Compliance programs are not just written standards and procedures that sit on a shelf in the main office of a practice, but are an everyday part of the practice operations. It is by integrating the compliance program into the practice culture that the practice can best achieve maximum benefit from its compliance program.

III. Conclusion

Just as immunizations are given to patients to prevent them from becoming ill, physician practices may view the implementation of a voluntary compliance program as comparable to a form of preventive medicine for the practice. This voluntary compliance program guidance is intended to assist physician practices in developing and implementing internal controls and procedures that promote adherence to Federal health care program requirements.

As stated earlier, physician compliance programs do not need to be time or resource intensive and can be developed in a manner that best reflects the nature of each individual practice. Many of the recommendations set forth in this document are ones that many physician practices already have in place and are simply good business practices that can be adhered to with a reasonable amount of effort. By implementing an effective compliance program, appropriate for its size and resources, and making compliance principles an active part of the practice culture, a physician practice can help prevent and reduce erroneous or fraudulent conduct in its practice. These efforts can also streamline and improve the business operations within the practice and therefore help to innoculate it against future problems.

Endnotes

1. For the purpose of this guidance, the term "physician" is defined as: (1) a doctor of medicine or osteopathy; (2) a doctor of dental surgery or of dental medicine; (3) a podiatrist; (4) an optometrist; or (5) a chiropractor, all of whom must be appropriately licensed by the State. 42 U.S.C. 1395x(r).

2. Much of this guidance can also apply to other independent practitioners, such as psychologists, physical therapists, speech language pathologists, and occupational therapists.

3. Currently, the OIG has issued compliance program guidance for the following eight industry sectors: hospitals, clinical laboratories, home health agencies, durable medical equipment suppliers, third-party medical billing companies, hospices, Medicare+Choice organizations offering coordinated care plans, and nursing facilities. The guidance listed here and referenced in this document is available on the OIG web site at http://www.hhs.gov/oig in the Electronic Reading Room or by calling the OIG Public Affairs office at (202) 619-1343.

4. The OIG has issued Advisory Opinions responding to specific inquiries concerning the application of the OIG's authorities, in particular, the anti-kickback statute, and Special Fraud Alerts setting forth activities that raise legal and enforcement issues. These documents, as well as reports from the OIG's Office of Audit Services and Office of Evaluation and Inspections can be obtained via the Internet address or phone number provided in Footnote 3. Physician practices can also review the Health Care Financing Administration (HCFA) web site on the Internet at http://www.hcfa.gov, for up-to-date regulations, manuals, and program memoranda related to the Medicare and Medicaid programs.

5. 31 U.S.C. 3729.

6. 42 U.S.C. 1320a-7a.

7. See Appendix D.II. referencing the Provider Self-Disclosure Protocol for information on how to conduct a baseline audit.

8. Physician practices with laboratories or arrangements with third-party billing companies can also check the risk areas included in the OIG compliance program guidance for those industries.

9. The OIG and HCFA are working to compile a list of basic documents issued by both entities that could be included in such a binder. We expect to complete this list later this fall, and will post it on the OIG and HCFA web sites as well as publicize this list to physician organizations and representatives (information on how to contact the OIG is contained in Footnote 3; HCFA information can be obtained at www.hcfa.gov/medlearn or by calling 1-800-MEDICARE).

10. Physician practices seeking additional guidance on potential risk areas can review the OIG's Work Plan to identify vulnerabilities and risk areas on which the OIG will focus in the future. In addition, physician practices can also review the OIG's semiannual reports, which identify program vulnerabilities and risk areas that the OIG has targeted during the preceding six months. All of these documents are available on the OIG's webpage at http://www.hhs.gov/oig.

11. Appendix A of this document lists additional risk areas that a physician practice may want to review and incorporate into their practice standards and procedures.

12. For example, Dr. X, an ophthalmologist, billed for laser surgery he did not perform. As one element of proof, he did not even have laser equipment or access to such equipment at the place of service designated on the claim form where he performed the surgery.

13. Billing for services, supplies and equipment that are not reasonable and necessary involves seeking reimbursement for a service that is not warranted by a patient's documented medical condition. See 42 U.S.C. 1395i(a)(1)(A) ("no payment may be made under part A or part B [of Medicare] for any expenses incurred for items or services which . . . are not reasonable and necessary for the diagnosis or treatment of illness or injury or to improve the functioning of the malformed body member"). See also Appendix A for further discussion on this topic.

14. Double billing occurs when a physician bills for the same item or service more than once or another party billed the Federal health care program for an item or service also billed by the physician. Although duplicate billing can occur due to simple error, the knowing submission of duplicate claims—which is sometimes evidenced by systematic or repeated double billing—can create liability under criminal, civil, and/or administrative law.

15. For example, Dr. Y bills Medicare using a covered office visit code when the actual service was a non-covered annual physical. Physician practices should remember that "necessary" does not always constitute "covered" and that this example is a misrepresentation of services to the Federal health care programs.

16. An example of this is when the practice bills for a service performed by Dr. B, who has not yet been issued a Medicare provider number, using Dr. A's Medicare provider number. Physician practices need to bill using the correct Medicare provider number, even if that means delaying billing until the physician receives his/her provider number.

17. Unbundling is the practice of a physician billing for multiple components of a service that must be included in a single fee. For example, if dressings and instruments are included in a fee for a minor procedure, the provider may not also bill separately for the dressings and instruments.

18. A modifier, as defined by the CPT-4 manual, provides the means by which a physician practice can indicate a service or procedure that has been performed has been altered by some specific circumstance, but not changed in its definition or code. Assuming the modifier is used correctly and appropriately, this specificity provides the justification for payment for those services. For correct use of modifiers, the physician practice should reference the appropriate sections of the Medicare Provider Manual. See Medicare Carrier Manual § 4630. For general information on the correct use of modifiers, a physician practice can consult the National Correct Coding Initiative (NCCI). See Appendix F for information on how to download the NCCI edits. The NCCI coding edits are updated on a quarterly basis and are used to process claims and determine payments to physicians.

19. This is the practice of coding/charging one or two middle levels of service codes exclusively, under the philosophy that some will be higher, some lower, and the charges will average out over an extended period (in reality, this overcharges some patients while undercharging others).

20. Upcoding is billing for a more expensive service than the one actually performed. For example, Dr. X intentionally bills at a higher evaluation and management (E&M) code than what he actually renders to the patient.

21. The official coding guidelines are promulgated by HCFA, the National Center for Health Statistics, the American Hospital Association, the American Medical Association and the American Health Information Management Association. See International Classification of Diseases, 9th Revision, Clinical Modification (ICD-9 CM)(and its successors); 1998 Health Care Financing Administration Common Procedure Coding System (HCPCS) (and its successors); and Physicians' CPT. In addition, there are specialized coding systems for specific segments of the health care industry. Among these are ADA (for dental procedures), DSM IV (psychiatric health benefits) and DMERCs (for durable medical equipment, prosthetics, orthotics and supplies).

22. The failure of a physician practice to: (i) document items and services rendered; and (ii) properly submit the corresponding claims for reimbursement is a major area of potential erroneous or fraudulent conduct involving Federal health care programs. The OIG has undertaken numerous audits, investigations, inspections and national enforcement initiatives in these areas.

23. " . . . for the diagnosis or treatment of illness or injury or to improve the functioning of a malformed body member." 42 U.S.C. 1395y(a)(1)(A).

24. For additional information on proper documentation, physician practices should also reference the Documentation Guidelines for Evaluation and Management Services, published by HCFA. Currently, physicians may document based on the 1995 or 1997 E&M Guidelines, whichever is most advantageous to the physician. A new set of draft guidelines were announced in June 2000, and are undergoing pilot testing and revision, but are not in current use.

25. The anti-kickback statute provides criminal penalties for individuals and entities that knowingly offer, pay, solicit, or receive bribes or kickbacks or other remuneration in order to induce business reimbursable by Federal health care programs. See 42 U.S.C. 1320a-7b(b). Civil penalties, exclusion from participation in the Federal health care programs, and civil False Claims Act liability may also result from a violation of the prohibition. See 42 U.S.C. 1320a-7a(a)(5), 42 U.S.C. 1320a-7(b)(7), and 31 U.S.C. 3729-3733.

26. The physician self-referral law, 42 U.S.C. 1395nn (also known as the "Stark law"), prohibits a physician from making a referral to an entity with which the physician or any member of the physician's immediate family has a financial relationship if the referral is for the furnishing of designated health services, unless the financial relationship fits into an exception set forth in the statute or implementing regulations.

27. See Appendix B for additional information on the anti-kickback statute.

28. The OIG's definition of "fair market value" excludes any value attributable to referrals of Federal program business or the ability to influence the flow of such business. See 42 U.S.C. 1395nn(h)(3). Adhering to the rule of keeping business arrangements at fair market value is not a guarantee of legality, but is a highly useful general rule.

29. See 42 U.S.C. 1320a-7a(a)(5).

30. In the OIG Special Fraud Alert "Routine Waiver of Part B Co-payments/ Deductibles" (May 1991), the OIG describes several reasons why routine waivers of these cost-sharing amounts pose concerns. The Alert sets forth the circumstances under which it may be appropriate to waive these amounts. See also 42 U.S.C. 1320a-7a(a)(5).

31. All physician contracts and agreements with parties in a position to influence Federal health care program business or to whom the doctor is in such a position to influence should be reviewed to avoid violation of the anti-kickback, self-referral, and other relevant Federal and State laws. The OIG has published safe harbors that define practices not subject to the anti-kickback statute, because such arrangements would be unlikely to result in fraud or abuse. Failure to comply with a safe harbor provision does not make an arrangement per se illegal. Rather, the safe harbors set forth specific conditions that, if fully met, would assure the entities involved of not being prosecuted or sanctioned for the arrangement qualifying for the safe harbor. One such safe harbor applies to personal services contracts. See 42 CFR 1001.952(d).

32. See OIG Special Fraud Alert "Joint Venture Arrangements" (August 1989) available on the OIG web site at http://www.hhs.gov/oig. See also OIG Advisory Opinion 97-5.

33. Physician practices should establish clear standards and procedures governing gift-giving because such exchanges may be viewed as inducements to influence business decisions.

34. There are various Federal regulations governing the privacy of patient records and the retention of certain types of patient records. Many states also have record retention statutes. Practices should check with their state medical society and/or affiliated professional association for assistance in ascertaining these requirements for their particular specialty and location.

35. The HHS-OIG "List of Excluded Individuals/Entities" provides information to health care providers, patients, and others regarding individuals and entities that are excluded from participation in Federal health care programs. This report, in both an on-line searchable and downloadable database, can be located on the Internet at http://www.hhs.gov/oig. The OIG sanction information is readily available to users in two formats on over 15,000 individuals and entities currently excluded from program participation through action taken by the OIG. The on-line searchable database allows users to obtain information regarding excluded individuals and entities sorted by: (1) the legal bases for exclusions; (2) the types of individuals and entities excluded by the OIG; and (3) the States where excluded individuals reside or entities do business. In addition, the General Services Administration maintains a monthly listing of debarred contractors, "List of Parties Debarred from Federal Programs," at http://www.arnet.gov/epls.

36. HCFA also offers free online training for general fraud and abuse issues at http://www.hcfa.gov/medlearn. See Appendix F for additional information.

37. As noted earlier in this guidance, another way for physician practices to receive training is for the physicians and/or the employees of the practice to attend training programs offered by outside entities, such as a hospital, a local medical society or a carrier. This sort of collaborative effort is an excellent way for the practice to meet the desired training objective without having to expend the resources to develop and implement in-house training.

38. Some publications, such as OIG's Special Fraud Alerts, audit and inspection reports, and Advisory Opinions are readily available from the OIG and can provide a basis for educational courses and programs for physician practice employees. See Appendix F for a partial listing of these documents. See Footnote 3 for information on how to obtain copies of these documents.

39. Currently, the OIG is monitoring a significant number of corporate integrity agreements that require many of these training elements. The OIG usually requires a minimum of one hour annually for basic training in compliance areas. Additional training may be necessary for specialty fields such as claims development and billing.

40. Instances of noncompliance must be determined on a case-by-case basis. The existence or amount of a monetary loss to a health care program is not solely determinative of whether the conduct should be investigated and reported to governmental authorities. In fact, there may be instances where there is no readily identifiable monetary loss to a health care provider, but corrective actions are still necessary to protect the integrity of the applicable program and its beneficiaries, e.g., where services required by a plan of care are not provided.

41. The physician practice may seek advice from its legal counsel to determine the extent of the practice's liability and to plan the appropriate course of action.

42. The OIG has established a Provider Self-Disclosure Protocol that encourages providers to voluntarily report suspected fraud. The concept of voluntary self-disclosure is premised on a recognition that the Government alone cannot protect the integrity of the Medicare and other Federal health care programs. Health care providers must be willing to police themselves, correct underlying problems, and work with the Government to resolve these matters. The Provider Self-Disclosure Protocol can be located on the OIG's web site at: www.hhs.gov/oig. See Appendix D for further information on the Provider Self-Disclosure Protocol.

43. In addition to whatever other method of communication is being utilized, the OIG recommends that physician practices post the HHS-OIG Hotline telephone number (1-800-HHS-TIPS) in a prominent area.

44. See Footnote 35 for information on how to access these lists.

Appendix A: Additional Risk Areas

Appendix A describes additional risk areas that a physician practice may wish to address during the development of its compliance program. If any of the following risk areas are applicable to the practice, the practice may want to consider addressing the risk areas by incorporating them into the practice's written standards and procedures manual and addressing them in its training program.

I. Reasonable and Necessary Services

A. Local Medical Review Policy

An area of concern for physicians relating to determinations of reasonable and necessary services is the variation in local medical review policies (LMRPs) among carriers. Physicians are supposed to bill the Federal health care programs only for items and services that are reasonable and necessary. However, in order to determine whether an item or service is reasonable and necessary under Medicare guidelines, the physician must apply the appropriate LMRP.[1]

With the exception of claims that are properly coded and submitted to Medicare solely for the purpose of obtaining a written denial, physician practices are to bill the Federal health programs only for items and services that are covered. In order to determine if an item or service is covered for Medicare, a physician practice must be knowledgeable of the LMRPs applicable to its practice's jurisdiction. The practice may contact its carrier to request a copy of the pertinent LMRPs, and once the practice receives the copies, they can be incorporated into the practice's written standards and procedures manual. When the LMRP indicates that an item or service may not be covered by Medicare, the physician practice is responsible to convey this information to the patient so that the patient can make an informed decision concerning the health care services he/she may want to receive. Physician practices convey this information through Advance Beneficiary Notices (ABNs).

B. Advance Beneficiary Notices

Physicians are required to provide ABNs before they provide services that they know or believe Medicare does not consider reasonable and necessary. (The one exception to this requirement is for services that are performed pursuant to EMTALA requirements as described in section II.A). A properly executed ABN acknowledges that coverage is uncertain or yet to be determined, and stipulates that the patient promises to pay the bill if Medicare does not. Patients who are not notified before they receive such services are not responsible for payment. The ABN must be sufficient to put the patient on notice of the reasons why the physician believes that the payment may be denied. The objective is to give the patient sufficient information to allow an informed choice as to whether to pay for the service.

Accordingly, each ABN should:

1. be in writing;

2. identify the specific service that may be denied (procedure name and CPT/HCPC code is recommended);

3. state the specific reason why the physician believes that service may be denied; and

4. be signed by the patient acknowledging that the required information was provided and that the patient assumes responsibility to pay for the service.

The Medicare Carrier's Manual[2] provides that an ABN will not be acceptable if: (1) the patient is asked to sign a blank ABN form; or (2) the ABN is used routinely without regard to a particularized need. The routine use of ABNs is generally prohibited because the ABN must state the specific reason the physician anticipates that the specific service will not be covered.

A common risk area associated with ABNs is in regard to diagnostic tests or services. There are three steps that a physician practice can take to help ensure it is in compliance with the regulations concerning ABNs for diagnostic tests or services:

1. determine which tests are not covered under national coverage rules;

2. determine which tests are not covered under local coverage rules such as LMRPs (contact the practice's carrier to see if a listing has been assembled); and

3. determine which tests are only covered for certain diagnoses.

The OIG is aware that the use of ABNs is an area where physician practices experience numerous difficulties. Practices can help to reduce problems in this area by educating their physicians and office staff on the correct use of ABNs, obtaining guidance from the carrier regarding their interpretation of whether an ABN is necessary where the service is not covered, developing a standard form for all diagnostic tests (most carriers have a developed model), and developing a process for handling patients who refuse to sign ABNs.

C. Physician Liability for Certifications in the Provision of Medical Equipment and Supplies and Home Health Services

In January 1999, the OIG issued a Special Fraud Alert on this topic, which is available on the OIG web site at www.hhs.gov/oig/frdalrt/index.htm. The following is a summary of the Special Fraud Alert.

The OIG issued the Special Fraud Alert to reiterate to physicians the legal and programmatic significance of physician certifications made in connection with the ordering of certain items and services for Medicare patients. In light of information obtained through OIG provider audits, the OIG deemed it necessary to remind physicians that they may be subject to criminal, civil and administrative penalties for signing a certification when they know that the information is false or for signing a certification with reckless disregard as to the truth of the information. (See Appendix B and Appendix C for more detailed information on the applicable statutes).

Medicare has conditioned payment for many items and services on a certification signed by a physician attesting that the physician has reviewed the patient's condition and has determined that an item or service is reasonable and necessary. Because Medicare primarily relies on the professional judgment of the treating physician to determine the reasonable and necessary nature of a given service or supply, it is important that physicians provide complete and accurate information on any certifications they sign. Physician certification is obtained through a variety of forms, including prescriptions, orders, and Certificates of Medical Necessity (CMNs). Two areas where physician certification as to whether an item or service is reasonable and necessary is essential and which are vulnerable to abuse are: (1) home health services; and (2) durable medical equipment.

By signing a CMN, the physician represents that:

1. he or she is the patient's treating physician and that the information regarding the physician's address and unique physician identification number (UPIN) is correct;

2. the entire CMN, including the sections filled out by the supplier, was completed prior to the physician's signature; and

3. the information in section B relating to whether the item or service is reasonable and necessary is true, accurate, and complete to the best of the physician's knowledge. Activities such as signing blank CMNs, signing a CMN without seeing the patient to verify the item or service is reasonable and necessary, and signing a CMN for a service that the physician knows is not reasonable and necessary are activities that can lead to criminal, civil and administrative penalties.

Ultimately, it is advised that physicians carefully review any form of certification (order, prescription or CMN) before signing it to verify that the information contained in the certification is both complete and accurate.

D. Billing for Non-covered Services as if Covered

In some instances, we are aware that physician practices submit claims for services in order to receive a denial from the carrier, thereby enabling the patient to submit the denied claim for payment to a secondary payer.

A common question relating to this risk area is: If the medical services provided are not covered under Medicare, but the secondary or supplemental insurer requires a Medicare rejection in order to cover the services, then would the original submission of the claim to Medicare be considered fraudulent? Under the applicable regulations, the OIG would not consider such submissions to be fraudulent. For example, the denial may be necessary to establish patient liability protections as stated in section 1879 of the Social Security Act (the Act) (codified at 42 U.S.C. 1395pp). As stated, Medicare denials may also be required so that the patient can seek payment from a secondary insurer. In instances where a claim is being submitted to Medicare for this purpose, the physician should indicate on the claim submission that the claim is being submitted for the purpose of receiving a denial, in order to bill a secondary insurance carrier. This step should assist carriers and prevent inadvertent payments to which the physician is not entitled.

In some instances, however, the carrier pays the claim even though the service is non-covered, and even though the physician did not intend for payment to be made. When this occurs, the physician has a responsibility to refund the amount paid and indicate that the service is not covered.

II. Physician Relationships with Hospitals

A. The Physician Role in EMTALA

The Emergency Medical Treatment and Active Labor Act (EMTALA), 42 U.S.C. 1395dd, is an area that has been receiving increasing scrutiny. The statute is intended to ensure that all patients who come to the emergency department of a hospital receive care, regardless of their insurance or ability to pay. Both hospitals and physicians need to work together to ensure compliance with the provisions of this law.

The statute imposes three fundamental requirements upon hospitals that participate in the Medicare program with regard to patients requesting emergency care. First, the hospital must conduct an appropriate medical screening examination to determine if an emergency medical condition exists.[3] Second, if the hospital determines that an emergency medical condition exists, it must either provide the treatment necessary to stabilize the emergency medical condition or comply with the statute's requirements to effect a proper transfer of a patient whose condition has not been stabilized.[4] A hospital is considered to have met this second requirement if an individual refuses the hospital's offer of additional examination or treatment, or refuses to consent to a transfer, after having been informed of the risks and benefits.[5]

If an individual's emergency medical condition has not been stabilized, the statute's third requirement is activated. A hospital may not transfer an individual with an unstable emergency medical condition unless: (1) the individual or his or her representative makes a written request for transfer to another medical facility after being informed of the risk of transfer and the transferring hospital's obligation under the statute to provide additional examination or treatment; (2) a physician has signed a certification summarizing the medical risks and benefits of a transfer and certifying that, based up on the information available at the time of transfer, the medical benefits reasonably expected from the transfer outweigh the increased risks; or (3) if a physician is not physically present when the transfer decision is made, a qualified medical person signs the certification after the physician, in consultation with the qualified medical person, has made the determination that the benefits of transfer outweigh the increased risks. The physician must later countersign the certification.[6]

Physician and/or hospital misconduct may result in violations of the statute.[7] One area of particular concern is physician on-call responsibilities. Physician practices whose members serve as on-call emergency room physicians with hospitals are advised to familiarize themselves with the hospital's policies regarding on-call physicians. This can be done by reviewing the medical staff bylaws or policies and procedures of the hospital that must define the responsibility of on-call physicians to respond to, examine, and treat patients with emergency medical conditions. Physicians should also be aware of the requirement that, when medically indicated, on-call physicians must generally come to the hospital to examine the patient. The exception to this requirement is that a patient may be sent to see the on-call physician at a hospital-owned contiguous or on-campus facility to conduct or complete the medical screening examination as long as:

1. all persons with the same medical condition are moved to this location;

2. there is a bona fide medical reason to move the patient; and

3. qualified medical personnel accompany the patient.

B. Teaching Physicians

Special regulations apply to teaching physicians' billings. Regulations provide that services provided by teaching physicians in teaching settings are generally payable under the physician fee schedule only if the services are personally furnished by a physician who is not a resident or the services are furnished by a resident in the presence of a teaching physician.[8]

Unless a service falls under a specified exception, such as the Primary Care Exception,[9] the teaching physician must be present during the key portion of any service or procedure for which payment is sought.[10] Physicians should ensure the following with respect to services provided in the teaching physician setting:[11]

- only services actually provided are billed;

- every physician who provides or supervises the provision of services to a patient is responsible for the correct documentation of the services that were rendered;

- every physician is responsible for assuring that in cases where the physician provides evaluation and management (E&M) services, a patient's medical record includes appropriate documentation of the applicable key components of the E&M services provided or supervised by the physician (e.g., patient history, physician examination, and medical decision making), as well as documentation to adequately reflect the procedure or portion of the services provided by the physician; and

- unless specifically excepted by regulation, every physician must document his or her presence during the key portion of any service or procedure for which payment is sought.

C. Gainsharing Arrangements and Civil Monetary Penalties for Hospital Payments to Physicians to Reduce or Limit Services to Beneficiaries

In July 1999, the OIG issued a Special Fraud Alert on this topic, which is available on the OIG web site at www.hhs.gov/oig/frdalrt/index.htm. The following is a summary of the Special Fraud Alert. The term "gainsharing" typically refers to an arrangement in which a hospital gives a physician a percentage share of any reduction in the hospital's costs for patient care attributable in part to the physician's efforts. The civil monetary penalty (CMP) that applies to gainsharing arrangements is set forth in 42 U.S.C. 1320a-7a(b)(1). This section prohibits any hospital or critical access hospital from knowingly making a payment directly or indirectly to a physician as an inducement to reduce or limit services to Medicare or Medicaid beneficiaries under a physician's care.

It is the OIG's position that the Civil Monetary Penalties Law clearly prohibits any gainsharing arrangements that involve payments by, or on behalf of, a hospital to physicians with clinical care responsibilities to induce a reduction or limitation of services to Medicare or Medicaid beneficiaries. However, hospitals and physicians are not prohibited from working together to reduce unnecessary hospital costs through other arrangements. For example, hospitals and physicians may enter into personal services contracts where hospitals pay physicians based on a fixed fee at fair market value for services rendered to reduce costs rather than a fee based on a share of cost savings.

D. Physician Incentive Arrangements

The OIG has identified potentially illegal practices involving the offering of incentives by entities in an effort to recruit and retain physicians. The OIG is concerned that the intent behind offering incentives to physicians may not be to recruit physicians, but instead the offer is intended as a kickback to obtain and increase patient referrals from physicians. These recruitment incentive arrangements are implicated by the Anti-Kickback Statute because they can constitute remuneration offered to induce, or in return for, the referral of business paid for by Medicare or Medicaid.

Some examples of questionable incentive arrangements are:

- provision of free or significantly discounted billing, nursing, or other staff services.
- payment of the cost of a physician's travel and expenses for conferences.
- payment for a physician's services that require few, if any, substantive duties by the physician.
- guarantees that if the physician's income fails to reach a predetermined level, the entity will supplement the remainder up to a certain amount.

III. Physician Billing Practices

A. Third-Party Billing Services

Physicians should remember that they remain responsible to the Medicare program for bills sent in the physician's name or containing the physician's signature, even if the physician had no actual knowledge of a billing impropriety. The attestation on the HCFA 1500 form, i.e., the physician's signature line, states that the physician's services were billed properly. In other words, it is no defense for the physician if the physician's billing service improperly bills Medicare.

One of the most common risk areas involving billing services deals with physician practices contracting with billing services on a percentage basis. Although percentage based billing arrangements are not illegal per se, the Office of Inspector General has a longstanding concern that such arrangements may increase the risk of intentional upcoding and similar abusive billing practices.[12]

A physician may contract with a billing service on a percentage basis. However, the billing service can not directly receive the payment of Medicare funds into a bank account that it solely controls. Under 42 U.S.C. 1395u(b)(6), Medicare payments can only be made to either the beneficiary or a party (such as a physician) that furnished the services and accepted assignment of the beneficiary's claim. A billing service that contracts on a percentage basis does not qualify as a party that furnished services to a beneficiary, thus a billing service cannot directly receive payment of Medicare funds. According to the Medicare Carriers Manual § 3060(A), a payment is considered to be made directly to the billing service if the service can convert the payment to its own use and control without the payment first passing through the control of the physician. For example, the billing service should not bill the claims under its own name or tax identification number. The billing service should bill claims under the physician's name and tax identification number. Nor should a billing service receive the payment of Medicare funds directly into a bank account over which the billing service maintains sole control. The Medicare payments should instead be deposited into a bank account over which the provider has signature control.

Physician practices should review the third-party medical billing guidance for additional information on third-party billing companies and the compliance risk areas associated with billing companies.

B. Billing Practices by Non-Participating Physicians

Even though nonparticipating physicians do not accept payment directly from the Medicare program, there are a number of laws that apply to the billing of Medicare beneficiaries by non-participating physicians.

Limiting Charges

42 U.S.C. 1395w-4(g) prohibits a nonparticipating physician from knowingly and willfully billing or collecting on a repeated basis an actual charge for a service that is in excess of the Medicare limiting charge. For example, a nonparticipating physician may not bill a Medicare beneficiary $50 for an office visit when the Medicare limiting charge for the visit is $25. Additionally, there are numer-

ous provisions that prohibit nonparticipating physicians from knowingly and willfully charging patients in excess of the statutory charge limitations for certain specified procedures, such as cataract surgery, mammography screening and coronary artery bypass surgery. Failure to comply with these sections can result in a fine of up to $10,000 per violation or exclusion from participation in Federal health care programs for up to five years.

Refund of Excess Charges

42 U.S.C. 1395w-4(g) mandates that if a nonparticipating physician collects an actual charge for a service that is in excess of the limiting charge, the physician must refund the amount collected above the limiting charge to the individual within 30 days notice of the violation. For example, if a physician collected $50 from a Medicare beneficiary for an office visit, but the limiting charge for the visit was $25, the physician must refund $25 to the beneficiary, which is the difference between the amount collected ($50) and the limiting charge ($25). Failure to comply with this requirement may result in a fine of up to $10,000 per violation or exclusion from participation in Federal health care programs for up to five years.

42 U.S.C. 1395u(l)(A)(iii) mandates that a nonparticipating physician must refund payments received from a Medicare beneficiary if it is later determined by a Peer Review Organization or a Medicare carrier that the services were not reasonable and necessary. Failure to comply with this requirement may result in a fine of up to $10,000 per violation or exclusion from participation in Federal health care programs for up to five years.

C. Professional Courtesy

The term "professional courtesy" is used to describe a number of analytically different practices. The traditional definition is the practice by a physician of waiving all or a part of the fee for services provided to the physician's office staff, other physicians, and/or their families. In recent times, "professional courtesy" has also come to mean the waiver of coinsurance obligations or other out-of-pocket expenses for physicians or their families (i.e., "insurance only" billing), and similar payment arrangements by hospitals or other institutions for services provided to their medical staffs or employees. While only the first of these practices is truly "professional courtesy," in the interests of clarity and completeness, we will address all three.

In general, whether a professional courtesy arrangement runs afoul of the fraud and abuse laws is determined by two factors: (i) how the recipients of the professional courtesy are selected; and (ii) how the professional courtesy is extended. If recipients are selected in a manner that directly or indirectly takes into account their ability to affect past or future referrals, the anti-kickback statute—which prohibits giving anything of value to generate Federal health care program business—may be implicated. If the professional courtesy is extended through a waiver of copayment obligations (i.e., "insurance only" billing), other statutes may be implicated, including the prohibition of inducements to beneficiaries, section 1128A(a)(5) of the Act (codified at 42 U.S.C. 1320a-7a(a)(5)). Claims submitted as a result of either practice may also implicate the civil False Claims Act.

The following are general observations about professional courtesy arrangements for physician practices to consider:

- A physician's regular and consistent practice of extending professional courtesy by waiving the entire fee for services rendered to a group of persons (including employees, physicians, and/or their family members) may not implicate any of the OIG's fraud and abuse authorities so long as membership in the group receiving the courtesy is determined in a manner that does not take into account directly or indirectly any group member's ability to refer to, or otherwise generate Federal health care program business for, the physician.

- A physician's regular and consistent practice of extending professional courtesy by waiving otherwise applicable copayments for services rendered to a group of persons (including employees, physicians, and/or their family members), would not implicate the anti-kickback statute so long as membership in the group is determined in a manner that does not take into account directly or indirectly any group member's ability to refer to, or otherwise generate Federal health care program business for, the physician.

- Any waiver of copayment practice, including that described in the preceding bullet, does implicate section 1128A(a)(5) of the Act if the patient for whom the copayment is waived is a Federal health care program beneficiary who is not financially needy.

The legality of particular professional courtesy arrangements will turn on the specific facts presented, and, with respect to the anti-kickback statute, on the specific intent of the parties. A physician practice may wish to consult with an attorney if it is uncertain about its professional courtesy arrangements.

IV. Other Risk Areas

A. Rental of Space in Physician Offices by Persons or Entities to Which Physicians Refer

In February 2000, the OIG issued a Special Fraud Alert on this topic, which is available on the OIG web site at www.hhs.gov/oig/frdalrt/index.htm. The following is a summary of the Special Fraud Alert.

Among various relationships between physicians and labs, hospitals, home health agencies, etc., the OIG has identified potentially illegal practices involving the rental of space in a physician's office by suppliers that provide items or services to patients who are referred or sent to the supplier by the physician-landlord. An example of a suspect arrangement is the rental of physician office space by a durable medical equipment (DME) supplier in a position to benefit from referrals of the physician's patients. The OIG is concerned that in such arrangements the rental payments may be disguised kickbacks to the physician-landlord to induce referrals.

Space Rental Safe Harbor to the Anti-Kickback Statute

To avoid potentially violating the anti-kickback statute, the OIG recommends that rental agreements comply with all of the following criteria for the space rental safe harbor:

- The agreement is set out in writing and signed by the parties.

- The agreement covers all of the space rented by the parties for the term of the agreement and specifies the space covered by the agreement.

- If the agreement is intended to provide the lessee with access to the space for periodic intervals of time rather than on a full-time basis for the term of the rental agreement, the rental agreement specifies exactly the schedule of such intervals, the precise length of each interval, and the exact rent for each interval.

- The term of the rental agreement is for not less than one year.

- The aggregate rental charge is set in advance, is consistent with fair market value, and is not determined in a manner that takes into account the volume or value of any referrals or business otherwise generated between the parties for which payment may be made in whole or in part under Medicare or a State health care program.

- The aggregate space rented does not exceed that which is reasonably necessary to accomplish the commercially reasonable business purpose of the rental.

B. Unlawful Advertising

42 U.S.C. 1320b-10 makes it unlawful for any person to advertise using the names, abbreviations, symbols, or emblems of the Social Security Administration, Health Care Financing Administration, Department of Health and Human Services, Medicare, Medicaid or any combination or variation of such words, abbreviations, symbols or emblems in a manner that such person knows or should know would convey the false impression that the advertised item is endorsed by the named entities. For instance, a physician may not place an ad in the newspaper that reads "Dr. X is a cardiologist approved by both the Medicare and Medicaid programs." A violation of this section may result in a

penalty of up to $5,000 ($25,000 in the case of a broadcast or telecast) for each violation.

Endnotes

1. HCFA has recently developed a web site which, when completed by the end of the year 2000, will contain the LMRPs for each of the contractors across the country. The web site can be accessed at http://www.lmrp.net.

2. The relevant manual provisions are located at MCM, Part III, §§ 7300 and 7320. This section of the manual also includes the carrier's recommended form of an ABN.

3. See 42 U.S.C. 1395dd(a).

4. See 42 U.S.C. 1395dd(b)(1).

5. See 42 U.S.C. 1395dd(b)(2) and (3).

6. See 42 U.S.C. 1395dd(c)(1)(A).

7. Hospitals and physicians, including on-call physicians, who violate the statute may face penalties that include civil fines of up to $50,000 (or not more than $25,000 in the case of a hospital with less than 100 beds) per violation, and physicians may be excluded from participation in the Federal health care programs.

8. 42 CFR 415.150 through 415.190.

9. 42 CFR 415.174

10. Id.

11. This section is not intended to be and is not a complete reference for teaching physicians. It is strongly recommended that those physicians who practice in a teaching setting consult their respective hospitals for more guidance.

12. This concern is noted in Advisory Opinion No. 98-4 and also the Office of Inspector General Compliance Program Guidance for Third-Party Medical Billing Companies. Both are available on the OIG web site at http://www.hhs.gov/oig.

Appendix B: Criminal Statutes

This Appendix contains a description of criminal statutes related to fraud and abuse in the context of health care. The Appendix is not intended to be a compilation of all Federal statutes related to health care fraud and abuse. It is merely a summary of some of the more frequently cited Federal statutes.

I. Health Care Fraud (18 U.S.C. 1347)

Description of Unlawful Conduct

It is a crime to knowingly and willfully execute (or attempt to execute) a scheme to defraud any health care benefit program, or to obtain money or property from a health care benefit program through false representations. Note that this law applies not only to Federal health care programs, but to most other types of health care benefit programs as well.

Penalty for Unlawful Conduct

The penalty may include the imposition of fines, imprisonment of up to 10 years, or both. If the violation results in serious bodily injury, the prison term may be increased to a maximum of 20 years. If the violation results in death, the prison term may be expanded to include any number of years, or life imprisonment.

Examples

1. Dr. X, a chiropractor, intentionally billed Medicare for physical therapy and chiropractic treatments that he never actually rendered for the purpose of fraudulently obtaining Medicare payments.

2. Dr. X, a psychiatrist, billed Medicare, Medicaid, TRICARE, and private insurers for psychiatric services that were provided by his nurses rather than himself.

II. Theft or Embezzlement in Connection with Health Care (18 U.S.C. 669)

Description of Unlawful Conduct

It is a crime to knowingly and willfully embezzle, steal or intentionally misapply any of the assets of a health care benefit program. Note that this law applies not only to Federal health care programs, but to most other types of health care benefit programs as well.

Penalty for Unlawful Conduct

The penalty may include the imposition of a fine, imprisonment of up to 10 years, or both. If the value of the asset is $100 or less, the penalty is a fine, imprisonment of up to a year, or both.

Example

An office manager for Dr. X knowingly embezzles money from the bank account for Dr. X's practice. The bank account includes reimbursement received from the Medicare program; thus, intentional embezzlement of funds from this account is a violation of the law.

III. False Statements Relating to Health Care Matters (18 U.S.C. 1035)

Description of Unlawful Conduct

It is a crime to knowingly and willfully falsify or conceal a material fact, or make any materially false statement or use any materially false writing or document in connection with the delivery of or payment for health care benefits, items or services. Note that this law applies not only to Federal health care programs, but to most other types of health care benefit programs as well.

Penalty for Unlawful Conduct

The penalty may include the imposition of a fine, imprisonment of up to five years, or both.

Example

Dr. X certified on a claim form that he performed laser surgery on a Medicare beneficiary when he knew that the surgery was not actually performed on the patient.

IV. Obstruction of Criminal Investigations of Health Care Offenses (18 U.S.C. 1518)

Description of Unlawful Conduct

It is a crime to willfully prevent, obstruct, mislead, delay or attempt to prevent, obstruct, mislead, or delay the communication of records relating to a Federal health care offense to a criminal investigator. Note that this law applies not only to Federal health care programs, but to most other types of health care benefit programs as well.

Penalty for Unlawful Conduct

The penalty may include the imposition of a fine, imprisonment of up to five years, or both.

Examples

1. Dr. X instructs his employees to tell OIG investigators that Dr. X personally performs all treatments when, in fact, medical technicians do the majority of the treatment and Dr. X is rarely present in the office.

2. Dr. X was under investigation by the FBI for reported fraudulent billings. Dr. X altered patient records in an attempt to cover up the improprieties.

V. Mail and Wire Fraud (18 U.S.C. 1341 and 1343)

Description of Unlawful Conduct

It is a crime to use the mail, private courier, or wire service to conduct a scheme to defraud another of money or property. The term "wire services" includes the use of a telephone, fax machine or computer. Each use of a mail or wire service to further fraudulent activities is considered a separate crime. For instance, each fraudulent claim that is submitted electronically to a carrier would be considered a separate violation of the law.

Penalty for Unlawful Conduct

The penalty may include the imposition of a fine, imprisonment of up to five years, or both.

Examples

1. Dr. X knowingly and repeatedly submits electronic claims to the Medicare carrier for office visits that he did not actually provide to Medicare beneficiaries with the intent to obtain payments from Medicare for services he never performed.

2. Dr. X, a neurologist, knowingly submitted claims for tests that were not reasonable and necessary and intentionally upcoded office visits and electromyograms to Medicare.

VI. Criminal Penalties for Acts Involving Federal Health Care Programs (42 U.S.C. 1320a-7b)

Description of Unlawful Conduct

False Statement and Representations

It is a crime to knowingly and willfully:

1) make, or cause to be made, false statements or representations in applying for benefits or payments under all Federal health care programs;

2) make, or cause to be made, any false statement or representation for use in determining rights to such benefit or payment;

3) conceal any event affecting an individual's initial or continued right to receive a benefit or payment with the intent to fraudulently receive the benefit or payment either in an amount or quantity greater than that which is due or authorized;

4) convert a benefit or payment to a use other than for the use and benefit of the person for whom it was intended;

5) present, or cause to be presented, a claim for a physician's service when the service was not furnished by a licensed physician;

6) for a fee, counsel an individual to dispose of assets in order to become eligible for medical assistance under a State health program, if disposing of the assets results in the imposition of an ineligibility period for the individual.

Anti-Kickback Statute

It is a crime to knowingly and willfully solicit, receive, offer, or pay remuneration of any kind (e.g., money, goods, services):

- for the referral of an individual to another for the purpose of supplying items or services that are covered by a Federal health care program; or

- for purchasing, leasing, ordering, or arranging for any good, facility, service, or item that is covered by a Federal health care program.

There are a number of limited exceptions to the law, also known as "safe harbors," which provide immunity from criminal prosecution and which are described in greater detail in the statute and related regulations (found at 42 CFR 1001.952 and www.hhs.gov/oig/ak). Current safe harbors include:

- investment interests;
- space rental;
- equipment rental;
- personal services and management contracts;
- sale of practice;
- referral services;
- warranties;
- discounts;
- employment relationships;
- waiver of Part A co-insurance and deductible amounts;
- group purchasing organizations;
- increased coverage or reduced cost sharing under a risk-basis or prepaid plan; and
- charge reduction agreements with health plans.

Penalty for Unlawful Conduct

The penalty may include the imposition of a fine of up to $25,000, imprisonment of up to five years, or both. In addition, the provider can be excluded from participation in Federal health care programs. The regulations defining the aggravating and mitigating circumstances that must be reviewed by the OIG in making an exclusion determination are set forth in 42 CFR part 1001.

Examples

1. Dr. X accepted payments to sign Certificates of Medical Necessity for durable medical equipment for patients she never examined.

2. Home Health Agency disguises referral fees as salaries by paying referring physician Dr. X for services Dr. X never rendered to the Medicare beneficiaries or by paying Dr. X a sum in excess of fair market value for the services he rendered to the Medicare beneficiaries.

Appendix C: Civil and Administrative Statutes

This Appendix contains a description of civil and administrative statutes related to fraud and abuse in the context of health care. The Appendix is not intended to be a compilation of all federal statutes related to health care fraud and abuse. It is merely a summary of some of the more frequently cited Federal statutes.

I. The False Claims Act (31 U.S.C. 3729-3733)

Description of Unlawful Conduct

This is the law most often used to bring a case against a health care provider for the submission of false claims to a Federal health care program. The False Claims Act prohibits knowingly presenting (or causing to be presented) to the Federal Government a false or fraudulent claim for payment or approval. Additionally, it prohibits knowingly making or using (or causing to be made or used) a false record or statement to get a false or fraudulent claim paid or approved by the Federal Government or it agents, like a carrier, other claims processor, or State Medicaid program.

Definitions

False Claim—A "false claim" is a claim for payment for services or supplies that were not provided specifically as presented or for which the provider is otherwise not entitled to payment. Examples of false claims for services or supplies that were not provided specifically as presented include, but are not limited to:

- a claim for a service or supply that was never provided.
- a claim indicating the service was provided for some diagnosis code other than the true diagnosis code in order to obtain reimbursement for the service (which would not be covered if the true diagnosis code were submitted).
- a claim indicating a higher level of service than was actually provided.
- a claim for a service that the provider knows is not reasonable and necessary.
- a claim for services provided by an unlicensed individual.

Knowingly—To "knowingly" present a false or fraudulent claim means that the provider: (1) has actual knowledge that the information on the claim is false; (2) acts in deliberate ignorance of the truth or falsity of the information on the claim; or (3) acts in reckless disregard of the truth or falsity of the information on the claim. It is important to note the provider does not have to deliberately intend to defraud the Federal Government in order to be found liable under this Act. The provider need only "knowingly" present a false or fraudulent claim in the manner described above.

Deliberate Ignorance—To act in "deliberate ignorance" means that the provider has deliberately chosen to ignore the truth or falsity of the information on a claim submitted for payment, even though the provider knows, or has notice, that information may be false. An example of a provider who submits a false claim with deliberate ignorance would be a physician who ignores provider update bulletins and thus does not inform his/her staff of changes in the Medicare billing guidelines or update his/her billing system in accordance with changes to the Medicare billing practices. When claims for non-reimbursable services are submitted as a result, the False Claims Act has been violated.

Reckless Disregard—To act in "reckless disregard" means that the provider pays no regard to whether the information on a claim submitted for payment is true or false. An example of a provider who submits a false claim with reckless disregard would be a physician who assigns the billing function to an untrained office person without inquiring whether the employee has the requisite knowledge and training to accurately file such claims.

Penalty for Unlawful Conduct

The penalty for violating the False Claims Act is a minimum of $5,500 up to a maximum of $11,000 for each false claim submitted. In addition to the penalty, a provider could be found liable for damages of up to three times the amount unlawfully claimed.

Examples

- A physician submitted claims to Medicare and Medicaid representing that he had personally performed certain services when, in reality, the services were performed by a nonphysician and they were not reimbursable under the Federal health care programs.

- Dr. X intentionally upcoded office visits and angioplasty consultations that were submitted for payment to Medicare.

- Dr. X, a podiatrist, knowingly submitted claims to the Medicare and Medicaid programs for non-routine surgical procedures when he actually performed routine, non-covered services such as the cutting and trimming of toenails and the removal of corns and calluses.

II. Civil Monetary Penalties Law (42 U.S.C. 1320a-7a)

Description of Unlawful Conduct

The Civil Monetary Penalties Law (CMPL) is a comprehensive statute that covers an array of fraudulent and abusive activities and is very similar to the False Claims Act. For instance, the CMPL prohibits a health care provider from presenting, or causing to be presented, claims for services that the provider "knows or should know" were:

- not provided as indicated by the coding on the claim;

- not medically necessary;

- furnished by a person who is not licensed as a physician (or who was not properly supervised by a licensed physician);

- furnished by a licensed physician who obtained his or her license through misrepresentation of a material fact (such as cheating on a licensing exam);

- furnished by a physician who was not certified in the medical specialty that he or she claimed to be certified in; or

- furnished by a physician who was excluded from participation in the Federal health care program to which the claim was submitted.

Additionally, the CMPL contains various other prohibitions, including:

- offering remuneration to a Medicare or Medicaid beneficiary that the person knows or should know is likely to influence the beneficiary to obtain items or services billed to Medicare or Medicaid from a particular provider;

- employing or contracting with an individual or entity that the person knows or should know is excluded from participation in a Federal health care program.

The term "should know" means that a provider: (1) acted in deliberate ignorance of the truth or falsity of the information; or (2) acted in reckless disregard of the truth or falsity of the information. The Federal Government does not have to show that a provider specifically intended to defraud a Federal health care program in order to prove a provider violated the statute.

Penalty for Unlawful Conduct

Violation of the CMPL may result in a penalty of up to $10,000 per item or service and up to three times the amount unlawfully claimed. In addition, the provider may be excluded from participation in Federal health care programs. The regulations defining the aggravating and mitigating circumstances that must be reviewed by the OIG in making an exclusion determination are set forth in 42 CFR part 1001.

Examples

1. Dr. X paid Medicare and Medicaid beneficiaries $20 each time they visited him to receive services and have tests performed that were not preventive care services and tests.

2. Dr. X hired Physician Assistant P to provide services to Medicare and Medicaid beneficiaries without conducting a background check on P. Had Dr. X performed a background check by reviewing the HHS-OIG List of Excluded Individuals/Entities, Dr. X would have discovered that he should not hire P because P is excluded from participation in Federal health care programs for a period of five years.

3. Dr. X and his oximetry company billed Medicare for pulse oximetry that they knew they did not perform and services that had been intentionally upcoded.

III. Limitations on Certain Physician Referrals ("Stark Laws") (42 U.S.C. 1395nn)

Description of Unlawful Conduct

Physicians (and immediate family members) who have an ownership, investment or compensation relationship with an entity providing "designated health services" are prohibited from referring patients for these services where payment may be made by a Federal health care program unless a statutory or regulatory exception applies. An entity providing a designated health service is prohibited from billing for the provision of a service that was provided based on a prohibited referral. Designated health services include: clinical laboratory services; physical therapy services; occupational therapy services; radiology services, including magnetic resonance imaging, axial tomography scans, and ultrasound services; radiation therapy services and supplies; durable medical equipment and supplies; parenteral and enteral nutrients, equipment and supplies; prosthetics, orthotics, prosthetic devices and supplies; home health services; outpatient prescription drugs; and inpatient and outpatient hospital services.

New regulations clarifying the exceptions to the Stark Laws are expected to be issued by HCFA shortly. Current exceptions articulated within the Stark Laws include the following, provided all conditions of each exception as set forth in the statute and regulations are satisfied.

Exceptions for Ownership or Compensation Arrangements

- physician's services;
- in-office ancillary services; and
- prepaid plans.

Exceptions for Ownership or Investment in Publicly Traded Securities and Mutual Funds

- ownership of investment securities which may be purchased on terms generally available to the public;
- ownership of shares in a regulated investment company as defined by Federal law, if such company had, at the end of the company's most recent fiscal year, or on average, during the previous three fiscal years, total assets exceeding $75,000,000;
- hospital in Puerto Rico;
- rural provider; and
- hospital ownership (whole hospital exception).

Exceptions Relating to Other Compensation Arrangements

- rental of office space and rental of equipment;

- bona fide employment relationship;

- personal service arrangement;

- remuneration unrelated to the provision of designated health services;

- physician recruitment;

- isolated transactions;

- certain group practice arrangements with a hospital (pre-1989); and

- payments by a physician for items and services

Penalty for Unlawful Conduct

Violations of the statute subject the billing entity to denial of payment for the designated health services, refund of amounts collected from improperly submitted claims, and a civil monetary penalty of up to $15,000 for each improper claim submitted. Physicians who violate the statute may also be subject to additional fines per prohibited referral. In addition, providers that enter into an arrangement that they know or should know circumvents the referral restriction law may be subject to a civil monetary penalty of up to $100,000 per arrangement.

Examples

1. Dr. A worked in a medical clinic located in a major city. She also owned a free standing laboratory located in a major city. Dr. A referred all orders for laboratory tests on her patients to the laboratory she owned.

2. Dr. X agreed to serve as the Medical Director of Home Health Agency, HHA, for which he was paid a sum substantially above the fair market value for his services. In return, Dr. X routinely referred his Medicare and Medicaid patients to HHA for home health services.

3. Dr. Y received a monthly stipend of $500 from a local hospital to assist him in meeting practice expenses. Dr. Y performed no specific service for the stipend and had no obligation to repay the hospital. Dr. Y referred patients to the hospital for in-patient surgery.

IV. Exclusion of Certain Individuals and Entities From Participation in Medicare and other Federal Health Care Programs (42 U.S.C. 1320a-7)

Mandatory Exclusion

Individuals or entities convicted of the following conduct must be excluded from participation in Medicare and Medicaid for a minimum of five years:

1) a criminal offense related to the delivery of an item or service under Medicare or Medicaid;

2) a conviction under Federal or State law of a criminal offense relating to the neglect or abuse of a patient;

3) a conviction under Federal or State law of a felony relating to fraud, theft, embezzlement, breach of fiduciary responsibility or other financial misconduct against a health care program financed by any Federal, State, or local government agency;

4) a conviction under Federal or State law of a felony relating to the unlawful manufacture, distribution, prescription, or dispensing of a controlled substance.

If there is one prior conviction, the exclusion will be for ten years. If there are two prior convictions, the exclusion will be permanent.

Permissive Exclusion

Individuals or entities convicted of the following offenses, may be excluded from participation in Federal health care programs for a minimum of three years:

1) a criminal offense related to the delivery of an item or service under Medicare or Medicaid;

2) a misdemeanor related to fraud, theft, embezzlement, breach of fiduciary responsibility or other financial misconduct against a health care program financed by any Federal, State, or local government agency;

3) interference with, or obstruction of, any investigation into certain criminal offenses;

4) a misdemeanor related to the unlawful manufacture, distribution, prescription or dispensing of a controlled substance;

5) exclusion or suspension under a Federal or State health care program;

6) submission of claims for excessive charges, unnecessary services or services that were of a quality that fails to meet professionally recognized standards of health care;

7) violating the Civil Monetary Penalties Law or the statute entitled "Criminal Penalties for Acts Involving Federal Health Care Programs;"

8) ownership or control of an entity by a sanctioned individual or immediate family member (spouse, natural or adoptive parent, child, sibling, stepparent, stepchild, stepbrother or stepsister, in-laws, grandparent and grandchild);

9) failure to disclose information required by law;

10) failure to supply claims payment information; and

11) defaulting on health education loan or scholarship obligations.

The above list of offenses is not all inclusive. Additional grounds for permissive exclusion are detailed in the statute.

Examples

1. Nurse R was excluded based on a conviction involving obtaining dangerous drugs by forgery. She also altered prescriptions that were given for her own health problems before she presented them to the pharmacist to be filled.

2. Practice T was excluded due to its affiliation with its excluded owner. The practice owner, excluded from participation in the Federal health care programs for soliciting and receiving illegal kickbacks, was still participating in the day-to-day operations of the practice after his exclusion was effective.

Appendix D: OIG-HHS Contact Information

I. OIG Hotline Number

One method for providers to report potential fraud, waste, and abuse problems is to contact the OIG Hotline number. All HHS and contractor employees have a responsibility to assist in combating fraud, waste and abuse in all departmental programs. As such, providers are encouraged to report matters involving fraud, waste and mismanagement in any departmental program to the OIG. The OIG maintains a hotline that offers a confidential means for reporting these matters.

Contacting the OIG Hotline

By Phone: 1-800-HHS-TIPS (1-800-447-8477)
By E-Mail: HTips@os.dhhs.gov
By Mail: Office of Inspector General
   Department of Health and Human Services
   Attn: HOTLINE
   330 Independence Ave., S.W.
   Washington, D.C. 20201

When contacting the Hotline, please provide the following information to the best of your ability:

- Type of Complaint:

Medicare Part A

Medicare Part B

Indian Health Service

TRICARE

Other (please specify)

- HHS Department or program being affected by your allegation of fraud, waste, abuse/mismanagement:

  - Health Care Financing Administration (HCFA)

    Indian Health Service

    Other (please specify)

Please provide the following information. (However, if you would like your referral to be submitted anonymously, please indicate such in your correspondence or phone call.)

Your Name
Your Street Address
Your City/County
Your State
Your Zip Code
Your email Address

- Subject/Person/Business/Department that allegation is against.

Name of Subject
Title of Subject
Subject's Street Address
Subject's City/County
Subject's State
Subject's Zip Code

Please provide a brief summary of your allegation and the relevant facts.

II. Provider Self-Disclosure Protocol

The recommended method for a provider to contact the OIG regarding potential fraud or abuse issues that may exist in the provider's own organization is through the use of the Provider Self-Disclosure Protocol. This program encourages providers to voluntarily disclose irregularities in their dealings with Federal health care programs. While voluntary disclosure under the protocol does not guarantee a provider protection from civil, criminal, or administrative actions, the fact that a provider voluntarily disclosed possible wrongdoing is a mitigating factor in OIG's recommendations to prosecuting agencies. Although other agencies may not have formal policies offering immunity or mitigation for self-disclosure, they typically view self-disclosure favorably for the self-disclosing entity. Self-reporting offers providers the opportunity to minimize the potential cost and disruption of a full-scale audit and investigation, to negotiate a fair monetary settlement, and to avoid an OIG permissive exclusion preventing the provider from doing business with Federal health care programs. In addition, if the provider is obligated to enter into an Integrity Agreement (IA) as part of the resolution of a voluntary disclosure, there are three benefits the provider might receive as a result of self-reporting:

- If the provider has an effective compliance program and agrees to maintain its compliance program as part of the False Claims Act settlement, the OIG may not even require an IA;

- In cases where the provider's own audits detected the disclosed problem, the OIG may consider alternatives to the IA's auditing provisions. The provider may be able to perform some or all of its billing audits through internal auditing methods rather than be required to retain an independent review organization to perform the billing review; and

- Self-disclosing can help to demonstrate a provider's trustworthiness to the OIG and may result in the OIG determining that it can sufficiently safeguard the Federal health care programs through an IA without the exclusion remedy for a material breach, which is typically included in an IA.

Specific instructions on how a physician practice can submit a voluntary disclosure under the Provider Self-Disclosure Protocol can be found on the OIG's internet site at www.hhs.gov/oig or in the Federal Register at 63 FR 58399 (1998). A physician practice may, however, wish to consult with an attorney prior to submitting a disclosure to the OIG.

The Provider Self-Disclosure Protocol can also be a useful tool for baseline audits. The protocol details the OIG's views on the appropriate elements of an effective investigative and audit plan for providers. Physician practices can use the self-disclosure protocol as a model for conducting audits and self-assessments.

In relying on the protocol for audit design and sample selection, a physician practice should pay close attention to the sections on self-assessment and sample selection. These two sections provide valuable guidance regarding how these two functions should be performed.

The self-assessment section of the protocol contains information that can be applied to audit design. Self-assessment is an internal financial assessment to determine the monetary impact of the matter. The approach of a review can include reviewing either all claims affected or a statistically valid sample of the claims.

Sample selection must include several elements. These elements are drawn from the government sampling program known as RAT-STATS.[1] All of these elements are set forth in more detail in the Provider Self-Disclosure Protocol, but the elements are (1) sampling unit, (2) sampling frame, (3) probe, (4) sample size, (5) random numbers, (6) sample design and (7) missing sample items. All of these sampling items should be clearly documented by the physician practice and compiled in the format set forth in the Provider Self-Disclosure Protocol. Use of the format set forth in the Provider Self-Disclosure Protocol will help physician practices to ensure that the elements of their internal audits are in conformance with OIG standards.

Endnote

1. Available through the OIG web site at http://www.hhs.gov/oas/ratstat.html.

Appendix E: Carrier Contact Information

Medicare

A complete list of contact information (address, phone number, email address) for Medicare Part A Fiscal Intermediaries, Medicare Part B Carriers, Regional Home Health Intermediaries, and Durable Medical Equipment Regional Carriers can be found on the HCFA web site at www.hcfa.gπov/medicare/incardir.htm.

Medicaid

Contact information (address, phone number, email address) for each State Medicaid carrier can be found on the HCFA web site at www.hcfa.gov/medicaid/mcontact.htm. In addition to a list of Medicaid carriers, the web site includes contact information for each State survey agency and the HCFA Regional Offices.

Contact information for each State Medicaid Fraud Control Unit can be found on the OIG web site at www.hhs.gov/oig/oi/mfcu/index.htm.

Appendix F: Internet Resources

Office of Inspector General—U.S. Department of Health and Human Services *www.hhs.gov/oig*

This web site includes a variety of information relating to Federal health care programs, including the following:

Advisory Opinions
Anti-kickback Information

Compliance Program Guidance

Corporate Integrity Agreements

Fraud Alerts

Links to web pages for the:

Office of Audit Services (OAS)

Office of Evaluation and Inspections (OEI)

Office of Investigations (OI)

OIG List of Excluded Individuals/Entities

OIG News

OIG Regulations

OIG Semi-Annual Report

OIG Workplan

Health Care Financing Administration
www.hcfa.gov

This web site includes information on a wide array of topics, including the following:

Medicare

National Correct Coding Initiative

Intermediary-Carrier Directory

Payment

Program Manuals

Program Transmittals & Memorandum

Provider Billing/HCFA Forms

Statistics and Data

Medicaid

HCFA Regional Offices

Letters to State Medicaid Directors

Medicaid Hotline Numbers

Policy & Program Information

State Medicaid Contacts

State Medicaid Manual

State Survey Agencies

Statistics and Data

HCFA Medicare Training
www.hcfa.gov/medlearn

This site provides computer-based training on the following topics:

HCFA 1500 Form

Fraud & Abuse

ICD-9-CM Diagnosis Coding

Adult Immunization

Medicare Secondary Payer (MSP)

Women's Health

Front Office Management

Introduction to the World of Medicare

Home Health Agency

HCFA 1450 (UB92)

Government Printing Office

www.access.gpo.gov

This site provides access to Federal statutes and regulations pertaining to Federal health care programs.

The U.S. House of Representatives Internet Library

uscode.house.gov/usc.htm

This site provides access to the United States Code, which contains laws pertaining to Federal health care programs.

Appendix D

Medicare Part B EDI Helpline

EDI Helpline is a regional number Medicare customers can call to access information and material regarding electronic data interchange.

Alabama Alaska Arizona Arkansas California Colorado Connecticut 205
988-2533 701
277-6781 701
277-6783
Option 1 501
378-2419 213
742-3996
or
800
222-2471 701
277-2655 203
639-3160

Delaware District of Columbia Florida Georgia Hawaii Idaho Illinois 972
766-5480 972
766-5480
904
634-4994 770
690-3040 701
277-6780 615
782-4505 618
993-4205

Indiana Iowa Kansas Kentucky Louisiana Maine Maryland 800
470-9630 800
407-0267 800
472-7135 800
470-9630 504
231-2163 781
749-7745 972
766-5480

Massachusetts Michigan Minnesota Mississippi Missouri Montana Nebraska 781

749-7745 618

993-4205 612

885-2889 804

327-7660 800

892-6048

800

447-7828

Ext. 8277 402

351-8476

or

402

398-3603

Nevada New Hampshire New Jersey New Mexico New York Upstate New York–BCBSWNY North Carolina North Dakota 701

277-6784 781

749-7745 717

763-6722 972

766-5480 212

721-1300

Ext. 360

or

212

476-6500 607

766-6439 336

605-6460 701

277-2655

Ohio Oklahoma Oregon Puerto Rico Pennsylvania Rhode Island South Carolina 614

277-6100 972

766-5480 701

277-6785 787

749-4949 717

763-6722 401

459-1700 803

788-9751

South Dakota Tennessee Texas Utah Vermont Virginia Washington 701

277-2655 615

782-4505 972

766-5480 800

333-6000 781

749-7745 804

327-2233 701

277-6782

West Virginia Wisconsin Wyoming 614

277-6100 608

221-7115 701

277-2655

Index